THE COMPLETE PROBLEM SOLVER

second edition

THE COMPLETE PROBLEM SOLVER

second edition

John R. Hayes

Department of Psychology
Carnegie-Mellon University

 LAWRENCE ERLBAUM ASSOCIATES, PUBLISHERS
1989   Hillsdale, New Jersey   Hove and London

Lawrence Erlbaum Associates, Inc., Publishers
365 Broadway
Hillsdale, New Jersey 07642

Library of Congress Cataging-in-Publication Data

Hayes, John R., 1940–
The complete problem solver.

Includes bibliographies and index.
1. Problem solving.   2. Thought and thinking.
I. Title.
BF441.H33 1989   153.4'3   88-7105.
ISBN 0-89859-782-X
ISBN 0-8058-0309-2 (pbk.)

Printed in the United States of America
10   9   8   7   6   5   4   3   2   1

Contents

Acknowledgments

This book is the result of many years' searching for a satisfactory way to teach a course on general problem solving skills. By general problem solving skills I mean skills that can be used by anyone in solving problems that occur in everyday life.

The idea that I should try to teach a problem solving course arose in a conversation with Herb Simon and Steve Rosenberg in 1974. The three of us decided that if we really knew something useful about problem solving, we ought to be able to teach it. Steve and I, accepting the challenge, put together an initial version of the course which we then taught to a mixed group of engineers and fine arts students at Carnegie-Mellon University. Our first version had many faults, but student response was still positive. I was sufficiently encouraged to continue. The course then underwent a long evolution as I borrowed ideas from a wide variety of sources and tested them in the classroom. Many of these ideas came from people who, at one time or another, have taught the course with me:

- Steven Rosenberg—who helped me to start the whole enterprise,
- Linda Flower—who made me see the relevance of problem solving to the crucial skill of writing,
- Lee Gregg—who encouraged me to think big about the course, and
- Lynne Reder—who added her sophistication in the fields of memory and decision making.

Other ideas came from people who were generous enough to contribute guest lectures. Delarese Ambrose spoke about how to get along in small groups; Edward Constant, about cultural influences in creativity; John Gatchnig, about recursive methods in problem solving; Douglas Lenat, about heuristics; David Meeker, about information retrieval; Robert Neches, about listening to lectures; John Payne, about decision making; Herbert Simon, about series completion problems; and Richard Teare, about problem solving in engineering.

I would like to add a special note to thanks to John Payne. It was through his example and encouragement that I added the section on decision making to the course—a section which many students have found extremely useful.

In teaching a course on problem solving skills, it is extremely important to provide students with close personal supervision. Teaching problem solving skills is a bit like coaching: The instructor needs to watch the students in action to be sure that they are performing the skills in the right way. As course enrollment increased, it became impossible for me to give this supervision myself. Instead, I relied on a group of teaching assistants—mostly undergraduates—who volunteered to supervise groups of about 15 students in weekly sections and to meet weekly with me to discuss section problems. The success of the course has depended very heavily on the efforts of the teaching assistants listed here:

Doug Bauman	Kevin Brown
Cynthia Berkowitz	Steve Ciampi
Sandra J. Bond	Aaron Clevenson
Barbara Madera Clevenson	Anne Lux
Dana Dunn	Bill Lyden
Suzanne Eckert	Marilyn Mantei
Carole Elm	John Maslany
Anna-Lena Ericsson-Neches	David Meeker
Becky Freeland	Ernie Prescott
Amy Gift	Greg Pisocky
Richard Gorelick	Susan Robinson
Mark Hanna	Mark Segal
Ron Kander	Lisa Thaviu
Anne Karcher	Judi Vitale
Rich Kleinhample	Philip Werner
Jeanne Kravanja	Ellen Zoll
Jamie Leach	

Jeanne Halpin has taught the course very successfully on her own. By doing so, she has demonstrated the important point that the course is genuinely "exportable."

Finally, I want to note the very important contributions of Sandra Bond. She has coordinated the complex mechanisms of the course: making sure that lectures got delivered, that grading got done, that TA's with difficulties got listened to, and that hundreds of students found their way to weekly section meetings. She served as a teaching assistant for many years, consistently receiving excellent evaluations from her students. In addition, she guest lectured on creativity in women. She has also contributed heavily in the preparation of this book. She typed the manuscript, drew the figures, edited and proofread the text, and did much of the research and writing for the final chapter. In short, a great deal of the work you see in this book is hers.

In appreciation, I dedicate this book to the many mentioned above who have contributed to this project.

Introduction

This book has two purposes. It is designed to provide you with skills that will make you a better problem solver, and to give you up-to-date information about the psychology of problem solving.

The first purpose is clearly a practical one, but I believe the second purpose is, too. It is important for people to know how their minds work. Certainly for humanistic reasons—knowledge of our human nature is valuable in itself—but it is also important because it provides us with a degree of flexibility which we might not otherwise have. If we can examine or own problem solving processes with some degree of understanding, then we have a better chance of improving them. Further, if we have some understanding of how people think, we can be more effective in helping others. Anyone who is to teach, or to tutor, or even to help a child with homework, can benefit from knowledge of how human problem solving processes work and how they can go wrong.

Early in my career as a psychologist, a student asked me about my special area of interest. I told him that I studied people's thinking processes. "Oh, thinking!" he said, "I know all about that. I'm a math major." Of course, he did know a lot about thinking—he knew about *how to do it,* at least in certain cases. Given a math problem, he could draw on a wealth of experience to help him find a solution. But if he were like most people, he would have a very difficult time articulating that wealth of experience; he knew how to think but he didn't know how to describe his own thinking. When they are faced with their first teaching task, whether in school or out, many professionals discover a vast difference between their ability to do what they do very well and their ability to describe what they do to others.

In this book, then, we hope to provide you with some skills that will help you to solve problems, but we also hope to provide you with some knowledge that will give you greater insight into what you are doing and an increased ability to understand others.

WHAT IS A PROBLEM?

If you are on one side of a river and you want to get to the other side but you don't know how, you have a problem. If you are assembling a mail-order purchase, and the instructions leave you completely baffled about how to "put tab A in slot B," you have a problem. If you are writing a letter and you just can't find the polite way to say, "No, we don't want you to come and stay for a month," you have a problem. Whenever there is a gap between where you are now and where you want to be, and you don't know how to find a way to cross that gap, you have a problem.

Solving a problem means finding an appropriate way to cross a gap. The process of finding a solution has two major parts: *1*. Representing the gap—that is, understanding the nature of the problem, and *2*. Searching for a means to cross it.

REPRESENTING THE GAP

If people fail to understand the nature of the gap, they may well set off in the wrong direction to search for the solution. Suppose you told a friend that you would give him $10,000 if he put his elbow in his ear. "Easy," your friend says; "I'll just cut off my elbow and put it in any ear you choose." Now you may question your friend's values, but you are also pretty sure that he understands the nature of the difficulty—the gap—that the problem presents. On the other hand, if your friend said, "Easy, I'll stand on a chair," you would suspect that he didn't really understand the nature of the difficulty.

Representing the gap isn't always easy. In fact, the main difficulty in many problems is just the difficulty of representing the gap. Consider the Driver's License Problem.

Problem 1. The Driver's License

When Tom and Bill applied for their drivers' licenses, they were asked their ages. Bill, who was a bit of a revolutionary, said they were both in their twenties and that was all he was going to reveal to a bunch of bureaucrats. The clerk insisted on more specific information so, to smooth things over, Tom added that they both had the same birthday, and that he was four times as old as Bill was when he was three times as old as Bill was when he was twice as old as Bill was. At this the clerk fainted and the two snatched up their licenses and disappeared. When the clerk came to and realized that he would have to complete his records some way or other he began to do a little figuring, and before long had found out how old the two were. Can you tell, too?

A typical reaction to this problem is to say, "What?" or beat a hasty retreat explaining, "I never was much good at puzzles." But the problem really isn't very difficult once we find an appropriate representation for it. In Chapter 1, we will discuss processes by which we come to understand the nature of a problem; we will show that the way we represent the gap can make an enormous difference in the difficulty of the problem; and we will provide some hints on how to represent problems to make them easier.

FINDING A SOLUTION PATH

Once we understand the nature of a problem, there are still many reasons why we may have difficulty in finding a solution to it. The problems below illustrate some of the most important reasons.

Problem 2. The Loser

A man once offended a fortune teller by laughing at her predictions and saying that fortune telling was all nonsense. He offended her so much, in fact, that she cast a spell on him which turned him into both a compulsive gambler and in addition a consistent loser. That was pretty mean. We would expect the spell would shortly have turned him into a miserable, impoverished wreck. Instead, he soon married a wealthy businesswoman who took him to the casino every day, gave him money, and smiled happily as he lost it at the roulette table. They lived happily in just this way ever after. Why was the man's wife so happy to see him lose?

The story poses a problem for most of us when we first see it. It would be no problem if the man were winning money. We know right away how to get from winning money to happy smiles, but to get from losing money to happy smiles *is* a problem—there is a gap that we can't immediately cross. How can losing money lead to happiness?

In trying to bridge the gap, people propose a variety of solutions:

"Perhaps she is so rich that she really doesn't care about the money."

"Perhaps she is becoming a nun and wants to give all her money away."

"Perhaps her crazy grandfather left a will which required her to lose all her money by 21 in order to inherit a billion."

"Perhaps she is a masochist."

These solutions vary in quality. The solution about the woman becoming a nun has the difficulty that it ignores her husband. A solution which seems to us better than all of these is this: When playing roulette, the man bets, say, on red and loses, as his spell requires. The woman, however, bets twice as much on black and wins. In short, she has turned her husband's misfortune into an advantage. His loss is their gain, and so the smiles. The gap is crossed.

The problem illustrates a very important process in problem solving—the process of invention. In many problems, lots of approaches are conceivable—some of them better than others. Typically, a person will try several approaches before hitting on a good one. If people can't think up any approaches, then they can't solve the problem.

Invention is an important problem solving process, but it isn't the only process required in solving problems. There are many problems in which invention is easy but the problem is still difficult.

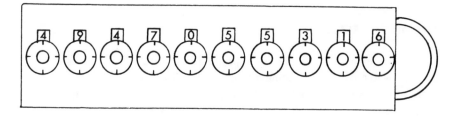

Problem 3. The Combination Lock

Suppose that you have the problem of opening the 10-dial combination lock shown above. Proposing possible solutions is easy. The dial setting shown may be a solution—and it may not. There is a total of 10^{10} or 10,000,000,000 or ten billion possible dial settings, any *one* of which may be the solution. This is where the difficulty of the problem lies—finding the single correct combination among ten billion possibilities. If we tried one combination every second, working day and night, it would take us 317 years to try them all. Some problems, then, like the Combination Lock Problem, are difficult to solve because we have to search for the solution among a very large number of alternatives.

The following problem is a difficult one, even though it involves neither invention nor examining large numbers of alternatives.

Problem 4. The Rational Investor

Suppose that you have a choice between a safe investment which yields a sure 25% return and a risky investment which gives you an even chance of either tripling your money or of losing it. Which investment is best?

The difficulty of practical decision making demanded by problems like this one lies in evaluating the alternatives. People are often unreliable when making such evaluations. If they choose from the same alternatives on several different occasions, the results may be quite inconsistent.

Which of the two investments is best depends in a complex way on the investor's financial circumstances. To evaluate the alternatives accurately, most people require explicit decision procedures such as those described in Chapter 9.

Some problems are difficult because we have trouble remembering where we are on our path to the solution. Try to solve problem #5 before reading further.

Problem 5. Cats Among Pigeons

Messrs. Downs, Heath, Field, Forest, and Marsh—five elderly pigeon fanciers—were worried by the depredations of marauding cats owned by five not less elderly ladies, and, hoping to get control of the cats, they married the cat owners.

The scheme worked well for each of them so far as his own cat and pigeon were concerned; but it was not long before each cat had claimed a victim and each fancier had lost his favorite pigeon.

Mrs. Downs' cat killed the pigeon owned by the man who married the owner of the cat which killed Mr. Marsh's pigeon. Mr. Downs' pigeon was killed by Mrs. Heath's cat. Mr. Forest's pigeon was killed by the cat owned by the lady who married the man whose pigeon was killed by Mrs. Field's cat.

Who was the owner of the pigeon killed by Mrs. Forest's cat?

(from Phillips, 1961)

Unless you are an expert in solving this sort of problem, you may have had some difficulty in keeping track of your place on your way to the solution. You may have found yourself asking questions like, "Wasn't Mrs. Marsh the lady who ate the cat that married Mr. Forest's pigeon?—Or was it the other way around?" Being able to remember your place on the solution path is a critical problem solving skill.

Consider Problem #6, but don't consider it for very long.

Problem 6. Who's Got the Enthalpy?

Liquid water at 212 °F and 1 atm has an internal energy (on an arbitrary basis)

of 180.02 Btu/lb$_m$. The specific volume of liquid water at these conditions is
0.01672 ft^3/lb$_m$. What is its enthalpy?

(from Smith and Van Ness, 1959)

Problem #6 is not a very difficult problem if you know something about thermodynamics. If you don't, however—if, for example, you haven't the foggiest idea what enthalpy is—then it's an impossibly hard problem. I present this problem not to make you feel bad, but to dramatize the extreme importance of knowledge in problem solving. If you are missing relevant knowledge, an easy problem may appear difficult or impossible. If your knowledge of math and science is weak, the problems that scientists solve may appear much harder to you than they really are. If the humanities or the arts are your weak suit, then people who can understand philosophy or who can interpret a musical score may seem magically intelligent to you. The moral is this: Much that passes for cleverness or innate quickness of mind actually depends on specialized knowledge. If you acquire that specialized knowledge, you too may be able to solve hard problems and appear clever to your less learned friends.

ORGANIZATION OF THE BOOK

The six problems given here illustrate six important aspects of human problem solving which we emphasize:

Problem 1: Representation
Problem 2: Invention
Problem 3: Search for the Solution Among Many Alternatives
Problem 4: Decision Making
Problem 5: Memory
Problem 6: Knowledge

The book is divided into four sections:

Section I. Problem Solving Theory and Practice (representing problems and searching for solutions)
Section II. Memory and Knowledge Acquisition
Section III. Decision Making
Section IV. Creativity and Invention

While the order in which you read Sections 1, 2, 3, and 4 is not critical for understanding, I do recommend that you read Section 1 first for an overview of the problem solving process.

REFERENCES

Phillips, H. *My Best Puzzles in Logic and Reasoning.* New York: Dover, 1961.
Smith, J. M., and Van Ness, H. C. *Introduction to Chemical Engineering Thermodynamics,* Second
Edition. New York: McGraw-Hill, Inc., 1959.

PROBLEM SOLUTIONS

Page xii. The Driver's License:
Tom is 24, Bill is 21
Page xv. Cats Among Pigeons:
Mr. Heath

I

PROBLEM SOLVING THEORY AND PRACTICE

1

Understanding Problems:
The Process of Representation

Usually when we solve a problem, we put most of our attention on the problem and very little attention on ourselves—that is, on what we are *doing* to solve the problem. If we did attend to our own actions, we might notice that they often occur in a characteristic sequence:

1. **Finding the Problem:** recognizing that there is a problem to be solved.
2. **Representing the Problem:** understanding the nature of the gap to be crossed.
3. **Planning the Solution:** choosing a method for crossing the gap.
4. **Carrying Out the Plan**
5. **Evaluating the Solution:** asking "How good is the result?" once the plan is carried out.
6. **Consolidating Gains:** learning from the experience of solving.

This sequence of actions is illustrated in the following problem.

Action	*Problem*
Finding the Problem	I observe Smith, who claims to be too poor to repay the $50.00 he owes me, buying round after round of drinks for his friends.
Representing the Problem	I conclude that Smith is not sufficiently serious about repaying his debt.
Planning the Solution	I consider a polite telephone call or a note remind-

	ing Smith of his indebtedness, but decide instead to ask three very large friends of mine to call on Smith in person.
Carrying Out the Plan	I call my friends, who then deliver my message to Smith.
Evaluating the Solution	Since Smith paid up rapidly without major bloodshed, I regard the problem as satisfactorily solved.
Consolidating Gains	I revise my rules for lending money to Smith and reflect on the value of having a few large friends.

In easy problems, we may go through these actions in order and without any difficulties. In hard problems, though, we may have to do a great deal of backtracking. For example, when we evaluate what we have done, we may decide that our solution is terrible, e.g., "Asbestos bread will not solve the burned toast problem!!" and go back to planning. Or while trying to execute a solution, we may discover something about the problem which will lead us to represent it in an entirely new way—"Oh, now I see what kind of a problem it is!" Retracing of this sort is characteristic of problems that are called "ill-defined." We will discuss these in much more detail later.

Our success as problem solvers depends on the effectiveness with which we can carry out each of the six actions just described. In this chapter, we will examine the nature of problem representations and the processes people use to form them. In addition, we will describe techniques for improving representations so that they make problem solving easier. In the next chapter we will discuss planning, executing, evaluating, and consolidating. We will delay the discussion of problem finding until the final section of the book because this topic is so closely related to the topic of creativity.

HOW DO PEOPLE UNDERSTAND PROBLEMS?

Suppose we were to spy on people as they were trying to understand a new problem, such as the Monster Problem below.

Monster Problem #1

Three five-handed extra-terrestrial monsters were holding three crystal globes. Because of the quantum-mechanical peculiarities of their neighborhood, both monsters and globes come in exactly three sizes with no others permitted; small, medium, and large. The medium-sized monster was holding the small globe; the small monster was holding the large globe; and the large monster was holding the medium-sized globe. Since this situation offended their keenly developed sense of symmetry, they proceeded to transfer globes from one monster to another so that each monster would have a globe proportionate to its own size.

Monster etiquette complicated the solution of the problem since it requires: *1.* that only one globe may be transferred at a time, *2.* that if a monster is holding two globes, only the larger of the two may be transferred, and *3.* that a globe may not be transferred to a monster who is holding a larger globe.

By what sequence of transfers could the monsters have solved this problem?

We might see people reading the problem over several times and pausing over the hard parts. We might see them drawing sketches or writing symbols on paper, and we might hear them mutter to themselves, something like: "Let's see . . . If a monster is holding two globes . . . What does this mean? . . ." If we were to ask people to "think aloud" as they worked on the problem, we would find that their reading, sketching, and muttering reflected a whirlwind of internal activities—imaging, inferencing, decision making, and retrieving of knowledge from memory—activities which are directed toward "understanding the problem." If we look in more detail, we would find that people are selecting information and imaging objects and relations in the problem. For example, after reading the first line of the Monster Problem, a person might form a visual image of three blobs, each touching a circle. The imagined blobs and circles, of course, correspond to the monsters and the globes, and touching in the image corresponds to the relation of holding. The images usually reflect some selection of information, e.g., the blobs may have no hands, or the circles may give no indication that the globes are crystaline.

To understand a problem, then, the problem solver creates (imagines) objects and relations in his head which correspond to objects and relations in the externally presented problem. These internal objects and relations are the problem solver's *internal representation* of the problem. Different people may create different internal representations of the same problem.

Frequently, problem solvers will make an *external representation* of some parts of the problem. They do this by drawing sketches and diagrams or by writing down symbols or equations which correspond to parts of the internal representation. Such external representations can be enormously helpful in solving problems.

The Relation of Internal and External Representations

Sometimes we can solve a problem using only an internal representation. For example, most of us can multiply 17 by 23 entirely in our heads and, with a little effort, get the right answer. Many problems, however, are very difficult to solve without the aid of an external representation. The Monster Problem and the Driver's License Problem in the Introduction are examples of such problems. While it is possible to solve the Monster Problem entirely mentally, it is very difficult to keep track of where you are in this problem without an external representation. You find yourself asking questions like, "Did I give the small globe to the big monster or didn't I?" In the Driver's License Problem, if you don't invent and write down a good algebraic notation, you are very likely to confuse such things as Tom's age *now* with his age at an earlier time.

External representations, then, are often very helpful in solving difficult problems. We should note, though, that external representations *can't help us at all unless we also have an internal representation of the problem.* Imagine that we are playing chess. In front of us the chess board and pieces provide a very useful external representation of the chess game. But when we make a move, we typically try it in our heads before making it on the board. Planning is done internally. Further, we couldn't make moves either in our heads or on the board if we didn't have an internal representation of how each piece moves. In short, intelligent play would be impossible without an internal representation.

In summary:

1. An internal representation is essential for *intelligent* problem solving. Internal representations are the medium in which we think, in the same way that words are the medium in which we talk. Without internal representations, we can't think through the solution of a problem, just as without words we can't speak.

2. Sometimes an internal representation is sufficient for solving. If we were very skillful, we could play "blindfold chess," that is, we could play using only our internal representation, but it wouldn't be easy.

3. For many problems, an external representation is *very* helpful. We will explore how external representations can help later in this chapter.

WHAT DO WE NEED TO REPRESENT IN AN INTERNAL REPRESENTATION?

Consider the Monster Problem discussed previously. If we are to solve this problem, there are four problem parts that we need to include in our internal representation:

1. **The Goal**—where we want the globes to be when we are done.
2. **The Initial State**—that is, which monsters have which globes at the beginning of the problem.
3. **The Operators**—the actions that change one problem state into another—in this case, passing globes back and forth; and
4. **The Restrictions on the Operators**—Monster Problem rules 1, 2, and 3.

Here is another problem:

Starting with the arrangement of dots shown below:

● ● ● ● _ ○ ○ ○ ○   *Initial State*

Try to produce this arrangement:

○ ○ ○ ○ _ ● ● ● ●   *Final State*

Given that a dot can move to an adjacent space on either side, e.g.,

○ ○←●   *Operator 1*

and a dot can jump over *one* other dot of either color into an empty space, e.g.,

● ○ ○   *Operator 2*

However, the white dots can only move to the left and the black dots to the right.

Restriction

Try to identify the goal, the initial state, the operators, and the restrictions in the following problem:

A farmer traveling to market took three possessions with him; his dog, a chicken, and a sack of grain. On his way, he came to a river which he had to cross. Unfortunately, the only available transportation was an old abandoned boat that would hold only himself and one of his possessions. Taking his possessions across one at a time posed a problem, however. If he left his very reliable dog with the chicken, the dog would very reliably eat the chicken. If he left the chicken with the grain, the chicken would eat the grain and then burst, improving neither of them.

How did the farmer manage to get all his possessions safely across the river?

While all four problem parts are essential in these two problems, this isn't always the case. All problems involve at least a goal, but many problems omit one or more of the other three parts. Suppose a friend says to us, "Get to my house at 10 o'clock." That statement specifies the goal you are to accomplish, but nothing else. It doesn't specify where you should start—north, south, east, or west. There is no special initial state. Further, it doesn't matter how you get there—you can walk, hop, skate, unicycle, take a cab, a helicopter, a large bird, anything—it doesn't matter—no operator is specified. Further still, no restrictions were specified—e.g., "If you hop, use only the left foot," or "If you come by bird, don't use a sparrow." Some other problem statements which specify only a goal are: "Be a success, my child," and, "Prove your point."

Some problems specify just initial state and goal: "Make a silk purse out of a sow's ear"; or initial state, goal, and restrictions: "Make a silk purse out of a sow's ear, but don't smell up the house." Others specify just goal and operators: "Paint a picture," or, "Get to my house by taxi"; or goal, operators, and restrictions: "Drive me home, but don't drive too fast." Finally, we have problems which specify goal and restrictions, e.g., "Build a fire but don't use matches."

To form an adequate internal representation of a problem, we must represent the goal of the problem, and in addition—for problems in which they are required—the initial state, the operators, and the restrictions.

HOW INTERNAL REPRESENTATIONS
ARE FORMED

At first, we might imagine that forming internal representations is a copying process in which the problem solver makes a sort of mental xerox of an external situation—reproducing everything in the external situation and adding nothing. In fact, an internal representation is far from being a copy. Forming a representation is a very active process in which the person adds and subtracts information, and interprets information in the original situation. When you read the Monster Problem, you may have pictured creatures arranged in a row either horizontally or vertically. You may have pictured them in the order they were mentioned in the text—medium, small, large—in order of size, or in some other order. However you pictured them, you *added details* to the representation. The problem said nothing at all about how the monsters were arranged. You may also have added shapes for the monsters such as those shown in Figure 1.

Figure 1.   A Representation of the Monster Problem

Selecting Information

While you probably added some details, you probably left others out. For example, your image of the problem situation probably didn't contain anything about "the quantum-mechanical peculiarities" of the monsters' neighborhood. Very likely you regarded this material as "just part of the cover story" and not really relevant to the solution of the problem. Further, you may have recognized that the number of monster hands is irrelevant and left that out of your representation as well. Relevance judgments such as these are useful because they allow us to pare our representations down to manageable size.

In a study exploring relevance judgments in problem solving (Hayes, Waterman, and Robinson, 1977), the experimenter read problems aloud which the subjects had not heard before and asked them to make relevance judgments. The problems were presented in small pieces so that the subjects could make separate judgments about each piece. A typical session for the "Allsports Problem" proceeded as follows:

Experimenter (reading problem): "I went to tea."

problem, and because you have a triangle problem *schema*, you know that you should use the Pythagorean theorem to solve it.

There are many familiar problem schemas. For example, there are schemas for distance-rate-time problems, triangle problems, interest problems, river-current problems, river-crossing problems, mixture problems, age problems, and many more. A problem schema is a package of information about the properties of a particular problem type. A schema for triangle problems, for example, may include information that:

1. The initial state will specify lengths of some of the sides of a right-angle triangle;
2. The goal will be to find the length of another side; and
3. The operator will involve application of the Pythagorean theorem.

There is a variety of "optimist" story which (inadvertently) illustrates the importance of our knowledge of problem schemas in representing problems.

Optimist Story 1

An optimist put a new kind of furnace in his house and found that it cut his heating bills in half. Delighted, he had another one installed, expecting that he would cut his fuel bill to zero.

Optimist Story 2

An optimist really likes his doctor except that every time he visits his office, he has to wait an hour to see him. Then a brilliant idea strikes him. He decides that if he takes two friends with him to help, he should only have to wait for 20 minutes.

Now, the peculiar thing about the optimists' thinking is not that they are failing to use knowledge, but rather that they are using the knowledge inappropriately. There are many situations in which it is true that if one of something does half a job, then two of them will do the whole job. If one can of paint covers half of the house, then two cans ought to cover the whole house. The optimist's error is that he has applied this schema to heating houses, where it is not appropriate.

The optimist in the second story uses a schema which is perfectly appropriate in "work" problems. If one person can do a job in an hour, three people ought to be able to do the job in 20 minutes. However, there are many activities that can't be hastened by having several people combine their effort. These include waiting, falling off cliffs, and maturing—If one boy reaches puberty at 12, could 12 boys reach puberty at one?

Problem schemas are an important part of the knowledge we use to solve problems. However, as the optimist stories show, we also need to know when the schemas are appropriate and when they are not.

INDIVIDUAL DIFFERENCES IN PROBLEM REPRESENTATION

Even when two people represent the same problem, they may well not represent it in the same way. A person who is very good at filtering out irrelevant detail may produce a very spare representation, as in Figure 2. Another person who is not good at filtering out irrelevant detail may produce a complex and ornate representation, as in Figure 3.

There are more differences between representations, though, than just the amount of detail they contain. One person may represent a problem in visual imagery, another in sentences, and a third in auditory images. If two people represent a problem in visual images, they may well not use the same images. For example, in imagining the monsters in the Monster Problem, some saw them arranged horizontally, some vertically, and some in a circle.

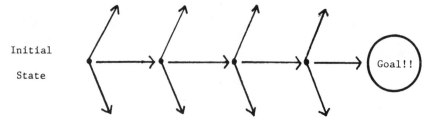

Figure 2. A Spare Representation

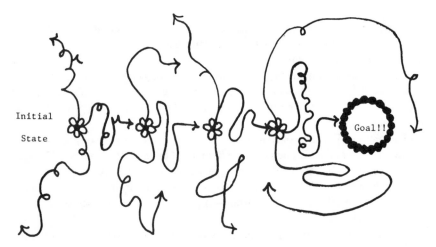

Figure 3. An Ornate Representation of the Same Problem

Our skill in problem solving depends in a very important way on our store of problem schemas. Each problem schema we know gives us a very valuable advantage in solving a whole class of problems—an advantage which may consist in knowing what to pay attention to, or how to represent the problem, or how to search for a solution, or all three. Clearly the more schemas we know, the better prepared we are as problem solvers.

While our problem skill depends on how many schemas we have, it also depends on the nature of those schemas. McDermott and Larkin (1978) have shown that novices in physics are more likely to have schemas that are tied to concrete aspects of the problem situation, e.g., "spring problem" schemas and "balance problem" schemas, whereas experts are more likely to have schemas tied to abstract physics principles, e.g., "energy" schemas and "moment of inertia" schemas.

In the same way, inexperienced math students are likely to use separate schemas for the following problems:

Mr. Lloyd and Mr. Russo

Mr. Russo takes 3 min. less than Mr. Lloyd to pack a case when each works alone. One day, after Mr. Russo spent 6 min. in packing a case, the boss called him away, and Mr. Lloyd finished packing in 4 more minutes. How many minutes would it take Mr. Russo alone to pack a case?

Saturated Fats

One vegetable oil contains 6% saturated fats and a second contains 26% saturated fats. In making a salad dressing how many ounces of the second may be added to 10 oz. of the first if the percent of saturated fats is not to exceed 16%?

They will use a "work problem" schema for the first and a "mixture problem" schema for the second. More experienced math students would include both of these problems in a "linear equations" schema.

Several years ago, I did some studies of the imagery people use to solve elementary math problems (Hayes, 1973). When I gave people long-division problems to do in their heads, I heard my subjects do a lot of talking to themselves: "Two-seventy-three into nine-forty-one, is two, and two times two-seventy-three is . . ." "Aha!" I said to myself. "Auditory images are important here." What really surprised me though was the behavior of subjects recruited from the faculty of the modern languages department. These subjects were people who were born in Europe but had been in the United States for many years and spoke excellent English. These subjects did a lot of talking, too, but in French, Spanish, Italian, Polish, or Latvian—whatever language they spoke when they originally learned division. One person told me that he did elementary mathematics in Catalan, his first language, and more advanced mathematics in Spanish, the language he used in his later schooling. Apparently many people use auditory imagery in solving arithmetic problems. In particular they use the sound of the language in which they originally learned arithmetic.

Visual imagery was also frequently used by people solving arithmetic problems. While doing problems in their heads, subjects reported visual images of the digits of the answer and of marks indicating borrowing or cancellation.

In one experiment, I presented subjects with the card shown in Figure 4, and asked them to add the numbers in their heads. I purposely did not leave any space on the card for them to write their answers, but then, since they were doing the problem in their heads, they didn't need any space to write the answer. In fact, 12 of the 16 subjects complained that there was no place to write the answer. Two of the subjects provided interesting solutions to this difficulty. One said that she suddenly realized that there was no reason that she couldn't write the answers *above* the problem. The other imagined a piece of paper scotchtaped to the bottom of the card.

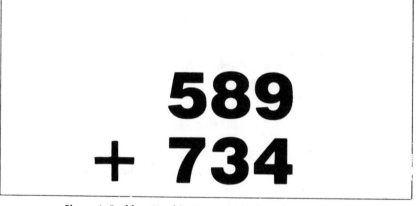

Figure 4. Problem Used in Hayes' Mental Math Experiment

Another subject, who learned her arithmetic in Hong Kong on an abacus, continually moved her fingers while solving arithmetic problems. As Hatano, Miyako, and Binks (1977) have shown, subjects who use the abacus to do arithmetic have difficulty doing mental arithmetic if they are prevented from using their fingers.

My most interesting subject was one who had very restricted vision and who, between fourth and twelfth grade, had relied entirely on Braille. When I questioned him about the imagery he used in doing arithmetic, he asked if I wanted to know about the "print" images, the Braille images, or the colors. In my best psychologist fashion, I maintained my upright posture and said, "Tell me about all of that."

In doing mental arithmetic, this subject could image numbers in the familiar form of numerals as Braille patterns, or as bars of color. Each digit had its own unique color, as did the days of the week (see Table 1). He could represent appointment times by a large patch of color for the day, with a small patch in the center for the hour. Thus, Tuesday at 3:00 was represented by a large patch of aqua with a small patch of pink in the center.

This phenomenon in which sensory images of one sort, e.g., colors or tastes, are strongly associated with sensory images of a different sort, e.g., shapes or sounds, is called "synthesia" and is fairly common. Perhaps you experience it yourself. One student told me that she associated colors with peoples names. "You know," she said, "like Michael is green." Another associated ice cream flavors with various kinds of laughter. She associated vanilla with a kind of high pitched giggle. Many people think of the week or the year as an oval or a distorted circle with days or months located at fixed places on the circle. Others have told me of spacial schemes for numbers, e.g., a spiral with "1" at the center and progressively larger numbers further from the center, and of colors systematically associated with musical notes.

One correspondent described what he called "song models", a kind of mental path for familiar songs. For example, "Silent Night" had a question mark shaped path starting at the bottom and moving toward the top. He wrote ". . . these 'song models' came about quite undeliberately, without any effort, and have no conscious purpose or use. For example, I don't use them deliberately to help me remember the songs. They rather just accompany my listening to a song, or singing it, or thinking about it, as a sort of image of the song. As the tune unfolds, I mentally proceed along the route."

We have observed that people use very diverse forms of representation even when they are solving simple problems. Numbers may be represented as the sound of words in one's native language. They may be represented as visual images

Table 1. One Subject's Color Associations

Numbers	Days of the Week	Months
0 = black	Monday = dark green	January = greenish white
1 = white	Tuesday = greenish white	February = redish yellow
2 = yellow (with	Wednesday = red orange	March = dark brownish red
some orange)	Thursday = light red	April = celery green
3 = pink	orange	May = light red orange
4 = blue	Friday = yellow	(like Thursday)
5 = yellow	Saturday = brown	June = green (lighter than
(paler than 2)	Sunday = greenish white,	Monday)
6 = dark green	but whiter than Tuesday	July = greener than April
7 = orange pink		August = red orange
8 = dark brown		(lighter than Wednesday)
9 = yellow (paler		September = orange with
than 5)		some red
		October = relatively pure
		white
		November = dark green, but
		not as dark as Monday
		December = darker than
		September

of print forms, Braille patterns, or colors. And they may be represented as finger movements. Most of our subjects used two or more of the forms. Thus, when they are representing a problem, people appear to have considerable choice in how they represent it. This choice is important because the form of representation that subjects choose can make a big difference in the difficulty they have in solving problems, and in the success they have in generalizing the solutions.

EXTERNAL REPRESENTATIONS

In many cases, an external representation is very helpful for solving problems. Drawing a sketch, jotting down lists, writing out equations, and making diagrams can help us to remember information and to notice new relations in the problem.

Consider the following rate problem:

> A car can average 20 mph up to Pike's Peak and 60 mph back down the same road. What is the average speed for the whole trip?

Some people will find this problem easy enough to solve in their heads. Others feel much more comfortable with pencil and paper—writing down relations as they occur to them and *not* trying to juggle all the facts in their heads at once. The scratch sheet of such a person might look like this:

(1) $\text{average rate} = \dfrac{\text{total distance}}{\text{total time}}$

(2) distance up = distance down = X

(3) total distance = 2X

(4) $\text{time} = \dfrac{\text{distance}}{\text{rate}}$

(5) $\text{time up} = \dfrac{X}{20 \text{ mph}}; \text{ time down} = \dfrac{X}{60 \text{ mph}}$

(6) $\text{total time} = \dfrac{X}{20} + \dfrac{X}{60}$

(7) $\text{average rate} = \dfrac{2X}{\dfrac{X}{20} + \dfrac{X}{60}} = \dfrac{2X}{\dfrac{60X + 20X}{20 \cdot 60}} = \dfrac{20 \cdot 60 \cdot 2X}{80X}$

(8) $\qquad\qquad = \dfrac{20 \cdot 60 \cdot 2}{80} = \dfrac{2400}{80} = 30 \text{ mph}$

Clearly this external representation is an enormous aid to memory. The problem solver can compute total time in lines 4 through 6 without having to remember total distance. In computing average rate in lines 7 and 8, he can apply each algebraic step without having to remember the effects of previous steps. Working without such an external representation would be very difficult for most people.

Other kinds of external representation can also be very useful memory aids. For example, matrix representation is very useful in solving identification problems such as this one:

Dickens, Einstein, Freud, and Kant

Dickens, Einstein, Freud, and Kant are professors of English, Physics, Psychology, and Philosophy (though not necessarily respectively).

1. Dickens and Freud were in the audience when the psychologist delivered his first lecture.
2. Both Einstein and the philosopher were friends of the physicist.
3. The philosopher has attended lectures by both Kant and Dickens.
4. Dickens has never heard of Freud.

Match the professors to their fields.

Our task is to match the professors to their fields. To do this, we construct a matrix as shown in Figure 5. Now, reading sentence 1, we conclude that the psychologist is neither Dickens nor Freud, so we put X's (indicating combinations ruled out) in two blocks as shown in the top matrix of Figure 6. In the second line, we learn that Einstein is neither the philosopher nor the physicist, and in the third line, that the philosopher is neither Kant nor Dickens, so we can fill in four more X's, as shown in the middle matrix of Figure 6. Now that leaves only Freud who could be the philosopher, so we put an O in the block corresponding to Freud and philosophy, and X out the other alternative fields for Freud (see remaining matrix, Figure 6). Proceeding in this way (though you may have some difficulty with the last few steps), you can identify the fields of all of the professors.

The matrix, like the notations in the previous problem, provides us with a great deal of help in remembering the results we have obtained in previous steps. Without such aids, some problems would be difficult or impossible to solve.

	English	Physics	Psychology	Philosophy
Dickens				
Einstein				
Freud				
Kant				

Figure 5. A matrix for the Dickens, Einstein, Freud, and Kant problem

After first step:

	English	Physics	Psychology	Philosophy
Dickens			X	
Einstein				
Freud			X	
Kant				

After second step:

	English	Physics	Psychology	Philosophy
Dickens			X	X
Einstein		X		X
Freud			X	
Kant				X

After third step:

	English	Physics	Psychology	Philosophy
Dickens			X	X
Einstein		X		X
Freud	X	X	X	O
Kant				X

Figure 6.   Steps for solving the Dickens, Einstein, Freud, and Kant problem

While external representations are clearly very useful as memory aids, they can help in other ways as well. As Paige and Simon (1966) have shown, some relations in problems are easier to discover when we use a diagram than when we don't. Think about the following problem for a moment and then examine Figure 7.

A car radiator contains exactly one liter of a 90% alcohol-water mixture. What quantity of water will change the liter to an 80% alcohol mixture?

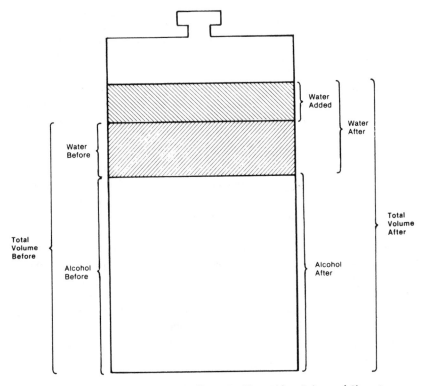

Figure 7. Representation of the Radiator Problem (After Paige and Simon)

Four relations which are important for solving the problem can be read directly from the diagram. These are:

ALCOHOL BEFORE = ALCOHOL AFTER
WATER AFTER = WATER BEFORE + WATER ADDED
TOTAL VOLUME BEFORE = ALCOHOL BEFORE + WATER BEFORE
TOTAL VOLUME AFTER = ALCOHOL AFTER + WATER AFTER

If any of these relations hadn't occurred to you after reading the problem text, the diagram could have given you a very useful hint.

Now, solve this problem before you proceed.

A board was sawed into two pieces. One piece was two-thirds as long as the whole board and was exceeded in length by the second piece by 4 ft. How long was the board before it was cut?

Did you notice the contradictory nature of the problem? Paige and Simon found that people who draw a diagram to represent this problem can use the diagram to discover its contradictory nature. People who do not draw a diagram are likely to miss the contradiction and some may be quite happy to accept an answer of −12 feet for the length of the board!

External representations, then, can be enormously useful both in remembering the details of a problem and in understanding the relations among its parts. You should *always* consider using them when you are solving difficult problems.

CHANGE AND GROWTH IN PRESENTATIONS

An important fact about a representation is that it can change or develop as we work on the problem. Often enough, when we start to solve a problem, there are some important parts that we are vague about or which have escaped us entirely. We may not fully understand the whole problem until we have worked on it for some time. When people start to solve the Monster Problem, they usually have a pretty clear understanding of the initial state, the goal, and the operator. Often though, they don't really understand the restrictions. As they try to make a move, we may hear them mutter, "If two globes are holding the same monster . . . No. That's not it." They may not achieve full understanding until they have been corrected several times for making illegal moves.

Imagine that you are faced with the following matchstick problem:

Matchstick Problem

Given 16 matches arranged in five squares like this

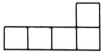

move just three sticks to form four squares.

When you first read the problem, it is reasonable to suspect that your representation of the goal will be very straightforward: you are looking for *any* arrangement of four squares, such as these:

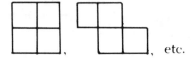

If your first several solution attempts fail, though, you may reexamine the problem statement to see if there is anything you overlooked. You may notice that 16 matches will make exactly four squares only if each match is used in one and only one square. Any arrangement in which a match serves as the side of two different squares won't work. This observation allows you to change your representation of the goal. Now you are searching for arrangements like this:

or this:

but not like this:

or this:

This new, more precise representation of the goal can help you to avoid false leads in your search for a solution.

I observed another example of change in representation firsthand when a friend challenged me to solve the Four Knights Problem. This problem involves a 3 × 3 chess board and four chess pieces—two white knights and two black knights, arranged as shown in Figure 8. The goal is to interchange the positions of the white and black knights using only legal knight moves. For those who aren't familiar with chess, Figure 9 shows the legal knight moves. The knight can move one space straight ahead and one space diagonally forward.

Unfortunately, I had never seen the Four Knights Problem before. However, on general principles, I set up some guidelines in searching for a solution. First, I decided to work with an external representation of the problem to help me keep my place. I used a 3 × 3 matrix like that shown in Figure 8, on which I pencilled the current position of each piece and erased the previous position. Second, I knew that if I moved pieces at random, I would have trouble remembering which

Figure 8. Original Position in the Four Knights Problem

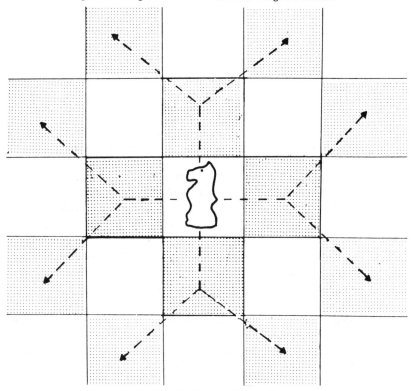

Figure 9. Eight Possible Knight Moves

paths I had already explored and which I had yet to explore. Further, I knew that even when I reached the goal, I might forget the path that had led there.* For these reasons, I made moves which would be easy to remember: I moved all four pieces one step clockwise, giving me the arrangement shown in Figure 10.

This result suggested absolutely nothing to me, so I moved all pieces one more step clockwise to yield the formation shown in Figure 11.

At this point, I recognized that I had rotated the original pattern by 90° and that if I just repeated what I had done up until now, the problem would be solved! Earlier I had thought small. In my representation, there was just one operator—the single knight's move. Now, because of the result I observed in the external representation, I added a larger operator to my representation—a macro-operator—consisting of eight knights' moves. Using the macro-operator, I could solve the problem in just two moves rather than 16.

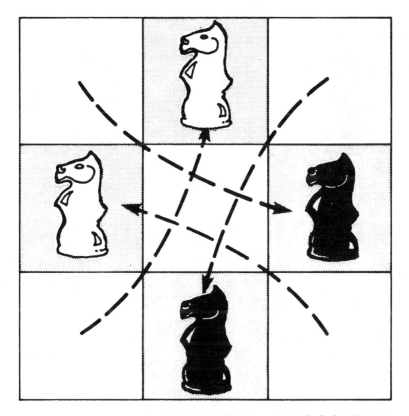

Figure 10. Four Knights Problem Rotated One Step Clockwise From Original Position

*(Question: Could I have used a better external representation?)

**Figure 11. Four Knights Problem Rotated Two Steps Clockwise
From Original Position**

Very often, then, we change our representation of a problem while we are
solving it. In many cases, these changes appear to be improvements which make
the problem easier to solve. If you are having difficulty in solving a problem,
it makes sense to consider changing your problem representation. A useful way
to proceed, as Polya (1945) has suggested, is to reexamine the problem statement very carefully. Perhaps we can make an inference which will help us
represent the goal more accurately as in the Matchstick Problem. Or perhaps we
can form a macro-operator as in the Four Knights Problem. Careful examination
of each of the four problem parts—initial state, goal, operators, and restrictions—
can suggest ways to improve our representation.

REPRESENTATIONS MAKE A DIFFERENCE

A problem may be difficult or impossible for us to solve in one representation, but much easier in another. For example, consider the Nine Dots Problem.

The Nine Dots Problem

Without raising your pencil from the paper, draw four straight lines so that each of the dots above is touched by at least one of the lines.

If you don't already know the problem, try to solve it before proceeding.

Some people have trouble because they have added a restriction to their representation which makes the problem unsolvable.* The restriction is that the lines should never extend beyond the square defined by the nine dots. Typical solution attempts for subjects adding this restriction are shown in Figure 12.

The first representation gave trouble because it added an extra restriction to the problem. Any representation that adds or deletes significant things from the initial state, from the goal, from the operators, or from the restrictions is very likely to give us serious trouble. We can avoid this trouble to some extent by checking our representation very carefully against the problem statement before we launch into any massive solution attempt.

Even when our representation of a problem is essentially correct, though, there are other ways to form a correct representation. Some of them are easier to use than others. Consider the following river-current problem.

A River-Current Problem

You are standing by the side of a river which is flowing past you at the rate of 5 mph. You spot a raft 1 mi. upstream on which there are two boys helplessly adrift. Then you spot the boys' parents 1 mi. downstream paddling upstream to save them. You know that in still water the parents can paddle at the rate of 4 mph. How long will it be before the parents reach the boys?

*See Wickelgren (1974) for an alternative interpretation.

One very natural way to represent the problem is to take the point of view of the observer standing by the side of the river. (The problem really sets you up to do this.) We can compute the speed of the boys with respect to the observer (5 mph downstream) and the speed of the parents with respect to the observer (5 mph—4 mph = 1 mph downstream). The difference in speed between the boys and their parents is four miles per hour. Thus, it should take half an hour to cover the two-mile distance.

An alternate and simpler way to represent the problem is to take the point of view of the boys on the raft. If we take this point of view, we can ignore the rate at which the boys and their parents are moving with respect to the observer. (The observer really *is* irrelevant in this problem.) In addition, we can ignore the rate of the current, since it is affecting the boys and their parents equally. (If this seems strange to you, remember that we routinely ignore motions that affect both parties equally such as the rotation of the earth on its axis and the motion of the earth around the sun.) All that is left is the rate at which the parents are paddling—four miles per hour. Thus, the new representation allows us to find the rate of approach in one step, while the old representation required three.

How people represent natural phenomena often determines how they act in practical situations. For example, as a child of four or five, I believed that electricity was a fluid that would run out of the light socket if a light bulb were not screwed into it. In my view, the light bulb acted as a kind of plug that stopped the flow of electricity. Although this representation was not good physics, I believed in it quite strongly and was upset when my parents ignored my advice to plug up an empty light socket. I was sure that we were going to be knee deep in wasted electricity.

The representation of electricity as a fluid has a more sophisticated adult version that doesn't require us to put bulbs in empty sockets and is actually quite useful. Gentner and Gentner (1983) found that there are two common ways for high school and first-year college students to represent electrical currents. One way is to think of electricity as a fluid and the other is to think of it as a moving crowd of people.

The Fluid Representation.   In this representation, electricity flowing through a wire is thought of as water flowing through a pipe. Electrical voltage is thought of as the pressure pushing the water through the pipe and electrical current, or amps, is thought of as the rate at which the water is flowing through the pipe, e.g., gallons per minute. Electrical resistance is thought of as a narrowing of the pipe that impedes the flow of water. A battery is thought of as a reservoir of water or as a pump pushing water through the pipe.

The Moving-Crowd Representation.   In this representation, electricity flowing through a wire is thought of as crowd of people (electrons) rushing down a corridor. The voltage corresponds to how hard the people are pushing and the current, or amps, to how many people pass through the corridor every minute. An electrical resistance is like a gate in the corridor that allows only a few people to pass at a time. People who represent electricity as a moving crowd, however, often have difficulty representing batteries.

Gentner and Gentner (1983) observed seven subjects who consistently used the fluid representation and eight who consistently used the moving-crowd representation. They found that people who used the fluid representation were consistently better at solving problems that involved complex arrangements of batteries than they were at problems that involved complex arrangement of resistances. The reverse was true for people who used the moving-crowd representation. How we represent a problem, then, is an important factor in determining what problems are hard and what are easy.

WORKING BACKWARDS

When you have trouble solving a problem head-on, it is often useful to try to work backwards. Working backwards involves a simple change in representation—or point of view—in which your new starting place is the original goal, and vice versa. Working backwards can be helpful because problems are often easier to solve in one direction than another. To see why this is so, consider Figure 14.

Suppose your problem is to get from X to Y. Starting from X, there are five equally promising paths to explore in searching for the solution. Starting from Y, however, there is just one path to X. In this case, then, solving backwards is easier than solving forwards.

Here is a problem which illustrates the usefulness of working backwards: You are given four black cards and four red cards from an ordinary deck. You have to arrange them in a stack, face down, so that you can deal them out as follows:

1. You place the top card on the table, face up. It is black.
2. You place the next card (now on the top of the deck) on the bottom of the deck.
3. You place the next card on the table, face up. It is red.
4. You place the next card on the bottom of the deck.

You proceed in this way—putting alternate cards on the table—until all the cards are dealt out. When you have finished, the pattern of cards on the table should look like Figure 15.

This is a moderately difficult problem if you try to solve it forwards. There are lots of possible arrangements of the cards (70 of them), and only one of the arrangements is right! If you work backwards from the final result, however, there is just one path to the correct arrangement. To work backwards, you have to reverse the original order of operations. Put the top card on the table, put the top card on the bottom, etc., becomes: Put a card from the table on top, put the bottom card on top, etc. When you apply this sequence of operations to the cards laid out on the table as shown above, you end up with a stack of cards arranged in the correct order.

Working backwards is useful in many practical situations. For example, suppose that you were writing a position paper to persuade the management of your

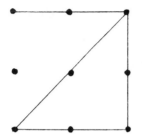 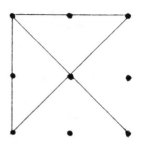

Figure 12. Typical Solution Attempts for the Nine Dots Problem

company to accept your pet idea. You might work forwards by writing a paper in which you present all those details and computations that you find so fascinating and firing it off to management. Or you might work backwards by saying to yourself, "Now hold on. What I'm trying to do is to convince management. If they're going to be convinced, what has to happen? I'll have to meet their objections. Now what are those objections likely to be?" By working backwards—by starting with your goal—you are more likely to write a convincing paper.

HYPOTHETICAL REASONING

Consider this problem:

Truthtellers and Liars

You are visiting a strange country in which there are just two kinds of people—truthtellers and liars. Truthtellers *always* tell the truth and liars *always* lie. You hail the first two people you meet and say, "Are you truthtellers or liars?" The first person mumbles something you can't hear. The second says, "He says he is a truthteller. He is a truthteller and so am I." Can you trust the directions that these two may give you?

A good way to solve this problem is to propose hypotheses. For example, you might say, "Suppose the first guy was a liar. What would he have have said then?" This is a hypothesis because, for the moment, you are purposely assuming something that wasn't stated in the problem—that is, that the first man was a liar. Now you work out the consequences of this hypothesis. "If the first man was a liar, he must have lied about himself and said that he was a truthteller." Now you try the alternative hypothesis: "Suppose he was a truthteller." The consequence of this hypothesis is that the first man would have to tell the truth about himself and say that he was a truthteller. The critical discovery that you can make by trying these hypotheses is that whether the first man was a truthteller or a liar, he must have *said* that he was a truthteller. The second man, then, must have been a truthteller, and so was the first man since the second man said so.

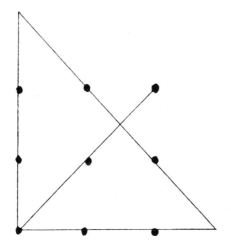

Figure 13. Solution of the Nine Dots Problem

This solution method is called hypothetical reasoning. It involves adding to the problem representation by making hypotheses and then working out the consequences of these hypotheses to learn more about the problem.

Hypothetical reasoning is useful in a very wide variety or practical situations. For example, suppose that a company manager is trying to decide whether to rent or to buy new office space. She might consider a variety of hypotheses in making her decision, e.g.,

"Suppose we use it for more than two years—then it will be cheaper to buy."

Or

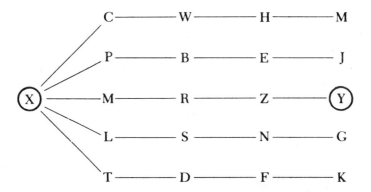

Figure 14. A Good Problem for Working Backwards

"Suppose there is a recession and we have to cut our staff. Then we would want to be able to get out fast, so renting would be better."

We will discuss ways to evaluate these hypotheses in the chapters on decision making.

ILL-DEFINED PROBLEMS

Many of the practical problems we encounter every day are ill-defined ones. That is, they are problems that we can't solve unless we take action to define them better. There are two sorts of actions we may have to take: we may have to make gap-filling decisions and we may have to jump into the problem before we can fully understand it. Here is an example of a problem that requires gap-filling decisions.

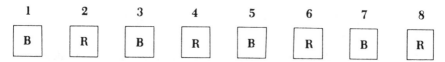

Figure 15.   Final Position in the Black/Red Card Problem

Just as you are about to leave your house for Christmas shopping, your sister rushes up to you and says, "I haven't had time to get anything for Mother. Would you mind getting something for her—Oh, just anything nice—for about 20 dollars—pleeese?" Your sister has solved her ill-defined problem by making it your ill-defined problem. To solve this problem, you will have to make some decisions. Would your mother prefer clothes? Books? Records? Suppose you decide on records. You still have many decisions to make. Is she really tired of Liberace? Will her punk rock phase last? When you finally choose a gift, your decisions will have contributed a great deal to the definition of this ill-defined problem.

It is easy enough to create an ill-defined problem. If you sit down at your local lunch counter and order "a milk shake, please, any flavor," you will have presented the counter people with an ill-defined problem. They may refuse to accept it, saying "I'm sorry, we can't help you unless you choose *some* flavor." Or they may accept the problem enthusiastically, reveling in the creative freedom you have provided them, and manufacture for you your first hot pastrami milk shake.

Since each problem solver may make different "gap-filling" decisions in solving the same ill-defined problem, each may, as a result, arrive at a different solution. These solutions may differ considerably in quality depending on the decisions the problem solver has made. Our skill in solving ill-defined problems, then, depends in an important way on our ability to make good gap-filling decisions.

The second action we may have to take to define an ill-defined problem is to jump into the problem before we fully understand it. Very often the real nature of a problem is hidden from us until we actually try to solve it. For example, suppose we have the task of writing a magazine article for ten-year-olds about abortion. The real nature of this problem probably won't be apparent to us until we begin writing. Then a multitude of difficulties will leap out at us. Will they know what the word "fetus" means? How can the question about when a fetus becomes a human be explained? Can they understand the problems that lead a woman to have an abortion?

Often with problems such as this one, we can't fully define the problem until we are nearly finished solving it.

Real-world problems are often ill-defined. For example, many of the problems that architects face are ill-defined. The architect's client may desire a building with a certain amount of floor space at a specified cost but may leave most of the other decisions about the building's design—its floor plan, its appearance, etc.—up to the architect. How well architects make these gap-filling decisions determines in large measure how good they are as architects. Similarly, professional problems faced by writers, painters, computer programmers, composers, lawyers, etc., are very often ill-defined ones. To solve such problems successfully, we must be prepared to make gap-filling decisions and to jump into the problems before we understand them.

CONCLUSION

Some problems are much easier to solve in one representation than another. If you are having difficulty solving a problem, consider changing the representation. First check to be sure your representation is correct. Then consider changing your point of view: Consider hypothetical reasoning or visual imagery; consider working backwards, making a gap-filling decision, changing straight lines into circles—anything that may yield a representation that is easier to work with. You may not find one, but if you are already having difficulty in solving the problem, you have relatively little to lose.

Summary

1. When we think through the solution to a problem, the things we think about are internal representations. Internal representations, then, are the medium of the problem solvers thought in the same sense that clay is the medium of the sculptor.

2. Our representation of a problem must include a representation of the goal, and may also include representations of an initial state, operators, and restrictions.

3. An internal representation is not a copy of an external situation. People

are very active when they form representations: They add information, delete information as irrelevant, and interpret information. The internal representation is very different from the external problem situation.

4. Knowledge of language and knowledge of the world are both important in interpreting problem information. Problem schemas are an especially important part of our world knowledge for interpreting problem information.

5. External representations can provide considerable aid in problem solving. In difficult problems, we should *always* consider using external representations.

6. There are large differences in the way different people represent the same information—some may use auditory imagery; others, visual imagery; still others, sentences, and so on.

7. These differences in representation can make an important difference in the difficulty of the problem. When problem solvers encounter difficulty, they should consider searching for a new problem representation.

REFERENCES

Gentner, D., and Gentner, D. R. "Flowing Water and Teeming Crowds: Mental Models of Electricity." In *Mental Models*, edited by D. Gentner and A. L. Stevens. Hillsdale, NJ: Lawrence Erlbaum, 1983.

Hatano, G., Miyako, Y., and Binks, M. G. "Performance of Expert Abacus Operators." *Cognition*, 5, 57–71, 1977.

Hayes, J. R. "On the Function of Visual Imagery in Elementary Mathematics." In *Visual Information Processing*, edited by W. Chase. New York: Academic Press, Inc., 1973.

Hayes, J. R., Waterman, D. A., and Robinson, C. S. "Identifying the Relevant Aspects of a Problem Text." *Cognitive Science*, 1(3), 297–313, 1977.

Hinsley, D. A., Hayes, J. R., and Simon, H. A. "From Words to Equations: Meaning and Representation in Algebra Word Problems." In *Cognitive Processes in Comprehension*, edited by P. Carpenter and M. Just. Hillsdale, NJ: Lawrence Erlbaum, 1977.

McDermott, J. R., and Larkin, J. H. "Representing Testbook Physics Problems." Proceedings of the Second National Conference of the Canadian Society of Computational Studies of Intelligence, Toronto, 1978.

Paige, J. M., and Simon, H. A. "Cognitive Processes in Solving Algebra Word Problems." In *Problem Solving: Research, Method and Theory*, edited by B. Kleinmuntz. New York: John Wiley & Sons, Inc., 1966.

Polya, G. *How to Solve It*, Second Edition. Princeton, NJ: Princeton University Press, 1957.

Wickelgren, W. A. *How to Solve Problems*. San Francisco: W. H. Freeman & Co., 1974.

Pages 6–7. The Eight Dots Problem

```
● ● ● ●     ○ ○ ○ ○
● ● ● ● ○   ○ ○ ○
● ● ●   ○ ● ○ ○ ○
● ●   ● ○ ● ○ ○ ○
● ● ○ ●   ● ○ ○ ○
● ● ○ ● ○ ●   ○ ○
● ● ○ ● ○ ● ○   ○
● ● ○ ● ○   ○ ● ○
● ● ○   ○ ● ○ ● ○
●   ○ ● ○ ● ○ ● ○
  ● ○ ● ○ ● ○ ● ○
○ ●   ● ○ ● ○ ● ○
○ ● ○ ●   ● ○ ● ○
○ ● ○ ● ○ ●   ● ○
○ ● ○ ● ○ ● ○ ●


○ ● ○ ● ○ ● ○   ●
○ ● ○ ● ○   ○ ● ●
○ ● ○   ○ ● ○ ● ●
○   ○ ● ○ ● ○ ● ●
○ ○   ● ○ ● ○ ● ●
○ ○ ○ ●   ● ○ ● ●
○ ○ ○ ● ○ ●   ● ●
○ ○ ○ ● ○   ● ● ●
○ ○ ○   ○ ● ● ● ●
○ ○ ○ ○   ● ● ● ●
```

33

Page 7.   The farmer crossing the river.

Here is one of the two solutions:

1. Take the chicken across and leave it on the far side.
2. Return to original side and take the dog across.
3. Leave the dog and take the chicken back.
4. Leave the chicken on the original side and take the grain across.
5. Leave the grain and go back to get the chicken.

Page 10.   Ahmed and George. 63.25 cubits.

Page 13.   Mr. Lloyd and Mr. Russo. Mr. Russo packs a case in 9 min.

Page 13.   Saturated fats. Ten ounces must be added.

Page 17.   Dickens, Einstein, Freud, and Kant.

Dickens is the English Professor
Kant is the Physics Professor
Einstein is the Psychology Professor
Freud is the Philosophy Professor

Page 20.   Matchstick Problem.

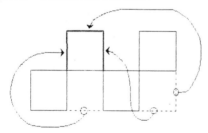

2

Search

Once people have arrived at a basic understanding of a problem—a preliminary representation of its goal, operators, etc.—they can launch into a search for the solution. In this chapter, we will describe that search process in its various forms and provide some practical guidelines which can help you in your own solution searches.

As a metaphor for the problem solver's search for solution, we imaging a person going through a maze. The entrance to the maze is the initial state of the problem and its exit is the goal. The paths in the maze, including all its byways and blind alleys, correspond to the *problem space*—that is, to all the sequences of moves available to the problem solver.

A factor which has an important effect on the difficulty of a maze is its size. Figure 1 shows six "tree" mazes which vary in branching, length, and size. A *tree maze* is one with no loops. The *size* of a maze is the total number of different paths from top to bottom. The mazes in the upper part of the figure branch twice at each choice point, while those in the lower part branch three times. This difference in branching doesn't make very much difference in size *if* the maze is short. If the maze is long, however, it makes an enormous difference. Notice that maze 6 is more than 50 times as big as maze 5.*

Familiar problems differ a great deal in size. The River Crossing Problem in the last chapter has a very small problem space, while the Combination Lock Problem in the Introduction has a huge one. Newell and Simon (1972) estimate that the size of the problem space for a typical chess game is 10^{120}. (They assume a game of 40 moves with branching of 20 alternatives per move.) It will

---

*If B is the degree of branching and L is length, then

$$size = B^L$$

help you to understand just how large a number 10^{120} is if you recognize that
the estimated number of atoms in the universe is only 10^{80}.

VARIETIES OF SEARCH

While most people are vaguely familiar with "trial and error" search, few
can describe other search methods. In fact, there are a great many search methods.
In this chapter, we will describe four general search methods:

Figure 1. Six Tree Mazes

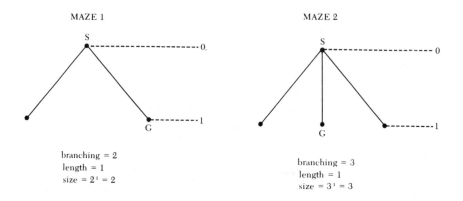

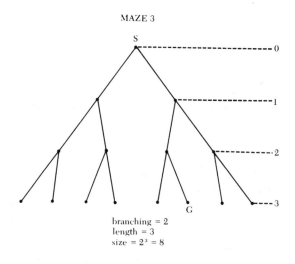

MAZE 4

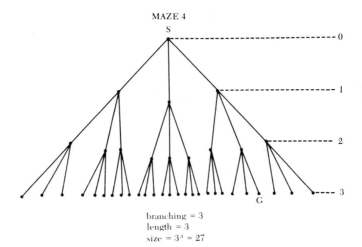

branching = 3
length = 3
size = 3^3 = 27

MAZE 5

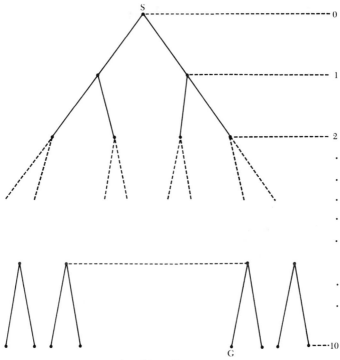

branching = 2
length = 10
size = 2^{10} = 1,024

MAZE 6

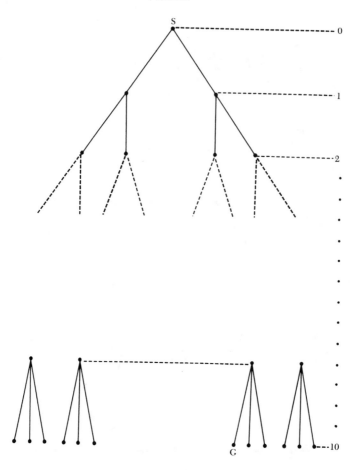

branching = 3
length = 10
size = 3^{10} = 59,049

1. Trial and Error
2. Proximity Methods
3. Fractionation Methods
4. Knowledge-based Methods

Understanding these strategies and their strengths and weaknesses is essential for choosing good problem solving procedures.

TRIAL-AND-ERROR SEARCH

The defining characteristic of trial-and-error search is that the searchers either don't have or don't use information that indicates to them that any path is more likely to lead to the goal than any other path. In a maze, trial-and-error searchers never know that they are on the right path until they open the last door and find themselves outside.

Trial-and-error search comes in two forms—*blind* and *systematic*. In blind search, the searchers pick paths to explore blindly, without considering whether they have already explored the path. In systematic search, the searchers keep track of the paths which they have already explored and choose to explore only unexplored paths. Because this method avoids multiple searches, systematic search is *twice* as efficient on the average as blind search.

A Dramatic Example

Suppose that you have 50 eggs in a bag balanced on your head. One of the eggs is brown and all the rest are white. Just as you are crossing a deep chasm by balancing on a fallen log, you hear a commanding voice say, "Stop where you are and show me the brown egg!" Since you have no idea what this maniac may do, you decide to pacify him. You reach into the bag with your one free hand and pull out an egg. It's white! What do you do now? If you put the white eggs back with the others and keep trying, you will be doing relatively inefficient *blind* search. On the average, it will take you 50 tries to find the brown egg and may take much longer. However, if you mark the eggs you have already examined in the only way you can, by tossing them into the chasm, you will be doing a relatively efficient *systematic* search. On the average, it will take you only 25 tries to find the brown egg, and it will never take more than 50. Since a little reflection suggests how truly demented this person must be, you decide to sacrifice your eggs and go for the quicker systematic search.

Trial-and-error search can be very useful for finding one's way in small mazes and for solving problems with small problem spaces. In the River Crossing Problem in Chapter 1, it is easy to search through all possible paths to find the solution. However, as the size of the problem space increases, the method becomes less and less useful. Trial and error is a reasonably comfortable strategy for opening a combination lock with one or even two dials. With three dials (1,000 paths), it gets a bit boring. With five dials (100,000 paths), we have to be pretty desperate to use it, and with 10 dials, as we pointed out in the Introduction, it is essentially useless unless you have a spare 317 years to invest.

Suppose you were passing through Pittsburgh, and you wanted to call your friend, Bill Miller. When you look in the phone book, you find that there are 180 William Millers listed. You could call them one after another until you found the right one, but it would be far more sensible to try another strategy. You could try to remember his middle initial or his address. Or you could try to reach a mutual friend who might have his number.

The moral here is very clear. Trial-and-error search is *not* efficient in large problems. If you find yourself doing trial-and-error search in a large problem, you should almost certainly stop and use a better method.

Sometimes (alas!) we don't have a choice. Trial and error may truly be the only method available. If so, you should consider very carefully whether solving the problem is worth the cost of the search. It may well not be!

PROXIMITY METHODS

Proximity search methods are in a sense just one step ahead of trial-and-error search. In proximity search, the searcher looks exactly one step ahead, while in trial-and-error search, the searcher doesn't look ahead at all. This one-step difference, however, makes an enormous difference in the effectiveness of the methods.

The two proximity methods we will discuss are "hill climbing" and "means-ends analysis." In both of these methods the basic question is, "What next step can I take that will bring me closer to the goal?" Neither method looks beyond that one step to see what difficulties lie ahead.

The Hill Climbing Method

Suppose that you are lost at night in a forest. You can't see a thing. You reason that if you were on the top of a hill you might be able to spot the light of a house or a campfire. Can you do any better than trial-and-error search to find the top of a hill? In fact, you can do much better! The hill-climbing method can greatly reduce the time you require to reach your goal. The method works like this:

1. You put out a foot to take a step.
2. If the step is up, you take it and repeat the procedure.
3. If the step is down, you pull your foot back, take a quarter turn clockwise, and try again.

4. If you have turned a full circle and have found nothing but steps down, you stop because you know you must be on the top of a hill.

Having completed the hill-climbing procedure, you can now look around for signs of civilization.

How efficient is the hill-climbing method compared to trial and error? Very efficient in hilly country. For example, if we were searching for a hilltop in an area 1,000 steps square, hill climbing would be about 1,000 times more efficient than trial-and-error search. The relative efficiency of hill climbing would be even greater for larger search areas.

Despite its efficiency, the hill-climbing method has some inherent weaknesses. To illustrate, let's pick up the example where we left off. Having reached the top of the hill, you look around and see nothing. Tired and discouraged, you fall asleep only to wake in full morning light. You look and find to your surprise that your hill is entirely surrounded by much taller hills. Now you can understand why you didn't see any signs of civilization last night. You wanted to be on a *tall* hill, but the hill-climbing method can't tell one hill from another. It took you to the top of the nearest hill and that happened to be a small one. If you want to be sure to find the highest hill, then you will have to supplement the hill climbing method with some other method that can choose among hills or use a different method entirely.

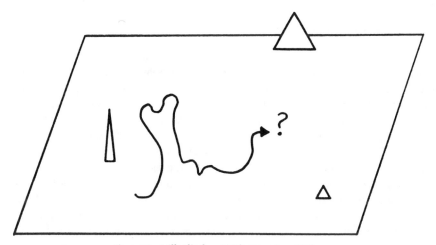

Figure 2. Hill Climber With Very Few Hills

Another problem with hill climbing is that it works well only when most of its search area slopes. If its search area is almost entirely flat with an occasional very steep peak (see Figure 2), the hill climber is very little better off than the trial-and-error searcher.

The hill-climbing method is important because it can be used and is used to solve a wide range of problems. Here are two everyday examples:

1. You are driving in a strange city and want to find the downtown area. At each corner you stop and look in all directions. You proceed in the direction that appears busiest.

In this example, the choice of streets corresponds to the choice of steps, and the amount of commotion on the streets corresponds to the height of the steps. Just as the method may take you to a low hilltop when you want the tallest one, it may also take you to a local shopping center when you want downtown.

2. A small child has readjusted your TV set so that it shows all sorts of interesting diagonal stripes. To return the set to its more traditional adjustment, you begin to twiddle knobs. That is, you choose a knob and turn it a little bit while watching the screen. If the pictures gets better, you do it again. If it gets worse, you move it a little in the opposite direction. When it gets worse when you move in either direction, you leave it where it is, having found the ''right'' adjustment. Then you do the same for the other knobs—that is, you ''hill climb'' to best adjustment with each knob. Since the adjustment of some knobs influences the adjustment of others, you may have to redo some of the knobs several times before you are able to get a decent picture.

After Hill Climbing, What?

In the problems we used to illustrate the hill-climbing method, the initial state and the goal differed in a single dimension, e.g., height, density of business, picture quality. Further, in each of these problems, the operators (if there was more than one) all worked in essentially the same way to change that single dimension, e.g., in the TV example, all of the knobs changed picture quality in roughly the same way. In many problems, though, we must deal with differences that have several dimensions and we must deal with them by using specialized operators—that is, operators that change one or a few of the dimensions but not all of them.

Imagine that you are a contractor building a house. The empty lot that you have right now differs in many dimensions from your goal. It doesn't have a foundation, walls or roof, plumbing, wiring, or paint. Further, your operators—masons, carpenters, plumbers, electricians, and painters—are specialized. Masons can build foundations and walls, but they can't paint. Electricians can put in wiring, but not roofs. When we were tuning the TV set, it was reasonable to try knobs at random to see what helped. In building a house, though, this strategy would be wasteful and foolish. If the house needed painting, we wouldn't randomly call in plumbers or carpenters to see if they helped. We would analyze what still needed to be done and search for an appropriate means to accomplish it. This is just what the technique of means-ends analysis does in solving problems.

Means-Ends Analysis

Means-ends analysis (Newell and Simon, 1972), like hill climbing, tries to reach the goal by taking a sequence of steps, each of which reduces the distance to the goal. The means-ends technique for doing this, however, is both more complex and more powerful than the hill-climbing technique. It can handle more complex differences and employs subgoals to help execute each step.

The technique involves three procedures:

Procedure	*Example*
1. Find a list of differences between the current state and the goal. (If you can't find any differences, report that the problem is solved.)	The house needs plumbing, wiring, and paint.
2. Take the first difference and find an operator appropriate for reducing it.	Try to hire a plumber.
If you can't find an appropriate operator, go to the next difference.	If the plumber is out of town, try to hire an electrician.
If you run out of differences to find operators for, report that you can't solve the problem.	If everyone is out of town for a builder's convention, give up—at least for now.
3. Compare the conditions for applying the operator with the current state to find a difference. (If there is no difference, of course, just apply the operator.)	The painter says he'll do the job, but he broke his ladder.
If there is a difference, try to reduce it.	Lend the painter your ladder.

Sometimes it is convenient to show the relation between means and ends in a means-ends table such as this:

	foundation	walls	roof	plumbing	wiring	painting
mason	X	X				
carpenter		X	X			
plumber				X		
electrician					X	
painter						X

Here is another example. Imagine that Vlad is a Slovak emigrant in the 1880's who is well trained in means-ends analysis. Vlad is traveling from his native village of Bicske, 35 miles west of Budapest, to Pittsburgh, Pennsylvania, to work in the steel mills. There are several means of transportation available which are suited to various purposes. These means and ends can be summarized as follows:

	ship	train	coach	trolley	walking
large ocean distances	X				
large land distances		X			
medium distances			X	X	
medium-small distances, urban areas				X	
small distances					X

Vlad looks in his atlas and discovers that Pittsburgh is separated from Bicske by a very large ocean. The means-ends table indicates that his original intention to take a stagecoach is out. Only a ship will do. The first travel agent he speaks to can arrange passage for him on a very nice ship to Calcutta. Vlad rejects this offer because his atlas shows that Calcutta is even farther from Pittsburgh than Bicske is. After all, his goal is to *reduce* the distance between him and Pittsburgh. The second agent offers him passage on a ship sailing from Bremen to New York.

Since New York is much closer to Pittsburgh than Bicske, Vlad buys a ticket for New York.

Now Vlad has identified an operator for reducing his distance from Pittsburgh—taking a ship from Bremen. But he can't apply it because the operator has a condition—he has to be in Bremen to sail. So Vlad sets up a subgoal—to get from Bicske to Bremen. Relying on his atlas and his means-ends table, he decides to take a train. Fortunately, he is able to buy a ticket for an express train form Budapest to Bremen. Here again, the operator imposes a condition—Vlad has to get to Budapest to take the train. So he sets up a new subgoal to get from Bicske to Budapest. Since Bicske is out in the sticks, the means-ends table tells Vlad that he has only one option, the stagecoach. Since the coach doesn't stop at Vlad's hovel, he has to set up one more subgoal—to get to the coach stop. His reliable means-ends table tells him to walk.

HILL CLIMBING AND MEANS-ENDS ANALYSIS: A COMPARISON

Both methods search for a next step which will reduce the distance to the goal. Means-ends analysis is a more powerful method than hill climbing because:

1. it can consider many dimensions of difference between the current state and the goal, and
2. it can set up a sequence of subgoals to help in accomplishing the next step.

Because both methods look only one step ahead, both have difficulty with blind alleys and detour problems. For example, in solving river-crossing problems, it is necessary at some point for the farmer to take one of his possessions back across the river away from the goal. Hill climbers, means-ends analyzers, and, not incidentally, people, have trouble with problems of this kind.

In the next section, among other things, we will discuss some procedures which can help us out of our difficulties with detour problems.

FRACTIONATION METHODS

A very powerful way to simplify the search for a solution is to break the problem into parts. Imagine that you are working your way through a tree maze that has a length of ten, and has two alternatives at each of ten choice points. In this maze, you would have to find the goal among 2^{10} or 1,024 alternatives. But notice how this situation would change if someone who knew the maze gave you the following hint. The last person to solve the maze lost his puppy halfway through the maze. The puppy is now sitting right in front of the door through which the solution path and his master passed. Now you can break the problem into two parts. As a *subgoal*, you first search for and rescue the puppy. Then, when you have found it, you can search for the exit from there. Breaking the problem into parts is a real advantage because solving the two subproblems is easier than solving the original problem. Figure 3 illustrates the point. Since you know that the puppy is located halfway through the maze, there are just 2^5 or 32 places where it may be. Once you find the puppy, there are just five more steps to reach the goal, and, therefore, just 32 alternative paths to the exit. To find the puppy and then find the goal will require us to examine no more than 32 + 32 or 64 alternatives. Without the hint, we would have to examine a maximum of 1,024 alternatives.

Where does this advantage come from? When we come to a door halfway through the maze and it doesn't have a puppy in front of it, we know that we don't have to explore any of the 32 paths which lie beyond. Since there are 31 doors without puppies, that means that we eliminate 31 × 32 or 992 paths.

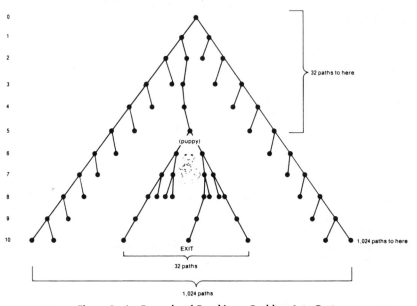

Figure 3. An Example of Breaking a Problem Into Parts

Breaking the problem into parts, then, has reduced the amount of search we have to do by a factor of $\dfrac{1024}{64}$, or 16. It is surprising what one little subgoal can do. Having several subgoals would help even more.

Clearly, if someone gives you a subgoal, as in the example just given, that will help you to solve the problem. But in most cases you aren't given subgoals. You have to find them for yourself. How can you do that?

Here, we list four methods for identifying subgoals: working in to the problem, abstracting, analyzing the goal, and using knowledge of problem schemas.

Working in to the Problem.   Suppose that you are trying to solve a problem like that represented in Figure 4. Working forward from *A*, you find that you can get to *M*, *B*, and *Q*. Working backward from *G*, you find that you can reach *K*, *F*, and *L*. At this point, your problem is to get from *M* or *B* or *Q* to *K* or *F* or *L*. If the route from *B* to *F* looks more promising to you than other routes, perhaps because of prior knowledge or planning ahead, then you can set the subgoal of getting from *B* to *F*. Working backward and forward into the problem, then, allowed you to indentify the smaller problem, getting from *B* to *F* as a subgoal of the larger problem of getting from *A* to *G*.

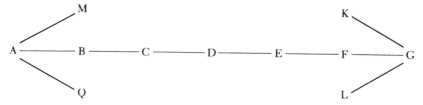

Figure 4. Problem: Get from A to G

Notice that you may set up subgoals in this way which are not useful. For example, suppose that you discover that you can get to *M* from *A*, and set up the subgoal to get from *M* to *G*. In fact, there is no path from *M* to *G* so that this subgoal can't be achieved. Subgoals are so useful in problem solving that it is almost always advisable to search for them, even though we sometimes find ones that are not useful.

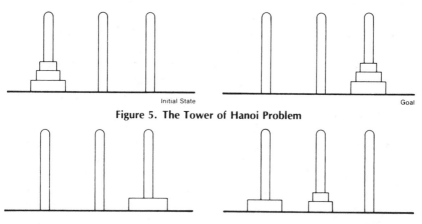

Initial State   Goal

Figure 5. The Tower of Hanoi Problem

**Figure 6. First Subgoal in the
Tower of Hanoi Problem**

**Figure 7. Second Subgoal in the
Tower of Hanoi Problem**

Analyzing the Goal.   Another way to find subgoals is to analyze the goal you are trying to reach. This process is illustrated in the Tower of Hanoi Problem shown in Figure 5. The problem is to move the disks from the left peg to the right peg with the following restrictions:

1. only one disk can be moved at a time, and
2. a large disk must never be placed on a small disk.

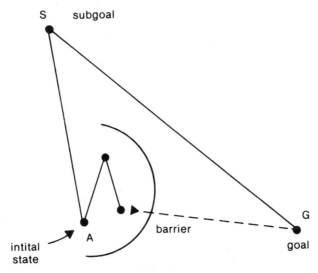

Figure 8. Subgoals Can be Used to Guide the Problem Solver Around Detours

Examining the goal, we can ask what part of the goal is the hardest to achieve. Since the second restriction constrains the small disk least, and the large disk most, we may reason that getting the large disk in place is the hardest part to achieve. Therefore, we set as our subgoal the state of affairs shown in Figure 6, with the other disks at unspecified locations. By comparing the subgoal with the initial state, we can see that the initial state could be transformed into the subgoal if the two smaller disks were removed. This suggests the second subgoal shown in Figure 7. Armed with these two subgoals, most find it quite easy to solve the problem.

The use of the subgoals in the Tower of Hanoi Problem illustrates a second very important function of subgoals: *subgoals can be used to guide the problem solver around detours.* Figure 8 illustrates this point. With the initial state at *A* and the goal at *G*, problem solvers using a distance-reducing method are bound to run into the barrier. However, if we provide a subgoal, *S*, to lead the problem solvers in a detour around the barrier, they can use their distance reducing methods first to get from *A* to *S* and then from *S* to *G*.

To see that the Tower of Hanoi Problem is a detour problem, look at Figure

9. The figure shows the complete solution, together with a measure of the distance from the goal at each step. Since the objective was to get three pegs off disk 1 and onto disk 3, distance to the goal was measured as follows:

$$\text{Distance} = \text{disks } on \text{ peg } 1 + \text{disks } off \text{ peg } 3$$

As you can see, the solution requires you to take two steps that increase the distance to the goal—goal step 3 and step 5. These detours disappear, however, if you use the two subgoals, S1 and S2, found by analyzing the goal. Figure 9 shows that traveling from the start to S1, from S1 to S2, and from S2 to the goal requires only forward moves. This situation is represented in Figure 10.

Abstracting.   Subgoals may also be identified through a process of abstracting from the original problem. Solving by abstraction involves three steps:

1. Dropping some of the constraints of the original problem, that is, abstracting from the original problem to produce a new, more general problem.
2. Solving the more general, less-constrained problem.
3. Adapting the solution of the more general problem so that it fits the constraints of the original problem.

For example, suppose that someone asks you, "How can I pick a good sports car in the $15,000 range?" You might respond, 'Well, first, if I were picking a sports car, [Here you temporarily drop the constraint about the price range.] I'd look at the repair records in *Consumer Reports*. [Here, you solve the generalized problem.] Then, I'd look to see if the price was close to what I wanted to spend." [Here, you adapt the solution to the original constraints.]

Let's illustrate "solving by abstraction" with another problem. Suppose that you are solving a problem with several restrictions, $X, Y,$ and Z. Since you are having trouble, you turn to the method of abstraction. With this method, you break the problem into parts. First, you drop some of the restrictions, say Y and Z, and solve the resulting "abstracted" problem. Next, you try to fix up this solution, so that restriction Y is satisfied. Finally, you try to fix the solution again so that the restriction Z is satisfied and the original problem is solved.

Let's illustrate this with a problem. Suppose that we are running a meeting of 16 people, males and females, from four companies and occupying four positions, as shown in Figure 11. Our problem is to organize four, four-person groups with the restrictions that each task group include:

1. a person from each company
2. a person from each position
3. two males and two females.

Solving this problem by abstraction, we start by solving it just for restriction 1. This solution, shown in Figure 12, is very easy to achieve.

Next we fix up the solution so that it satisfies restriction 2. This solution, shown in Figure 13, is also easy to achieve. As we can see, however, the proposed solution does not balance all of the groups by sex. Groups 2 and 4 are balanced but 1 and 3 are not. However, this solution can be fixed up by exchanging the two people from companies *A* and *C* in group 1 with those in group 3.

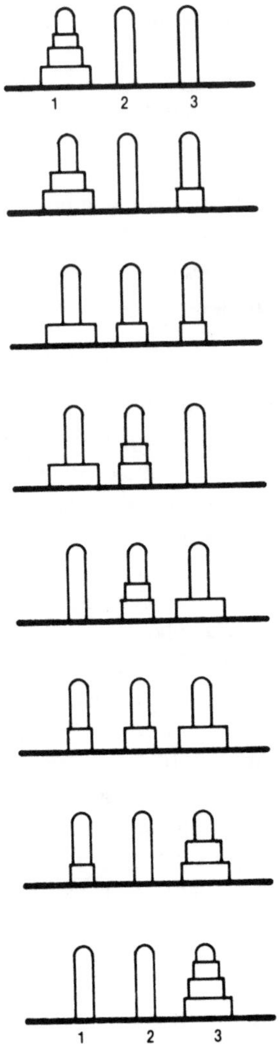

	Distance to Goal	Direction	Subgoals	Distance to Subgoal or Goal
0	6			4
1		forward		3
2	3	forward		1
3	4	back	*S1	0
4	2	forward	*S2	4
5	3	back		3
6	2	forward		1
7	0	forward		0

Figure 9. Solution to the Tower of Hanoi Problem

"Using Knowledge of Problem Schemas to Identify Subgoals." Finally, and perhaps most important, we can set up useful subgoals when we are dealing with familiar classes of problems. When we are writing an essay, we know that we can break the task into parts—research, brainstorming, organization, writing a draft, revising, getting outside criticism. We know this because we are familiar with writing tasks. In the same way, in solving geometry problems, we know that drawing a figure is often a useful subgoal, and in solving identification problems (see p. 11), we know that setting up a matrix is a helpful first step.

USING KNOWLEDGE IN PROBLEM SOLVING

Previously, we saw how problem solvers can apply knowledge of problem schemas as an aid in finding subgoals. This is just one instance of the importance of the problem solver's knowledge of problem solving. Actually, it is a very rare event for a person to solve a problem without making some use of their own knowledge of language or the way the world works or of problem types or solution strategies. Here, we will discuss a number of important ways in which people use their knowledge to solve problems.

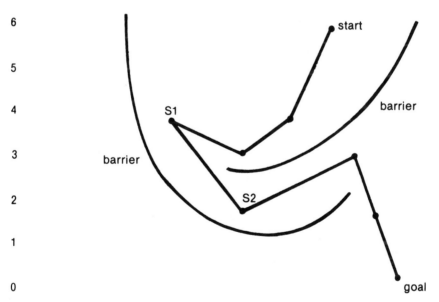

Figure 10. Distances to the Goal in the Tower of Hanoi Problem

Learning Solution Paths

If you knew that you were going to have to run the same maze 50 times, you would certainly make a point of trying to learn useful things about the maze.

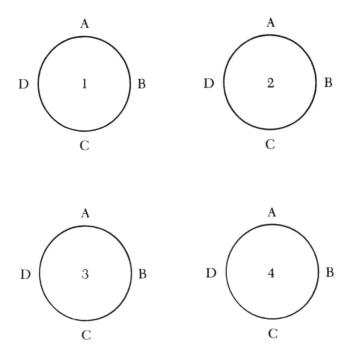

A,B,C,D are companies
1,2,3,4 are tables

Figure 11.   Solving by Abstraction for Restriction 1

For example, you would try to recognize blind-alley entrances so as not to stumble into them again. You would probably try to remember the move just before the end, and on a particularly successful run you might want to remember your first few moves as well. As you gain experience with the maze, the old patterns will grow and new ones will be added until they blend together to cover the whole solution path. As the patterns grow, the number of errors you make will decrease until finally you can run the maze perfectly.

Clearly, learning part or all of the solution path can reduce the difficulty of search enormously. It's fortunate that this is so, for otherwise we would all waste a great deal of time finding our way home at night.

Learning Solution Strategies

Much of our knowledge of solution strategies is acquired rather unsystematically through our daily experience in solving problems. However, the problem

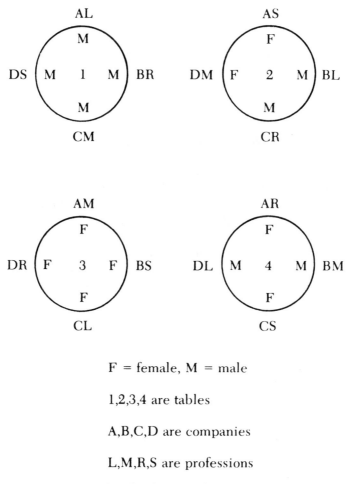

F = female, M = male

1,2,3,4 are tables

A,B,C,D are companies

L,M,R,S are professions

Figure 12. Solving by Abstraction for Restrictions 1 and 2

solving technique called *Searching for Auxiliary Problems* helps us to solve problems by providing a systematic way to search for and learn appropriate solution strategies. It works like this. When we have difficulty with a problem, we can try to pose a related, easier auxiliary problem for ourselves. We do this because by solving the easier problem, we hope to learn something that will help us solve the harder problem.

For example, consider the Eight Dots Problem in Chapter 1. We can create an easier auxiliary problem quite handily in this case just by reducing the number of dots. Solve the Eight Dots Problem by first solving this one:

● _ ○

then this one:

● ● _ ○ ○

and then this one:

● ● ● _ ○ ○ ○

As you solve each problem, be careful to notice anything you learn that helps you to solve the next harder problem.

Frequently you can create an easier auxiliary problem by reducing the number of elements in the problem or the number of constraints. Searching for auxiliary problems is closely related to the process of solving by abstraction because both involve dropping constraints from the original problem. The difference is that in solving the abstraction, we focus on producing a solution that is close to the one we are looking for. Our intent is to fix up the solution produced by abstraction so that it works for our original problem. In solving an auxiliary problem, on the other hand, we focus not on producing a particular solution but rather on learning methods and strategies for solving the whole class of problem.

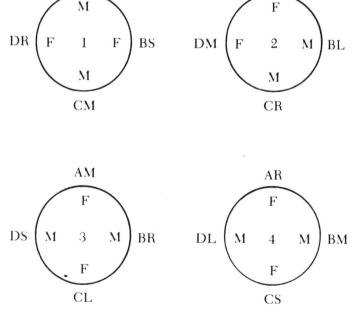

Figure 13. Solution of the Abstraction Problem

Pattern Matching

Much of the knowledge we use in problem solving is in the form of patterns, that is, of familiar states of the world. For example, in social situations, we can recognize the complex patterns of voice and facial expression that indicates whether the person we are talking to is angry, sad, happy, or bored. If we recognize the pattern, we can deal much more appropriately with the person than if we do not.

Playing 50 games of chess or of poker isn't like running the same maze 50 times. Each chess game and each poker game is unique. Still, there are many patterns to be learned which can be useful in later play, e.g., standard chess gambits and end-game situations.

The importance of such patterns in chess has been demonstrated by de Groot and by Simon and his collaborators in a significant series of studies. These investigations were sparked by a surprising discovery made by de Groot (1965), who was trying to answer the question, "Why are chess masters better than weaker players?"

It was commonly believed that when chess masters chose a move, they either examined more alternatives than weaker players or examined the alternatives in greater depth—that is, they looked further ahead than weaker plears. De Groot found that neither of these beliefs was true. Both masters and weaker players typically examined between 30 and 50 moves, and both searched to a depth of two or three moves on the average. The only thing that seemed really different about the masters' play was that they made better moves!

While conducting his investigations, de Groot noticed a curious thing. If the chess masters looked at a chess position for only a few seconds, they could remember it remarkably well—far better than weaker players. The masters' ability to remember chess positions wasn't a general memory skill. When they were asked to remember random arrangements of chess peices, they did no better than the weaker players. Their superior ability to remember chess positions depended specifically on their superior knowledge of chess.

This observation of de Groot stimulated a series of studies by Simon and his collaborators that provide us with a reasonably clear explanation for the master's superior ability to find good moves.

1. Chess masters can remember briefly exposed chess positions because they have a very large number of chess patterns stored in memory. These patterns allow the master to remember a chess position as a combination of a small number of fairly large patterns already familiar to them. Less experienced chess players must try to remember chess positions as a large number of smaller patterns—a more difficult task.

Simon and Gilmartin (1973) tested this theory by computer simulation. They constructed a program, called MAPP, which remembered chess board positions by comparing them to patterns stored in its memory. Given about 1,000 patterns, MAPP did better than chess beginners but only half as well as masters. On the

basis of their simulation, Simon and Gilmartin estimate that masters have between 10,000 and 100,000 chess patterns stored in memory.

2. Chess masters can find better moves than weaker players for a given amount
of search because the chess masters have a larger collection of patterns stored
in memory. They can recognize better than weaker players that a particular pattern on the chess board requires a particular response. They may recognize, for
example, that a board positon is similar to one in a game they are familiar with,
e.g., "Oh, this is life Game 3 of Fischer versus Spassky." This recognition will
often suggest a move similar to one in the original game.

How long does it take a chess master to learn the patterns on which his skill
is based? Simon and Chase (1973) estimate that to become a grand master requires from 10,000 to 50,000 hours staring at chess positions. They note that
no one has reached the grand master level with less than about a decade's intense
preoccupation with the game.

Search Algorithms

Sometimes when we are searching for the solution to a problem, we use procedures that are often useful, but are by no means guaranteed to produce the solution of the problem. Such procedures are called *search heuristics*. Hill climbing,
means-ends analysis, and looking for auxiliary problems are all examples of search
heuristics. For some classes of problems, though, there are procedures which,
if correctly applied, are guaranteed to yield the right solution. These procedures
are called *algorithms*.

The long-division procedure is an example of a search algorithm. When you
recognize that you are dealing with a division problem, you can apply the method
and be sure of getting the answer. You can solve division problems by trial-and-
error search, but it is very inefficient with complex problems. If I asked you to
divide 19 into 323, you could carry out a systematic trial-and-error search as
follows:

$$
\begin{aligned}
&\text{``}19 \times 1 = 19. \text{ No, that's not it.} \\
&\;\;19 \times 2 = 38. \text{ No, that's not it.} \\
&\;\;19 \times 3 = 57, \text{ etc.''}
\end{aligned}
$$

Clearly the long-division algorithm is better.

We all learn a number of search algorithms in school. We learn about "com-
pleting the square" in algebra, "balancing equations" in chemistry, the "right-
hand rule" in physics, the Pythagorean theorem in geometry, and so on.

A search algorithm which you may now know is the *maze algorithm*. The maze
algorithm insures that when you enter a maze, you will *always* be able to find
the exit. The algorithm is very simple. As you enter the maze, put your hand
on the wall, *and keep it there* as you walk through the maze. Try the algorithm
with the maze shown in Figure 14. Imagine first that you are walking through

the maze with your right hand on the wall. Then try it using your left hand.

Notice that you took a different path to the exit when you used your left hand than when you used your right hand. Either hand will work, but it is important not to switch hands! If you switch from right to left when you get to the arrow (see Figure 14), you will *never* get out of the maze. The advantage that the maze algorithm gives is that it insures that you won't get caught wandering in circles through the maze.

The split-half method is another search algorithm and a very useful one. It is used by electricians, mechanics, electronics technicians, and others to locate troubles in faulty equipment. As an example of its use, suppose that your front doorbell doesn't work. You find that it isn't getting current, even though the power supply in the kitchen is working fine. There must be a break somewhere in the 20 feet of wall between the kitchen and the front door. You want to locate the break with a minimum of damage to your house. Using the split-half technique, you make a hole halfway between the kitchen and the bell, and test the wire for current. If there is current, then the break must be between the hole and the front door. Applying the technique again, you make a second hole half-way between the first hole and the bell. If you didn't find current on your first test, the break must be between the hole and the kitchen. In this case you would have made the second hole halfway between the first hole and the kitchen. If you make holes that are about three inches across, you should never have to make more than six of them to find the break, as shown in Figure 15.

Figure 14. A Practice Maze for the Maze Algorithm

PLANNING

Up to now, we have been discussing search methods but we haven't said much about where that search takes place. You may have assumed that the search methods were being applied first in the problem solver's imagination but that needn't be the case. Many search methods can be carried out in the practical world rather than the imagination. Hill climbing, for example, could be carried out on a lunar hill by a space robot with no imagination at all. And a submarine robot could use the maze algorithm to keep itself out of trouble while exploring underwater caves. In these examples, search and execution are the same thing. We will reserve the term "planning" for those cases in which search is carried out in some representation of the world, such as a drawing or the problem solver's imagination, rather than in the real world. In planning, search and execution are separate.

In common sense terms, planning is the process of thinking before acting—of looking before we leap. Perhaps the best way to think about planning is to consider it as a process that involves *both* representation and search. More particularly, it is a process in which the problem solver takes advantage of the problem representation to exercise more effective search strategies.

Let's start with an example to illustrate how planning works. Suppose that I wanted to drive to the National Bison Range. I could simply climb into my car in Pittsburgh with no plan at all and start driving, trusting that the road signs would guide me to my destination. With enough driving, of course, I would eventually find the National Bison Range, but, the chances are, it would be a very long and expensive trip. I could save myself much of this expense if I did a little planning before I started. For example, I might consult my Atlas. There, in the index, I would discover the valuable fact that the National Bison Range is in Mon-

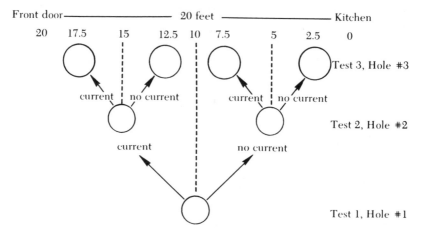

Figure 15. Using the Split-half Algorithm to Locate a Current Break

tana. With a little search through the map of Montana, I could find that the National Bison Range is very close to Ravalli and not too far from Missoula. With these facts and the U.S. map, I could plan a fairly direct route from Pittsburgh through Chicago and Minneapolis to Fargo, Billings, and Missoula.

It is obvious in this case that planning is enormously helpful. It is so helpful, in fact, that no sensible person would undertake this trip without first doing some planning. But just why does planning help us to solve problems? We might be tempted to say that planning helps because it allows us to find an efficient way to solve the problem. The statement is true but it isn't very deep. It says nothing at all about *how* planning helps us to find efficient ways to solve problems. To understand how planning works, we need first to draw a clear distinction between the task environment and the planning environment. By the task environment, we mean the real-world context in which the task is to be performed. For the task of driving to the National Bison Range, the most important part of the task environment is the extensive network of roads connecting various places in the United States. By the planning environment, we mean a symbolic representation that can substitute for the real world when we are thinking about the problem. It might be a sketch on paper, or the solid models that industrial designers often use in designing a product, or it might simply be images in our mind. In our example, the most important parts of the planning environment are the maps of Montana and the U.S. For the construction engineer, the task environment is the world of bricks, beams, and anxious clients, while the planning environment is the drafting board. For the chess player, the task environment is the chess board and the opponent. The planning environment is an imagined chess board in which the player can try out moves and replies without revealing them to the opponent.

Once the problem solver has established a planning environment by representing the task in drawings, imagination, or some other convenient medium, he or she can begin to search in the planning environment for a solution to the problem. In our example, the search involves examining maps first to identify the initial state, Pittsburgh, and the goal, the National Bison Range, and then to find practical routes connecting them. The output of the planning process is, reasonably enough, a plan. The plan describes, in more or less detail, a procedure that one could execute in the task environment to solve the real problem. In our example, the plan is the list of names of cities we choose to travel though on the way to the National Bison Range, e.g., Chicago, Minneapolis, etc. Each city name is the name of a subgoal for the problem solver to accomplish on the way to the main goal. Plans often consist of a sequence of subgoal names.

Plans may vary a great deal in specificity from task to task. In chess, the plan is often complete in the sense that it specifies the sequence of moves to be taken step by step. That is, the plan may be isomorphic to the sequence of moves to be taken. In the National Bison Range task, the plan is sketchier in that it specifies some but not all of the actions to be executed. For example, the plan specifies that one must travel in order from Chicago to Minneapolis to Fargo to Billings, etc. but it leaves out details such as finding specific highways and stopping for gas. The subgoals must be carried out in a specific order, however, if the plan is to be effective. In other cases, the plan may consist of an unordered list of subgoals. For example, a grocery list is a plan to buy a number of items at the store but it doesn't matter whether we buy the lemons or the mozzarella first. Plans, then, vary from very explicit directions to carry a specific set of operations in a specific order to vague directions to accomplish some subgoals in any order and anyhow.

To summarize, planning consists of three steps:

1. Representing the real task in a planning environment, e.g., on paper or in the planner's imagination.
2. Exploring the planning environment to find a way to solve the problem. This exploration may involve imaginary actions, as when we think about what to say in a lecture while we are taking a shower, or it may involve physical actions such as drawing sketches of room arrangements before moving the furniture.
3. Selecting a solution path. The path selected in the planning environment is called the plan.

Once the plan has been constructed, one can attempt to execute it in the task environment. With luck, the plan will work and the problem will be solved with a gratifying saving of effort. Sometimes, however, plans fail. On our way to Montana, we may encounter a roadblock or a washed out bridge that wasn't shown on the map. In playing chess, our opponent may accidentally make a brilliant move. Or we may simply make a mistake! In such cases, we will have to go back to the map, or to the drawing board, or to our imagination with the new information to repair our plan or to make a new one and hope for better luck.

WHY PLAN?

When we plan, we translate problems from the real world to the planning environment and back. Why should this be a help? Translating from one representation to another isn't necessarily useful. Translating English word problems into Turkish won't help unless you are more fluent in Turkish than English. Why then should translating from the task environment to the planning environment be useful? We believe that there are three differences between task and planning environments which can account for the utility of planning: reversibility, economy, and flexibility.

Reversibility

There are a number of task environments in which moves once made can't be unmade. Chess is an example. Chess rules specify that once we commit ourselves to a move on the board, we can't take the move back no matter how disastrous it turns out to be. In business, when we sign a contract, we can't legally unsign it. When we mail an irritated note to a friend, we can't retrieve it from the mail box when we cool down. However, moves in planning environments are almost alway reversible. If we think about making a chess move or about signing a contract, we can always change our mind. And writing outraged letters to our friends that we never mail is a time-honored way to preserve our sanity. Planning, then, can help us to avoid disastrous errors.

Economy

In many cases, it is much less expensive to make a move in the planning environment than it is to make the corresponding move in the task environment. It is less costly to scan the map from Pittsburgh to Chicago than it is to drive there. It is less costly to draw a wall than to build it. As a result, we can generally save a great deal of effort by searching for solutions in the planning environment before executing them in the task envornment. In the planning environment, we can explore and eliminate blind alleys, such as driving to Missoula by way of Saskatoon, without expending any gasoline. Further, we can optimize our solution inexpensively in the planning environment. That is, after we identify one plan for solving the problem, e.g. one route to the National Bison Range, we can identify others to see which is best. If we were doing the task only once, it wouldn't make sense to optimize in the task environment. For example, once we got to the National Bison Range, it wouldn't make sense to say, "Well, let's go back to Pittsburgh and see if we can find a faster route."

Flexibility

When we represent a task in the planning environment, we often have options about how the task is represented. This flexibility in representing the task means that a number of powerful problem solving procedures are available to us in the planning environment that may not be available in the task environment. For example, we can work backwards in planning a route from Pittsburgh to the National Bison Range. That is, we can represent the real goal, the National Bison Range, as the starting place and the real starting place, Pittsburgh, as the goal. However, we don't have that flexibility in the task environment. As a practical matter, we *have* to start in Pittsburgh and drive west.

Another very important example is that we can use abstraction in the planning environment but not in the task environment. An architect planning a hotel will typically begin with very crude drawings that take into account only the most abstract properties of the structure to be built. He or she may draw circles to indicate the general positions of the major units, e.g., the registration area, dining areas, kitchen, guests rooms, recreation areas, etc., with arrows indicating traffic flow. These drawings provide no hint either of the shape or the appearance of the structures to be built. Later in the design process, drawings become progressively more detailed and specific until the final drawings become, literally, blueprints for construction. This sort of planning by abstraction is impossible in the task environment. Architects can't *build* abstract structures of unspecified shape in indefinte locations. All real structures are concrete and definite and don't allow the sort of abstraction that is possible in a sketch.

Planning, then, helps us to perform tasks in three ways:

1. It allows us to avoid irreversible errors, e.g., telling that traffic cop what we think about his ancestry.
2. It allows us an inexpensive way to explore alternate methods for performing a task.
3. It allows us to employ a range of powerful problem solving procedures which are not available in the task environment, e.g., working backward, hypothetical reasoning, abstraction, etc.

SUMMARY: SEARCHING FOR SOLUTIONS

We have discussed four general methods for searching for problem solutions:

• Trial and error
• Proximity methods
• Fractionation methods, and
• Knowledge-based methods.

1. Trial-and-error search is useful only in small problem spaces. Systematic trial-and-error search is twice as efficient as blind trial-and-error search.
2. Proximity methods attempt to solve problems by selecting a step at a time, each of which reduces the distance to the goal.
   a. The hill-climbing method sees just one kind of difference between the current state and the goal, e.g., height, picture quality. All its operators have the same effect—to change that difference.
   b. Means-ends analysis can handle many kinds of differences in the same problem. It employs specialized operators which have different effects on the differences. If it runs into difficulties in applying an operator, it can set up a sequence of subgoals to reduce that difference.
   All proximity methods have trouble with detour problems.
3. Fractionation methods involve breaking the problem into a sequence of smaller parts, that is, by setting up subgoals. Subgoals make problems easier

to solve because they reduce the amount of search required to find the solution, and they may guide the problem solver around a detour.

We can set up subgoals by working part way into the problem, analyzing the goal to be achieved, dropping some of the problem restrictions and solving the "abstracted" problem, or using knowledge of familiar problem types.

4. Knowledged-based methods use information stored in the problem solver's memory to guide the search for solution. Problem solvers may set out to acquire the needed knowledge when they have difficulty. For example, they may solve an auxiliary problem to learn how to solve the one they are having difficulty with. Or problem solvers may use information already known to them, as when a chess player uses stored chess patterns, a puzzle enthusiast recognizes a problem type and applies a problem schema, or a mechanic applies a search algorithm such as the split-half technique.

5. Planning is a process in which the problem solver takes advantage of a problem representation to exercise more effective search strategies.

EXECUTING THE SOLUTION PLAN

Once we have planned a solution to a problem, we have to carry it out. Sometimes execution of the plan is quite easy. In the Driver's License Problem, for example, the hard part is figuring out what equations we want to solve. Carrying out the solution is routine algebra. We need only take care not to make dumb mistakes which will spoil our brilliantly conceived plan. (Dumb mistakes give people far more trouble than they may care to admit.)

In other cases, execution is by no means trivial. For example, after we have planned an essay, we find that turning our plan into smoothly flowing sentences or even into marginally intelligible scrawl is very difficult indeed. Frequently the plan has to be modified or in some cases abandoned entirely. Our attempts at execution send us scurrying back to the drawing board to devise a new plan. With luck, we will have learned enough from our disastrous attempt to execute the old plan that our new plan will have a better chance of success.

Executing the solution provides us with a very valuable check on the adequacy of our plans. Sometimes students will look at the problems at the end of a chapter and decide that since they know how to solve them, they needn't bother with the drudgery of actually executing the solutions. Sometimes the students are right, but sometimes they miss an excellent opportunity to discover that they were wrong.

EVALUATING THE SOLUTION

How do we know when we have gotten the right answer to a problem? If we are rushed, we may do little more than guess that what we have *looks* like an answer. The problem said "Solve for X," and here we have X on one side and everything else on the other side, so that's the answer.

This quick glance at the answer to see if it has the general shape of a solution may be the best we can do when we are rushed, but it can hardly be viewed as an adequate evaluation. If a druggist were weighing out a medication for us, we would not only want him to check carefully to see that his measured quantities corresponded to the quantities in the prescription. We might even want him to be sure that the prescription he is using is the one with our name on it!

The critical question in evaluation is this: "Does the answer I propose meet all of the goals and conditions set by the problem?" Thus, after the effort of finding a solution, we must turn our attention back to the problem statement and check carefully to be sure our solution satisfies it.

In easy problems, we may be tempted strongly to skip evaluation because the probability of an error seems small. In some cases this can be costly. This can be shown by the following problems from Whimbey and Lochhead (1980). Solve them before proceeding.

1. There are 3 separate, equal-size boxes, and inside each box there are 2 separate small boxes, and inside each of the small boxes there are 4 even smaller boxes. How many boxes are there altogether?

   a. 24   *b.* 13   *c.* 21   *d.* 33   *e.* some other number

2. Ten full crates of walnuts weigh 410 lb. while an empty crate weighs 10 lb. How much do the walnuts alone weigh?

   a. 400 lb.   *b.* 390 lb.   *c.* 310 lb.   *e.* 420 lb.

3. Three empty cereal boxes weigh 9 ozs. and each box holds 11 ozs. of cereal. How much do 2 full boxes of cereal weigh together?

   a. 20 ozs.   *b.* 40 ozs.   *c.* 14 ozs.   *d.* 28 ozs.   *e.* 15 ozs.

4. Cross out the letter after the letter in the word *seldom* which is in the same position in the word as it is in the alphabet.

5. In how may days of the week does the third letter of the day's name immediately follow the first letter of the day's name in the alphabet?

   a. 1   *b.* 2   *c.* 3   *d.* 4   *e.* 5

(From *Problem Solving and Comprehension*, Fourth Edition. Reprinted by permission of LEA.)

While these problems are not difficult, it is easy to make mistakes while solving them, and the mistakes are revealing, Whimbey and Lochhead (1982) point out the following common errors:

In problem 4, many people cross out the "d" rather than the "o" in "seldom." One can imagine that these people have become so involved in the processes of finding the letter with the same position in the alphabet as in the word that they forget that their task is to cross out the letter *after* it. Evaluation could have revealed the error.

In problem 2, a frequent error is to answer 400 pounds. The difficulty appears to lie in representing the problem incorrectly—that is, in failing to notice that there are 10 10-pound boxes. In evaluating, then, it's important to evaluate our representation as well as our solution.

While evaluation is useful in solving simple problems, it is even more useful in solving complex ones. Suppose we have the task of writing an essay on "Endangered Species" for an audience of 10-year-olds. Like the people solving problem 4, we may become so involved in one part of the problem, e.g., expounding our theories of ecology, that we completely forget that we are supposed to write to a 10-year-old audience. While writing, we must continually evaluate what we write to be sure that it satisfies all the requirements of our writing task.

Some problems have unique solutions. We either get them right or we get them wrong. Other problems have a whole range of solutions, some better than others. Problems of this sort pose an especially difficult evaluation task—the task of determining how good our solution is. In the chapters on decision making, we will discuss techniques which can help you to carry out this task.

Sometimes special decision-making procedures don't help. What we may really need is an outside opinion. We will discuss just one practical case here—the case of writing. When we write an essay, we often write about things of special interest to us—things we know a great deal about. Because of our special knowledge, it may be very difficult for us to put ourselves in the position of our audience—to imagine what it would be like not to understand things we consider obvious.

Recognizing the difficulty we have in evaluating our own writing, the sensible thing to do is to seek the help of others. Asking a friend to read aloud what we have written and to tell us what it means can be a horrifying but extremely educational experience.

Testing writing out on the audience for which it is intended is a very simple idea with obvious advantages, but very few people do it. Major corporations and governmental agencies put a great deal of money and effort into producing instruction manuals and other documents to inform the public, yet rarely consider testing those documents on the audience for which they were intended.

We intend our writing to be understood. To evaluate whether or not it can be understood, we should routinely take it to others for criticism.

CONSOLIDATION

Think of the last time you solved a difficult problem. When the solution finally came to you, your strongest emotion was probably one of great relief. At such times, we are likely to say to ourselves, "Whew! Thank God I'm through with that!" and turn our attention to more relaxing thoughts. It is just at this point, though, that we can gain most from the process of *consolidation*—that is, from reflecting on the problem-solving experience we have just been through and learning from it.

When we struggle with a hard problem, we may start off in a hundred wrong directions, explore numerous blind alleys, miss critical clues, and only slowly come to recognize what's important about the problem and what is not. As we make progress, we may make important changes in our representation, detect faulty assumptions or discover useful detours. After a week has passed, or perhaps even after a few hours, we will be able to remember very little of this complex process. We recognize the problem but forget why we found it so difficult.

Consolidation is best done when our memory of the problem-solving process is still very fresh in our minds. How do we do it? The basic question to be answered is, "What can I learn from the experience of solving this problem?" The following more specific questions may help us to answer this one:

1. Why was this problem difficult?
2. Was it hard to find an appropriate representation?
3. Was it difficult for me to keep my place in the problem?
4. Was it hard to find a solution method?
5. Was there a detour?
6. Why did I miss critical clues?
7. Did I make false assumptions?
8. Should I have used a different representation?
9. What mistakes did I make?
10. Did I make important discoveries about representation, methods, detours?
11. If so, how did I make them?
12. Are there other problems similar to this one?
13. Could they have been solved in the same way?

Of course, different questions may be appropriate for different problems. The particular questions are not important. What is important is that you reflect on the problem-solving process, ask questions about it, and learn from the experience. If you make it a habit to consolidate immediately after problem solution, you can take advantage of a wealth of information which would otherwise be lost to you.

REFERENCES

de Groot, A. D. *Thought and Choice in Chess*. The Hague: Mouton, 1965.
Newell, A., and Simon, H. A. *Human Problem Solving*. Englewood Cliffs, NJ: Prentice-Hall, Inc. 1972.

Simon, H. A., and Chase, W. G. "Skill in Chess." *American Scientist, 61*, 394–403, 1973.
Simon, H. A., and Gilmartin, K. "A Simulation of Memory for Chess Positions." *Cognitive Psychology, 5*, 29–46, 1973.
Whimbey, A., and Lochhead, J. *Problem Solving and Comprehension: A Short Course in Analytical Reasoning*, Second Edition. Philadelphia, PA: The Franklin Institute Press, 1980.

PROBLEM SOLUTIONS

Page 64.

1. d. 33
2. c. 310 lbs.
3. d. 28 ozs.
4. Cross out the letter "o"
5. c. 3
   - Mon
   - Tue
   - Wed
   - Thu
   - Fri
   - Sat
   - Sun

3

Protocol Analysis

In this chapter we introduce the technique of *protocol analysis*—cognitive psychology's most powerful tool for tracking psychological processes. First, we will answer the question, ''What is a protocol?'' Then we will work through several examples to show how protocols may be analyzed.

WHAT IS PROTOCOL?

A protocol is a description of the activities, ordered in time, in which a person engages while performing a task.

A protocol, then, is a description, but not every description of a task performance is a protocol. Often we describe tasks mentioning only their outcomes or goals. We may say, for example, ''My Great Dane, Spot, persuaded me to give him his supper.'' This description tells us that the dog did one or more things to get food, but it doesn't say what these things were or in what order they occurred. The description, therefore, is *not* a protocol. The description below *is* a protocol, however.

Experimenter: [seated at dinner table cutting into his steak]

Spot: [seated directly behind the experimenter, his chin resting on the experimenter's shoulder. Spot watches intently as the steak is being cut.]

Exp: [skewers a large piece of steak with his fork]

Spot: [tail wags, stomach rumbles ominously]

Exp: [begins to raise fork to mouth]

Spot:	[places paw on experimenter's arm and looks intently into experimenter's eyes]
Exp.	"Spot!"
Spot:	[removes paw, continues to watch intently]
Spot:	[drools into experimenter's shirt pocket]
Exp:	[abandons own dinner and feeds dog]

This is a protocol because it lists Spot's activities and the order in which they occurred. In the same way, when we collect protocols of people solving problems, we are not just interested in the answers they give us, but, more importantly, in the sequence of things they do to get those answers. They do things—such as draw diagrams, make computations, and ask questions—in a particular order.

We will describe three kinds of protocols here: *motor* protocols, *eye movement* protocols, and *verbal* protocols. All three kinds have proved to be very useful for describing psychological processes, but in this chapter our main interest will be in the third kind—verbal protocols.

MOTOR PROTOCOLS

To obtain motor protocols, we observe the obvious physical activities of our subjects—activities such as walking, picking things up, and reaching. The "Spot" protocol was largely a motor protocol. The motor protocol below, collected by Köhler (1925, p. 174), describes the activities of Sultan, an ape, as he solved a simple problem.

(March 26th): Sultan is squatting at the bars, but cannot reach the fruit, which lies outside, by means of his only available short stick. A longer stick is deposited

outside the bars, about two metres on one side of the objective, and parallel with the grating. It can not be grasped with the hand, but it can be pulled within reach by means of the small stick (see Figure 1). Sultan tries to reach the fruit with the smaller of the two sticks. Not succeeding, he tears at a piece of wire that projects from the netting of his cage, but that, too, is in vain. Then he gazes about him; (there are always in the course of these tests some long pauses, during which the animals scrutinize the whole visible area). He suddenly picks up the little stick once more, goes up to the bars directly opposite to the long stick, scratches it towards him with the 'auxiliary,' seizes it, and goes with it to the point opposite the objective, which he secures. From the moment that his eyes fall upon the long stick, his procedure forms one consecutive whole, without hiatus...

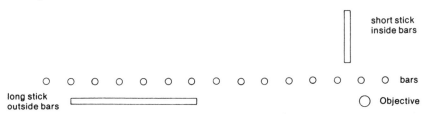

Figure 1. Köhler's Experimental Arrangement of Two Sticks Reprinted by permission of Routledge & Kegan Paul Ltd. from *The Mentality of Apes,* by W. Köhler.

Köhler used the observation that the solution occurred suddenly to argue that Sultan's solution process involved "insight." Further, Köhler used the observation that the solution ran off smoothly and continuously to argue that Sultan "knew what he was doing" from the moment of insight.

Motor protocols are especially valuable for use with subjects who have limited language abilities—for example, children and animals.

EYE-MOVEMENT PROTOCOLS

An eye-movement protocol is a record of the places in a scene where the subjects fix their gaze as they perform a task. In some cases, we can obtain sufficiently accurate information about eye movements just by looking at the subjects, as Fantz (1961) has done, to see if they are looking left or right. In other cases, we must use sophisticated equipment such as an eye-movement camera (Mackworth and Thomas, 1962) to obtain precise eye positions.

Figure 2 shows the eye movements of an expert chess player during the first

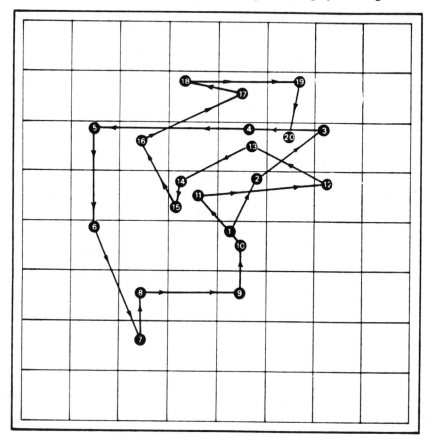

Figure 2. Record of Eye Movements for the First Five Seconds Reprinted from *Soviet Psychology*, Vol. 5, 1966, by permission of the publisher, M.E. Sharpe, Inc., White Plains, NY 10603.

five seconds of examining the chess position shown in Figure 3 (Tichomirov and Poznyanskaya, 1966). Using these data, Simon and Barenfeld (1969) argued that the chess expert was examining attack-and-defense relationships among the pieces. Eye-movement protocols have also been used to study tasks such as reading (Carpenter and Just, 1978) and solving number puzzles (Winikoff, 1966).

VERBAL PROTOCOLS

In a verbal, or "thinking aloud" protocol, subjects are asked to say aloud everything they think while performing the task. They are asked to say everything that occurs to them, no matter how trivial it may seem. Even with such explicit instructions, however, subjects may forget and fall silent—completely absorbed in the task. At such times the experimenter will say "Remember, tell me everything you are thinking."

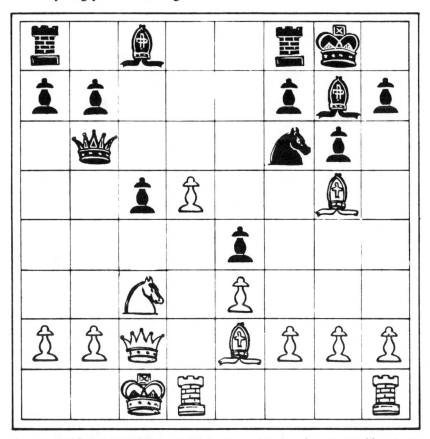

Figure 3.   Middle Game Position Used by Tichomirov and Poznyanskaya Reprinted from *Soviet Psychology*, Vol. 5, 1966, by permission of the publisher, M.E. Sharpe, Inc., White Plains, NY 10603

As examples we will show two verbal protocols, in which subjects solve water-jug problems. These require that the subject measure out a specified quantity of water using three jugs, as shown in Figure 4.

One typical water-jug problem requires the subject to measure out 31 quarts when Jug A will hold 20 quarts; Jug B, 59 quarts; and Jug C, 4 quarts. The problem can be solved in four steps as follows:

1. Fill Jug B.
2. Fill Jug A from Jug B, leaving 39 quarts in B.
3. Fill Jug C from B, leaving 35 quarts in B.
4. Empty C and fill it again from B, leaving the desired quantity, 31 quarts, in B.

When you analyze a protocol it is helpful to have already done the task yourself. So, before you begin to analyze Protocol I, try to solve this problem:

Water Jugs

Measure 100 qts. given Jug A, holding 21 qts.; Jug B, holding 127 qts.; and Jug C, 3 qts.

When you have found the solution, solve the problem in Protocol I, if you have not already done so.

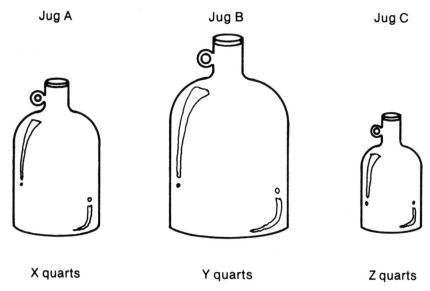

Jug A	Jug B	Jug C
X quarts	Y quarts	Z quarts

Figure 4. Non-calibrated Jugs Used to Solve the Water Jug Problem

Protocol I

Problem: Given Jug A, which contains 9 qts.; Jug B, 42 qts.; and Jug C, 6 qts., measure out exactly 21 qts.

Subj = Subject   Exp = Experimenter

Subj: (1) "Uh, the first thing that's apparent is half of B is, is the uh, the

       (2) amount that you want."

Exp: (3) "Uh huh."

Subj: (4) "Um, you can't get 21 from just multiplying up A or C.

       (5) You get 18 and 18 respectively, that's as close as you can get,

       (6) I guess. Um, so I'll try to think of the different combinations that

       (7) might . . . come up with a surplus . . . or deficit of the 21 quarts . . . and

       (8) nine and six are, 15 . . . if you took two nines and two sixes, you'd have 30 which

       (9) would leave you . . . and pour them into the 42 container, you'd have a,

   (10) an open space of a, 12, which means nothing. How about . . . see . . . now I'm

   (11) trying to think of how close to 42 you can get with a nine and the six quantities.

   (12) You can get . . . I forget the seven table. It's been a long time since I've

   (13) had to multiply or anything so you'll have to give me some time. Um,

   (14) nine times five is 45 . . . hm, six times seven is 42, I think. Is that right?"

Exp: (15) "Uh huh."

Subj: (16) "OK, so you can, uh . . . Fill B with C, evenly . . . "

Exp: (17) "You could . . . "

Subj: (18) "So, . . . if you were to take . . . 36 . . . hm, oh, uh, six times four is 24 . . . and if you, uh,

   (19) What I'm trying to get rid of is, is, three quarts there . . . "

Exp: (20) "Good."

Subj: (21) "So if you were to, um . . . still 24. I, I was trying to think possibly,

   (22) some way, of . . . the difference between the six and the nine is three quarts. I

   (23) was trying to think of . . . a way to uh . . . oh, how about . . . you put the three, six

   (24) quart quantity into the 42 bottle, which is 18, then the run off, from

   (25) pouring a nine into a six which is three and 18 is 21.

Exp: (26) "Good."

AN EXAMPLE OF PROTOCOL ANALYSIS

Now, let's examine Protocol I in detail and try to make some reasonable guesses about what the subject is doing.

In his first sentence, the subject mentions something that appears to be irrelevant to solving the problem. He mentions the fact that the desired amount (21 quarts) is just half the quantity contained in Jug B. Now, division is a very useful operation in many algebra problems. In this problem, if we could divide Jug B in half, the problem would be solved. But alas! There is no division operation in water-jug problems. All we can do is add and subtract the quantities in Jugs A, B, and C. Why, then, does the subject notice that the desired quantity is half of B? The simplest answer seems to be that he is confusing water-jug problems (perhaps because he isn't thoroughly familiar with them) with the more general class of algebra problems. If this answer is correct, we would expect that the subject would stop noticing division relations as he gains more experience with water-jug problems. In fact, that is what happened.

In line 3, the experimenter does just what the experimenter is supposed to do— that is, he is noncommital. In general, the experimenter should answer only essential questions and remind the subject to keep talking.

From lines 4 and 5, we can guess that the subject has successively added nines to get nine, 18, 27 . . . and sixes to get six, 12, 18, 24 . . . and realized that neither sequence includes 21. From lines 6 through 10, we can see that the subject begins to consider combinations of nines and sixes which may be added together to obtain interesting sums, or subtracted from the 42-quart container to obtain interesting differences. While considering sums, the subject fails to notice that the sum 6 + 6 + 9 solves the problem.

In lines 11 through 14, the subject tries to find out if 42 quarts can be obtained by adding nines and sixes. The answer is positive, but it doesn't help the subject to find a solution. It appears to be a "blind alley." In this section, the subject indicates several times that he doesn't feel confident about multiplication.

In lines 15 and 17, the experimenter provides the subject with a small amount of information by confirming his uneasy suspicion that six times seven equals 42. On occasion, the experimenter must decide whether or not to provide information the subject requests. In this case, since the experimenter was really interested in water jug problems rather than in arithmetic, he decided to supply an arithmetic fact.

In lines 18 and 19, the subject realizes that if he had a way to subtract three quarts from 24 quarts, he could solve the problem. In line 20 the experimenter appears to slip by providing the subject with approval, when he would better have remained silent. In line 21, the subject is still thinking of working from 24 quarts. In line 22, he discovers a way to add (rather than subtract) three quarts by pouring A into C and catching the overflow. In lines 23 and 24, he decides to work from 18 quarts rather than 24 quarts and then (on line 25) immediately solves the problem.

Now, let's stand back from the details of the protocol to see if we can characterize the whole problem-solving process that the subject went through. Before reading further, review the discussion of the protocol and then try to characterize the problem-solving process yourself.

One way to characterize the problem-solving process is to describe it as a search for an operator or a combination of operators to solve the problem. (In this case, the operators are arithmetic procedures such as division and subtraction). In Figure 5, where we have diagrammed this search process, we can see that search proceeds, generally, from simple to complex—that is, from single operators to complex combinations of operators.

Up until line 18, the subject's search for a solution could have been guided by the problem statement. That is, by reading the problem statement, the subject could have decided that what was needed to solve the problem was some combination of algebraic operators. Up to line 18, he could simply be trying one combination after another. We call this "forward search"—a search suggested by the problem statement alone. In lines 18 and 19, however, the subject formulates a goal on the basis of his difficulties in solving the problem. He notes that he hasn't been able to get closer to the answer than three quarts and attempts to find an operator that will subtract three quarts. This goal depends not just on the problem statement but also on the subject's experience in trying to solve the problem—that is, on his distance from the goal. It is a form of means-ends analysis in which the subject attempts to find a means to the end of reducing his distance from the goal.

	lines protocol	operator applied	outcome	comment
forward search	1-2	divide by 2	fail	operator not available
	4-5	add 9's	fail	
	4-5	add 6's	fail	the subject apparently doesn't try all combinations because he fails to notice that 6 + 6 + 9 = 21
	6-8	add 9's and 6's	fail	
	7-10	add 9's and 6's and subtract from 42	fail	
means-ends analysis	18-19	notice difficulty	succeed	the subject notices the operators above got him no closer to 21 than 24; he sets the goal of finding an operator to subtract 3
	22	overflow 9 into 6	fail	
	23-25	add 6 three times and overlow 9 into 6	succeed	

Figure 5. The Search Process Used for Solving the Water Jug Problem

The whole solution process then consists of

1. An initial phase of forward search through an increasingly complex sequence of operators, followed by
2. A phase of means-ends analysis in which the subject succeeds in finding a solution.

In analyzing a protocol, we attempt to describe the psychological processes that a subject uses to perform a task. To do this, it is useful to be familiar both with the properties of the task and with the problem solver's component psychological processes. In analyzing the water-jug protocol above, knowing that the task required algebraic operators and that human problem solvers often use processes of forward search and means-ends analysis helped us to recognize how the subject had organized these processes in his search for a solution. In the same way, when we analyze other protocols, knowledge of other tasks and of other psychological properties will be useful. This is not to say that we must already understand a performance before we can analyze it. It is just that when we do understand some things about the performance, we can use them very profitably to learn other things.

In analyzing Protocol II, knowledge of the psychological phenomenon of set is very helpful.

Protocol II

Problem: Given Jug A, which contains 23 qts., Jug B, 49 qts., and Jug C, 3 qts., measure out exactly 20 qts.

Subj: (1) "Uh, . . . I'm adding and subtracting here,"
Exp: (2) "Say what you're adding and subtracting."
Subj: (3) "O.K. Well, 23 and 49 . . . is . . . uh . . . reminds me when
        (4) we keep score when we play cards. 26 . . . oh, OK. Er it
        (5) would be easy enough. You take . . . um . . . OK. How do we
        (6) get this into water and jugs now? . . . because you could take a . . .
        (7) which is 23, and pour it into C which is three, there we go,
        (8) pour it into C which is three, and 20 would be what would go . . .
        (9) right into B."
Exp: (10) "Good."

The problem used in this protocol can be solved in either of two ways. It can be solved by the procedure B—A—2C, or it can be solved by the simpler procedure: A—C. Just before solving this problem, the subject worked a series of six problems, all of which required the procedure B—A—2C for solution. As a result, we would expect the subject to show a set to use the B—A—2C procedure. As lines 6 through 9 show, the subject actually solves the problem by the A—C procedure. However, if we look back to lines 3 and 4, we see that the subject's first problem solving attempt was to subtract A from B. This suggests that he started to use the B—A—2C procedure even though he didn't carry it through. Clearly, analyzing the protocol gives us evidence about the subject's solution process that we can't get just by looking at the answer.

AGE PROBLEMS

The protocol of an age problem illustrates again the usefulness of knowledge of task demands and component psychological processes for understanding human performance. As in many problems, part of the difficulty of age problems lies in keeping track of relevant information. Unless problem solvers are very careful in labeling information, they are likely to confuse a person's age at one time with the same person's age at a different time. For example, problem solvers who have only a single label which they use both for "Mary's age now" and "Mary's age then"—let us say "Mary" or "M"—are very likely to confuse Mary's age now with Mary's age then. This is just what happens in this age-problem protocol.

Protocol III

Problem: John is now twice as old as he was when Mary was 3 years older than he is now, but he is only half as old as Mary is at present. Now how old are they?

Subj: (1) "Um, um, John is now twice as old as he was when Mary was
(2) three years older than he is now. But he is only half as old as Mary
(3) At present. Um, um, three years older is the only number supplied,
(4) so I'm going to start working from there. I guess, and uh, . . ."
Exp: (5) "What are you thinking?"
Subj: (6) "I get absolutely nothing from those questions.
(7) "I am drawing a blank at the moment, um, I am trying to sort out John
(8) and Mary, I guess, here, because, the words don't lend themselves to
(9) be deciphered into, like, two neat little John and Mary columns, um,
(10) and it's hard. OK. John is twice as old . . . now . . . than when he was when
(11) Mary was three years older than him . . . OH wow! Um, but he is only half
(12) as old as Mary at present . . . so, um, John equals, um, now I'm trying
(13) to think of a . . . I don't know why it just occurred to me that maybe if
(14) I plugged John and Mary and the information into little, little, you
(15) know, John equals Mary plus three, or something like that, you know,

(16) little X, Y?''
Exp: (17) "Uh Huh."
Subj: (18) "I don't know what you call them."
Exp: (19) "Equations."
Subj: (20) "Equations. OK. Got to warn you, I flunked math in sixth grade. So um,
(21) um, Ah . . . John is now twice as old as he was when Mary was three years
(22) older than he is now . . . OK, so John equals . . . um, Mary and three . . . , which
(23) doesn't do me any good, and he is only half as old as Mary at present,
(24) so I have to know how much John is worth first, here, and, uh, . . . Mary is
(25) three years older than he is . . . , and half as old as Mary at present. Um,
(26) Mary is three years older than he is now, but he is only half as old as
(27) Mary at present . . . so he has to be um . . . Mary is three years older than
(28) he is now . . . and Mary is twice his age. Then he's got to be three years
(29) old.''
Exp: (30) "All right."

ANALYSIS OF THE PROBLEM

To solve this problem, it is necessary to distinguish four quantities—John's age now (JN), John's age then (JT), Mary's age now (MN), and Mary's age then (MT). Three equations can be derived from the problem statement.

$JN = 2\ JT$ [John is twice as old now as he was then.]
$MT = JN + 3$ [Mary then was three years older than John is now.]
$JN = \frac{1}{2}\ MN$ [John now is half as old as Mary now.]

In addition, because we know that John and Mary age at the same rate, we can derive a fourth equation:

$JN - JT = MN - MT$ [The difference between John's age now and John's age then is the same as the difference between Mary's age now and Mary's age then.]

Armed with these equations, those adept at algebra can determine that John's age now is six and Mary's age now is 12.

Now, let's see what our subject has done. From lines 15 through 29, she frequently confuses John's and Mary's ages now with John's and Mary's ages then.

In fact, nowhere in the protocol is there any evidence that she ever makes the now-then distinction. In lines 27 and 28, she derives two equations:

$$\text{Mary} = \text{John} + 3, \text{ and}$$

$$\text{Mary} = 2 \times \text{John}$$

The second one is correct, but the first is not because it confuses Mary's age then with Mary's age now. The subject then solves these equations and concludes, incorrectly, that John's age now is three.

PROTOCOL ANALYSIS, MORE GENERALLY CONSIDERED

As we have seen, protocol analysis can be used as an aid in understanding a wide variety of tasks from simple problem solving by apes to complex performances such as solving algebra word problems and playing chess. Typically though, protocols are incomplete. Many processes occur during the performance of a task which the subject can't or doesn't report. The psychologist's task in analyzing a protocol is to take the incomplete record provided by the protocol, together with his knowledge of human capabilities, and to infer from these a model of the underlying psychological processes by which the subject performs the task.

Analyzing a protocol is like following the tracks of a porpoise. Occasionally, the porpoise reveals itself by breaking the surface of the sea. Its brief surfacings are like the glimpses of the underlying mental process which the protocol affords us. Between surfacings, the mental process, like the porpoise, runs deep and silent. Our task is to infer the course of the process from these brief traces.

Some have shown concern that thinking-aloud protocols may distort or interfere with the mental processes which we want to observe. Sometimes subjects complain that it is hard to think about doing the task and to talk at the same time. While these difficulties typically disappear with a little practice, they force us to take the questions of distortion and interference seriously. Fortunately, Ericsson and Simon (1979) have provided a thorough and thoughtful review of the evidence on this issue. They have found that:

1. there is no evidence that thinking-aloud protocols collected under the sorts of conditions we described above distort or interefere with subjects' thinking when they are performing tasks; and
2. thinking-aloud protocols very closely reflect the thought processes that occur during task performance.

However, they also conclude that, under *special circumstances*, thinking-aloud can interfere with the subjects' thought processes. In the usual thinking-aloud procedure, the experimenter asks the subjects to say whatever is on their minds. If instead of the usual procedure, the experimenter tells the subects what to talk about, they may be forced to pay attention to things they would ordinarily have ignored. Suppose, for example, that we gave subjects a number problem and asked them to tell us every time they thought of an odd number while solving it. Ordinarily, they might pay no attention at all to whether a number was odd or even in solving the problem. With our instructions, not only must they pay special attention to odd numbers, but they may also develop the sneaking suspicion that odd numbers are important for the solution whether they are or not.

We conclude that as long as we avoid telling our subjects what to think about, thinking-aloud protocols can provide us with a fairly clear, undistorted window into human thinking processes.

PRACTICAL APPLICATIONS

Although we have described protocol analysis as a research tool, it is important for you to realize that you can adapt it for your personal use. Imagine that you are having trouble with a particular type of problem either in school or at work. It might be a writing problem or a problem in, say, accounting or law. You have read all the available instruction manuals, and you have asked people to help you. Unfortunately, their advice just confuses you. They say things like, "Oh, sure. It's easy. You just rearticulate the frames, adjust for marginal liquidity at compound interest, and stir until slightly thickened."

How can you get out of your dilemma? One very effective thing you can do is to watch an expert solve one of these problems. An ideally cooperative expert would let you tape record a thinking-aloud protocol. However, you may have to satisfy yourself just watching him or her scribbling out the successive parts of the solution. If you can, of course, you should take notes so you can remember the sequence of events. Perhaps all you will be able to do is to write a sequence of numbers to indicate the order in which notes were scribbled on the expert's scratch pad. In any case, just watching another person solving a problem can be remarkably helpful. In fact, Whimbey and Lochhead (1982) recommend that thinking aloud be used as a routine classroom exercise to teach problem-solving skills.

In the next section, we present two rather difficult problems together with a detailed description of how some problem solvers successfully solved them. Try to solve each problem before reading the solution. If you manage to solve the problem, compare your solution to the one in the text. If you can't solve it, try to understand how the problem solver whose solution process is described in the text avoided or overcame the difficulties that you experienced.

The Handshaking Problem*

A social psychologist was interested in the custom of handshaking. He noticed that some people are more inclined than others to shake hands when they are introduced. One evening when he and his wife had joined four other couples at a party, he took advantage of the occasion to collect data. He asked each of the other nine people at the party how many people they had shaken hands with during the introductions. He received a different answer, from zero through eight, from each of the nine people. You can assume that husbands and wives don't shake hands with each other during introductions, and, of course, people don't shake hands with themselves. Given this information, find out how often the psychologist's wife shook hands.

Many people find it hard to believe that this problem can be solved with only the little information given, but it can. Try it.

---

*This problem was described to me by R. Bhaskar.

When I first encountered this problem, I had no idea how I was going to solve it. Despite this, I decided to jump in by trying to represent what I knew in a systematic way. I chose the matrix shown in Figure 6 to represent the facts.

Next, I decided arbitrarily (gap-filling decision) to represent the person who shook hands eight times as H1. Equally arbitrarily, I assumed that that person was the husband in couple 1. My only justification for making this particular decision was that I had to make *some* decision in order to proceed. I entered X's in the first row and first column in Figure 7 for each person H1 shook hands with. The zeros indicate that H1 shook hands neither with himself nor with his wife.

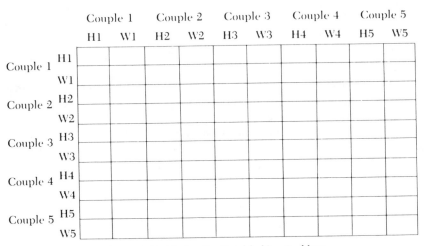

Figure 6. Matrix for the Handshaking Problem

At this point, jumping in yielded the first important insight into the problem. Since everyone but H1's wife shook hands at least once, she is the only person who could have shaken hands zero times. So I filled in zeros for W1 row and column. Next I arbitrarily chose H2 to be the person who shook hands seven times. I inserted zeros in the table to indicate that H2 shook hands neither with himself nor his wife, and I put X's in H2's row and column to indicate that he shook hands with the remaining six people as shown in Figure 8.

Now, jumping in led me to a second discovery. Everyone but H2's wife had shaken hands twice. So she was the only person who could have shaken hands just once. This discovery suggested a pattern. In the first two couples, eight was paired with zero and seven with one. I hypothesized that in the remaining cou-

		Couple 1		Couple 2		Couple 3		Couple 4		Couple 5	
		H1	W1	H2	W2	H3	W3	H4	W4	H5	W5
Couple 1	H1	0	0	X	X	X	X	X	X	X	X
	W1	0									
Couple 2	H2	X									
	W2	X									
Couple 3	H3	X									
	W3	X									
Couple 4	H4	X									
	W4	X									
Couple 5	H5	X									
	W5	X									

Figure 7. Step One in Solving the Handshaking Problem

		Couple 1		Couple 2		Couple 3		Couple 4		Couple 5	
		H1	W1	H2	W2	H3	W3	H4	W4	H5	W5
Couple 1	H1	0	0	X	X	X	X	X	X	X	X
	W1	0	0	0	0	0	0	0	0	0	0
Couple 2	H2	X	0	0	0	X	X	X	X	X	X
	W2	X	0	0							
Couple 3	H3	X	0	X							
	W3	X	0	X							
Couple 4	H4	X	0	X							
	W4	X	0	X							
Couple 5	H5	X	0	X							
	W5	X	0	X							

Figure 8. Proceeding to Fill in the Matrix to Solve the Handshaking Problem

ples, six would be paired with two, five with three, and four with four. Working out the details (executing the solution) proved that the hypothesis was correct.

It was only at this point that I had the critical fact that I needed to solve the problem—the fact that four was paired with four. The social psychologist asked the other people how often they had shaken hands, and found only one person who had shaken hands four times. He, himself, must be the other person who shook hands four times. We can conclude then that his wife shook hands four times.

This problem demonstrates as well as any I know the value of jumping into a problem and making gap-filling decisions in solving what for me at least was a *very* ill-defined problem.

The Christmas Tree Problem*

Arrange 10 Christmas trees in five straight rows of four trees each. Again, try to solve the problem before reading further.

We will describe how two subjects solved this problem in similar but slightly different ways. Problem solver #1 approached the problem cautiously. First, she asked the experimenter if it was important that the trees were Christmas trees rather than oaks or maples. The experimenter assured her that the type of tree was not relevant. Next, she was concerned that the problem might involve some sort of trick in representation, e.g., that the numbers be represented as Roman numerals, so that "five rows of four" might be five lines making up the Roman numeral IV as below:

Again, the experimenter ruled out this possiblity.

Subject #2 less cautiously, simply assumed that the problem involved no such catches. Fortunately for him, it didn't.

At this stage in problem solving, both subjects recognized that arranging ten trees in five rows of four required putting some trees in more than one row. To accomplish this, both settled down to arranging and rearranging dots on paper (see below).

```
              •   •   •   •                        •
     •   •   •              •   •   •   •        •     •
  •   •   •   •             •                  •   •   •
     •   •   •             •                •   •   •   •
```

*This problem was described to me by C. Berkenkotter.

Both subjects started by considering rectangular arrays first and then proceeded to experiment with triangles. When these early attempts failed to yield a quick solution, both subjects attempted to change the representation of the problem by redefining "row." Both argued (independently) that a row of five could be viewed as two rows of four as below:

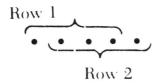

After several unsuccessful tries, Subject #1 abandoned this approach, but Subject #2 persisted and proposed the following solution.

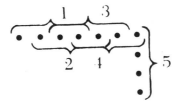

The experimenter asked Subject #2 to search for a more elegant solution.

Both subjects then returned to the first problem representation—the one involving non-overlapping rows. After considerable experimentation, Subject #1 produced this solution.

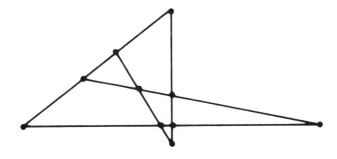

Subject #2 reexamined the problem statement. While previously he had attended most specifically to "five *rows* of *four*," now he shifted his attention to "*five* rows of four." This change in emphasis led him to search for interesting figures with five parts. This search soon turned up the star which suggested Subject #2's solution.

REFERENCES

Carpenter, P. A., and Just, M. A. "Reading Comprehension as Eyes See It." In *Cognitive Processes in Comprehension*, edited by M. Just and P. Carpenter, Hillsdale, NJ: Lawrence Erlbaum, 1978.

Ericsson, K. A., and Simon, H. A. *Thinking-aloud Protocols as Data*. CIP Working Paper #397, Carnegie-Mellon University, Pittsburgh, March, 1979.

Fantz, R. L. "The Origin of Form Perception." *Scientific American, 204,* 66–72, 1961.

Köhler, W. *The Mentality of Apes.* London: Routledge and Kegan Paul, Ltd., 1925.

Mackworth, N. H., and Thomas, E. L. "A Head-Mounted Eye-Marker Camera." *Journal of the Optical Society of America, 52,* 713–716, 1962.

Simon, H. A., and Barenfeld, M. 'Information-processing Analysis of Perceptual Processes in Problem Solving." *Psychological Review, 76,* 473–483, 1969.

Stoehr, T. "Writing as Thinking." *College English, 28,* 411–421, 1967.

Tichomirov, O. K., and Poznyanskaya, E. D. "An Investigation of Visual Search as a Means of Analyzing Heuristics." *Soviet Psychology, 5,* 2–15, 1966.

Van Nostrand, A. D. "Writing and the Dialogue of Disciplines."*Personalized System of Instruction Proceedings*, Brown University, Providence, RI, 1976.

Whimbey, A., and Lochhead, J. *Problem Solving and Comprehension*, Fourth Edition. Hillsdale, NJ: Lawrence Erlbaum, 1982.

Winikoff, A. *Eye Movements as an Aid to Protocol Analysis in Problem Solving.* Unpublished doctoral dissertation, Carnegie-Mellon University, 1966.

PROBLEM SOLUTION

Page 74. Water Jugs
Fill B; Fill A from B; Fill C from B twice.
100 quarts now remains in B.

4

Writing As Problem Solving

My purpose in this chapter is to show that the problem solving concepts and ideas that we have been discussing in the first three chapters can be applied very usefully to the understanding of writing. In fact, one important way to view writing *is* as problem solving. Indeed, when we find we have to write, we experience a gap between where we are now—faced with a threatening piece of blank paper—and where we want to be—the author of a more or less satisfactory text. In many cases the gap appears enormous.

ANALYZING WRITING PROCESSES

Because writing is very complex, we have divided the writer's world into three major parts to help us analyze the problem solving processes involved in writing. These are the task environment, the writer's long-term memory, and the writing process (see Figure 1). The task environment and the writer's long-term memory may be viewed as the context in which the writing process operates.

The Task Environment

The task enironment includes everything outside the writer's skin that may influence the performance of the writing task. It includes the writing assignment, such as, information from one's teacher or boss indicating what we have to write about, to what purpose, and in what form. It may also include information about how seriously the task must be taken. That information may be conveyed by the teacher's stern expression or by other indications of the task's importance. Writ-

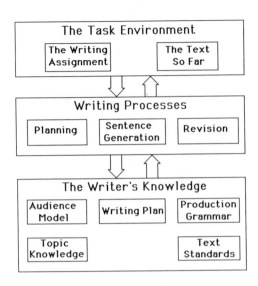

Figure 1. The Hayes–Flower Model

ing a letter to close $1 million deal is far more likely to inspire our best writing efforts than is writing a letter home.

Once writing has begun, the task environment also includes the text that the writer has written so far. This text has an important influence on the writing process because the writer refers to it repeatedly as writing procedes. We have to make the new sentences and paragraphs fit with the ones we have already written. We find ourselves reading and rereading what we have just written to help us know what to write next. The next time you write an essay, notice how frequently you read your own sentences.

The fact that writing is influenced by its own output, that is, by the text written so far, is an important and special feature about writing that differentiates it from some problem solving tasks and connects it to some others. Tasks like industrial design and computer programming are also strongly influenced by their output. For example, suppose that an industrial designer is designing a telephone headpiece. He or she will first sketch some designs and then build a solid model of the most promising one. The designer will then evaluate the look and feel of the model to determine what needs to be modified or added just as the writer evaluates the sound and sense of the text to determine what needs to be modified or added.

The Writer's Long-Term Memory

Writers' long-term memories contain enormous amounts of knowledge that they can draw on while writing. Skilled writers know about a wide variety of topics, e.g., baseball and history, and about the properties of many different audiences, e.g., children and Republicans. Further, skilled writers have a good deal of knowledge about language, e.g., grammar and diction, and writing formats, e.g., narration, exposition, etc. Writers must depend heavily on their long-term memories in all aspects of writing. Because each writer's knowledge is different, it is convenient for purposes of analysis, to separate the information that long-term memory provides to the writing process from the writing process itself.

The Writing Process

Evidence from protocol analysis (Hayes and Flower, 1980), indicates that writing consists of three major subprocesses that we have called "planning," "sentence generation," and "revising." These processes correspond closely to the stages of problem solving described at the beginning of Chapter 1. The planning process in writing includes the two problem solving stages that were called "representation" and "planning" in Chapter 1. In planning to write, the writer represents the task to be performed e.g., "I have to tell Auntie that I really liked the sweater she sent me for Christmas. Furthermore, I better sound sincere." Here, the writer is concerned primarily with the goal component of the representation. In addition to representing the writing task, the writer plans a sequence of steps or subgoals intended to accomplish the task, e.g., "First, I'll explain why I waited until summer to write. Then, I'll tell her how often I wear it." In writing, then, planning includes such activities as determining what writing task needs to be done, setting goals, thinking of things to say, and deciding on an order of subtasks. The output of these processes is a writing plan.

The sentence generation process in writing corresponds to the stage called "execution" in Chapter 1. It takes the writing plan and puts it into action. That is, it takes the subgoals formed by the planning process, e.g., "Tell them about the problems of unwanted children", and turns them into complete English sentences, e.g., "Can you imagine what it is like for a small child to live with a parent who regards her smallest request as a major annoyance? Many children. . . . " Sentence generation turns the writing plan into text.

The revision process in writing corresponds to the stages called "evaluation" and "consolidation" in problem solving. In revising, writers examine their text and attempt to improve it by determining how well it fits the rules of good form, e.g., grammar, spelling, and clarity, how well it expresses what they wanted to say, and what it suggests to them that might be better to say. We include the consolidation stage here because we find that during writing and especially during revision, writers often consolidate their ideas. That is, they find unexpected relationships or inconsistencies, and make new inferences or generalizations that had not occurred to them before. For example, while writing about his job, a software engineer said, "I hadn't realized until now that writing is something like computer programming."

It may seem odd to you that a person could find surprising relations and even contradictions in their own knowledge. Remember, however, that when we acquire new information, we normally don't check it carefully against what we already know. In writing, we may dredge up facts and opinions that we learned at various times and for various proposes—facts and opinions that we have never thought about before at the same time. Thus, writing can be an important learning experience because it provides writers with an opportunity to interrelate facts and to evaluate and extend their ideas.

THE ORGANIZATION OF WRITING PROCESSES

It would be quite natural to imagine that the writing processes occur in a fixed sequence. That is, we might think that writers first plan what they want to write; then, when planning is finished, they write out a complete draft; and finally, they revise the completed draft one or more times to produce the finished paper. Actually, when we observe real writers at work, we find that the writing processes are almost always interwoven with each other in a complex way. There are at least three causes for this mixing of processes.

1. *Some writer's composing strategy.* Some writers compose by trying to write the perfect first sentence; then, to follow it with the perfect second sentence, and so on. This means that they plan, generate, and very carefully revise each sentence before going on to the next one and thus interweave the three processes while writing a text. I used to write this way until I realized that it was rather inefficient. That is, I found that in later drafts of my papers, I was editing out sentences that I had spent enormous amounts of time perfecting—tinkering with them to get them to sound just right. Now, I try to produce a rough first draft quickly and spend time polishing a section only if I am pretty sure that it is going to be part of the final text. I found that this change in strategy saved me a great deal of time and effort.

In writing as in problem solving generally, there are often alternative strategies for reaching the same goal. Some are more effective or more efficient than others. Good problem solvers are aware of these alternatives and choose wisely among them. If writers are alert to the alternative strategies available to them, they can increase the effectiveness and efficiency of their writing.

2. *Process interrupts.* Editing is the part of the revision process concerned with detecting and correcting errors. Editing appears to have priority over other writing processes in the sense that it can interrupt other ongoing processes in order to correct errors. In the two examples here, the writers were engaged in planning. The editing process (indicated by italics) interrupted planning to correct an error of meaning in the first case and grammar in the second. "The problem is to make the uses more 'general and acceptable' . . . *that's the wrong word . . . I mean 'important seeming.' '' '' '' . . .* the idea is that one has a special marker that—*which*—means 'stop'.''

3. *Writing processes may be nested within other writing processes.* To understand how one writing process can be nested within another, consider the com-

pleted essay shown on pages 105–106. In the first draft of this essay, the first two sentences were "Personal satisfaction is the major motivation for writing my papers and reports. When I feel that I've written a high-quality or professional paper to be submitted for grading, it is not manditory for the teacher to have the same opinion." These are the first and seventh sentences of the final draft. When the writer read the first draft during revision, she decided that the reader would have trouble with the transition between these sentences. To solve the problem, she planned, wrote, and revised a mini-essay of five sentences (sentences 2 through 6 in the final essay) to be included between these sentences. Thus, planning, sentence generation, and revision were nested within the process of revising the first draft.

ANALYSIS OF WRITING PROCESSES

In the remainder of this chapter, we will discuss the major writing processes in greater detail. Much of the writing research we will report has employed thinking aloud protocols similar to those discussed in Chapter 3. A typical writing protocol study proceeds as follows: Subjects arrive at the experimental session knowing that they will be assigned a topic on which to write an essay and that the whole procedure will take about an hour. Further, they know that they will be asked to think aloud while writing. They are specifically not told beforehand what the topic of the essay is to be so that all of their planning for writing will occur during the experimental session. Each subject is run separately, seated in a quiet office with a desk, pencil, paper, and tape recorder. The experimenter instructs the subjects to say everything they are thinking aloud, and to say aloud whatever they read or write. Further, subjects are asked to save all their notes and drafts and to delete material by crossing it out rather than by erasing it. The experimenter then gives the subject an envelope containing the writing assignment—that is, the topic and the intended audience. The subject then busily sets to work writing and commenting roughly as follows: "Well, opening up the envelope. OK. Whew, this is a killer! Write about abortion pro and con for *Catholic Weekly*. Oh, boy. How am I going to handle this?, etc. This continues for about an hour until the subject says something like, "Well, that's it. Goodbye tape recorder [click]."

The data from such a study consists of a verbatim transcript of the tape recording (with all the "um" 's and pauses and swearing left in) together with the essay and all the notes and drafts the writer has generated along the way. These materials are then examined in considerable detail for evidence that might reveal something of the processes by which the writer has created the essay. In general, these data are very rich in information about writing processes. The writer's protocols give many clues about their goals and plans, e.g., "I really want to change their minds about this"; about how they compose sentences, e.g., "It's important that we . . . uh . . . It's important that we . . . What?"; and about their strategies for revising, e.g., "Better make it simpler."

PLANNING IN WRITING

Planning to write consists of setting the major writing goals to be accomplished, e.g., the topic to be discussed, the intended effect on the audience, etc., of deciding what should be said, that is, the specific content, and organizing the content into a reasonable sequence.

Goal Setting. Writing, like other forms of problem solving, is goal directed. That is, the various things that people do while writing are aimed at accomplishing the major goals that they themselves establish, usually early, in the writing session. These goals, of course, will be influenced by the writing assignment, but even so writing tasks are typically quite ill defined. Even when we are assigned a very specific topic to write about, e.g., "Sensory imagery in Keats' poems," we still have to make a great many decisions on our own to define a specific writing problem and to proceed with its solution. For example, if we were to write on the 'sensory imagery' topic, we would have to decide on the major points we wanted to make. Do we just want to say that there *is* sensory imagery in Keats' poems and illustrate it? Or do we want to say that it is different from other poet's imagery? Or similar to some other poets? Once we have chosen our major points, we will still have to choose examples, craft sentences, choose appropriate words, etc. In short, our own decisions will be evident in every part of our essay. To understand how very ill-defined writing tasks are, consider this. If two students turned in identical solutions to a physics problem, no one would be very surprised. However, if two students turned in identical papers in history, it would be taken as clear evidence of cheating. Writers contribute so much from their own resources to the task of writing, that no one would believe that two writers would independently write exactly the same essay. The most important thing to notice about writers' goals is that the writers *create* them in response to the writing situation. Some of the writers' goals concern topic. For example, an engineer writing about his job says, "I've got to show how I am improving the steam turbine and why it's important." Other goals concern the demands of the writing task, e.g., "If I want to get an 'A', I'd better write at least ten pages." Still other goals concern adapting the text to the audience. For example, the engineer, in thinking about writing to a lay audience, said, "Better keep it simple." Another writer who was writing about the role of women in business to a potentially hostile audience of business men said, "I'll write this as if I were one of them."

Generating Content. When the writer has decided on a general topic, then he or she can begin to think about specific content. Many writers find it useful to "brainstorm" at this point (see Chapter 11). By brainstorming, we mean the process of trying to produce ideas freely, without editing or criticism. If we were to listen in on a writer's brainstorming session, it might sound like this. "Let's see, what do I want to say about writing? . . . uh . . . Revision is important . . . even though a lot of people don't do it. Planning is a must! Got to talk about that. What about writing with computers? and writer's block? etc.''

Organizing

Typically, brainstorming leads to a jumble of ideas in no particular order. To complete the writing plan the writer needs to impose structure on this chaos by putting the ideas in a sensible order. Listening in on writing protocols at such times, we hear writers saying things like, "Let's start with this. It'll grab them" and "This will make a strong final point."

When they are well carried out, these processes can result in a writing plan that is an enormous help in producing a successful text. However, this is not to say that everyone plans in this way when they write. In particular, novice writers spend much less time in planning to write than do experts. Indeed, some seem to plunge into writing without having any very clear idea about where they are going. Further, novices' planning is generally less complicated than that of experts. For example, the novice may plan simply to "tell them what I know about X" whether that knowledge is appropriate for the audience or not. For example, one novice, writing about his job to a teenage female audience, described the inner workings of a steam turbine in sufficiently loving detail to make his audience scream, "Gag me with a spoon!" This practice of dumping facts is the "knowledge telling" strategy that Bereiter and Scardamalia (1987) describe as common in pre-college writers. Experts typically form more complex plans, not just to tell knowledge, but to make a point, to discuss an issue, to capture the reader's interest, to overcome an objection, etc. In general, experts are far more likely to consider their audience when they plan than are novices.

Overall, it appears that experts' superiority in writing depends in a very important way on the greater sophistication of their planning processes.

SENTENCE GENERATION

Kaufer, Hayes, and Flower (1986) studied sentence generation by examining thinking aloud protocols of 12 writers as they were composing essays. Six of the writers were experienced composition teachers and six were average college writers. The top part of Figure 2 (taken from Kaufer et al., 1986) is a protocol segment in which the writer was composing and writing down the sentence shown at the bottom of the figure. Read through the protocol to see if it reminds you of your own process for composing sentences.

Figure 2 shows the most common features of sentence generation that were observed in these studies. First and most important, the writers composed sentences by proposing and evaluating sentence parts. Items 1, 4, 6, 7, 9, 12 and

17 are proposed sentence parts. On the average, the sentence parts for the 12 writers were a little over 9 words in length.

> "The best thing about it is(1) -- what?(2) Something about using my mind(3) -- it allows me the opportunity to(4) -- uh -- I want to write something about my ideas.(5) -- to put ideas into action(6) --or -- to develop my ideas into(7)-- what?(8) -- into a meaningful form?(9) Oh, bleh! -- say it allows me(10) -- to use(11) -- Na --allows me -- scratch that. The best thing about it is that it allows me to use(12) -- my mind and ideas in a productive way.(13)"

Figure 2. Protocol Segment from a Writer Composing a Sentence

Items 10, 13, and 15 indicate that sentence parts are being evaluated. For example, "Oh, bleh" suggests that the writer didn't think much of item 9. Items 2 and 8 suggest memory searches. It is very common for writers to ask themselves questions such as, "What do I want to say?", "What do I mean?", "What did he do?", or simply "What?". Questions such as these appear to reflect memory search processes in which the writer is trying to find the appropriate information or the right word to be used in constructing the sentence. Items 3 and 5, in which the writer specifies an objective she has for the sentence she is composing, appear to reflect local goal setting—that is, setting goals within the sentence. Items 11, 14, and 16 are instances in which the writer reread previously composed sentence parts. Overall, the writers were about eight times as likely to reread a part of the sentence they were currently composing as they were to read a previously composed sentence. This suggests that during sentence generation, the writers' attention is directed more toward the coordination of parts within the current sentence than toward the coordination of the current sentence with sentences previously written. Generally, Kaufer, et al. (1986) found that expert and average writers resembled each other fairly closely in the way they generated sentences. Both constructed sentences by proposing and evaluating sentence parts, both accepted about 75% of the parts they propose, and both engaged in questioning themselves, in local goal setting, and in rereading sentence parts. The groups differed, however, in two ways. The experts wrote significantly longer essays (785 words vs. 464 words for average writers). Further, the experts proposed significantly longer sentence parts (11.2 words vs. 7.3 words for average writers). Part of the expert's skill, then, appears to be the ability to handle language in larger units than average writers.

In contrast to the fluency shown by experts, the sentence generating processes of poor writers may be interrupted frequently by difficulties with low level processes such as spelling and grammar. Figure 3 illustrates this sort of difficulty in a student who had been referred to a writing clinic for help. Spelling, forming letters, and even the simple matter of handling a pencil occupy so much of the writer's attention that he has considerable difficulty remembering where he was in the sentence he was trying to write. Clearly, writers differ widely in their ability to translate writing plans into sentences.

> All right -- I've got to remember to print nicely here. Uh, I work at CMU as a hardware technician in the Digital Lab -- I should rephrase it. -- say -- uh-- I work -- no -- yeah -- I work at Carnegie Mellon -- must be able to go ahead and spell this out so they'll know what I'm talking about -- keep breaking the top of the pencil off -- [inaudible] never see -- uh -- as a hardware -- I hope the person reading this can read it -- actually -- all right, so -- technition -- um -- All right -- a hardware -- Well, this is actually not -- wait a minute -- this spelling word is wrong -- hardware t-e-c-h-n-c-i-a-n -- I believe that's it -- uh -- Okay -- Almost lost my train of thought. --

Figure 3. Protocol Segment by a Poor Writer Composing an Essay

REVISION

Murray (1978), reviewing the testimony of eminant writers, concluded that for them, "writing is rewriting." Here, Murray is describing the tendency of skilled writers to spend far more time in revising their work than in producing the original draft. On the other hand, Bracewell, Scardamalia, and Bereiter (1978) found that fourth graders hardly revise at all, that eighth graders' revisions hurt more than they help, and that for 12th graders, helpful revisions narrowly outnumbered harmful ones. Bridwell's results were a bit more positive. She found that 12th graders' second drafts were considerably better in "general merit" and mechanics than their first drafts. Pianko (1977) reported that college freshman devote less than 9% of their composing time to rereading and revising. Clearly, writers differ widely in the amount they revise. In general, it appears that the more expert the writer, the greater proportion of writing time the writer will spend in revision.

The time spent on revision, however, is not the only difference between experts and novices. Experts appear to define the task of revision differently than novices do. Stallard (1974) found that only 2.5% of 12th graders' revisions were focused above the word and sentence level. Bridwell (1980), who also studied 12th graders, found about 11% of revisions above the sentence level. Sommers (1980) found that college freshmen "understand the revision process as a rewording activity. . . . They concentrate on particular words apart from their role in the text." In contrast, experienced writers " (p. 381) describe their primary objectives when revising as finding the form or shape of their argument." Further Sommers found that "the experienced writers have a second objective; a concern for their readership" (p. 384). Hayes, Flower, Schriver, Stratman, and Carey (1987) found that expert revisors differed from novices in the following ways:

Experts usually read the whole text through before starting revision, whereas the novices started revision after reading the first sentence.

Novices attended almost exclusively to local (work and sentence level) problems, whereas experts attended both to local and global problems.

Faigley and Witte (1983), who studied changes in meaning resulting from revision, found that experts were more likely to change meaning through revision than were novices. They observed that the revisions of inexperienced college writers resulted in changed meaning in 12% of cases; the revisions of experienced college writers, in 25% of cases; and the revisions of adult writers, in 34% of cases. These results suggest that expert revisors define the task of revisions as being more global and more focused on meaning and audience than do novices.

Detection and Diagnosis of Text Problems

Two skills that are extremely useful to revisors are *detection* skills—that is, skills used to identify text problems, e.g., "Oops! This doesn't sound right"—and *diagnosis* skills—that is, skills used to characterize text problems, e.g., "This is too formal. There are too many passive sentences." Expert writers appear to be better than novices in both kinds of skill.

Hayes et al. (1987) found that experts detected about 1.6 times more problems in a faulty text than did novices. Further, of the problems they detected, experts were able to diagnose 74%, whereas novices were able to diagnose only 42%—a ratio of 1.7:1. Experts, then, showed a clear advantage over novices both in the detection and in the diagnosis of text problems. Superiority in these two skills gives experts much greater flexibility in revision than novices have.

To appreciate this point, one needs to recognize two important facts about revision:

1. *Diagnosis is not an obligatory step in revision.* Diagnosis is heavily emphasized in composition classes. Students are taught to identify faulty parallelism, dangling modifiers, wordiness, etc. However, writers often revise without diagnosing. For example, Hayes et al. (1987) found many instances, both in experts and in novices, in which the revisor detected problems in the text and rewrote the problematic sections without bothering to diagnose the problems. In a typical instance, the revisor encounters a horrible text filled with grammatical blunders and atrocities. He says, "This is truly ghastly," reads the text for its main points and rewrites them in his own words, completely ignoring the faults in the original text. We will call this approach to revision without diagnosis the "rewrite" strategy.

The most common alternative strategy is to diagnose the text problems and to fix them. Here, the revisor examines the text carefully to identify the nature of its faults. For example, if the author has written, "I like many winter sports such as swimming, ski weekends and to skate", the revisor may say, "Aha! Another parallelism problem," and revise it to read "I like many winter sports such as swimming, skiing, and skating." We will call this the "revise" strategy.

2. *Whether rewriting or revising is preferable depends on the text.* (a) If it is important to preserve as much of the original text as possible, then the revise strategy is probably best. For example, if you are required to edit something that your boss has written and is moderately proud of, you do it very gently, saving as much of her original wording as possible. Here revision is the appropriate strategy. On the other hand, if it isn't important to save the original text, then rewriting may be the best strategy. For example, if you are reworking something that you, yourself wrote in an alcoholic stupor, you may be well advised to set fire to the original text and to rewrite it from the beginning. (b) If there are a great many problems in the original text, diagnosing and fixing may be very expensive. With such texts, rewriting may be the best strategy. In a text with few faults, revision will probably be more efficient than rewriting.

Because experts have strong skills in both detection and diagnosis, they can typically exercise either the rewrite or the revise strategy and therefore can choose the strategy they feel will be most efective. Novices, on the other hand, often find that their lack of skills limit their strategic choices. Experts, then, have more strategic options than do novices.

ADJUSTING THE TEXT TO THE AUDIENCE

If writers are to be successful in communicating to an audience, they have to adjust their writing to the reader's needs. Writers have to be careful not to write over the reader's head, that is, over their vocabulary level or beyond their knowledge. Further, writers must try to make the text interesting to the audience or it may never be read at all! For example, if we were to write an article about a teachers' strike for sixth-grade children, we might have to explain or 'write around' words such as 'arbitration' and 'grievance'; we might have to fill in gaps in our readers' knowledge such as why teachers might want to strike; and we might have to take special pains to interest the audience, e.g., "Suppose you came to school one morning and none of the teachers was there."

Expert writers are clearly better than novices at adjusting to the audience, but the task is a difficult one for all writers. There are at least two major reasons that this is so. First, the writer's own knowledge may blind him or her to what would confuse a reader. Second, the writer may not have a good internal representation of the reader and, thus, be unable to anticipate the readers' needs.

The Problem of the Writer's Knowledge

A common task writers do is to revise a text so that is intelligible to nonexperts. One problem that arises in doing this is that if the writers are subject matter experts, as they often are, they may have difficulty in guessing what the nonexpert might find confusing about the topic. This is a familiar problem that turns up not only in writing but in teaching and in ordinary conversation as well. The common wisdom is that experts have learned the elements of their field so long ago that they have forgotten that their hard earned knowledge is more than common sense shared by everyone, e.g., that "everyone knows that." If this explanation is correct, then we would expect that prior knowledge of the content of any text would make it more difficult for the revisor to detect faults in that text. To test this hypothesis, Hayes, Schriver, Spilka, and Blaustein (1986) asked freshman to underline parts of unclear texts that they judged would cause comprehension problems for other freshmen readers who did not know the subject matter. One of the two groups of subjects, which we will call the "high knowledge" group, had read and evaluated a clear version of the text before they evaluated the unclear version. As a result, they had knowledge of the content of the unclear version when they were trying to predict what parts of it would be unclear to other readers. The other group of subjects, which we will call the "low knowledge" group, did not read the clear version first and therefore had little knowledge of the content of the unclear version when they were making their predictions. On the average, the low knowledge group discovered 50% more problems in the unclear text than did the high knowledge group. This study shows, then, that subject matter experts' knowledge *can* make them insensitive to the comprehension problems their readers may have. In addition, it shows that this knowledge effect takes place in a matter of minutes rather than months or years. That is, within minutes after revisors acquire knowledge that helps them to understand a text, they become insensitive to the problems that someone else without their newly acquired knowledge would have in understanding the text.

We all know, of course, that there *are* people who can explain things well even though they are experts. We are currently exploring what it is that distinguishes these individuals from the rest of us. We hope to identify strategies that they use to predict the reader's comprehension problems so that we can teach them to other writers.

Problems Due to an Inadequate Representation of the Reader

To revise a text for an audience is a very complex task. It requires the revisor to represent the goals of the text, to represent the intended audience, to predict how well the audience will respond to the text, and to propose better ways to accomplish those goals when the revisor perceives the text to be faulty. It is not obvious that expert revisors operating on their intuitions can accomplish this task optimally. Duffy, Curran, and Sass (1983) found that when professional writing firms revised documents for clarity, the results were frequently disappointing when the original and revised documents were compared in tests of comprehension.

Swaney et al. (1981) asked a group of four expert writers to revise four public documents so that they could be understood by a general audience. The documents included a warranty, an auto insurance form, and an employee benefits brochure. The writers, working as a group, put in 100 hours in trying to improve the documents. Comprehension tests on the original and the revised documents showed that the designers' efforts had improved the comprehensibility of three of the documents but made the last one worse. Overall, the result was a positive one—the writers had helped more than they had hurt—but it wasn't nearly as positive as one would like.

When the writers were shown the sorts of trouble that the readers were having with their texts, they were genuinely surprised. These results made it clear that the writers were operating under severe disadvantages. They did not have an adequate internal representation of the reader to guide their writing. Further, they were writing without any direct feedback from the target audience. Swaney et al. (1981) decided to try to help their writers by giving them direct feedback from their readers through reading protocols. The intention was to show the writers how their writing actually worked with the target audience. The writers then revised the document using the protocols. That is, they read thinking-aloud protocols of readers attempting to comprehend the document and used these protocols to identify features of the text that required improvement. The document was then revised in the light of the protocols. After three revision cycles, the protocols revealed no further problems in the text. Comprehension tests showed that the text was now significantly clearer than the original (16% errors vs. 46% errors).

The result is both a sensible one and a very practical one. It makes good common sense to go directly to the audience for information about readers' comprehension needs rather than relying on the writer's intuition. It is a very practical result because it can be applied quite directly to the improvement of documents. Based on these results, Swaney et al. developed a procedure for writing clear documents called Protocol Aided Revision. With this procedure, the writer produces a draft that is then tested on a reader from the intended audience. The writer uses the audience feedback to produce a second draft and so on until the readers no longer have major difficulties in comprehending the text. In fact, Swaney et al. appplied the technique to produce a prize-winning computer manual.

Schriver (1984) noticed that writers who use Protocol Aided Revision claim that it has changed their writing and that, in particular, it has made them more sensitive to their audience's needs. Following up on this suggestion that protocols can improve the writer's representation of the reader, Schriver has constructed a sequence of 10 lessons for writers. In each lesson, students are asked to read a flawed text and to predict the sorts of troubles the reader would have in comprehending the text. Next, the students read a thinking-aloud protocol of a reader who is trying to comprehend the text. The students then revise their predictions of reader difficulties. They proceed in this manner for each of the ten lessons.

Results have been very encouraging. After training, writers detect nearly twice as many reader problems as before. After approximately six lessons, the writers begin to predict reader problems accurately before they see the protocols and no longer need protocols on new texts. This line of work appears to have considerable promise not just for writers but for training audience sensitivity more generally, e.g., for training speakers how their talks will be received and for training literature teachers how their students will respond to assigned texts.

WRITING CAN HELP THINKING

The writer, part of who's protocol is reproduced below, was a volunteer who knew that she was to engage in a writing study for about an hour. She knew that she would be asked to "think aloud" as she produced a short essay. She did not know the topic, however, until she arrived for the tape recording session.

Protocol IV

Problem: Write a short essay on why you write papers at Carnegie-Mellon University.

S: (1) "OK, um, the issue is motivation and the problem of writing papers. For
   (2) me, motivation here at Carnegie-Mellon is the academic pressure and grades that
   (3) are involved, so I'd better put that down . . . and grades . . . um, they kind of
   (4) compel me, that's really what motivation is, um, kind of to impel or start or
   (5) a, momentum. (Pause) OK, I suppose from the academic pressure of the grades,
   (6) I'm not sure whether, I think personal satisfaction is important, but I'm not
   (7) sure whether that stems from academic pressures and grades, or whether—I
   (8) would say personal satisfaction is a major issue. OK, um, Oh."
E: (9) "What are you thinking?"
S: (10) "I'm trying to think of the first sentence to start with. Um, maybe something
   (11) like, personal satisfaction is the major motivating force in the writing of my
   (12) papers and reports. OK, I'm trying to think of . . . OK, I want to somehow get it into
   (13) the academic pressures now. Um, well maybe not so soon. OK. Not only do I get
   (14) satisfaction from my grades, but I also get satisfaction in turning in something
   (15) that is good quality. So, if I'm happy when I write a good paper, it really doesn't
   (16) matter what kind of grade I get back on it, if I'm happy with it. So, um, um,

(17) let's see. Um, what are the—I'm thinking of, I'm trying to relate personal
(18) satisfaction between academic pressure and the grades, but I'm not really
      sure
(19) how to do it, how to branch it. I'm really having a hard time getting started.
(20) Well, maybe I'll just write a bunch of ideas down, and maybe try to con-
      nect them after
(21) I finish. OK. When I feel that I've written a high quality, and I put in paren-
(22) theses, professional, paper, um, to be graded, when I submit it, the grade
      is not
(23) always necessary for the teacher to have the same. OK, that's kind of ___;
(24) I'll check with that one. OK, and—let's see what else. Um, but
(25) of course, the reason I'm writing the paper in the first place is for the grade,
(26) or to relate that back. Those two ideas are very interlocked—maybe that's
      not
(27) the right term.''

Analysis of the Protocol

In analyzing this protocol fragment, we will call attention to just one class
of processes which we consider especially significant—understanding processes.
What we refer to here as understanding processes are what Stoehr (1967) calls
"thinking," and Van Nostrand (1976) describes as a "learning process." Evidence that understanding processes are at work may be seen in changes in the
writer's understanding of the topic as writing proceeds. In lines 1 through 3, the
writer identifies motivation with grades. In lines 6 and 7, she introduces the idea
of personal satisfaction but is not at all sure that this is a source of satisfaction
distinct from grades. In lines 8 through 12, personal satisfaction is given a very
important role, but it is not clear how the writer relates it to grades. In lines 13
through 15, two sources of personal satisfaction are identified: grades and the
production of high-quality work. A relation between the two sources of satisfaction is specified in lines 15 and 16 and again in lines 21 through 23. The relation
is that if the work is of good quality, a grade is not necessary for satisfaction.
In lines 24 and 25, a contradictory relation is noted—that is, that grades are the
initial motivator for all essay writing. In lines 26 and 27, these relations are
described as "interlocked" rather than as contradictory. The contradiction between the relations is recognized later in the protocol. In large measure, the final
essay is concerned with the resolution of this conflict.

The Completed Essay

Personal satisfaction is the major motivating force in the writing of my papers and reports. The emphasis on 4.0's here at Carnegie-Mellon University causes grades to become an instinctive motivator for myself. Acquiring good grades does, in fact, give me personal satisfaction.

The initial motivator in the outset of writing a paper is the fact that a grade will be attached to it upon completion. I feel that my role as a student requires all of my efforts to be put forth into course work, which includes the writing of papers.

After I begin writing a paper, the grade emphasis diminishes and a higher level of personal satisfaction takes over. When I feel that I've written a high-quality or professional paper to be submitted for grading, it is not mandatory for the teacher to have the same opinion. But of course, this somewhat contradicts my earlier statement that the motivation for writing paper is to achieve the ultimate goal—a good grade.

Thus, the combination of the grade "initiator" and later a higher level of personal satisfaction is what motivates me to write my college papers and reports.

In the course of writing the essay, the subject's understanding of the topic changed radically. At first, she believed her motivation had a single source. By the end of the essay she recognized that it had two sources which were related in a complex way. Writing in this case clearly involved understanding processes.

REFERENCES

Bereiter, C., and Scardamalia, M. (1987). *The psychology of written composition.* Hillsdale, NJ: Lawrence Erlbaum Associates.

Bracewell, R., Scardamalia, M., and Bereiter, C. (1978). The development of audience awareness in writing. *Resources in Education,* October, 1978. 154–433.

Bridwell, L. S. (1980). Revising strategies in twelfth grade students' transactional writing. *Research in the Teaching of English, 14*[3], 107–122.

Duffy, T., Curran, T., and Sass, D. (1983). Document Design for Technical Job Tasks: an Evaluation. *Human Factors, 25,* 143–160.

Faigley, L., and Witte, S. (1983). Analyzing revision. *College Composition and communication, 32,* 400–414.

Hayes, J. R., and Flower, L. S. (1980). Identifying the organization of writing processes. In L. Gregg and E. Steinberg (Eds.), *Cognitive Processes in Writing: An Interdisciplinary Approach.* Hillsdale, NJ: Lawrence Erlbaum Associates.

Hayes, J. R., Flower, L. S., Schriver, K. A., Stratman, J., and Carey, L. (1987). Cognitive Processes in Revision. In S. Rosenberg (Ed.) *Advances in Psycholinguistics, Volume II: Reading, Writing, and Language Processing.* Cambridge, England: Cambridge University Press.

Hayes, J. R., Schriver, K. A., Spilka, R., and Blaustein, A. (1986). *If its clear to me it must be clear to them.* Paper presented at the Conference on College Composition and Communication, New Orleans.

Kaufer, D., Hayes, J. R., and Flower, L. S. (1986). Composing Written Sentences. *Research in the Teaching of English, 20,* 121–140.

Murray, D. M. (1978). Internal revision: A process of discovery. In C. R. Cooper and L. Odell (Eds.), *Research on Composing: Points of Departure.* Urbana, IL: National Council of Teachers of English.

Pianko, S. (1979). Description of the composing process of college freshman writers. *Research in the Teaching of English*, 13, 5–22.

Schriver, K. A. (1984). *Revising computer documentation for comprehension: Ten lessons in protocol-aided revision* (Tech. Rep. No. 14). Pittsburgh, PA: Carnegie Mellon University, Communication Design Center.

Sommers, N. (1980). Revision strategies of student writers and experienced writers. *College Composition and communication*, 31, 378–387.

Stallard, C. (1974). An analysis of the writing behavior of good student writers. *Research in the Teaching of English*, 8, 206–218.

Stoehr, T. (1967). Writing as Thinking. *College English, 28*, 411–421.

Swaney, J. H., Janik, C. J., Bond, S. J., and Hayes, J. R. (1981). *Editing for comprehension: Improving the process through reading protocols.* Carnegie Mellon University, Document Design Project Technical Report #14.

Van Nostrand, A. D. (1976). Writing and the Dialogue of Disciplines. *Personalized System of Instruction Proceedings,* Providence, RI: Brown University.

II

MEMORY AND KNOWLEDGE ACQUISITION

5

The Structure of Human Memory

Each of us has several memories which hold different kinds of information for different lengths of time. We have a long-term memory which will hold great quantities of information—such as our knowledge of a language—for many, many years. We have a short-term memory which will hold about seven numbers or letters for roughly 15 seconds; in addition, we have a number of *very* short-term sensory memories. For example, we have a visual sensory memory which can hold an image of 9 to 10 letters but for less than a second. In the following sections, we will discuss the properties of each of these three kinds of memory in detail.

THE RELATIONSHIP BETWEEN SENSORY MEMORIES, SHORT-TERM MEMORY, AND LONG-TERM MEMORY

Figure 1 provides us with a framework for understanding human memory. Messages, received mostly by eye or ear, are stored for very short periods of time in sensory stores. If we attend to them, the messages will be transferred to short-term memory. Otherwise they are lost.

Once the message has entered short-term memory, we can keep it there by repeating it to ourselves—that is, by rehearsal. Otherwise it will be lost within a few seconds.

Later in this chapter, we will discuss how messages are transferred to long-term memory by a process called elaborative rehearsal.

Information enters through our senses and is held very briefly (for less than a few seconds) in sensory memories associated with each sense. If we attend to

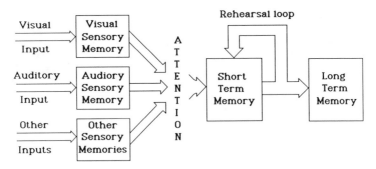

Figure 1. A framework for understanding human memory

the information in one of the sensory memories, it will enter short-term memory (STM) where we can maintain it without rehearsal for, at most, about 20 seconds. If we do rehearse it, that is, if we repeat the information to ourselves (as we do when we are trying to remember a phone number until we can dial it) we can keep the information in short-term memory for a longer time. However, only small amounts of information can be held in STM—about seven independent items. Information can be transferred from our short-term memory to our long-term memory (LTM) by a process called elaborative rehearsal that makes connections between the new information to be learned and information already in long-term memory. In contrast to the limited capacity of STM, we can hold vast amounts of information in LTM and we can store it there for very long periods of time— that is, for years or decades. Having whizzed through this tour of human memory structure, we will now return for a more leisurely examination of each of the components.

SENSORY MEMORIES

The sensory memories are very short-term memories associated with each sense. That is, there is one sensory memory for vision, one for hearing, etc. It is believed that the sensory memory retain information in raw (uncategorized or unprocessed) form. That is, they contain simple sensory information such as color and position but not complex characteristics that require reference to learned patterns in LTM, e.g., "That's the number five." For this reason, sensory memories are also called *pre-categorical.*

Many psychologists believe that the major purpose of the sensory memories is to retain raw sensory information long enough so that it can be processed appropriately. Visual patterns must be held long enough so that they can be recognized as belonging to a category, e.g., a letter, a word, a face, etc. Auditory patterns must be held long enough to allow accurate interpretation of sentences. For example, the sentence, "You believe him" has a very different meaning if the word "him" is said with a rising rather than a falling inflection. Understanding this sentence, then, requires that pitch information must be stored at least briefly.

Evidence that sensory memories really are part of our memory structure comes from a large number of studies. The best known of these were designed by Sperling (1960). In Sperling's study, subjects were shown a three-by-three matrix of letters (such as that shown in Figure 2) very briefly and asked to report all the letters they had seen. Typically, subjects could remember between four and five letters or about 50%. Sperling wondered whether this meant *1.* only four or five letters ever made it into memory, or *2.* that, possibly, all the letters got into memory but that the last four or five were forgotten while the first four or five were being reported. To see which hypothesis was correct, Sperling devised a partial reporting experiment in which the subjects had to try to remember all of the letters but were required to report only some of them.

Figure 2. An array of letters similar to those used by Sperling

In the partial reporting study, the subjects again saw a three by three matrix of letters exposed very briefly. Immediately after the matrix disappeared, Sperling sounded either a high, medium, or low tone to signal the subjects to report either the top, middle, or bottom row of letters. Notice that the subjects would have to try to store all nine of the letters because they couldn't tell beforehand which row they would be asked to report. Sperling reasoned that if all the letters were recorded in memory, then the subjects should be able to score close to 100% when they were asked to report on a row that the experimenter chose at random. (Very little should be forgotten in the time required to report just three letters.) On the other hand, if only half of the letters got into memory, then subjects shouldn't be able to do better than about 50% correct. In fact, the subjects were almost 100% accurate in making their partial reports. These results indicate that the subjects were able to retain all nine letters after they disappeared from sight— but not for very long. By the time the subjects could report four or five of them, the rest had been forgotten.

To find out exactly how long the letters were held in the visual memory, Sperling varied the partial reporting experiment as follows: Rather than sounding the tone (the partial reporting signal) immediately after the letter matrix disappeared, he sounded it with various delays up to one second in length. When the tone was delayed by as much as a second, the advantage of partial reporting was lost. Thus, the visual memory appears to hold information for less than a second.

As we noted earlier, it has been suggested that sensory memories hold only unprocessed sensory information—that is, just the information that is in the raw physical stimulus. If this suggestion is correct, then the visual memory could contain information about the position or color of the letters in the matrix, but could not contain information about whether the symbols are letters or digits. (To distinguish letters from digits, we have to process the information by comparing it to patterns in long-term memory.) It follows further that only properties of the unprocessed physical stimulus can provide effective partial reporting cues. (If the subject is to succeed in reporting only the green objects in the sensory memory, then the property green has to be stored in the sensory memory.) Thus, instructions to give partial reports based on position or color should improve performance but instructions based on learned categories, which are stored in long-term memory, should not. In fact, Banks and Barber (1977) showed that color can be used successfully as a partial reporting cue and Sperling found that when subjects were presented a matrix of mixed numbers and letters, a cue to report just the numbers or just the letters didn't improve performance.

The visual sensory memory, then, is a very short-term memory (lasting less than one second) which contains unprocessed or pre-categorical information.

After Sperling's work had revealed the visual memory, researchers looked for a corresponding very short-term store for auditory information. Moray, Bates, and Barnett (1965) performed a partial reporting experiment on memory for spoken letters that was quite parallel to Sperling's experiment. They asked subjects to listen to two, three, or four simultaneous messages (lists of one to four letters) presented through two to four loudspeakers located in different directions from the listener as shown in Figure 3. The visual arrays in Sperling's experiment, which consisted of three letters presented in each of three rows, were matched by auditory arrays in the Moray et al. study that consisted of up to four letters presented on each of two to four loudspeakers. The loudspeakers were used in this study as cues for partial reporting in the same way as rows were used in the Sperling experiment. Just as readers can narrow their focus to a single row, listeners can focus on a single source of sound. They can attend to one of several loudspeakers in the same way that we can attend to one of several conversations at a party.

In the Moray et al. (1965) experiment, the subjects in the whole report condition were required to report all the letters they heard from all the speakers. In the partial report condition, they had to listen to all of the speakers but they only reported the letters from the speaker designated by a light that was lit after all the letters had been heard. As in the Sperling study, subjects performed consistently better in the partial report condition than in the whole report condition.

To determine how long information remains in the auditory register, Darwin, Turvey, and Crowder (1972) varied the time of presentation of the partial report signal from zero to four seconds after the presentation of the simultaneous messages. Their results, shown in Figure 4, indicate clearly that partial reports were superior to whole reports when the signal was delayed by two seconds. Notice,

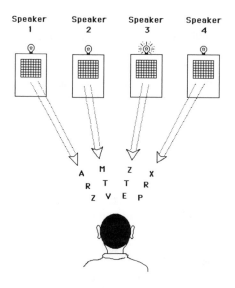

Figure 3. Experimental arrangement for the Moray, Bates, and Barnett study.

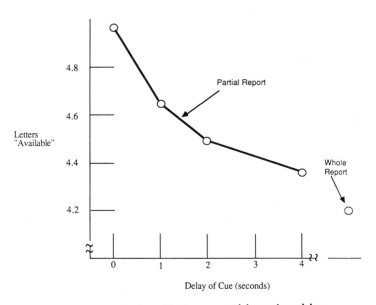

Figure 4. Number of letters reported for various delays.

however, that this superiority disapears when the signal is delayed by as much as four seconds. The auditory sensory memory, then, appears to hold information for about two seconds. The auditory sensory memory, then, is a very short-term memory lasting about two seconds.

Although it has been suggested that there are sensory memories for each of the senses, very little research has been conducted other than on vision and hearing.

Attention

Normally, the sensory memories contain a great deal of information—a flood of sights, sounds, smells, etc. coming from the outside world. However, most of this information *does not* enter short-term memory. Most of it decays and is lost forever. Information is transferred from the sensory memories to short-term memory only when it is specifically attended to.

Attention is a limited resource in the sense that we can attend to only one source of information at a time. As we noted previously, when you are in the midst of a party, you may hear several conversations going on at the same time—all of them putting information into your auditory memory. Although you are engaging in one conversation, you are aware of the other conversations only as background noise. However, although you are aware that the conversations are happening, you are not aware of very much else about them. You would likely be able to tell (if asked) whether the speakers were male or female. However, you would not know what the other conversations were about or even if they were being carried on in English. If your name were mentioned by the group behind you, however, you would likely switch your attention to that conversation to find out whether you were being praised or damned. One's own name is a very powerful (categorical) attention getter. Although your attention is switched to the new conversation, you will no longer be able to understand what your former conversational partners are saying now. Without your attention, their words will still enter your auditory memory, but within a couple of seconds, they will be lost without ever having been understood.

What we want to emphasize here is that attention is indeed a limited resource. If there are five conversations within earshot, you can't attend to all of them or to two or three and ignore the rest. You can attend to any of them, but *only one at a time*.

Evidence for this discussion, fortunately, does not come entirely from cocktail parties, but from a careful series of studies employing a task called *shadowing*. In the shadowing task, the experimenter presents two simultaneous voices to the subject through earphones, one voice in each ear. The subject's job is to listen to one of the voices and to repeat it, or "shadow" it, with as little delay after hearing as possible. When shadowing, subjects are usually just a word or two behind the voice they are listening to. Shadowing is a useful task in this kind of research because it allows the experimenter to be sure that the subject is attending to the voice he or she is supposed to attend to. In Cherry's (1953) studies, subjects knew whether the unshadowed voice was there, whether it was a real voice or just a buzz, and whether the voice changed from male or female. The subjects, then, could report on certain physical features of the unshadowed voice. However, they did not know what the unshadowed voice was saying, what language it was being said in, or whether the language had changed during the experiment. Moray (1959) found that subjects couldn't report any of the words said by the unshadowed voice, even if they were repeated over and over.

When we *do not* attend to information in our sensory memories, we don't process it and we don't understand it. But what happens when we do attend to it? The most plausible current opinion is that in attending, we attempt to recognize the information in the sensory memories by comparing it to patterns already in long-term memory. That is, we try to determine whether the images we see or the sounds we hear match a known pattern in long-term memory. The pattern might be a letter, a word, a face, a tune, the odor of camomile tea, or any sort of information, trivial or not, that you might have squirreled away in your long-term memory.

The task of matching sensory information to patterns in long-term memory may sound easy—like matching the square peg to the square hole—but in many practical cases it is not. Very often, the sensory information resembles more than one pattern in LTM and none of them exactly. Speakers may pronounce the same words differently. When a Texan says "pen," it may sound like "pin"; and when a Bostonian says "heart" it may sound like "hat" as in "My fawthuh had a hat attack." People are always saying mysterious things to us that we have to try to understand using whatever information we can bring to bear. Just how sensory information is matched to patterns in LTM is a matter now actively being investigated. One interesting suggestion is embodied in the HEARSAY speech recognition program (Reddy and Newell, 1974).

HEARSAY is a computer program that accepts spoken language as input and produces a typed version of what it has heard as output. In order to do this, it compares the incoming speech signal to knowledge of three different sorts: *acoustic knowledge*—knowledge of English speech sounds and English words; *syntactic knowledge*—knowledge of English grammar; and *semantic knowledge*—knowledge of what is meaningful or sensible to say. Each of these three types of knowledge is handled by a separate module in HEARSAY. The important thing to notice is how these modules cooperate with each other in order to understand the spoken message.

The task set for HEARSAY was to type out chess moves spoken by people playing the game shown in Figure 5. We should note that interpreting spoken chess moves is easier than interpreting general conversation because chess moves have a relatively limited grammar and vocabulary (just 31 words). "Pawn to King four" is a chess move, but "King to pawn four" and "Pawn to Albuquerque, New Mexico" are not. Despite the limited grammar and vocabulary, though, there are still 108 different legal ways to say, "Bishop to Queen Knight three."

Even if a move is grammatically all right, it may be illegal or unwise. HEARSAY's Semantic module contains a chess-move evaluation program that tells it which moves are legal given the current state of the board (there are about 40 legal moves in a typical chess position) and which of the legal moves are good ones. To illustrate how HEARSAY's sources of knowledge cooperate in interpreting speech, we will work through an example in which the person playing 'white' in the game shown in Figure 5 announced the move "Bishop to Queen Knight three." HEARSAY starts very reasonably by trying to identify the first word of the sentence. The syntax module proposes 13 words that would be grammatically legal. The semantics module rules out two of these because they are not part of any legal move. The acoustics module then examines each of the remaining words to see how well each of them matches the speech signal. The Acous-

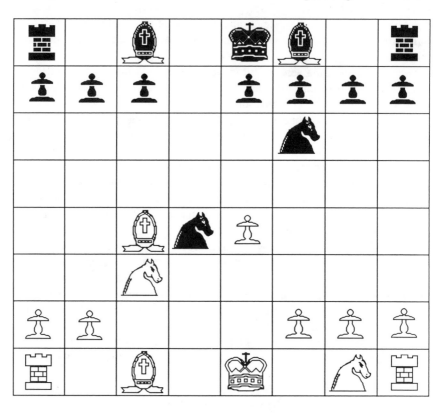

Figure 5. The chess game in the HEARSAY study.

tics module then prints out its evaluation of each of the candidate words. In this instance, the correct word "Bishop" has the highest evaluation and, therefore, is tentatively chosen by HEARSAY as the first word of the sentence. HEAR-SAY now procedes by the same method to try to identify the remaining words in the sentence. Things procede smoothly with HEARSAY identifying "Bishop to Queen . . .": when a mistake occurs. Of five candidates for the next word, the acoustic module rates the correct word "Knight" second after the word "three." This may seem an odd error to make—confusing "knight" for "three." It happens because HEARSAY can interpret the "n" sound that begins "knight" with the "n" sound that ends "queen" and the "t" sound that ends "knight" with the "t" like sound that begins "three." Because "three" scored higher than "knight," HEARSAY now tries to complete the sentence, "Bishop to Queen three. . . ." Looking for the next word, the syntax module proposed seven possible words, but most of them were unacceptable to the semantics module. The Acoustics module examined the few words that were acceptable to both of the other modules. It found that none of them matched the speech signal very well. As a result, "Bishop to Queen three . . ." was given a low rating and was replaced as the best candidate sentence by the correct "Bishop to Queen Knight. . . ." From this point forward, HEARSAY succeeds in identifying the remainder of the message without error. The most important point to notice here is that in recognizing the message contained in the sensory data, HEARSAY not only matched the data against stored letter and word sound patterns, but also made use of grammatical and semantic knowledge as well. The importance of these other sources of knowledge is illustrated in Figure 6, which shows that recognition of both words and sentences is greatly enhanced by supplementing acoustic knowledge with syntactic and semantic knowledge. It is reasonable to believe that humans use interacting sources of knowledge, in the same way that HEARSAY does, when they are interpreting each other's speech.

	Accuracy	
Knowledge Sources Used	% Words Recognized	% Sentences Recognized
Acoustic Phonetics only	40%	0%
Acoustics and Syntax	65%	14%
Acoustics, Syntax, and Semantics	88%	46%

Figure 6.   HEARSAY's success using various knowledge sources.

Summary: Sensory Memories

1. Visual sensory memory can store 9 to 10 symbols for less than one second.
2. Auditory sensory memory can hold about 5 symbols for less than four seconds.
3. If we attend to information in sensory memory, it enters short-term memory. Otherwise, it is forgotten.
4. Attending to information in the sensory memories is believed to involve recognizing that information by matching it to information in long term memory.
5. The HEARSAY program provides a model of how sensory information might be matched to information of various sorts in long-term memory.

SHORT-TERM MEMORY

Although it isn't appropriate to describe short-term memory as the most important memory—we would be quite thoroughly crippled by the loss of any of our memories—short-term memory is where the action is. It is the place where information is manipulated, where inferences are made, and where problems are solved. For this reason, it is also called "working memory." Klatzky (1980) has described short-term memory as a work bench where information recognized in the sensory registers and information retrieved from long-term memory may be processed and put to work.

Information in STM is subject to two important constraints: STM will hold only a limited amount of information and it will hold that information only for a limited period of time.

Memory Span

A phenomenon that reveals the limited capacity of STM is memory span. In a memory span test, the experimenter reads a list of unrelated items, such as letters or digits, to the subject just once. The subject then attempts to repeat the list just as it was presented, e.g., the same items in the same order. By presenting lists of varying lengths, the experimenter can determine the length of the list that the subject can repeat correctly half the time. This length is the subjects memory span. A typical adult memory span for letters is about seven.

The reader who is interested in measuring memory span can use the lists provided in Table 1. To conduct a memory span measurement, you should first provide yourself with a friend who is willing to have his or her memory span measured and a watch that measures seconds. Then you explain the memory span task to your subject roughly as follows: "I am going to read you a list of unrelated letters at the rate of one letter a second. I will start with a list of four letters and increase the length of the list by one letter with each trial. I will raise my hand when I start the list and lower it when I finish so that you will know when you have heard the whole list. At that point, you should try to repeat the list just as you heard it." When the subject is ready, say "Here are four letters." Then read the first list at a uniform rate of one letter per second. After your subject responds, procede to the next list saying "Here are five letters," etc. Don't go more than one or two lists beyond the point at which the subject begins to make errors so as to minimize frustration and embarrassment.

Table 1. Random Numbers for Memory Span Test

Length	Series 1	Series 2	Series 3
4	0 8 2 4	1 2 7 9	8 2 6 9
5	4 1 6 2 3	1 4 6 0 3	1 4 5 0 8
6	9 0 7 8 9 6	7 2 3 4 9 5	2 4 1 2 7 9
7	3 0 7 1 2 8 3	8 4 9 2 6 0 7	6 4 1 3 2 6 1
8	5 4 3 7 5 9 8 0	6 9 7 8 3 5 1 7	0 6 2 9 4 8 3 8
9	4 2 1 6 9 2 1 0 8	5 3 1 8 0 9 2 9 2	9 0 8 1 3 5 8 0 1
10	5 4 6 7 4 0 2 1 9 3	1 5 6 8 2 4 0 5 1 2	4 2 8 6 5 1 3 9 1 2
11	8 5 7 2 9 6 1 5 3 5 8	6 8 3 0 9 7 4 6 3 5 7	4 7 9 0 3 8 6 8 5 3 5
12	2 7 6 0 8 1 4 9 3 6 0 4	0 1 8 2 4 9 3 2 0 7 6 3	3 9 4 2 6 3 9 4 1 8 0 6

Figure 7. Three Chinese Ideographs: "A Flight of Butterflies"

Memory span studies usually require the subject to work through several sets of lists like those in Table 1. Typically, the subject gets the very short lists right 100 percent of the time and the very long lists zero percent of the time. The subject's memory span is the length of the list that he can repeat correctly 50 percent of the time. A typical memory span for adults is between seven and eight numbers. If we performed the memory-span test using letters, we would get about the same results as for numbers. The average memory span for letters is about 7.2.

Memory "Chunks"

The memory span for familiar words is a bit less than that for letters—5.86. However, this span is surprisingly large when we consider how many letters are contained in 5.86 words. An average word has about five letters. When people remember five or six words, they are remembering 25 or 30 letters—a number far beyond their memory span for letters.

Why can people remember so many more letters when they are combined in words than when they are presented separately? The reason is that we store information in "chunks." A chunk is a package of information that is treated as a unit. Letters are sometimes treated as units and sometimes not. When letters are presented in an unrelated way as in the list XZLPTR, each letter acts as an independent unit. Thus this list would be remembered as the six chunks "X," "Z," "L," "P," "T," and "R." When letters are combined into familiar words, as in the list

PEACH   MAP   RIVER   FLIGHT

they don't function as individual units. These 19 letters function as four units and would be remembered as the chunks "peach," "map," "river," and "flight." Such observations led George Miller (1956) to conclude that the capacity of short-term memory is 7 ± 2 *chunks*, not 7 ± 2 *letters*. When several letters are combined in each chunk, we can hold many more letters in short-term memory than when there is only one letter per chunk.

Where Do Chunks Come From?

A person's ability to remember in chunks depends on that person's knowledge. If you wanted to remember a list containing the Swahili word for lemon, *ndimu*, you would probably have to remember three chunks—*en*, *dee*, and *moo*—rather than the single chunk you would need for *lemon*. The syllables *en*, *dee*, and *moo* are familiar as units of pronunciation in English; therefore, we can remember them as chunks. The combination *en-dee-moo*, however, is not a familiar unit for English speakers, so we can't remember it as a chunk. *Ndimu* is a chunk for Swahili speakers because it is as familiar to them as *lemon* or *parsnip* is to us.

Each character in a Chinese ideograph (Figure 7) can be remembered as a chunk to those fluent in Chinese. For those of us who are not capable of reading Chinese, each character appears to be complexes of four to 10 lines and squiggles, each of which must be remembered as a chunk.

Figure 8.   2:1 Recoding

Chunks come in many shapes and sizes. Whenever we recognize a pattern in information, we can break the information down into chunks and remember it more easily. For example, familiar sentences can be chunks. The list of words in Table 2A is hard to remember, but the same list is easy to memorize when it is reorganized into maxims, as in Table 2B.

Table 2. Maxims as Chunks

A. Words in bizarre sequence:

For I see there's one old basket like all of my regret in your country eyes don't fool an I shoot one but the fool that you have put to life till their eggs don't give no whites.

B. The same words in familiar maxims:

I regret that I have but one life to give for my country.
Don't put all your eggs in one basket.
There's no fool like an old fool.
Don't shoot till you see the whites of their eyes.

Groups of letters can be chunks even if they don't form words. DDT, IBM, RSVP, and USSR are examples of familiar letter clusters that we treat as chunks. Familiar dates such as 1066 and 1492 are examples of number chunks. Telephone numbers that are easy to chunk, such as 707-1776, are easy to remember for that reason.

Recoding

Sometimes messages can be recoded so that we can get more information into each chunk. Smith (reported in Miller, 1956) has shown a dramatic effect of recoding on memory span for binary digits.* Smith first determined that his subject, who was unusually good at short-term memory tasks, could hold 15 binary digits in immediate memory. That is, he could listen to and repeat back a list like this:

$$1\text{-}0\text{-}1\text{-}1\text{-}0\text{-}1\text{-}0\text{-}0\text{-}0\text{-}1\text{-}1\text{-}0\text{-}1\text{-}1\text{-}0$$

Next he drilled his subject thoroughly in several recoding schemes. In the 2:1 recoding scheme, the subject first grouped the list of digits in pairs and then recoded each pair by the rule shown in the box labeled "2:1 Recoder" in Figure 3.

The subject stored the names of the pairs rather than the original binary digits in short-term memory. Thus, he had to remember only six pair names rather than 12 binary digits. When asked to recall, the subject decoded the pair names and attempted to report the original list of binary digits. This sequence of events is also shown in Figure 8. In the 3:1 recoding scheme, the subject grouped the list of digits into triplets and then recoded each triplet by the rule in the box labeled "3:1 Recoder" in Figure 9. With this scheme, the subject stored the four names of the triplets—5-5-0-6—rather than the 12 binary digits. In addition, 4:1 and 5:1 recoding schemes were also taught.

---

*Binary digits are sequences of zeros and ones.

When the recoding schemes had been mastered, the subject's memory span for binary digits was again tested. This time the subject recoded the binaries as he listened to them and then decoded them again when he repeated them. The result was that all of the recoding schemes improved the memory span for binaries. With 3:1 recoding, he remembered about 33 binaries, and with 5:1 recoding, more than 40.

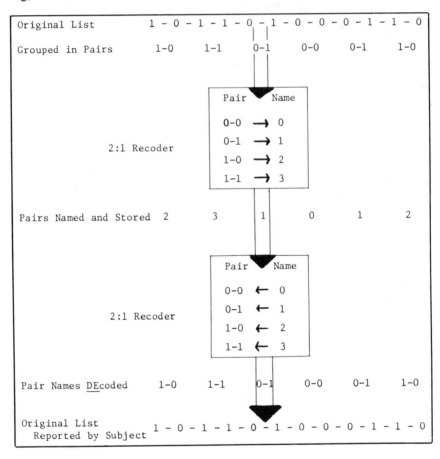

Figure 8. 2:1 Recoding

Recently, Chase and Ericsson (1979) reported memory-span results for a subject who uses a complex scheme for recoding decimal digits as times for running races. This subject can remember up to 81 decimal digits.

Searching for Chunks

Chunking is an activity—it is something that we do—although we are often

completely unaware that we are doing it. Chunking involves noticing, but sometimes we fail to notice a pattern in the material we are trying to learn. This fact
was demonstrated very nicely in experiments by Bower and Springston (1970).
In both experiments, subjects studied and immediately tried to recall lists of letters. There were two sorts of lists—lists like TV IBM TWA USSR—in which
the chunks are easy to find—and lists like IC BMF BIU SAOK—where the chunks
are a little harder to find. (Be sure you do find them or you will miss an important point.) In one study, the groups were formed by inserting pauses in spoken
lists. In the other, they were formed by changing the size or the color of the letters in printed lists. In both of the experiments, the subjects remembered more
letters from the easy-to-find lists than from the hard-to-find ones—and the differences were big—in some cases, more than 40 percent. The experimenters were
able to show that the subjects were not making use of the chunks in the hard-to-
find lists. If the subjects had made use of the chunks that were present in the
lists, they would have remembered more.

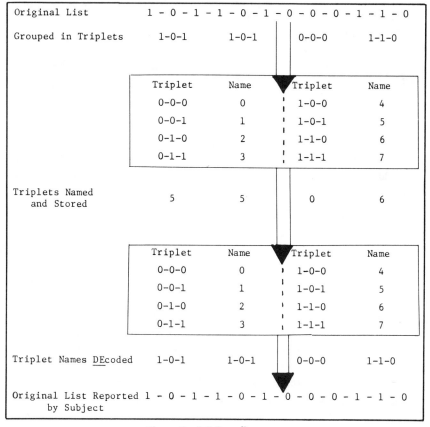

Figure 9. 3:1 Recoding

It is clear that we can make learning and remembering easier by searching consciously for chunks in the material we are studying.

Forgetting and Short-Term Memory

There are two ways we can lose information from short-term memory: by *displacement* and by *decay*.

Displacement

Imagine yourself as a novice waiter who believes that good waiters keep orders in short-term memory. You take the order of your first customer: mussels, borscht, spaghetti, rice, asparagus, pickles, and cocoa. "Very good, sir," you say, not really meaning it, but confident that the order is safely stored in short-term memory. As you walk away, the customer says, "And a side of zucchini, waiter!" Now you're in trouble. Your short-term memory holds seven chunks and zucchini makes eight. You remember the zucchini, but it has pushed something else out of STM. You have no idea what it was. But you know that at some point the customer is going to say, "Waiter, where is my _____?"

This is forgetting by *displacement*. Because short-term memory holds a limited number of chunks, putting a new chunk in when it is full will push an old chunk out.

Decay

Information is lost very quickly from STM if we don't rehearse it. This fact we demonstrated clearly in an experiment by Peterson and Peterson (1959). The Petersons asked their subjects to remember just three letters—a triplet of consonants such as "PTK"—for less than a minute. This seems like a very easy task. However, between hearing the letters and the test, the subject had to count backwards by three's as fast as possible. The interchange between the experimenter and the subject went as follows:

Experimenter: "RXB, 471"
Subject: "471, 468, 465, 462, . . ." [light signaling test] "RXB"

Counting backwards, if it is done rapidly, prevents rehearsal quite effectively. You can convince yourself of this by trying it.

The results of the Petersons' study are shown in Figure 10, and they are surprising. After seven seconds, the subject's chances of getting the triplet right are 50/50, and after 18 seconds, only one in 10. The conclusion is obvious: Even a simple message in STM will decay in less than 20 seconds and be lost if it is not refreshed by rehearsal.

Rehearsal

We can maintain a message in short-term memory for quite some time through rehearsal. A common way to rehearse a message is to say it over and over to ourselves. Suppose we want to make a phone call in a public place where the phone book is in one place and the phone is in another. We all know what to do: We look up the number and repeat it over and over while we race madly to the phone, avoiding people who might ask us a question that could wipe the number out of our heads.

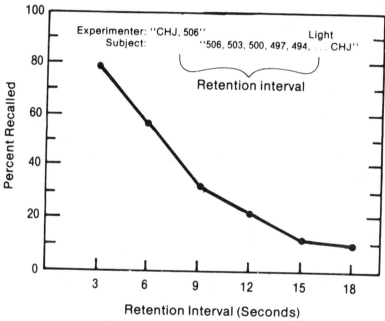

Figure 10.   **Trigram Recall After Various Intervals Filled With Backward Counting**
From *The Psychology of Learning and Memory* by Douglas L. Hintzman, W. H. Freeman and Company, copyright © 1978.

Surprisingly, young children may not know this rehearsal strategy. Keeney, Cannizzo, and Flavell (1967) found that some first-grade children rehearsed and some didn't. Those who rehearsed did better in short-term memory tests than those who didn't. However, when the non-rehearsers were told to rehearse, their performance improved to the level of the children who rehearsed on their own.

With uninterrupted rehearsal we can keep a phone number in short-term memory for a long time. Just how long would appear to depend on the persistence with which the person continues to rehearse. There is currently no Guinness World Record time for holding a telephone number in STM, but perhaps someone desiring eternal fame will soon establish one.

Summary: Short-Term Memory

1. A chunk is a package of information that we treat as a unit because we recognize it as a familiar pattern.
2. Short-term memory can hold 7 ± 2 chunks.
3. By actively searching for chunks in the material we want to learn, we can make learning easier.
4. By continuous rehearsal, we can keep a message in short-term memory for long period of time.
5. Without rehearsal, information in STM will decay within 20 seconds.

LONG-TERM MEMORY

There are two dramatic ways in which long-term memory differs from short-term memory. First, while short-term memories last for less than 20 seconds, long-term memories can last for a lifetime. A very old man may be able to recall where he sat in his first-grade classroom and what his teacher looked like. Second, while short-term memory can hold only 7 ± 2 chunks, the capacity of long-term memory is practically unlimited. Long-term memory contains our knowledge of our language and of the faces of the people we know. It contains our knowledge of how to find our way around the city, how to order in a restaurant, how to do algebra, and how to peel a banana. I could go on, but it should be clear already that the amount of information in long-term memory is huge.

The topic of long-term memory can be divided quite naturally into three phases: first, an *encoding* phase in which we put information into memory; second, a *storage* phase; and finally, a *retrieval* phase in which we recover the information we stored (see Figure 11). It is necessary to understand all three of these phases if we are to understand how to improve long-term memory. We will discuss the phases in reverse order, dealing first with retrieval, then storage, and leaving the most complicated topic—encoding—for last.

ENCODING   ⟹   STORAGE   ⟹   RETRIEVAL

Figure 11. The Three Phases of Long-term Memory

Retrieval

Even though we have some fact, such as a name or date, stored in our memory, that doesn't mean we can get at the information whenever we want it. We have all felt the frustration of recognizing people at parties but being completely unable to dredge up their names—certainly not in time for introductions. Often we feel that the name is "on the tip of (our) tongue." We may be sure that it has three syllables and begins with "B" and we know that if someone told us the name we would recognize it immediately.

Roger Brown and David McNeill (1966) have studied the "tip of the tongue" phenomenon in people trying to remember words. They read definitions of infrequently used words to subjects who were asked to respond by writing down the corresponding word. For example, they would read "a navigational instrument used in measuring angular distances, especially the altitude of sun, moon, and stars at sea." Some of the subjects had no idea what word this defines, while some others were immediately able to write down "sextant." The interesting subjects, though, were the ones who could not immediately write down the answer, but who felt that it was just "on the tip of (their) tongue." These subjects were encouraged to give all the information they could about the word: What are its first letters? How many syllables does it have? What does it rhyme with? About half were able to identify the first letter correctly, and about half knew the number of syllables in the word. Many of these subjects did eventually remember the correct word.

Read through the list of definitions below and see if you experience the "tip of the tongue" phenomenon yourself. If you do, try to guess the first letter of the word and the number of syllables it contains.

1. An iron block on which metal objects are hammered into shape.
2. A lensless photographic method that uses laser light to produce three dimensional images.
3. A short witty pointed statement.
4. Standing out from the rest, notable, conspicuous, prominant.
5. Hard to rouse to action, cool, stolid, calm.
6. A visionary scheme for an idealized society.
7. An abnormal fascination with the dead.
8. A remedy to counteract a poison.
9. A giant with one eye in the middle of his forehead.
10. The horizontal crosspiece over a door.

If you find yourself stuck in the "tip of the tongue" state, the answers are on the next page.

The "tip of the tongue" phenomenon illustrates clearly that even though we have information in memory, we can't always get at it when we want.

Retrieval Tasks

Psychologists have invented a variety of ways to test memory. Some of these methods put the burden on the subjects to show what they know, while others reveal knowledge that the subjects themselves can't report and indeed are unaware they possess.

Suppose that you asked subjects to memorize the following list:

Derby	Hut	Edna
Carp	Beret	Orange
Jane	Peach	Flounder
Apple	House	George
Church	Grape	Skyscraper
Trout	Hat	Fez
Frank	Cod	

Let's assume that you read this list to them in order, one word at a time, and that you read it through completely three times before you tested the subjects' memory. There are many ways that you could test the subjects' knowledge. We will discuss four methods: uncued recall, cued recall, recognition, and savings.

Uncued recall. The critical feature of uncued recall tasks is that the subjects are required to reproduce the material they have learned with no aids. There are two common kinds of uncued recall tasks: *serial recall* and *free recall.*

If you ask the subjects to write down the words *in the order* in which they heard them, you will be testing by the method of serial recall. If the subjects write CARP-DERBY rather than DERBY-CARP, they get two wrong. Remembering the number of your combination lock is an everyday example of a serial recall task. You have to remember the numbers *and* their order.

If you let the subject write down the words in any order, then you are testing by the method of free recall. Free recall is easier for the subjects than serial recall because they can be scored correct even though they don't remember the order of the words. Being asked to say who was at a party or meeting is a common free recall task. The order in which you mention the people doesn't matter.

Cued recall. If you gave the subjects hints which they tried to recall (Remember any fish names? Does anything rhyme with fig?), then you would be using the method of cued recall. A common example of a cued recall task is the party situation in which you have to remember people's names when you see them. The face is the cue to the name which you must try to recall. A cued recall task can be made harder or easier by changing the cues. The second list of cues in Table 3 would probably be more helpful than the first.

Table 3. Cue Lists

General Category Cues	Specific Category Cues	Rhyme Cues
living things	fish	harp
food	fruit	teach
names	first names	tank
clothing	head gear	bat
man-made structures	buildings	lurch

Categories can serve as very powerful retrieval cues. Tulving and Pearlstone (1966) demonstrated this in an experiment in which the subjects learned lists of words which could be grouped into categories. For example, the words "bomb," "table," "carrot," "cannon," "potato," and "chair" can be grouped into the categories "weapons," "furniture," and "vegetables."

Two groups of subjects studied lists which consisted of 48 words in 12 categories. Group 1 was asked to recall as many words as they could. Group 2 had the same task but they were also given the names of the categories to help them. People in Group 1 remembered about 19 of the words, while people in Group 2 remembered nearly 30. The people in the two groups remembered about the same number of words in each category—2.6 out of 4—but Group 2 remembered words in many more categories—11.5 categories for Group 2, but only 7.3 for Group 1. The advantage that having the category names gave to Group 2, then, was that it increased the number of *categories* they remembered. Notice that if Group 1 remembered any words in a category, then they remembered as many as Group 2. This suggests that remembering one word in a category reminds the person the whole category just as hearing the category name does. We can imagine ourselves trying to recall the words, saying to ourselves, "CH. . .CH something—CHAIR! Oh, yeah! And bed and table!"

This tendency to remember things in clusters from the same category was clearly demonstrated by Bousfield (1953). He asked subjects to study a list of 60 words from the four categories; animals, names, professions, and vegetables. The categories were scrambled to produce lists like this: giraffe, Otto, baker, turnip, Noah, celery, Bernard, camel, florist, etc. The subjects were asked to recall as many words as they could in any order that occurred to them. In their responses, the subjects would recall first a group of items from one category, pause, and then recall a group of items from another category, etc. Remembering an item seemed to cue recall for other items in the same category.

Recognition. You could also test your subjects' memory for 20 words by asking them to pick them out of a larger list which consists of the 20 old words mixed with 20 new ones that weren't on the list they studied. These new words are called "foils." The subjects' task is to go through the 40 words, marking them either "old" if they recognize them as part of the studied list, or "new" if they do not. This is a recognition task, which is generally easier than a recall task.

The difficulty of a recognition task varies with the nature of the foils. We would expect our subjects to do better if the foils were different from those items on the original list. For example, if the old list were made up of names of fruit, and the foils were all Italian words, the recognition task would be simple.

Recognition tasks in real life can be more complicated: If you go to the airport to meet someone you have met only once before, you have a difficult recognition task in picking that person out of the crowd. If your laundry gets mixed with someone else's at the laundromat, you also have a recognition task.

Savings. If instead of testing your subjects right after learning, you tested them a week or a month later, they would probably get very low scores on any of the tests we have discussed. They might even claim that they remembered absolutely nothing about the lists. Even so, by using the savings method you could probably show that they still retained something of their earlier learning. With the savings method, we measure how long it takes the subject to relearn the old list in comparison to learning a comparable new list. If it takes the subjects seven repetitions to relearn the old list and 10 to learn the new, then relearning time is 70 percent of learning time, and the savings score is 30 percent.

People who have to repeat a course are often surprised by how much easier the course is the second time around. Even if they flunked the course the first time, being in the same learning situation reveals knowledge they didn't suspect they had.

One study showed that a child may retain a good deal of information even from very early experiences. When his son was between 15 months and three years old, H. E. Burtt (1941) read passages to him from Sophocles in the original Greek. He repeated each passage about 90 times. When the child was 8½, he learned both old and new passages and showed a savings score of 27 percent for the old. By the time the child was 14, the savings score dropped to eight percent, and at 18, to zero percent.

The four recall tasks have been presented here in increasing order of sensitivity to the subjects' knowledge. For a given degree of learning, we would expect our subjects to score worst in uncued recall tasks, better in cued recall tasks, and still better in recognition tasks. The savings method is the most sensitive of all since it may reveal knowledge even when the subject scores zero on all of the other tasks.

We will make use of the fact that some retrieval tasks are easier than others when we discuss memory techniques in the next chapter. Some memory tech-

133

niques work by changing a harder retrieval task into an easier one, e.g., by changing an uncued recall task into a cued recall task.

Summary: Retrieval

1. Even though information is stored in our memory, we can't always retrieve it, as the "tip of the tongue" phenomenon shows.
2. Retrieval tasks vary in difficulty in the following order:

                Uncued recall   (most difficult)

                Cued recall

                Recognition

                Savings   (least difficult)

For a given degree of learning, we would get the best score on a savings test and worst on an uncued recall test.

Storage

Suppose someone gives you a message that you will have to act on tomorrow, such as: "When you take the dog to the cleaners, tell them to use less starch." Between the time you encode the message and the time you have to recall it, you would hope that the information will remain stored, peaceful and undisturbed, in long-term memory. However, lots of things can happen to an unsuspecting memory trace. If you were hit on the head shortly after receiving the message, you might suffer from retrograde amnesia—a condition in which memories of events experienced just before the blow are lost. This phenomenon reminds us dramatically that the memory trace has a physical basis within our brains and that it can be disturbed by a gross physical event like a blow on the head.

If anything happens to our memory trace, though, it is far more likely to happen through interference than through retrograde amnesia. Interference occurs when learning one thing makes it difficult for us to remember something else. Psychologists distinguish between two kinds of interference—*proactive* and *retroactive*. In proactive interference, something learned earlier makes it difficult to remember something learned later. For example, if last week you had gotten the message, "When you get the dog from the cleaners, tell them the starch was just right," this message might be confused with the current message and cause proactive interference. The effect of proactive interference can be quite large. Greenberg and Underwood (1950) asked people to learn 20 lists of word pairs—one list every two days. For the first list, they found that in 24 hours, subjects forgot about 20 percent of the pairs that they had learned. With each successive list they learned, they forgot more in 24 hours until on their twentieth list they forgot nearly 80 percent in 24 hours. Each successive list suffers from more proactive interference than did the previous one. This can make the difference between remembering four out of five items and forgetting four out of five items.

In retroactive interference, something learned later makes it difficult to remember something which was learned earlier. Thus, if after your first message about the dog, you received a great many other messages about dogs and laundries, these could cause retroactive interference which would greatly increase your chances of forgetting the original message.

Retroactive interference was demonstrated in a cued recall experiment by Barnes and Underwood (1959). The subjects first learned list A-B (see Table 4) so that when they were given the A items they could repeat the B items. Then they began to study the A-C list (see Table 4). Notice that the A items in the A-B list are exactly the same as the A items in the A-C list. In learning the A-B list, the subjects learn ZUT-USEFUL and in learning the A-C list, they learn ZUT-BROWN. Between practice sessions on the A-C list, the subjects were tested by presenting the A list and asking them to give *both* the B and the C items. As practice on the A-C list continued, cued recall for the B items declined from 100 percent to little more than 50 percent after 20 A-C practice trials. Clearly retroactive interference had a very marked effect.

Can memories decay simply through the passage of time? Earlier psychologists thought so. Thorndike (1914), for example, believed that memories got weaker through disuse. When psychologists came to understand the effect of interference on memory, they began to doubt that they needed decay to explain memory losses. McGeoch (1932), for example, said, "Time, in and of itself, does nothing." Many modern psychologists believe that retroactive and proactive interference are sufficient to account for all of the forgetting attributed to decay. The issue, however, is still in doubt, as Hintzman (1978) points out.

How can we reduce the effects of interference? Our main weapons against it are *overlearning* and *reviewing.*

Suppose that it would take you 10 hours of study to learn a topic well enough to score 100 percent on a quiz given immediately after study. If you studied 15 hours, we would say that you had put in 50 percent overlearning, and if you studied 20 hours, 100 percent overlearning. The effect of overlearning is to reduce forgetting. Kreuger (1929) showed that if material was overlearned by 50 percent or 100 percent, it was better recalled over the next week or two than if it was not overlearned. Further, even after a month, the subjects show a 20 percent savings score with overlearning, while without it, they show none.

Reviewing information also protects it against interference (Underwood, 1964). The more frequently we refer to information, the more likely we are to retain it. Telephone numbers we call frequently survive interference from the many other numbers we may dial in a typical week. Clearly, if students would review the course material frequently during the term, they could avoid that dreadful question, "Where have I heard about that before?" that so often comes up during final exams.

NEXT TIME YOU TAKE THE DOG TO THE CLEANERS, TELL THEM TO USE LESS STARCH.

Table 4. Nonsense Syllable/Adjective Pairs

Nonsense Syllable	Adjective	Nonsense Syllable	Adjective
A	B	A	C
ZUT	useful	ZUT	brown
PUM	dark	PUM	humble
BIP	early	BIP	tall
SEG	green	SEG	happy
YAD	new	YAD	easy
LUS	short	LUS	frequent
VOB	helpful	VOB	hot
KIJ	tough	KIJ	wet
WOF	sad	WOF	wide
RUP	distant	RUP	lively

Summary: Storage

1. Much of our forgetting can be attributed to interference from other learning.
2. When things learned earlier interfere with memory for things learned later, we speak of proactive interference.
3. When things learned later interfere with memory for things learned earlier, we speak of retroactive interference.
4. The effects of interference can be reduced through overlearning and review.

Encoding

At one time, psychologists believed that we could transfer information into long-term memory simply by rehearsing it. Now they recognize that in order to fix an item in long-term memory, we must do something more complicated than just repeating it over and over. We must rework the item or elaborate on it by asking questions about it, making associations, creating images, etc. Simple rehearsal which will keep an item in short-term memory is called "maintenance rehearsal." Rehearsal with reworking and elaboration is called "elaborative rehearsal" (Craik and Watkins, 1973; Reder, 1980).

In this section, 1. we will describe the evidence that maintenance rehearsal isn't sufficient to put information into long-term memory, and 2. we will discuss the processes which do help to fix information in long-term memory.

There is a difficulty in showing that simple repetition isn't sufficient to fix information in long-term memory. The difficulty lies in getting people to do repetition without also elaborating. If subjects suspect that they may be tested on what they are repeating, they may almost automatically do whatever they usually do that helps to put the material into LTM, such as form images or make associations. Craik and Watkins (1973) were able to devise a task in which the subjects apparently don't elaborate on what they are rehearsing. The subjects were asked to listen to a list of words, similar to that shown in the left-hand column of Table 5. The words were read to them one at a time. The subjects' task was to report the last word in the list which began with the letter "G". To do this, the subjects waited for a word beginning with G. When a target word was presented, the subjects rehearsed it (since it might be the last one) until another target word, if any, appeared (see the right-hand column in Table 5). When the new target word appeared, it replaced the old one as the word being rehearsed. From the subjects' point of view, there was no point in putting the old target words into long-term memory, since their task was to report only the current target. Notice that by varying the spacing between target words from zero to twelve words, the experimenters were able to control the amount of rehearsal given to each word.

However, after the subjects had worked through a number of word lists like that shown in Table 5, the experimenters unexpectedly asked them to recall as many words as possible from all the lists. The critical finding was that words which were rehearsed for a long time, as during a 12-word interval, weren't remembered any better than words which were rehearsed for a short time, as during a zero-word interval. Maintenance rehearsal appeared to have no effect in fixing information in long-term memory. Other studies by Craik and Watkins (1973, Experiment II) and Jacoby (1974) also support this conclusion.

We have taken the trouble to emphasize this point because it is of considerable practical importance. Some students spend a great deal of effort on maintenance rehearsal of their lessons in the mistaken belief that it will fix informa-

Table 5. Craik and Watkins' Task

Word List Read to Subject	Target Word Rehearsed by Subject
1. daughter	——
2. oil	——
3. rifle	——
4. garden	garden
5. grain	grain
6. table	grain
7. football	grain
8. anchor	grain
9. giraffe	giraffe
10. harp	giraffe
11. lake	giraffe
12. bike	giraffe
13. purse	giraffe
14. milk	giraffe
15. issue	giraffe
16. shadow	giraffe
17. chair	giraffe
18. nail	giraffe
19. job	giraffe
20. trip	giraffe
21. elbow	giraffe

From Craik and Watkins, "The Role of Rehearsal in Short-term Memory," in the *Journal of Verbal Learning and Verbal Behavior*, 12, 1973. Reprinted by permission of the authors.

tion in their memory. These students would do far better by using the encoding procedures described below.

Elaboration

I suggested above that in order to get information into long-term memory, we must elaborate it. However, I didn't say very specifically what elaboration is. Perhaps the best way to understand elaboration is to think of it as a process that forms connections—either within the material to be learned, or between the material to be learned and other things we already know. The more connections the material has, the more likely we are to be able to remember it. We might think of an elaborated memory as a satchel with lots of handles. The more handles it has, the easier it is to get hold of.

In the following sections I will describe some techniques for elaborating memories.

Inputs and Representations.   Imagine that you are at a party and that you are being introduced to someone. At that moment you are exposed to a great deal of information all at once. Much of the information comes from the outside, through sensory channels. There is visual information—the appearance of the person's face and clothing, and the confused party scene around him. There is auditory information—the sound of the person's voice, the voice of your host introducing him, and noises in the room. There is information from the muscle senses—you have been standing for hours and would very much like to sit down—and there is osmic or smell information—a faint fragrance of perfume and tobacco.

In addition to this sensory information, there is semantic information—that is, meanings you derive from the sensory information that are not themselves sensory in character. For example, your host says, "Meet my son, the doctor." Later, even though you can't remember the sensory information—the inflections of the host's voice or his particular wording—you still remember the meaning, that he has a son and the son is a doctor. Similarly, the sensory information of a faint fragrance may be processed to produce a question of meaning far more complex than the scent which triggered it: "Why is this guy wearing Chanel #5?"

Corresponding to the various forms of information input there are forms of internal representation. Remembering a visual image of a face is much like looking at a face. Usually, we can tell the difference between a sensory image and a memory image, but Perky (1910) showed that people can be fooled into accepting a real external picture as something they are imagining. Similarly, remembering an auditory image of a friend's voice is much like listening to a real voice.

A particular form of internal representation, e.g., a visual image, is typically better for remembering some kinds of information than for remembering other kinds. Visual images are good for remembering pictures but not for remembering tunes. Auditory images are good for tunes but terrible for sunsets.

Representation and Elaboration. One obvious way to elaborate on a message is to use more than one form of representation to code it. When reading, for example, we might construct visual images of the people and actions described in the text in addition to our usual semantic coding of the material. There is a great deal of evidence demonstrating that imagery is a powerful memory aid. Levin (1973) taught fourth-grade children to image what they were reading and showed that it helped them to remember the material. Paivio and Csapo (1973) showed that it is easier to learn a list of words such as "alligator" and "accordian" which are easy to image than words such as "ability" and "afterlife" which are hard to image. In the next chapter, we will describe a number of memory techniques that depend on visual imagery.

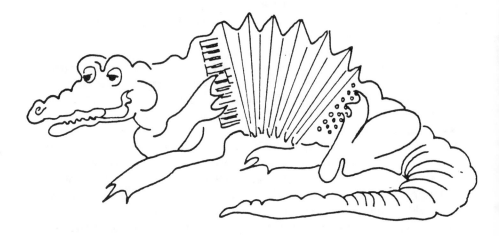

While imagery can be a very powerful memory aid, not every sort of image is helpful. To help them learn a list of word pairs, Bower (1972) asked his subjects to form either of two kinds of images: interacting images and separated images. To form an interacting image for the pair "dog-bicycle" the subjects might picture a dog riding a bicycle. To form a separated image, they would picture a dog on the left and a bicycle on the right in such a way that the two objects didn't interact. Bower found that with interactive images, subjects given the first half of each pair could remember 71 percent of the pairs. With separated images, they remembered only 46 percent—no more than subjects who simply repeated the pairs without imaging. Interactive images, that is, images which form connections, are a useful memory aid. Separated images are not.

Elaboration is possible within a single form of representation because we can use that form in more than one way to code a message. Suppose, for example, that we wanted to form an image for an abstract word like "agreement." We might picture two people shaking hands, or we might picture a paper marked "agreement," or we might picture two people shaking hands *and* exchanging a paper marked "agreement."

Elaborating by Answering Questions. Suppose that you are halfway through a mystery story and a friend who has already read it begins to harass you with questions such as:

Did you notice how the Countess was dressed after the murder?
Did you figure out why the butler walked with a limp?
Did you wonder why Sir Aubrey always wore a scarf?

Assuming that you restrain the impulse to throw the book at your friend, you will probably change the way you represent the story to yourself as you read. Now you will notice how people are dressed and how the butler walks, and try to find connections between these things and the murder. The questions, then, will cause you to elaborate your representation.

Craik and Tulving (1975) performed an experiment to find out how elaborations induced by questions would influence memory. They believed that elaborations involving semantic codes would improve memory more than elaboration of visual or auditory codes. The subjects' task was to answer questions about a sequence of words. The subjects would be given a question such as, "Is the word in capital letters?" before each word. They answered "yes" or "no" and went on to the next question. Typical questions and responses are shown in Table 6.

The typeface and rhyme questions might be expected to induce visual and auditory elaboration respectively, and the category and sentence questions might be expected to induce semantic elaboration. After the subjects worked through 40 question-word pairs, they were unexpectedly tested. The test required the subjects to examine a list consisting of the original words mixed with 40 new ones and to check the words they had seen before.

Table 7 shows that the sentence and category questions led to better recognition than the rhyme and typeface questions. This result is consistent with Craik

Table 6. Typical Questions and Responses in the Craik and Tulving Experiment

Level of processing	Question	Answer	
		Yes	No
Visual	Is the word in capital letters?	TABLE	table
Auditory	Does the word rhyme with WEIGHT?	crate	MARKET
Category	Is the word a type of fish?	SHARK	heaven
Sentence	Would the word fit the sentence: "He met a _____ in the street?"	friend	CLOUD

From Craik and Tulving, "Depth of Processing and the Retention of Words in Episodic Memory," in the *Journal of Experimental Psychology,* 104, 1975. Copyright 1975 by the American Psychological Association. Reprinted by permission.

Table 7. Percent of Words Correctly Identified in the Craik and Tulving Experiment

Question Type:	Typeface	Rhyme	Category	Sentence
Percent Correct:	16	57	78	89

and Tulving's belief that semantic elaboration would aid memory more than visual or auditory elaboration.

Noticing Categories. As we discussed earlier, categories are a very powerful retrieval cue. If we notice categories in the material we are learning, we can increase our chances of remembering it.

Jacoby (1974) showed this by arranging a situation in which one group of subjects was more likely to notice categories in a list than another. He showed both groups a long list of words which contained such categories as birds, vegetables, etc. As each word was shown, Group 1 was asked to say whether it was a member of the same category as the immediately preceding word. Group 2 was asked to say whether it was in the same category as *any* preceding word. Thus, if words like "parrot" and "finch" occurred in the list five words apart, we would expect that Group 2 would be more likely to notice the category "birds" than would Group 1. On a surprise recall test, Group 2 remembered much more than Group 1. The learner is well advised to notice category relations in the material being learned.

Hierarchies. Much of the information we deal with every day is organized in categories, and frequently those categories are themselves organized in hierarchies. For example, minerals can be arranged in a hierarchically organized set of categories as shown in Figure 12. We know that attention to categories can aid learning. What about attention to hierarchical organization? Bower, Clark, Lesgold, and Winzenz (1969) have studied just such hierarchically organized material. In fact, Figure 12 is one of the eight hierarchies they studied. The subjects in their experiment learned either by seeing the complete hierarchy all at once on each of the four trials (whole method) or by seeing level 1 and 2 of the hierarchy on trial 1; levels 1, 2, and 3 on trial 2; and all four levels on trials 3 and 4 (progressive method). Further, in some cases the organization of the material was meaningful as in Figure 12, and in others it was random, as in Table 8.

Table 8. Random Organization of Mineral Information

STONES			METALS	
Precious	Alloys	Rare	Masonry	Common
limestone	ruby	copper	emerald	iron
bronze	sapphire	marble	silver	diamond
aluminum	granite	steel	lead	slate
	platinum		brass	gold

Meaningful organization made a big difference in the number of words recalled. On the first trial, subjects in the meaningful condition remembered more than three times as many words as those in the random condition. Performance of subjects in the meaningful condition was perfect by the third trial, while subjects in the random condition still knew less than half of the words on the third trial. Further, learning the top three levels of the hierarchy first, as in the progressive method, helped subjects to learn the words on the fourth level. On their first exposure to the words on the fourth level, subjects using the whole method learned 60 percent of the words, while subjects using the progressive method learned 77 percent. Attending to the hierarchical organization of the material to be learned is clearly a powerful learning aid.

Use of Examples. Examples are typically at the very lowest levels in the hierarchical structure of a text or a lecture. Nonetheless, they can be very important for understanding the information presented. Pollchik (1975) asked subjects to read a 100-sentence text describing seven psychological defense mechanisms. In addition, he gave some of the subjects two one-sentence examples illustrating each of the mechanisms. To test their knowledge of the defense mechanisms, subjects were asked to identify the mechanism involved in each of 20 cases. Subjects who had had examples as part of their instruction correctly identified 16.4 of the 20 cases. Subjects who had not seen the examples as part of their instruction identified only 9.9 of the cases. Examples, then, are an important aid to instruction.

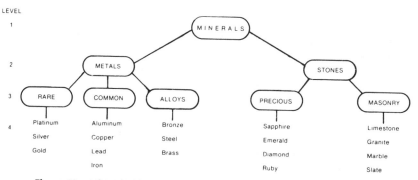

Figure 12. Minerals Arranged Hierarchically Reprinted from the *Journal of Verbal Learning and Verbal Behavior*, Vol. 8, 1969, by permission of the author, Gordon H. Bower, and the publisher, Academic Press, Inc.

Summary: Encoding

1. Maintenance rehearsal isn't sufficient to put information into long-term memory. Elaborative rehearsal is necessary.
2. There are several distinct memory codes: auditory, visual, semantic, etc.

3. Elaborative rehearsal may involve:
   - use of extra codes, such as imagery
   - answering questions
   - noticing categories
   - attending to hierarchical structure
   - seeing principles illustrated in examples

CONTROLLING YOUR OWN LEARNING PROCESS

Up to this point we have discussed the processes of encoding, storage, and retrieval separately. In this section, we will describe how people can use one of these processes to control another. For example, we will describe how retrieval can profitably be used to control information about success and failure at encoding.

When you are studying, you can make decisions about how to spend your study time. If you are lucky, you can choose to spread the effort you spend on a subject out over weeks or months. If you aren't lucky, you may find yourself cramming all your effort into the last few hours available before an exam or some other deadline. You can choose to employ any of a wide variety of strategies in learning, e.g., you can encode information in many ways. You may choose to spend 100 percent of your study time in reading and rereading the material you are trying to learn, or you may choose to spend some of your time testing yourself. Your decisions about how to spend your time help determine the efficiency of your learning.

In general, spreading your study effort out over a period of time is more efficient than cramming. That is, if you distribute your effort, you can learn a topic in less time than with massed practice. Figure 13 shows Lyon's (1914) results comparing massed and distributed practice for tasks which vary in difficulty. The advantage of distributed practice increases as the task becomes more difficult.

A study by Thorndyke and Stasz (1980) on map learning illustrates the importance of strategy selection. The subjects were given six two-minute study periods in which to learn place names and spatial information from a map. After each study period, they drew and labeled as much of the map as they could remember. The subjects varied considerably in their success in this learning task and in the strategies they used in performing it. The authors found important differences in the way good and poor learners approached the task. First, they found that good learners employed better strategies for encoding spatial information. They frequently used visual imagery, pattern encoding (e.g., "It looks like a house"), and relational encoding (e.g., "Those two streets are parallel"). Second, the good learners were more effective in using self-evaluation to control their learning. The good learners were more likely than the poor learners to evaluate where their knowledge was weak. The poor learners were more likely to spend time

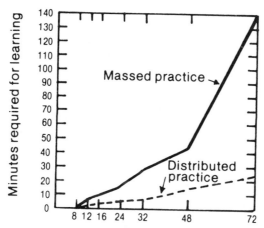

Figure 13.   Massed Versus Distributed Practice in Relation to Length of List Learned Reprinted from *Foundations of Psychology*, Boring, E. G., Langfeld, H. S., and Weld, H. P. By permission of John Wiley and Sons, © 1948.

confirming what they did know. In evaluating themselves, the good learners were more accurate (96 percent correct) than the poor learners (82 percent correct). Further, when the good learners discovered that they didn't know something, they were more likely to take immediate action to learn it (95 percent) than were the poor learners (75 percent). These three differences taken together add up to a very considerable difference in the effectiveness with which good and poor learners use self-evaluation to control learning.

In a second study, Thorndyke and Stasz (1980) showed that the spatial coding and self-evaluation strategies which the good learners use could be taught to other subjects and that doing so markedly improved the subjects' map learning performance.

The Thorndyke and Stasz study shows that self-evaluation is important, but how much of your study time, if any, should you devote to testing yourself? Gates (1917) investigated this question and came up with a surprising answer. His results, shown in Figure 14, indicate that people may learn best when they spend up to 80 percent of their study time in testing themselves.

Summary: Control of Learning Process

People can influence their own learning processes and have a great deal to gain by doing so. By 1. choosing to distribute practice, 2. selecting appropriate learning strategies, and 3. using evaluation of progress to control study, people can significantly increase their learning effectiveness.

CONCLUSION

Basic research on human memory provides us with a great deal of useful in-

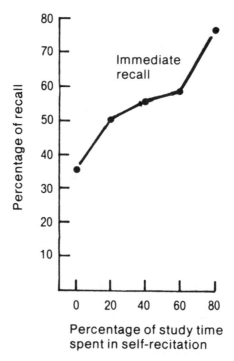

Percentage of study time
spent in self-recitation

Figure 14. Effects on Recall of Spending Various Proportions of Study Time in Attempting Retrieval Rather Than in Silent Study, for Tests Given Immediately After Study From *Introduction to Psychology*, Seventh Edition, edited by E. R. Hilgard, R. L. Atkinson, and R. C. Atkinson. By permission of Harcourt Brace Jovanovich, Inc., © 1979.

formation. It indicates the importance of chunking in using our limited capacity short-term memories effectively. Further, it provides a number of guiding principles for the efficient use of long-term memory. For example, it has shown the importance of elaboration for learning, the value of overlearning and rehearsal for maintaining information in storage, and the usefulness of cueing in recall. In addition, research reveals that people can become more effective learners if they learn to monitor and control their own learning processes.

REFERENCES

Banks, W. P., and Barber, G. Color information in iconic memory. *Psychological Review*, 1977, *84*, 536–546.

Barnes, J. M., and Underwood, B. J. " 'Fate' " of First-list Associations in Transfer Theory." *Journal of Experimental Psychology*, 58, 97–105, 1961.

Bousfield, W. A., "The Occurrence of Clustering in the Recall of Randomly Arranged Associates." *Journal of General Psychology*, 49, 229–240, 1953.

Bower, G. H., "Mental Imagery and Associative Learning." In *Cognition in Learning and Memory*, edited by L. W. Gregg. New York: Wiley, 1972.

Bower, G. H., Clark, M. C., Lesgold, A. M., and Winzenz, D. "Hierarchical Retrieval Schemes in Recall of Categorized Word Lists." *Journal of Verbal Learning and Verbal Behavior, 8*, 323-343, 1969.

Bower, G. H., and Springston, F. "Pauses as Recoding Points in Letter Series." *Journal of Experimental Psychology, 83*, 421-430, 1970.

Brooks, L. R. "Spatial and Verbal Components of the Act of Recall." *Canadian Journal of Psychology, 22*, 349,368, 1968.

Brown, R., and McNeill, D. "The 'Tip of the Tongue' Phenomenon." *Journal of Verbal Learning and Verbal Behavior, 5*, 325-337, 1966.

Burtt, H. E. "An Experimental Study of Early Childhood Memory: Final Report." *Journal of Genetic Psychology, 58*, 435-439, 1941.

Chase, W. G., and Ericsson, K. A. *A Mnemonic System for Digit Span: One Year Later.* Unpublished report, Carnegie-Mellon University, 1979.

Cherry, E. C. Some experiments on the recognition of speech with one and two ears. *Journal of the Acoustical Society of America.* 1953, *25*, 975-979.

Craik, F. I. M., and Tulving, E. "Depth of Processing and the Retention of Words in Episodic Memory." *Journal of Experimental Psychology, 104*, 268-294, 1975.

Craik, F. I. M., and Watkins, M. J. "The Role of Rehearsal in Short-term Memory." *Journal of Verbal Learning and Verbal Behavior, 12*, 599-607, 1973.

Darwin, C. T., Turvey, M. T., and Crowder, R. G. An auditory analogue of the Sperling partial report procedure: Evidence for brief auditory storage. *Cognitive Psychology*, 1972, *3*, 255-267.

Gates, A. I. "Recitation as a Factor in Memorizing." *Archives of Psychology, 40*, 1917.

Greenberg, R., and Underwood, B. J. "Retention as a Function of Stage of Practice." *Journal of Experimental Psychology, 40*, 452-457, 1950.

Hintzman, D. L. *The Psychology of Learning and Memory.* San Francisco: W. H. Freeman, 1978.

Jacoby, L. L. "The Role of Mental Contiguity in Meory: Registration and Retrieval Effects." *Journal of Verbal Learning and Verbal Behavior, 13*, 483-496, 1974.

Keeney, T. G., Cannizzo, S. R., and Flavell, J. H. "Spontaneous and Induced Verbal Rehearsal in a Recall Task." *Child Development, 38*, 953-966, 1967.

Klatzky, R. L. *Human Memory: Structures and Processes.* San Francisco: W. H. Freeman, 1975.

Kreuger, W. C. F. "The Effect of Overlearning on Retention." *Journal of Experimental Psychology, 12*, 71-78, 1929.

Levin, J. R. "Inducing Comprehension in Poor Readers: A Test of a Recent Model." *Journal of Educational Psychology, 65*, 19-24, 1973.

Lyon, D. L. "The Relation of Length of Material to Time Taken for Learning, and the Optimum Distribution of Time." *Journal of Educational Psychology, 1-9*, 85-91 and 155-163, 1914.

McGeoch, J. A. "Forgetting and the Law of Disuse." *Psychological Review, 39*, 352-370, 1932.

Miller, G. A. "The Magical Number Seven, Plus or Minus Two: Some Limits on Our Capacity for Processing Information." *Psychological Review, 63*, 81-97, 1956.

Moray, N. Attention in dichotic listening: Affective cues and the influence of instructions. *Quarterly Journal of Experimental Psychology*, 1959, *11*, 56-60.

Moray, N., Bates, A., and Barnett, T. Experiments on the four-eared man. *Journal of the Acoustical Society of America*, 1965, *38*, 196-201.

Paivio, A., and Csapo, K. "Picture Superiority in Free Recall: Imagery or Dual Coding?" *Cognitive Psychology, 5*, 176-206, 1973.

Perky, C. W. "An Experimental Study of Imagination." *American Journal of Psychology, 21*, 422-452, 1910.

Peterson, L. R., and Peterson, M. J. "Short-term Retention of Individual Verbal Items." *Journal of Experimental Psychology, 58*, 193-198, 1959.

Pollchik, A. *The Use of Embedded Questions in the Facilitation of Productive Learning.* Ph.D. Dissertation, Vanderbilt University.

Reddy, R., and Newell, A. "Knowledge and its representation in a speech understanding system." In L. W. Gregg (Ed.), *Knowledge and Cognition.* Hillsdale, New Jersey: Lawrence Erlbaum, 1974.

Reder, L. M. "The role of elaboration in the comprehension and retention of prose: A critical review." *Review of Educational Research*, *50*(1) 5-53, 1980.

Sperling, G. The information available in brief visual presentations. *Psychological Monographs*, 1960, *74* (Whole No. 498).

Thorndike, E. L. *The Psychology of Learning*. New York: New York Teacher's College, 1914.

Thorndyke, P. W., and Stasz, C. "Individual Differences in Procedures for Knowledge Acquisition from Maps." *Cognitive Psychology*, *12*, 137-175, 1980.

Tulving, E., and Pearlstone, Z. "Availability Versus Accessibility of Information in Memory for Words." *Journal of Verbal Learning and Verbal Behavior*, *5*, 381-391, 1966.

Underwood, B. J. "Forgetting." *Scientific American*, *3*, 155-162, 1964.

Problem Solutions

Page 129. "Tip of The Tongue" Phenomenon

1. anvil
2. holograph
3. epigram
4. salient
5. phlegmatic
6. utopia
7. necrophilia
8. antidote
9. cyclops
10. lintel

6

Using Memory Effectively

Usually when we think of memory, we think of information that is stored inside the head. In this chapter, we want to emphasize that, while some of the information available to us is stored inside the head, much of it is stored outside. Solving practical problems typically requires us to use both internal *and* external memory. Our effectiveness in practical memory tasks is often determined by our success in managing the relation between internal and external memory. If the answer to our problem is in a reference book in the library, it won't help us at all unless we have sufficient knowledge *in our heads* to be able to find the book.

In this chapter, we will describe strategies for using both internal and external memories effectively. First, we will describe several mnemonic techniques— that is, procedures for storing information rapidly in internal long-term memory— and we will provide practice exercises in their use. When you have mastered this section, you should be able at one hearing to learn a list of 20 words presented at the rate of one word every five seconds. In addition, you should be able to learn foreign language vocabulary at the rate of one word a minute. We will place heaviest emphasis in this chapter on mnemonic techniques. Next, we will discuss the use of external sources of information, such as libraries and reference books. Finally, we will discuss notes and reminders—that is, self-generated external memory aids such as lecture notes, and describe their use in solving particular memory problems.

MNEMONIC TECHNIQUES: THE NEED

External memory aids are very useful in a wide variety of situations. There are many practical situations, however, in which it is either necessary or very convenient for us to have information stored in our memories.

Imagine yourself at a cocktail party; your host steers you to a group of people standing together who cordially introduce themselves. You immediately whip out your pad and pencil and write down their names and distinguishing features, in order to remember their names and faces. Rumors immediately circle that you are *a*. a narcotics agent, *b*. an emissary from the CIA, or *c*. a divorce lawyer looking for evidence. Obviously, this use of external memory does not reflect good social manners and is not encouraged.

The previous example is one of the most common situations requiring internal memory skills. In social and business meetings, we are expected to store name-face connections internally. The "What was your name again?" routine certainly isn't flattering, and eventually it becomes insulting. Numerous other examples can be cited. In speaking a foreign language, most of the vocabulary and grammar rules must be stored internally. As a practical matter, one can use a dictionary only rarely in conversation. The same applies to writing. Efficiency of writing is greatly reduced if you must consult the dictionary frequently to check spelling. Also, typing speed suffers horribly if you have to make frequent reference to the keyboard. In football, you have to remember the plays, and on the stage, you must remember your lines. In many school situations, such as test taking, the task is exactly that of storing information internally.

Some students take the view that there is no purpose in learning information contained in textbooks because one can always look it up. There are some cases in which this view is justified. We *don't* want to memorize tables of logarithms or trigonometric functions. However, there are many cases in which this view is not justified. Imagine visiting a doctor who has a great medical library but doesn't know the contents. You say, "Doc, I hurt right here." Doc says, "Right there, eh! OK, I have no idea what that means, but I'll hit the medical books right away to see if I can turn anything up. I'll give you a call in a few weeks if we're going to need any tests."

Finally, there are situations in which external memory would be better but we just don't have pencil and paper available at the moment. It is for situations like these that we recommend using the seven memory aids we are about to describe, as well as such variations and combinations of them as you may invent for your own special needs.

In the sections which follow, we describe seven types of mnemonic techniques or memory aids:

1. acronyms and acrostics
2. rhyme-keys
3. multiple-keys
4. the method of loci
5. the keyword method

6. the image-name technique, and

7. chaining.

THE BASIS OF MNEMONIC TECHNIQUE

The effectiveness of mnemonic techniques depends on four memory principles: 1. indexing, 2. switching to an easier memory task, 3. chunking, and 4. elaboration. The last three principles should be familiar to you from reading Chapter 4. Switching to an easier memory task refers to the sequence of retrieval tasks ordered from most to least difficult: uncued recall, cued recall, recognition, and savings. The most usual application of this principle in mnemonics is to change an uncued recall task into a cued recall task.

Indexing, the only principle not discussed in Chapter 4, is familiar to you in another context. Dictionaries contain an enormous amount of useful information in the form of words paired with their definitions. This information would be very hard to retrieve if the words were arranged at random. Fortunately, dictionaries are indexed. That is, they are arranged in an orderly way (alphabetically) so that we can quickly find the word we are interested in without an exhaustive search.

More generally, an index is any organized set of cues to information. In memory, an index is an organized set of cues (in the sense of cued recall) to information in memory. The rhyme-key method, discussed below, provides an excellent illustration of the application of indexing in mnemonics.

As you read about each technique, try to identify the memory principles on which it relies.

Acronyms and Acrostics

If you try to remember the names of the Great Lakes without help (that is, as a free recall task), you may experience some difficulty. However, if you know that the first letters of the names spell the word *HOMES*, you may find the task much easier. *HOMES* is the kind of memory aid called an *acronym*. An acronym is a word or phrase made entirely of letters which are cues to words we want to remember. Often the cues are the first letter or first syllable of the words we want to remember. Other examples of acronyms are shown in Table 1 (items 2, 3, and 4).

An *acrostic* is a sentence or rhyme in which the first letter of each word is a cue. In the acrostic, "True virtue means dull company," the first letter of each word is a cue to a sequence of terms relating to the magnetic compass: "*t*rue, *v*ariation, *m*agnetic, *d*eviation, *c*ompass." Other examples of acrostics are shown in Table 1 (items 6 and 7).

Table 1. Acronyms and Acrostics

Memory Aid	Type	Application
HOMES	Acronym	The names of the Great Lakes (*H*uron, *O*ntario, *M*ichigan, *E*rie, *S*uperior)
ITCHE (pronounced "itchy")	Acronym	Words designating the four memory principles (*I*ndexing, *T*ask switching, *Ch*unking, *E*laboration)
ROY G. BIV	Acronym	The colors of the rainbow (*R*ed, *O*range, *Y*ellow, *G*reen, *B*lue, *I*ndigo, *V*iolet)
FACE	Acronym	The notes represented by the spaces of the G-clef
True virtue makes dull company.	Acrostic	A sequence of navigation terms to be remembered in order (*T*rue, *V*ariation, *M*agnetic, *D*eviation, *C*ompass)
Every good boy does fine.	Acrostic	The notes represented by the lines of the G-clef
On old Olympus topmost top, a Finn and German viewed a hop.	Acrostic	Used to remember the first letters of the cranial nerves (*O*ptic, *O*lfactory, *O*culomotor, *T*roclear, *T*rigeminal, *A*bducens, *F*acial, *A*uditory, *G*lossopharyngeal, *V*agus, *A*ccessory, *H*ypoglossal)

Exercises

Invent acronyms or acrostics for each of the following:

1. A doubled consonant is preceded by a short vowel.
2. The first 13 states of the union in order of their admission to the union: Delaware, Pennsylvania, New Jersey, Georgia, Connecticut, Massachusetts, Maryland, South Carolina, New Hampshire, Virginia, New York, North Carolina, and Rhode Island.
3. The names of the Great Lakes in order of size: Ontario, Erie, Michigan, Huron, Superior.
4. Geological periods of the Paleozoic era from earliest to most recent: Cambrian, Ordovician, Silurian, Devonian, Mississippian, Pennsylvanian, Permian.
5. The planets in order of distance from the sun: Mercury, Venus, Earth, Mars, Jupiter, Saturn, Uranus, Neptune, Pluto.

The Rhyme-Key Method

This method is useful for remembering lists of ordered or unordered items such as shopping lists or check lists. To use the method, you must first memorize the list of key words rhymed with the sequence of digits shown in Table 2.

Table 2. Digits and Rhymed Key Words

Digit	Rhymed Key Word
one	gun
two	shoe
three	tree
four	door
five	hive
six	bricks
seven	heaven
eight	gate
nine	mine
ten	hen

Suppose that we want to remember a shopping list consisting of the following items: onions, coffee, bananas, soup, spaghetti, cola, eggs, bread, and milk. With the rhyme-key method, we will create an image relating the items on the shopping list to the sequence of rhymed key words. Thus the first item, "onions," might be associated to the key word "gun" through an image of a gun shooting a hole in an onion or an image of a gun shooting onions as bullets. Any image that depicts a striking interaction between the rhymed key word and the object to be remembered will do. When the first image is created, the second item is is related to the key word rhymed with two, and so on. Thus, we might picture a shoe filled with ground coffee, a banana hanging on a tree, a door inset with dozens of soup cans, or bees carrying strands of limp spaghetti to their hive, a boy throwing bricks at cola bottles, clouds (in heaven) shaped like eggs, a gate set into the side of a loaf of bread, and milk pouring from the mouth of a mine.

If the method is to work well, you must first have Table 2 thoroughly memorized, and you must generate vivid interactive images relating the items to be remembered to the key words.

Exercises

Study the rhymed key pairs shown in Table 2 until you can reproduce them rapidly and easily. Then memorize the following shopping lists using the rhyme-key method:

1. hat, gloves, shoes, needles, glasses, umbrella, pen, gift wrap, scotch tape, razor blades
2. perch, cheese, ginger root, salt, onions, cashews, sandwich bags, steak, cookies
3. thread, curtains, light bulbs, saw blades, fuses, masking tape

Multiple-Key Method

This method is a variation of the rhyme-key method and is especially useful for remembering telephone numbers. The method requires a fair amount of intial effort. Table 3, or a similar chart of your own device, must be thoroughly memorized. The effort involved in learning Table 3 is less than it appears at first glance, since the key for each digit can be learned as a single image, and the four words in the key rhyme with the corresponding digit. To illustrate, the four key words for zero, or "naught," can be stored in a single image of a hot daughter who is standing on her newly-bought yacht. Further, the last column in Table 3 is identical to the last column in Table 2, which you already know.

Table 3. A Chart for Using the Multiple-Key Method

Digit	Modifier	Actor	Act	Object-Place
0 (nought)	hot	daughter	bought	yacht
1	funny	nun	runs	gun
2	blue	gnu	flew	shoe
3	wee	me	skis	tree
4	snoring	whore	tore	door
5	jive	wife	arrives	hive
6	quick	hick	fix	bricks
7	raving	Kevin	severs	heaven
8	crated	Beethoven	inflates	gate
9	fine	lion	dines	mine

The hard part of remembering a telephone number is remembering the last four digits. So we will concentrate on that first. To remember the number 963-8725, we will take the last four digits in order and code them as a modifier, an actor, an act, and an object or place. Thus, 8725 becomes "crated Kevin flew to a hive." Notice that the order of the numbers is important in determining the image. The number 7528 becomes "a raving gnu arrives at the gate," and the number 5872 becomes "a jive Beethoven severs a shoe." Articles and prepositions can be inserted to assure the grammaticality of the phrase.

The exchange (the first three digits of a telephone number) is often easy to remember without a memory aid since the numbers we call most frequently— local numbers—either have the same exchange or are divided into a very few exchange areas. If you do want to use a memory aid for remembering an exchange, however, the method requires one modification—a symbol for a missing number. We will use the image of a hole to represent a missing number. Thus the number 963 can be represented as "a fine hick skis into a hole."

Exercises

1. Recite the list of images for the digits.

2. Generate images (and words, when possible) for the following numbers:
   a. 2893
   b. 5106
   c. 7454
   d. 8888
3. Generate images for the following numbers:
   a. 555-1212 (directory assistance—information)
   b. (292) 456-1414 (the White House)
   c. 391-9500 (the "time" number)
4. Memorize this social security number (or your own):
   420-14-3170
5. Memorize π to nine places:
   3.14159265

The Method of Loci

This method, like the rhyme-key method, is especially useful for remembering unrelated lists of objects. Because it retains items in a specific sequence, it is also useful for memorizing items that must be mixed in a definite order, such as ingredients in a recipe, or chemicals in a laboratory experiment. The method is of very ancient origin and was used by Roman orators when delivering speeches.

To use the method of loci, you must select a place such as a house or a building that you are very familar with. Next choose a convenient starting place such as a front door or main entrance and imagine yourself walking slowly through the building. As you walk, choose a sequence of 20 distinct loci—clearly defined places like a sofa or a refrigerator—where you can imagine putting the objects you are trying to remember. To avoid confusion, do not cross your path; that is, "walk" in each area only once. Figure 1 shows the house that I use and my chosen path through it with 20 loci. The first locus is the front door; the second, a radiator, the third, the refrigerator, etc. It is important, if the method is to work well, that you identify a unique path with a well-defined starting place and a very definite set of loci so that when you are retrieving information you can repeat exactly the same sequence of loci that you used when storing the information.

To apply the method of loci in learning a list of items such as those shown in Table 4, you must associate the items of the list successively to the sequence of loci. Thus, since the first item is an umbrella, and my first locus is the front door, I imagine the umbrella stuck into the middle of the door. I imagine the second item, the sea gull, squatting uncomfortably on the radiator; the third item, the watermelon, falling out of the refrigerator, etc.

It helps in using the method to break your loci into groups of five. If you use a square house for your loci, a convenient and natural way to do this is to place five loci along each of the four walls of the house. Breaking the loci up in this way makes it easier to retrieve a single item in the middle of the list. For example, if you want to retrieve item 12, you can jump ahead to locus 10 at one corner of the house and then "walk" two loci.

Exercises

1. Make a diagram of your loci similar to Figure 1.
2. Memorize the following recipe using the method of loci:

Veal Cutlets—Parma Style

Beat six veal cutlets lightly to flatten them. Sprinkle with salt and fry in butter on both sides in a heavy frying pan. Sprinkle the cutlets with ¼ pound chopped

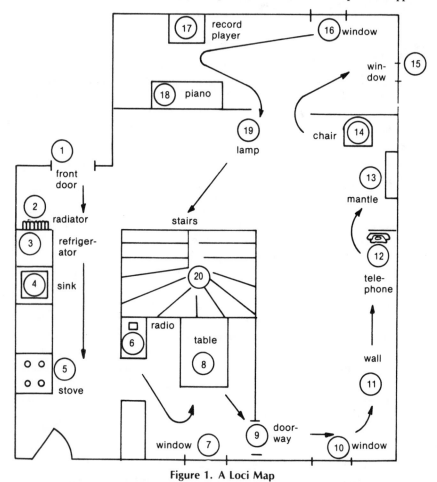

Figure 1. A Loci Map

ham, 2-3 sprigs chopped parsley, ¼ cup grated parmesan cheese, and 2½ tablespoons marsala wine. Serve as soon as the cheese begins to melt.

Table 4. A Word List To Practice the Method of Loci

1. umbrella	11. railroad tie
2. sea gull	12. brick
3. watermelon	13. hippopotamus
4. Picasso painting	14. fire
5. elephant	15. dog
6. telephone	16. pizza
,7. cricket	17. uncle
8. waterfall	18. candlestick
9. automobile tire	19. spinach
10. snow shovel	20. ivy vines

3. Memorize the following lists:

List 1

1. an egg
2. Thomas Jefferson
3. a freight train
4. a water glass
5. the Thames River
6. cotton candy
7. a rose bush
8. Ty Cobb
9. a fountain
10. Beethoven's Second Symphony
11. a horse
12. an ice cream cone
13. philosphy
14. Ghana
15. a pencil
16. a carrot
17. the Pacific Ocean
18. Galileo
19. an automobile tire
20. jello

List 2

1. cheese
2. Budapest
3. John Milton
4. thread
5. a yak
6. cadmium
7. a door
8. the Antarctic
9. tennis
10. a robin
11. jurisprudence
12. a vacuum cleaner
13. Spiro Agnew
14. The Pyrenees
15. maple syrup
16. a light bulb
17. Bulgaria
18. summer
19. honesty
20. Cezanne

Repair manual. If you have trouble with the method—that is, if you find you remember less than 17 or 18 out of 20 items—try the following:

1. *Recheck your loci.* Make another diagram of your loci and check it against the diagram you made in Exercise 1. Be sure that you know without any doubt exactly what your loci are and what order they come in.
2. *Be sure that you are generating striking interactive images.* If you are storing the item "towel" at the locus "sink," don't just place the towel there neatly folded and looking as if it belonged. Make the towel and the sink interact. Imagine that the water is turned on and it is soaking the towel. If you are storing the umbrella on the stove, let the stove set fire to the umbrella.

The method of loci has proved itself quite effective in improving memory for lists. Seventy-five of my students were given a memory test both before and after learning the method of loci. In both cases, the students heard a list of 20 items read only once at the rate of one item every seven seconds. The median score on the pre-test was 7; on the post-test, 17. The difference was very reliable statistically.

Some students have expressed concern that the method of loci will become less and less effective as one continues to use it to learn successive lists. The worry is that images constructed for remembering earlier lists will become confused with images for the current list, and that this confusion will grow as the number of lists we learn by this method increases. Confusions of this sort sometimes occur in using the method, but I don't believe that they constitute an important limitation. To test my belief, I asked people to use the method several times in succession. They learned a list, were tested on it, immediately learned a second list, were tested on the second list, and so on. I reasoned that learning the lists in immediate succession would cause more confusion than would learning lists widely separated in time. Thus, this test should be a severe one for the method of loci. The results are shown in Table 5. Clearly the method holds up quite well even under this severe test.

Table 5. Results of Using the Method of Loci To Learn Successive Lists

	Successive Lists Learned					
Subject	1	2	3	4	5	6
1	20	20	16	19	20	19
2	19	20	17	15	18	14
3	18	20	20	18		
4	20	19	20			
5	16	13	16	12	14	14

The Keyword Method

The keyword method is especially useful for learning foreign language vocabulary. We will illustrate the method by applying it in learning the meanings of the list of Italian words in Table 6. Consider the first Italian word, *agnello*. The Italian pronunciation [AN YELL' OH] sounds quite similar to the English words "ANN YELLOW," our chosen keywords for *agnello*. Next we will relate the keywords to the English translation: "lamb." To do this we can create an image of a girl, Ann, leading a bright yellow lamb. The second word, *pomidoro* [PALM EE DOOR' OH], sounds like the English words "BALMY DOOR" or "BOMB HIS DOOR." For the first keyword, we could imagine a doorway in a tropical region surrounded by palm trees and tomato plants. For the second keyword we could imagine a man's door being bombarded with exploding tomatoes.

Table 6. Italian Menu Words

Word in Italian	Pronunciation	Key Word	English Meaning
ag nel' lo	an yell' oh	ann yellow	lamb
bis tec' ca	biss tech' ah	bee sticker	steak
for mag' gio	for modge jo	for mod joe	cheese
ci pol' le	chee pole a	cheap ollie	onions
pom i dor' o	palm ee door oh	balmy ⎱ door / palmy ⎰	tomatoes
man' zo	mon zo	man sew	beef
rip i en' o	ree pee-a' no	rip piano	stuffed
tor' ta	tore tah	(ex) tort a	cake
in sa la' ta	in sah lah' tah	it's a lotta' (salad)	salad
uo' va	woe vah	woven	eggs
mai al' e	mah yah' lay	my alley	pork, pig
car cio' fi	car choh' fe	car show fee	artichokes
me lan zan' e	meh lahn zahn' a	zany melon	eggplant
vi tel' lo	vee tell' oh	v telly	veal
pol' lo	pole' low	polo	chicken
fun' ghi	foon ghee	fun geese	mushrooms
pes' ce	pesh shay	passion	fish
bi an' co	bee yon' co	bee uncle	white
sal sic' ce	sahl see chay	sol's itchy	sausage
ros' so	row sow	row sow	red

The keyword method, then, consists of two steps: First, one selects as a keyword an English word that resembles the foreign word in pronunciation. As is the case in using "bomb his door" as a keyword for *pomidoro*, the resemblance need not be perfect. Second, one creates a striking interactive image relating the keyword and the English meaning. The images must be actively related, as we saw in the last chapter, to promote retrieval.

Exercise 1

In Table 6, we have suggested keywords for each of the 20 Italian words. Spend about 10 minutes, using the keyword method, to learn all 20 of the Italian words. Be sure to generate an interactive image relating the keyword with the English meaning. This is a crucial step in the keyword method. Then cover the page so that only the Italian words are showing and test yourself.

Table 7. Arabic Menu Words

Word in Arabic	Keyword	English Meaning
loo'bee	blue bean	green beans
ba mi'a	bomb	okra
koo'sa	clues	green squash
wa'rak	war rock	leaves
a reesh'	a reach	grape
la'ban	lob bun	yogurt
kib'bee	k b	meat and wheat
na yee'	navy	raw
ta boo'lee	table leg	mixture
ba'ba ga nouge'	papa canoes	mashed eggplant
hom'mos	home moss	chick peas
bit' hen'ee	bit any	sesame
bas zel'la	buzz ella	sweet peas
mi'shee	mishmosh	stuffed
mal foof'	male foot	cabbage leaves
na mool'	a mule	butter cookie
na mu'ra	no more	coconut cake
ke na'fee	can offer	shredded wheat cake
niss oo niss	not so nice	half and half
bak la'wa	bake lava	honey pastry

Exercise 2

Study the Arabic menu words in Table 7 for 10 minutes by the keyword method (time yourself). Then test yourself by covering all but the Arabic words.

Generating Keywords

In the two exercises above, we have provided keywords for you. Now, to make the technique more generally useful, you should practice generating keywords for yourself. Table 8 shows 20 German words, their pronunciations, and their meanings. Spend 20 minutes studying these words by the keyword method, generating your own keywords. Then test yourself by covering the page so that only the German words are showing.

When keywords are provided, we estimate that it takes a typical student about 30 seconds per word to memorize a list of foreign language words by the keyword method. When keywords are not provided, the same task takes about 60 seconds per word.

The method appears to work well for most students. Eighty-five of my students were given 10 minutes to learn the Italian words shown in Table 6 (which they had not seen before), with the keywords provided. Given a posttest, 66 percent got all 20 correct, 19 percent got 18 or 19 correct, and 15 percent got 17 or fewer correct.

Worries. Some people have expressed concern that by using the keyword method, the language student's memory will be cluttered with meaningless keywords which, while useful for intial learning, will later interfere with the natural use of language. Atkinson (1975), who has pioneered research on the use of this method, has investigated this problem. He finds in general that the student's consciousness of the keywords fades as familiarity with the language increases. Thus it appears that the keyword, which is useful for intial learning, disappears without harmful after-effects, like a builder's scoffolding when it is no longer needed.

Table 8. German Words

German Word	Pronunciation	English Word
abend	ah-bent	evening
ei	eye	egg
essen	ess-en	to eat
flugzeug	flook-tsoyk	airplane
frühstück	free-schteeck	breakfast
gasthof	gahsst-hahf	hotel
kartoffel	kart-off-el	potato
kellner	kel-ner	waiter
mittag	mit-tahg	noon
morgen	morg-en	morning
nicht	nikt	not
rouchen	rowk-en	to smoke
stadt	shtahtt	city
strasse	shtrahs-e	street
trinken	trink-en	to drink
wann	vahnn	when
wo	vok	where
zeit	tsite	time
zeitung	tsy-toong	newspaper
zug	tsook	train

A second frequently expressed worry relates to pronunciation. Since the keyword provides only an approximation to the correct pronunciation of the foreign word, some have been concerned that students using the method may learn incorrect pronunciations which will later be hard to unlearn. This is certainly a problem to be avoided in using the method. Singer (1976) has shown, however, that the keyword method can actually be used as an aid in avoiding errors in pronunciation. For example, in learning the French word *le pantalon*, her students would typically have mispronounced the first syllable of the word by using a short "a". "Le pantalon" looks like "pant," not "pont," as it should be pronounced. By choosing the keyword, "Pontiac" the mispronunciation was avoided.

The keyword method may also be used to learn spelling. Suppose you wanted to learn to spell the words *peasant*, *exercise*, and *determine*. First, you must identify an English word (or words) which contains the "hard-to-spell" part of the target word. Where possible, the keywords may contain the whole word. Thus, we get the keywords, "PEAS ANT" for *PEASANT*, "TEN" for *EXISTENCE*, and "DETER MINE" for *DETERMINE*. Next, you must construct an image or story relating the keywords to the target word. Thus, for the first word, we may construct the sentence, "Peasants eat peas with ants on them"; for the second, "Existence has ten minus one letters"; and for the third, "The coal company wants to dig a hole in my front yard but I am determined to deter the mine." This technique has been described in detail by Shefter (1976) in his book, *Six Minutes a Day to Perfect Spelling*.

Exercise

Use the keyword method to learn the following spelling words:

acceptable
cameos
courtesy
extraordinary
jurisdiction
mausoleum
pigeon
sovereign

The Image-Name Technique

This procedure is most frequently used for learning people's names, but it can also be used for associating paintings with their titles, or, more generally, images with names.

Let's suppose you want to learn the names of some people. The image-name technique involves analyzing both the face and the name, and then searching for any relation between the two that can be found. Analysis of the face involves searching for individual features such as closely-set eyes, high hairline, large ears, or heavy eyebrows, or for overall impression such as "reminds me of a weasel," or "looks like a judge." The features that you attend to should be permanent ones that are likely to be present when you meet the person again. Clothes or changeable jewelry would not help you learn the name permanently.

Analysis of the name involves identification of parts, rhymes, and puns. Any relation that you can find between the analysis of the face and the name is fair game. Figures 2 and 3 show one subject's analysis of two names and faces and the relations he found between them.

"HE LOOKS LIKE BEETHOVEN WITH A HAIRCUT."

Exercise

Apply the image-name technique the next time you meet someone new.

The image-name technique is harder for most people than the techniques discussed previously. Prior to learning the image-name technique, 75 students in my Problem Solving course were able to remember a median of six name-face pairs in a list of 20. After learning the technique, they were able to remember a median of 10.5 name-face pairs. While this improvement is less impressive than the improvement with the method of loci, it is very reliable statistically. Of the 75 students, 66 showed some improvement after learning the method.

Repair manual. If you are having trouble with the image-name technique, the difficulty may come from inadequate analysis of the names and faces. This aspect of the technique requires considerable effort and concentration if it is to work consistently well. You shouldn't expect memorable relations between names and faces to spring into consciousness easily. Often you will have to dig for them. Practice helps here.

A final word of wisdom. The technique won't help at all if you don't use

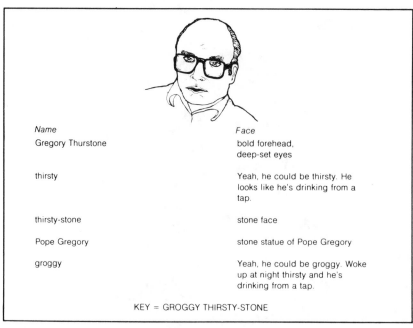

Name	Face
Gregory Thurstone	bold forehead, deep-set eyes
thirsty	Yeah, he could be thirsty. He looks like he's drinking from a tap.
thirsty-stone	stone face
Pope Gregory	stone statue of Pope Gregory
groggy	Yeah, he could be groggy. Woke up at night thirsty and he's drinking from a tap.

KEY = GROGGY THIRSTY-STONE

Figure 2. Using the Image/Name Technique to Learn Gregory Thurstone's Name

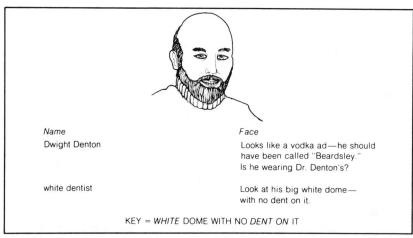

Name	Face
Dwight Denton	Looks like a vodka ad—he should have been called "Beardsley." Is he wearing Dr. Denton's?
white dentist	Look at his big white dome— with no dent on it.

KEY = *WHITE* DOME WITH NO *DENT ON* IT

Figure 3. Using the Image/Name Technique to Learn Dwight Denton's Name

164

it. To get the benefit of the technique you have to get in the habit of applying it when you meet new people.

Chaining

In all of the techniques we have discussed so far, the memory cue and the content retrieved were distinct. In the chaining technique, each portion of the content as it is retrieved serves as the cue for the next retrieval. With this technique, the user constructs a story that incorporates each element of a list to be remembered in turn. Thus, to remember the list: fudge, Toronto, Napoleon, pin, eater, tent, brick, flower pot, river, and hot dog, we can create a story like the following: "Once there was a piece of fudge made in Toronto. It was eaten by Napoleon and gave him a pain in the stomach that felt like a pin. He pulled it out and threw it at an anteater who was frightened and ran into a tent where it hit its head against a brick that was just inside, and knocked over the flower pot on top, which rolled down to the river and floated next to an old hot dog."

This technique is useful for the same range of tasks as the method of loci, i.e., remembering ordered or unordered lists of objects. Kohut (1976) compared these two methods for memorizing multiple lists. He asked subjects to hold six lists in memory at the same time, three memorized by the method of loci and three by the chaining method. He tested for recall of the lists after all six had been memorized. In the tests, the subject was given the first word of the list and asked to recall the rest. Kohut found that the two methods were about equally good if the subject had to remember both the correct position and the correct list to be scored correct. However, the method of loci was better if the subject just had to remember the correct position of the word in its list and not which list it was on. The chaining method was better if the subject just had to get the list right but not the position.

WHY DO THE MNEMONIC TECHNIQUES WORK?

As we noted earlier, the mnemonic techniques depend on four memory principles for their effectiveness:

1. *I*ndexing,
2. Switching to an easier memory *t*ask,
3. *Ch*unking, and
4. *E*laboration.

Acronyms and acrostics make use of two of the principles. The acronym ITCHE, for example, is a chunk which helps us remember cues to the four memory principles. These cues change what would otherwise be a free recall task into a cued recall task. Acrostics work in the same way. Thus, acronyms and acrostics depend on chunking and on switching to an easier memory task.

The rhyme-key method makes use of a numerical index—the numbers from one to ten—to cue highly imageable key words—gun, shoe, etc. The keywords are associated with the items to be remembered by forming interactive images—a process of elaboration. The multiple-key method depends on the same principles as the rhyme-key method, as does the method of loci. However, the method of loci uses a spatial rather than a numerical index.

The keyword method, the image-name technique, and the chaining method all depend on elaboration of various sorts. In the chaining method, the elaboration may be largely semantic—we try to tell ourselves a meaningful story about items to be remembered—and in the keyword method, it may be largely visual, e.g., images of tomatoes thrown at doors. The image-name technique encourages both auditory and visual elaboration.

Table 9 lists the seven mnemonic techniques together with the memory problems they are applied to and the memory principles they employ.

Constructing Memory Schemes

We have presented a number of schemes that can be used to aid memory. These schemes are each useful in themselves in a variety of situations. However, the reader would be missing a major value of these schemes and an important reason for presenting them, if he failed to realize that they illustrate just a few of the many possible memory schemes. The reader should realize that he himself can construct others.

The schemes we have presented differ in a number of ways. Some of the schemes employ memorized keys while others require the user to generate his own keys. Some have single keys; others, multiple keys. Some schemes use auditory imagery, others require visual imagery, and so on. If you have a special memory need, you may find that none of the schemes we have presented is quite appropriate to it. Suppose you want a memory scheme for use in playing bridge. None of the schemes we have presented is especially adapted to remembering the cards yet to be played in a bridge hand. What would you do to put such a scheme together? A way to begin would be to try to answer two questions:

1. What is special about the bridge situation?
2. What aspects of known memory schemes match the special aspect of the bridge situation?

To answer the first question, we may note that bridge has four players; they are associated with the compass directions—north, south, east, and west; there are two hands which don't need to be remembered—self and dummy; some cards are more important than others; and the cards are characterized by two

Table 9. Seven Mnemonic Techniques, Their Applications, and the Memory Principles Involved in Their Use

Name	Application	Memory Principles Used
Acronyms and Acrostics	permanent storage of important lists and rules, e.g., shopping lists; not used for temporary storage	chunking, task
Rhyme-Key	arbitrary lists of 10 items or less (ordered or unordered)	numerical indexing, elaboration
Multiple-Key	multi-digit numbers, e.g., telephone numbers	numerical indexing, elaboration
Method of Loci	arbitrary lists (ordered or unordered); length limited by loci list	spatial indexing, elaboration
Keyword Method	vocabulary learning	elaboration
Image-Name	learning names of people, works of art	elaboration
Chaining	arbitrary lists (ordered or unordered)	elaboration

dimensions—suit and value. These properties of the bridge task suggest some features we might want to include in a useful memory scheme. The spatial coding of the four players suggests the use of a modified method of loci with a locus for each of the compass directions. The fact that the cards have two dimensions suggests a pair of memorized keys—one for suit and one for value. Since the values are the digits one through ten and Jack, Queen, and King, the rhyme-key for digits might easily be augmented to provide the key for value. Since the rhyme-key is focused on nouns, perhaps the suit key should be focused on adjectives to allow easy combinations of the keys in images. Can a useful scheme be constructed with these properties? We don't know. We leave that question to the interested reader.

Exercises

Design a memory scheme based on an analysis of the memory task of one of the following:

1. chemical nonmenclature
2. biological classifications
3. appointments
4. geological eras
5. resister color-coding
6. traffic laws
7. cultural history

USING EXTERNAL SOURCES

There is an enourmous amount of useful information stored in such external sources as textbooks, magazines, journals, newspapers, microfilm, and so on. There is so much useful information, in fact, that we often have considerable trouble sifting through what is available to find what we want. Fortunately, there are many guides or *indexes* to available information which can aid us in our search. Knowing the right indexes is an important prerequisite to work in many fields. For example, physicians should be able to use the *Cumulative Medical Index*, and psychologists should know how to locate psychological studies through *Psychological Abstracts*.

Using Indexes

The questions we may need to ask when doing research in the library are very diverse, and so are the sources of information needed to answer them. The card catalog is one index to these sources, but typically we need many more. Among the most generally useful indexes* are:

1. *World Almanac and Book of Facts*
2. *Statistical Abstract of the United States*
3. *Webster's Third New International Dictionary of the English Language Unabridged*
4. *Encyclopedia Americana*
5. *Reader's Guide to Periodic Literature*
6. *New York Times Index*

If there are any of these references which you have never used, you should make a point of finding them in the library and examining their contents.

One of the most valuable resources of a library is the staff of research librarians. Research librarians are familiar with a large number of indexes to information—many unfamiliar to most people—which allow them to answer a stupifying variety of questions. Below are some samples of the kinds of questions research librarians must handle and the reference sources (indexes) which may be used to answer them.*

Q: What does A.C.R.L. mean?
A: Look in the *Acronyms, Initialisms, & Abbreviations Dictionary*.
Q: I know part of a poem; how can I find out what it is so that I can get a copy?
A: *Granger's Index to Poetry* (indexed by title *and* first line)
Q: What does the symbol of the pyramid on the back of the dollar bill signify?
A: *Collier's Encyclopedia*, v. 11. This appears under the subject of the "Great

---

*These lists were prepared by Ms. Dorothea Thompson, Reference Librarian, Hunt Library, Carnegie-Mellon University.

Seal of the United States.'' Any attempt to locate this information under the headings of "dollar" or "currency" or "money" will be futile.

Q: How many steel workers belong to labor unions?

A: *Directory of National Unions and Employee Associations*

Q: Where can I find the address of the company that makes my slide-o-matic windows?

A: *Thomas Register*, v. 7 (brand names and index)

Q: How many houses in the Pittsburgh area have central air-conditioning?

A: *U.S. Census of Housing, Census Tracts, Pittsburgh, PA.*

Q: Where can I buy a good map of Dekalb County, Georgia?

A: *10,000 Map and Travel Publications Reference Guide*

The important point to notice is that there are many obscure indexes. The index most appropriate to solving your problem may be one you never dreamed existed, and a quick question to your research librarian might lead you to it.

Exercises

Find appropriate indexes to help you answer the following questions:

1. Is there a poster of the Coneheads in print?
2. What do yaks eat?
3. On what day did Estes Kefauver die?
4. Who is on the Board of Directors of Marvel Comics?
5. What is Spiro Agnew doing now?

Notes and Reminders

People make frequent use of notes and reminders in everyday memory tasks. We are familiar with them in the form of shopping lists, lecture notes, and the proverbial string around the finger. Some commonplace reminders, however, may escape our notice. For example, we may routinely use a finger to keep our place in a telephone book or in our reading but never think of it as a memory aid. We are even less likely to notice that eye position can be used as a memory aid. When you are following a person in a crowd, it is essential to try to keep him in sight. If you lose sight of him for a moment, it is important to look for him close to the place you saw him last.

The sorts of notes we make while doing arithmetic computations or solving other problems are of great practical importance and illustrate how aids to memory can also be aids to problem solving. Think how much harder it is to multiply 2,749 by 9,472 when you have to do all of the work in your head than when you can write down the partial results as you work, or how much harder it may be to solve a physics or geometry problem without first drawing a diagram. We discussed the function of diagrams and other forms of representations in more detail in Chapter 1.

In the next chapter, we will discuss techniques for taking lecture notes which can improve learning efficiency for many students. Here we will discuss just one practical application of reminders which can be helpful to that pitiable segment of humanity known as "the absent-minded"—those people who regularly arrive at their offices to discover that their office keys are at home. There really is a difference in the degree of absent-mindedness among people. In one study (Wilkins and Baddeley, 1978) people were asked to punch a time clock four times a day—8:30 A.M., 1:00 P.M., 5:30 P.M., and 10:00 P.M. This is a task similar to that of remembering to take your medicine at the right time or remembering to put more coins in your parking meter before the meter maid discovers how long it's been since you last did so. The study showed consistent differences among people in the degree of lateness with which they punched the clock.

Can absent-mindedness be helped? We hope so. In many cases, the trouble seems to result from failure to pay attention at certain critical times. A critical time is a time just before we take an action that is hard to reverse—like traveling to work or to Tahiti; mailing a package (Did I remember to take off the price tag?); or revealing information (Oops, I think that *was* a secret!). One way we can help ourselves to notice the critical times is to use a landmark that is connected with the critical time. For example, the front door is an excellent landmark to use for remembering what we want to take to work. If we would just stop for a moment at the front door to review what we will need during the day, we could avoid many annoying attacks of absent-mindedness. The act of sealing a package is a good landmark for reminding us to ask questions like, "Did I include everything I should have?" For the absent-minded surgeon, sewing the patient back up should trigger questions such as, "Do I know where all my scissors are? Or my wrist-watch? Or my shoes?"

Absent-mindedness may strike even when we *do* stop at the front door and try to remember what we should take with us. It's hard to remember *everything* we should take. In such situations, *checklists* can be very useful. A checklist is simply a list of items we may want to remember. A checklist for leaving the house might look like this:

car keys
briefcase
office keys
cats (Have they been fed?)
garbage (Is it out?)
wallet
checkbook

socks

pants

If some day you forget a new item, e.g., your pen, you can simply add it to the list. If the checklist can be associated with a landmark, e.g., taped to the front door where you will see it when you leave, it is likely to be more effective.

SUMMARY

1. In solving problems, we make use both of internal and of external memory.
2. Mnemonic techniques are procedures we use for putting information rapidly into long-term memory.
   a. These techniques depend on four memory principles:
      * Indexing
      * Switching to an easier memory task
      * Chunking
      * Elaboration
   b. Seven mnemonic techniques, their applications, and the memory principles they depend on are summarized in Table 9.
   c. If the available memory techniques don't suit our needs, we should consider inventing new techniques that do.
3. To find information in external memory, e.g., books, libraries, we depend on indexes.
   a. Reference librarians can often provide us with an index to the information we need.
4. Notes and reminders are external memory aids we construct for ourselves.
   a. They can be used to aid us in learning and in problem solving.
   b. They can be used to reduce absent-mindedness.

REFERENCES

Acronyms, Initialisms, and Abbreviations Dictionary, Sixth Edition. Detroit: Gale Research Company, 1978.

Atkinson, R. C. "Mnemotechnics in Second-language Learning." *American Psychology, 30*, 821–828, 1975.

Collier's Encyclopedia. New York: P. F. Collier, 1975.

Directory of National Unions and Employee Associations. U.S. Department of Labor. Bureau of Labor Statistics, Bulletin #1937.

Encyclopedia Americana. New York: Americana Corporation, 1977.

Granger's Index to Poetry. New York: Columbia University Press, 1978.

Kohut, W. "A Comparison of the Method of Loci and Chaining for Memorizing Multiple Lists." Unpublished manuscript, Carnegie-Mellon University, 1976.

Miller, G. A. "The Magical Number Seven, Plus or Minus Two: Some Limits on Our Capacity for Processing Information." *Psychological Review*, *63*, 81–97, 1956.

New York Times Index. New York: The New York Times Company, 1980.

Reader's Guide to Periodical Literature. New York: The H. W. Wilson Company, 1978.

Shefter, H. *Six Minutes a Day to Perfect Spelling*. New York: Pocket Books, 1976.

Singer, G. "Enjoying Vocabulary Learning in Junior High: The Keyword Method." *Canadian Modern Language Review*, *34*, 80–87, 1977.

Statistical Abstract of the United States. Washington, D.C.: U.S. Department of Commerce, Bureau of Census, 1979.

10,000 Map and Travel Publications Reference Guide. Hollywood, CA: Travel Centers of the World, 1978.

Thomas Register of American Manufacturers, 67th Edition. New York: Thomas Register, 1977.

U.S. Census of Housing. Washington, D.C.: U.S. Department of Commerce, Bureau of Census, Government Printing Office, 1970.

Webster's Third New International Dictionary of the English Language, Unabridged. Springfield, MA: G. & C. Merriam Company, 1961.

Wilkins, A. J., and Baddeley, A. D. "Remembering to Recall in Everyday Life: An Approach to Absent-mindedness." In *Practical Aspects of Memory*, edited by M. M. Gruneberg, P. E. Morris, and R. N. Sykes. London: Academic Press, 1978.

World Almanac and Book of Facts. New York: Newspaper Enterprise Association, 1980.

7
Learning Strategies

Nearly everyone uses learning strategies, but some people clearly make better and more extensive use of them than others. Differences in the way people perform in learning situations, either in school or on the job, may depend more on differences in their learning strategies than on differences in their ability. For example, Goldman and Hudson (1973) found that college students with high, middle, and low grade-point averages differed in learning strategies but not in ability.

If learning strategies are so important, why do we hear so little about them? There are at least two answers to this question. One is that the learning strategies we use may be so familiar and automatic that we are almost unaware of them. For example, we all rehearse information when we want to remember it. It seems such a natural thing to do that we hardly think of it as a strategy. In Chapter 4, though, we saw that some first-grade children had not yet learned to rehearse. When they were taught to rehearse, their memory performance improved. Rehearsal, then, isn't innate. It is a strategy we have to learn. Most of us learned it so long ago that we don't remember learning it.

The second reason we don't hear much about learning strategies is that research on learning strategies is quite new. There is still a great deal to learn about them. However, we do know that instruction in learning strategies can improve people's ability to learn.

In this chapter, we will 1. discuss seven basic learning strategies, 2. describe some practical learning systems which make use of these basic strategies, and 3. describe some special techniques for learning difficult topics.

BASIC LEARNING STRATEGIES

The seven basic learning strategies we will discuss are:

1. The structuring strategy
2. The context strategy
3. Monitoring
4. Inferencing
5. Instantiation
6. Multiple coding
7. Attention management

Fundamental research underlying many of these strategies has already been described in Chapter 4.

The Structuring Strategy

The strategy of information structuring requires you to search actively for relations in the learning material. The relations may reveal categories, hierarchies, networks, or other information structures that will help you to understand and remember the material.

For example, suppose that you are reviewing for a test on Chapter 5 by learning the following list:

1. Elaboration
2. Displacement
3. Cued recall
4. Retroactive interference
5. 7 ± 2
6. Tip of the tongue
7. Recognition
8. Maintenance rehearsal
9. Proactive interference
10. Savings
11. Chunks
12. Uncued recall

Table 1 shows the category structure of the list, and Figure 1 shows its hierarchical structure.

The chapter has a theme—the structure of human memory—with some major topics under the theme. The topics in turn have subtopics under them, and these subtopics may have subtopics of their own. At the lowest level, we typically find examples and specific studies that illustrate points made in higher levels.

In general, it is a good principle to list related topics under a single heading in the hierarchy. For example, the various topics under the heading "retrieval" are grouped together in Chapter 4. Separating these topics would have two unfortunate effects:

1. It would be more difficult to make comparisons and contrasts among similar topics, e.g., the difference between recognition and recall might be missed.
2. It would be harder to identify the hierarchical structure of the text.

Table 1. Items Arranged by Categories

Short-term Memory	Encoding	Storage	Retrieval
7±2	Elaboration	Retroactive interference	Tip of the tongue
			Uncued recall
Chunks		Proactive interference	
			Cued recall
Displacement			
			Recognition
Maintenance rehearsal			
			Savings

If you can't find the hierarchical structure of a lecture or text, either it is poorly constructed or you have not fully understood it. In either case, you are likely to have difficulty in remembering the material.

Using the structuring strategy shouldn't be viewed simply as a matter of identifying structure. It can and sometimes should involve restructuring. If a sentence, paragraph, or larger text is hard to understand because of poor organization, you may need to reorganize it in order to understand it. Readers often do this when reading very difficult texts (see Flower, Hayes, and Swarts, 1979).

Examining relations in the material to be learned can lead you to discover more complex structures than hierarchies. For example, if we look at authority relations in a company, we will find a hierarchy like that shown in Figure 2. However, if we look at communications, we are very likely to find a complex *network* like that shown in Figure 3. The network differs from a hierarchy because it contains loops. For example, there is a communication loop from the president to A to F and back to the president. If there were a similar authority loop, the company would be in big trouble.

Rhetorical Structure

Bartlett (1978) made an important practical application of the structuring strategy in teaching students how to profit from their reading, by having them describe

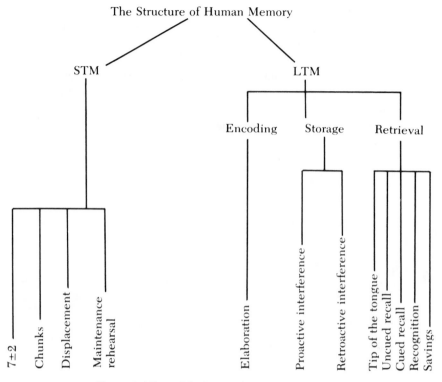

Figure 1. Hierarchical Organization of Chapter 4.

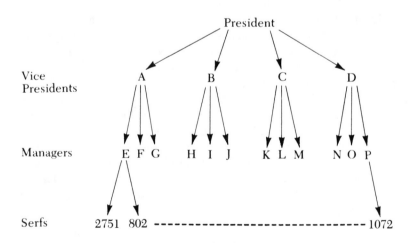

Figure 2. Authority Relations in an Imaginary Company

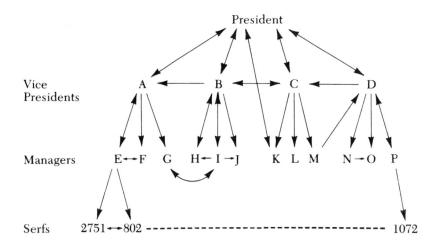

Figure 3. Communications Network in an Imaginary Company

the *rhetorical structure* of the text, or how the author organized it to achieve its major purpose. Four common rhetorical structures are described by Meyer and Freedle (1978):

> Attribution: Attribution is used to relate a description of a person, place, thing, event, quality or abstraction of that thing which it describes.
> Covariance: Covariance indicates a causal relationship serving as an *antecedent* to another serving as the *consequent* . . . either the antecedent or the consequent can be in the superordinate . . . position.
> Response: Response has three subtypes. One . . . can be a *question* and its *answer*. The second has arguments that are a *remark* and a *reply* to it. The arguments of the third are a *problem* and its *solution*.
> Adversative: Adversative . . . relates what did not happen to what did happen, or what does not exist to what does exist.

Bartlett (1978) has taught ninth-grade children how to identify rhetorical structure as a way to improve their ability to learn from their reading. In a series of five one-hour class sessions, the students learned to identify

1. the main idea of the passage, and
2. which of the four rhetorical structures the author used to get the idea across.

This quiz illustrates the skills the students were expected to acquire:
Underline the sentence containing the main idea. Circle the top-level organization used by the writer.

1. Martha was worried about her health. The doctor had told Martha that her

system was overtaxed. As a result she tried to rest more and to eat at regular times. She knew her lifestyle had to change.
a) description   c) problem-solution
b) before-as a result   d) favored view vs. opposite view

2. Pollution is a problem for our rivers. Polluted rivers are eyesores. They are also health hazards. One solution is to stop the dumping of industrial waste.
a) description   c) problem-solution
b) before-as a result   d) favored view vs. opposite view

3. Our class reunion was held last year. We saw many old friends there. The business of the meeting was kept to a minimum. We spent most of our time socializing.
a) description   c) problem-solution
b) before-as a result   d) favored view vs. opposite view

4. Despite the argument that smoking is harmful, many claim it is not so. Certainly, smoking has been related to lung cancer, high blood pressure, and loss of appetite. But, for some people smoking may relieve tension.
a) description   c) problem-solution
b) before-as a result   d) favored view vs. opposite view

The students were told that finding the organization (the rhetorical structure) was the key to getting the author's message. To recall that message, they were told:

Our strategy involves two steps. In reading, we find the organization the writer used. In recalling, we use the same organization. This is a strategy to improve memory. The strategy is called *using top-level organization.*

Students who had had this training were compared to a group of students who had not. Both groups were asked to read passages such as that shown below. After reading, the subjects were asked to write down all they could remember about the passage. The experimental group remembered nearly twice as much as the controls.

The Early Railroads*

Two contrasting views on the usefulness of railroads existed for early Americans. American men of business were quick to recognize the promise of railroads, and by 1830 several companies had been formed to construct railroad lines in the United States. Both the South Carolina Railroad and the Baltimore and Ohio Railroads, America's earliest lines, commenced operations in 1830. The first American locomotive engines were built and delivered in the same year. Most of the early railroads were short lines—the longest in the United States was also the longest in the world, 136 miles. Railway development proceeded rapidly. In the first six years, more than a thousand miles of track were laid, and railroads began to run trains in eleven states.

*From Bartlett, 1978.

In the 1850's, rail service was extended to the Mississippi River. Except for the bulkiest of goods, railroads became the most economical form of transportation within the United States. Traveling by water between New York City and Detroit in the 1850's took ten days; by rail, the same trip required only four days.

Railroads were not popular with everybody. Farmers complained that the noise frightened their cattle, and that sparks from the engines set their fields afire. Some physicians feared that the human body could not endure travel at speeds so high as 30 miles an hour. Canal companies tried to keep railroads from building lines that might compete with canals.

Since knowing the structure of the text we are reading can help us to learn, it makes sense to look actively for clues to structure before we begin reading. If we preview the text quickly by reading indexes, headings, and topic sentences, and glancing at pictures, we can often anticipate the main topic, subtopics, and the author's general approach. The clues we use to identify structure before we read are called *advanced organizers* (Ausubel, 1960). Attending to them can make learning a good deal easier.

Since cues to structure can help us when we are reading, we should remember to provide them for our readers when we are writing. This means first, that our writing should have structure, and second, that we tell the reader what it is. The use of headings, clear paragraphs, and topic sentences can ease your readers' task greatly. Also, there is nothing disgraceful about telling your reader straight out what you are up to, e.g., "First, I will discuss the arguments for capital punishment, then I will try to refute each of them." Your reader may well appreciate the help.

The Context Strategy

In the structure strategy, we search for relations within the material to be learned. In the context strategy, we search for relations between the things to be learned and the things we already know. Recognizing such relations can make learning a great deal easier. In Chapter 2, we found that chess masters make extensive use of their chess knowledge to help them learn new chess positions. When we read a puzzle, we have a much easier time learning its details if we can relate it to similar problems we have seen before. If we already know how to fix lawnmower motors, we will have an easier time learning how to fix outboard motors. Often, the things we want to learn suggest a great deal of related knowledge. In such cases, we don't need a context strategy because the context is obvious.

In other cases, when the problem seems strange or when little related knowledge suggests itself, we may want to use the context strategy—that is, we may want to search for analogies or old knowledge to help us learn the new material. This situation may arise when we start a new course or take a new job. Here, some time spent searching for relevant knowledge may pay off handsomely.

A situation in which the context strategy is frequently useful is in finding the meanings of unfamiliar words. We have a great deal of knowledge about word meanings in the form of word roots. If it occurs to us to use this knowledge, we can often guess the meaning of a new word. Although many of the relevant word roots are Latin or Greek, one doesn't need to know either of these languages in order to do the analyses. All of the necessary information can be found in any good English dictionary.

In learning foreign language vocabulary, one can guess the meanings of words like arbe (tree) and vin (wine) by noticing their relations to the roots of the English words arbor and vine. The meanings of the English words, of course, may be learned in the same way. For example, we can guess the meaning of the word *pericardial* if we relate it to roots of words like perimeter and cardiac.

Spelling can also be made easier by knowledge of word roots. For example, spelling words like *pneumonia, pneumatic, psychology,* and *psychomotor* is easier if we know that "pneumo" is a root for lung and "psycho" the root for mind.

Monitoring

Certainly one of the most powerful of the learning strategies is *monitoring*. This is the strategy in which learners test themselves to find out what they have and have not learned. Then they use that information to guide study and promote learning.

One way to monitor is to test yourself after you have completed a unit of study. For example, after reading an article, you could write down all you remember about the article and then check your response against the original. Another way is to ask yourself questions *while* you are reading. Asking a question focuses your attention on a part of the text and makes it more likely that you will learn that part. By asking yourself many questions while you read, you should be able to learn the text more rapidly than if you don't ask questions. As we saw in Chapter 4, it may be useful to spend as much as 80 percent of your study time in such self-testing activities.

What sort of questions should you ask? If your objective is just to get the facts, the questions can be quite superficial: "Why did Roosevelt decide to run as a third party candidate?" or, "What were the names of the first railway companies?" If your objective is to evaluate the text or to deepen your understanding of it, then you should employ the *inference strategy*, which requires you to ask more penetrating questions.

Inferencing

This strategy is related to monitoring because it involves asking questions about the material studied, and it is related to contextualizing because, typically, it explores the relation of other knowledge to the material being learned. Its objective, however, is to generate inferences about the material in order to evaluate its truth or importance, to work out its implications, or to deepen understanding.

Carrying out this strategy involves asking probing questions, such as: "Is the author biased?" or, "Can I think of a counter-example?" or, "How would the argument seem if the roles were reversed?" In Chapter 10, we will describe some critical thinking techniques that can help you to find "penetrating questions."

Instantiation

Often, when we are having trouble understanding something that someone is telling us, we will say, "Can you give me an example of that?" This is an example of the *instantiation strategy*. We saw in Chapter 5 that examples help us to learn. In the instantiation strategy, we seek out examples that illustrate the materials we are trying to master. We can do this in two ways:

1. We can pay careful attention to the examples that others give us in lectures, in textbooks, or in answer to questions such as, "Can you give me an example of that?" and
2. We can try to create examples for ourselves. It is common for people to do this when they are reading a difficult text. In a recent study by Flower, Hayes, and Swarts (1980), people were asked to think aloud as they read a difficult federal regulation and tried to understand it. The protocols were peppered with examples the readers created for themselves in an effort to understand. Here is an instance.
   [The subject reads "ineligible concerns," and then says] "Say that if a fellow has a bar and he's selling moonshine which is not taxed . . ."

Multiple Coding

The essence of the multiple-coding strategy is to represent the information we want to remember in more than one way. We can do this by paraphrasing, forming images, weaving the material into a story, and by many other ways. For example, suppose we wanted to remember the information in the following sentence:

"Brave Worm finished first; Fig Newton, second; and King Kong, third." We could paraphrase this as: "The win, place, and show horses were Brave Worm, Fig Newton, and King Kong." We could form an image of a worm with its chest stuck out sitting on a fig newton held by King Kong, or we could create a story about the first of a line of brave worms which all by itself ate two fig newtons and a third of King Kong.

Any of these methods of multiple coding should make the information easier to recall.

Attention Management

Far and away the most important cause of failure to learn is failure to study. If you haven't read an article, you may well experience some difficulty in answering questions about it.

We all have limited time and we may often have difficulty in finding the time to do the reading that is expected of us. Some people, though, seem to have more difficulty than others. Differences in performance on the job or in the classroom may depend more on differences in the amount of time invested than on differences in ability.

Some people have a very poor idea of where their time goes. You may be one of these. For example, do you know how many hours a week you spend reading to learn? Do you know how many hours you spend watching TV? Do you know how much of your time is spent being polite to people who are interrupting what you really want to do? If you did know, you might be sufficiently horrified to do something about it. Appendix I describes some procedures that can help with time management.

Concentration

Perhaps you are putting in enough time on your learning tasks but you are working very inefficiently. For example, you may dutifully sit down for a long study session and find that you have terrible trouble concentrating. Often when we are reading, we discover that we haven't been paying attention. Our eyes were scanning line after line, but our mind was far away. We have no idea what the last few pages were about. This can be a very annoying problem when we are trying to meet a deadline, such as a test in the morning or a meeting after lunch. We can't spare the time but we can't seem to concentrate either! Appendix I provides some suggestions that can help you solve concentration problems.

STUDY SYSTEMS

Study systems are organized approaches to learning, especially to learning from reading. There are many different study systems; typically they involve some rule or sequence for applying some of the basic learning strategies, and many include problem-solving strategies as well.

Survey Q3R

One of the most widely used study systems is the Survey Q3R system devised by Robinson (1946). The five steps in this system—survey, question, read, recite, and review—are described in Robinson's own summary (Robinson, 1946):

SURVEY   1. *Glance over the headings in the chapter to see the few big points which will be developed.* This survey should not take more than a minute and will show the three to six core ideas around which the rest of the discussion will cluster. If the chapter has a final summary paragraph this will also list the ideas developed in the chapter. This orientation will help you organize the ideas as you read them later.

QUESTION 2. Now begin to work. *Turn the first heading into a question*. This will arouse your curiosity and so increase comprehension. It will bring to mind information already known, thus helping you to understand that section more quickly. And the question will make important points stand out while explanatory detail is recognized as such. This turning a heading into a question can be done on the instant of reading the heading, but it demands a conscious effort on the part of the reader to make this query for which he must read to find the answer.

READ 3. *Read to answer that question*, i.e., to the end of the first headed section. This is not a passive plowing along each line, but an active search for the answer.

RECITE 4. Having read the first section, look away from the book and try briefly to *recite the answer to your question*. Use your own words and name an example. If you can do this you know what is in the book; if you can't, glance over the section again. An excellent way to do this reciting from memory is to jot down cue phrases in outline form on a sheet of paper. Make these notes very brief!

NOW REPEAT STEPS 2, 3, AND 4 ON EACH SUCCEEDING HEADED SECTION. THAT IS, TURN THE NEXT HEADING INTO A QUESTION, READ TO ANSWER THAT QUESTION, AND RECITE THE ANSWER BY JOTTING DOWN CUE PHRASES IN YOUR OUTLINE. READ IN THIS WAY UNTIL THE ENTIRE LESSON IS COMPLETED.

REVIEW 5. When the lesson has thus been read through, *look over your notes to get a bird's-eye view* of the points and of their relationship *and check your memory* as to the content by reciting on the major subpoints under each heading. This checking of memory can be done by covering up the notes and trying to recall the main points. Then expose each major point and try to recall the subpoints listed under it.

Survey QR3 makes use of three of the seven strategies. The survey step is an example of the structuring strategy. The question step involves monitoring, but Robinson intends it also to facilitate structuring and to provide context by making contact with previous knowledge. The reciting step involves both monitoring and structuring, and the review step is simply monitoring.

Dansereau's MURDER System

The acronym MURDER (remember acronyms?) stands for the six parts of Dansereau et al.'s (1979) study system: *M*ood, *U*nderstand, *R*ecall, *D*igest, *Ex*pand, and *R*eview.

1. *Mood*. The first step of MURDER is setting the mood for study. Dansereau sees two major problems in setting the right mood. One is creating a positive attitude—that is, somehow overcoming the fear and loathing of study.

The second is coping with distractions, e.g., your roommate practicing elephant mating calls. Both of these problems are attention management problems, which are treated in Appendix I under the heading "Concentration."

2. *Understand.* In using the system, you are encouraged when first reading a text to mark any parts of the text you don't understand. During the "Digest" step, you attend to the marked parts which are still unclear to you after further reading. In learning to use the system, you are trained to locate the problem—a difficult word, sentence, or paragraph—and to break it into parts, e.g., you are trained to break a difficult word into its roots. If the meaning is still not clear, you are encouraged to look at the context of the difficulty to find related information, and if all else fails, to consult outside sources, e.g., dictionaries, research librarians, etc. The "Understand" and "Digest" steps, then, involve a problem-solving strategy—fractionation—and a learning strategy—the context strategy.

3. *Recall.* After initial reading, you are instructed to recall the information you have been reading about and to transform it using one (or possibly both) of the following substrategies:

   1. *Paraphrase-imagery.* This is just the multiple-coding strategy described above.

   2. *Networking.* You identify relations in the materials to be learned, such as "part of," "example of," and "leads to." This is an instance of the structuring strategy described above.

4. *Digest.* This step has already been described under "Understand."

5. *Expand.* In this step, you ask and answer three kinds of questions.

   1. If you could talk to the author, what sorts of questions or criticisms would you raise?

   2. How can the material be applied?

   3. How could you make the material more understandable and interesting to others?

   Clearly, the learning strategy involved here is inferencing.

6. *Review.* Here, you review your errors with the intent of finding their causes and making appropriate changes in your study habits. The relevant strategy here is monitoring.

The MURDER system, then, makes use of all of the learning strategies except instantiation.

Dansereau tested the MURDER system by comparing 38 college students who took a 12-week learning strategies class with 28 students who did not take the class. Learning performance was measured three times in each group: once before the class began, once halfway through, and once after the course was completed. The measurement involved reading a 3,000 word passage and then taking a test on its contents one week later. After training, the experimental group performed between 14 and 18 percent better than the untrained control group.

Dansereau also tested the networking strategy separately from the whole system. He found that after six hours of training, the experimental group remembered 34 percent more main ideas than the untrained control group, but about the same number of details.

B. F. Jones and her colleagues (1979) have developed a study system to improve the reading skills of disadvantaged children in the fifth through eighth grades in Chicago public schools. Students are taught a carefully sequenced set of learning strategies in a *mastery learning* format. Mastery learning means that each student must have mastered all of the strategies taught so far, as indicated by passing a test, before being allowed to study the next strategy. The strategies include multiple coding, e.g., visualizing words in analogies; structuring, e.g., differentiating main points and details; contextualizing, e.g., finding the meaning of an unfamiliar word from other information in the text; and inferencing, e.g., differentiating opinion from fact in what is read.

Jones et al. find that their learning strategies yield much greater improvement in the student's reading comprehension scores than does more traditional instruction.

In his book *Knowledge as Design* (1986), Perkins has proposed another study system in which students are encouraged to ask the following questions when acquiring new knowledge:

1. What is its purpose?
2. What is its structure?
3. What are model cases of it?
4. What are arguments that explain and evaluate it?

While Perkins' study system has not been evaluated, the questions he proposes seem likely to promote the structuring and context strategies as well as instantiation and inferencing.

SPECIAL TECHNIQUES FOR HARD CASES

In this section, we will show how the learning strategies can be applied in learning topics which many people find difficult, e.g., zoological categories, physics equations, and cultural history. Of course, there are so many different topics that we can't hope to cover them all. Our intention here is simply to provide a few illustrations of how the learning strategies can be applied. We hope that these examples will help you to apply the learning strategies when you encounter difficult learning situations.

The first topic will illustrate the application of the structuring and context strategies.

Learning Categories In Zoology

Suppose that you wanted (or needed) to learn material like the zoological phyla, classes, and orders with associated properties and examples, as shown in Table 2.

At first sight, the strange and complex names of the categories may seem a terrible barrier to learning. In fact, if we use them in the right way, the names become a key to a great deal of knowledge we already have stored—knowledge that can be connected to the new material to help us in learning it.

On the right-hand side of Table 2 are the roots of the category names. Some of them, like "cnida" and "echino" are unfamiliar to most of us, but many are parts of words we are already familiar with, e.g., *proto*type, pyro*canthus* (fire thorn), *arth*ritis, *den*tist, etc. These roots should be easy to learn because we can connect them to knowledge we already have.

When we know the meanings of the roots, the category name gives us a thumbnail description of the animals in the category. Since mollus means "soft," Mollusca seems a very reasonable name for clams and oysters. We can imagine what the Acanthocephali (Acantho = Thorny, Cephali = Heads) will look like, and we can guess that lobsters might well be Arthropoda (Artho = Jointed, Poda = Feet)

One of the most important facts about categories in zoology is that they are hierarchically organized, as shown in Figure 4. We could learn the categories without paying attention to the hierarchy, but learning would be more difficult and much less meaningful. For example, a person who doesn't understand the hierarchical organization can't figure out that birds are more closely related to reptiles than to sponges.

The structure shown in Table 2 reflects several important principles of zoology. For example, the phyla are organized by a principle of complexity. The simplest of the phylas, the Protozoa, consist of single cells. The next level of complexity involves multicellular phyla like Porifera and Cnidaria which have tissues but no organs. More complex phyla have organ systems of varying degrees of elaborateness.

A second organizing principle for the phyla is the principle of encephalization. By encephalization, we mean an increasing importance of the head. As we progress from unorganized blobs to people, we find an increasing preference for head-first motion, with an increasing concentration of sensory systems and neural centers at the head end. Simple phyla like Protozoa and Cnidaria show little encephalization. We find increasing encephalization with increasing complexity as we move from Platyhelminthes to Annelida to Chordata.

Other organizing principles for the categories in Table 2 involve changes in specific organ systems. Changes in the digestive tract provide one of the most fundamental of the organizing schemes for the phyla. The two least complex phyla, Protozoa and Porifera, have no digestive tract at all. The most complex of the phyla, the Molluscs, Annelids, Arthropods, Echinoderms, and Chordates, have well-developed digestive systems with a true coelum. A true coelum is a space

Table 2. Zoological Categories

	Name	Example	Meaning
Phylum	**Protozoa**	amoeba	proto (primitive, original) + zoa (animal)
	Porifera	sponge	poros (passage, pore) + ferre (to bear)
	Cnidaria	jellyfish	cnida (nettle, stinging cell)
	Platyhelminthes	flatworms	platy (flat) + helminthes (worm)
	Acanthocephala		acantho (thorny) + cephalus (head)
	Mollusca	clam	mollus (soft)
	Annelida	earth worm	annulus (ring)
	Arthropoda	spiders, crabs	arthro (jointed) + poda (legs)
	Echinodermata	starfish	echino (spiny) + dermus (skin)
	Chordata (Vertebrates)	cat, people	chorda (string, cord)
Class	**Agnatha**	lampreys	a (no) + gnathos (jaw)
	Placodermi	(extinct)	placo (plates) + dermus (skin)
	Osteichthyes	salmon	ostio (bony) + ichthyes (fish)
	Chondrichthyes	sharks, rays	chondro (cartilage) + ichthyes (fish)
	Amphibia	frogs	amphi (on both sides, around)
	Reptilia	reptiles	reptilia (from repere; to crawl)
	Aves	birds	avis (bird)
	Mammalia	mammals	mamma (breast)
Order	**Monotremata**	duck-billed platypus	mono (one) + trema (hole)
	Marsupialia	opossum, kangaroo	marsupium (little bag)
	Insectivora	shrew	insectum + vorare (to devour)
	Dermoptera	flying lemurs	dermus (skin) + pteron (wing)
	Chiroptera	bats	chirus (hard) + pteron (wing)
	Edentata	anteaters, sloths	e (without) + dentum (teeth)
	Proboscoidia	elephants	proboscis

188

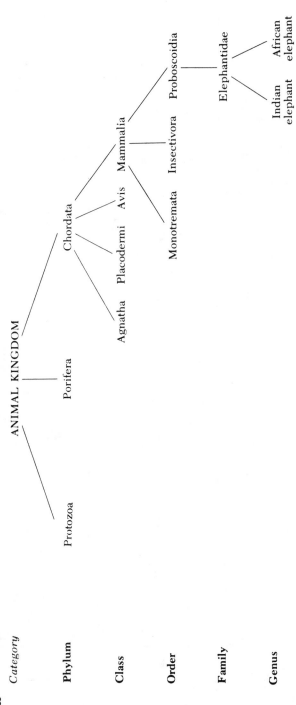

Figure 4. Hierarchical Organization of Zoological Categories

separating the digestive tract from the body wall which is lined with special tissue called peritoneum. Cnidaria and Platyhelminthes, which are a step above the sponges in complexity, have a digestive tract but no coelum. The Acanthocephala, which lie between the Platyhelminthes and the Molluscs, have a pseudocoelum—that is, a space which is like a coelum but which is not lined with peritoneum.

In the same way that the digestive system provides grouping and ordering for the phyla, the circulatory system provides groupings and ordering for the classes of vertebrates. Fish have two-chambered hearts, amphibians have three-chambered hearts, and reptiles, birds, and mammals have four-chambered hearts.

In general, the various organizing principles such as encephalization and complexity order the categories in ways that are consistent with each other and with an overall principle of evolutionary development.

In zoology, then, understanding the structure of the categories is closely related to understanding the science itself.

To see that the learning strategies really help to learn zoology, consider this example. Suppose you were to hear that the imaginary phylum "Platypoda" was considered the immediate evolutionary descendant of the Annelida. You would know immediately that the members of the phylum are characterized by flat feet; that they are moderately complex, with well-developed organ systems, a definite head-to-tail orientation, and a digestive system with a true coelum. That is really quite a lot of information to get from a name and a position in an ordering.

These learning strategies are very important in biological sciences, medicine, geology, chemistry, and many other areas of knowledge.

LEARNING MATHEMATICAL FORUMULAS

Suppose that you have an assignment that requires you to learn formulas of the sort typically found in physics or engineering texts. There are a number of procedures you can use to make this task easier and more meaningful. We will describe one which makes use of the multiple coding and context strategies.

Physical Interpretation of Equations

One of the most powerful procedures for learning and understanding equations is the process of physical interpretation. By physical interpretation we mean the process in which people make use of knowledge of a physical situation, perhaps in the form of sketches or visual images, to help them understand or learn an equation.

One way we can use physical interpretation is to help us remember whether a quantity should be placed in the numerator or denominator of an equation.

Before describing how this works, let me mention a property of equations which the math haters in the audience may either have forgotten or never learned in the first place. Consider this arbitrary equation:

$$X = \frac{(A \cdot B) + C}{(D + E)F}$$

How does X change with A, B, C, D, E, and F?
The fact I want you to notice is that

1. X gets *bigger* as A, B, and C get bigger *because those quantities* are in the numerator, and
2. X gets *smaller* as D, E, and F get bigger *because those three quantities* are in the denominator.

Now, suppose that you wanted to remember the equation for the force of gravity between two objects. You know that the force, F, is equal to some combination of G, a constant, M_1 and M_2, the masses of the objects, and r, the distance between them. You think it might be

a. $F = GM_1M_2r^2$ or

b. $F = \dfrac{GM_1M_2}{r^2}$ or perhaps

c. $F = \dfrac{Gr^2}{M_1M_2}$

Physical interpretation might involve imagining ourselves floating in space holding two large globes apart. If either of the globes were very heavy, we would expect that it would be harder to hold them apart that if both were light. Since force increases as either of the masses (M's) increases, the masses must be in the numerator. (Why?)

As we push the globes farther apart, the force of attraction between them will decrease as the force of attraction between two magnets decreases as we pull them apart. Since force decreases as distance, r, increases, r must be in the denominator. (Why?)

Of the three equations above, only (b), $F = \dfrac{GM_1M_2}{r^2}$, satisfies these relations. It is, in fact, the correct equation.

A slightly more complex example involves the equation for the capacity of a condenser:

$$C = \frac{kA}{4\pi D}$$

A condenser is a device for storing an electrical charge. It consists of two metal plates placed close to each other but not touching, as shown in Figure 5. A condenser works, that is, stores electricity, more easily than say, the average doorknob, for two reasons:

1. Charges of the same sign repel each other and they repel more strongly the closer they are. Therefore, it is more difficult to put a charge onto a plate with a small area, where the electrons are crowded, than onto a plate with a large area where the electrons can spread out.

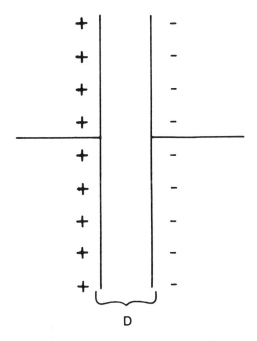

Figure 5. A Diagram of a Condenser

2. Charges of opposite sign attract each other, and they attract more strongly
   the closer they are. The fact that the opposite charges are close together
   in a condenser means that there is an attractive force holding the charge
   on the condenser which in part counteracts the forces by which the charges
   of the same kind on each plate repel each other. Now, back to the equation:

$$C = \frac{kA}{4\pi D}$$

The capacity of the condenser, C, is a measure of how easy it is to place a given
charge on the condenser. A is the area of the plates and D is the distance between
them. (k is a constant which varies with the material between the places and won't
concern us here.) It is clear from what we have said above that capacity must
increase as the area of the plates increases and as the distance between the plates
decreases. A therefore must be in the numerator of the equation and D in the
denominator.

Physical interpretation can also help us learn the values of constants in equations. Consider the equation for the volume of a sphere:

$$V = \frac{4}{3} \pi r^3$$

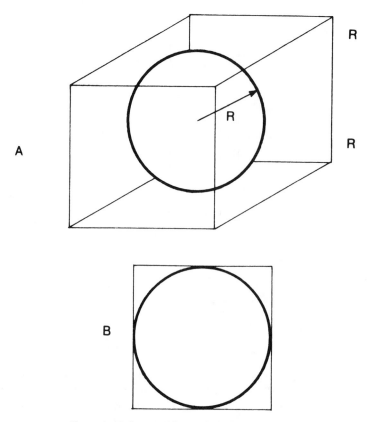

Figure 6. Sphere Inside a Cube from Two Angles

In the constant $4/3\pi$ reasonable? To estimate what the constant ought to be, imagine that the sphere is inside a cube just 2r on a side, as shown in Figure 6. The sphere just touches the cube at a few points. There is a fair amount of empty space between the sphere and the cube. We might estimate that half of the space inside the cube is occupied by the sphere. Now, since the side of the cube is 2r, its volume is

$$(2r)^3 = 8r^3$$

Therefore, we estimate that the volume of the sphere is roughly half of that, or

$$4r^3$$

Now since π is approximately 3, $4/3\pi$ is approximately 4, which is about right. In the same way, considering the equation for the surface area of the sphere,

$$A = 4\pi r^2$$

we can ask whether or not the constant 4π is reasonable. To estimate the correct value, imagine a square 2r on a side into which the sphere will just fit, as shown in Figure 7. This square has an area of

$$(2r)^2 = 4r^2$$

Now imagine trying to cover the sphere with the square. By noting that one square won't cover even a half of the sphere, we might estimate that it will take about three squares to cover the sphere. The total area, then, would be about

$$3 \text{ times } 4r^2$$

Thus, $4\pi r^2$ is about right.

The method of physical interpretation works well for estimating many constants. Try to apply it in the following exercises.

Exercises

1. Use physical interpretation to show that the constants in the following equations are about right.

$$C = 2\pi r$$

where C is the circumference of a circle and r is its radius.

$$V = 1/3\pi \ r^2 h$$

Where V is the volume of a right circular cone, r is the radius of its base, and h is its height.

Learning Cultural History

In fields like zoology and physics which have well-developed theories, it is relatively easy to find strong organizing principles to aid learning and comprehension. In the humanities, however, where theories are not as well developed, organizing principles may be harder to find. Consider the task of learning information about cultural history, that is, information about the relations of art, science, music, politics, etc., over a period of time. We can get help in organizing such material by relating it to artistic movements such as classicism or romanticism, to religious movements, such as the Reformation or the counter-Reformation, or to political events, such as the succession of the British monarchs. Often people seem to apply such organizing principles very narrowly. Thus, a person may know that baroque music preceded romantic music and that Louis XIV preceded Napoleon, but he may have no idea what sort of music was being composed during either man's reign.

In general, college students seem to have difficulty organizing people and events in time. The test shown in Table 3 was administered to the freshman class enter-

Table 3. History Test Results

	Percentage of students recognizing	Absolute average error in years
1. Bach	99%	117
2. Dante	94	195
3. Louis XIV	93	79
4. Giotto	26	109
5. Hieronymus Bosch	20	140
6. Marco Polo	99	120
7. Shakespeare	100	73
8. Napoleon	99	67
9. Elizabeth I	93	95
10. Gutenberg	64	139
11. Disraeli	58	60
12. Cromwell	86	89
13. Ben Franklin	100	13
14. Van Gogh	98	150
15. Lavoisier	40	102
16. Mozart	98	140
17. Machiavelli	77	112
18. Rembrandt	98	105
19. Darwin	99	64
20. Jane Austen	60	43
21. Wagner	70	101
22. Newton	99	133
23. Scarlatti	24	148
24. Chaucer	90	126

Timeline: 1100 — 1200 — 1800 — 1900 — 51

HISTORY TEST: INSTRUCTIONS

This is a test of your ability to identify the times of historically important people.

The test sheet contains a time line extending from 1100 AD to 1900 AD and a list of 51 names. Try to identify the time of each of the people on the list by writing the number of the person (1 for Bach, 2 for Dante, etc.) at a point on the time line which corresponds to the time at which the person was an adult. As an example, number 51, George Washington, has already been placed on the time line. Any time which falls between a person's twentieth birthday and his death will be counted as correct.

If you do not recognize a name, cross out that name. If you do recognize a name, put it some place on the time line, even if you have to guess.

No.	Name		
25.	Tintoretto	20	155
26.	Henry VIII	100	91
27.	Copernicus	91	163
28.	Delacroix	38	125
29.	Galileo	96	175
30.	Milton	71	126
31.	Martin Luther	98	120
32.	Gainsborough	41	104
33.	Debussy	65	141
34.	Vermeer	37	94
35.	Fielding	36	95
36.	Dostoievski	73	66
37.	Van Eyck	45	210
38.	Leonardo daVinci	98	90
39.	Beethoven	99	132
40.	Hogarth	25	128
41.	Richard the Lionhearted	94	176
42.	Tennyson	87	127
43.	El Greco	70	122
44.	Marie Antoinette	96	115
45.	Goya	60	126
46.	Descartes	83	143
47.	Byron	77	93
48.	Calvin	86	119
49.	Jonathan Swift	82	68
50.	Thomas Aquinas	67	207
51.	George Washington		

Time line: 1300 1400 1500 1600 1700

195

ing Carnegie-Mellon's College of Humanities and Social Sciences in September, 1973.

How did the humanities freshmen do? First, everyone recognized the name of Benjamin Franklin. Furthermore, nearly three-quarters were able to place him accurately on the time scale. Other historic persons who were universally recognized were Shakespeare, Henry VIII, Bach, Napoleon, Newton, Darwin, and Beethoven. However, the average error in placing people on the time scale was in excess of a century—and this was just for people recognized. More than a quarter of the students did not recognize the names Byron, Milton, Wagner, El Greco, and Debussy, and more than 75 percent failed to recognize Scarlatti and Tintoretto.

The judgments reveal a curious "time warp" in the students' perception of history. Famous composers as a group are placed about 140 years early and famous scientists are placed about 130 years early. In contrast, political and religious leaders are placed about 45 years late.

The magnitude of the warp suggests that there is something faulty in the student's perception of his culture. After all, a slippage of six or seven generations makes some very surprising contemporaries. For example, the average judgments make Debussy and Franklin contemporaneous, and they make Newton a few years older than Henry VIII.

One approach to structuring a body of knowledge such as this is to provide a set of landmarks. In learning our way around a city, we typically make use of tall buildings, parks, or other distinctive features to keep us oriented to the overall plan of the city (Lynch, 1960). In the same way, we can provide ourselves with landmarks for learning cultural history. The matrix shown in Table 4 is a framework of landmarks for learning the relations of art, science, and politics between 1400 and 1900. It is organized by time and by field. In constructing the matrix we divided time into 50-year intervals and defined six major fields. For each time interval, we tried to find a notable individual in each field who made his most important contribution during that time interval. Thus, Mozart was chosen as a composer active between 1750 and 1800 and Galileo, as a scientist active between 1600 and 1650. While the 50-year interval provides only a rather crude specification of time, we believe that students using the matrix should be able to make time estimates which are considerably more accurate than the students we tested who were in error on the average by more than a century.

The work involved in learning a matrix such as that shown in Table 4 is considerable. To make the task of learning it a bit easier and more palatable, we have provided the list of connections shown in Table 5.* These connections relate pairs of people in the matrix through an easy-to-remember bit of biographical information. For example, knowing that Voltaire's mistress translated Newton's works into French makes it easier to remember that the time of Voltaire closely followed that of Newton.

The matrix provides a framework for relating people and events in cultural history and the connections are an aid in learning the matrix. Once the matrix

---

*Because of its length, Table 5 has been placed at the end of this chapter, followed by Table 6.

has been learned it can help us to organize knowledge we have which is not contained in the matrix. Most of us have at least some information that can be related to the matrix. For example, we may know that Marie Antoinette knew Mozart as a child or that she was beheaded in the French Revolution. We may know that the British chemist Priestly was involved in a controversy with Lavoisier. These facts would allow us to identify these people as figures of the late 1700's and as contemporaries of Kant and Goethe. Further, knowing the matrix can help us to relate new information to what we already know. When we hear, for example, that the great plague which killed more than 15 percent of the population of London occurred in 1695, we realize that it could have killed both Purcell and Newton.

The technique of using a matrix of landmarks can, of course, be applied to other areas of history such as American history, music history (Table 6), and literary history. It can also be applied to topics in which time is not an important dimension, as in learning one's way about a city.

Summary

We have described seven basic learning strategies, each of which can provide us considerable help in learning. These are:

1. The structuring strategy
2. The context strategy
3. Monitoring
4. Inferencing
5. Instantiation
6. Multiple coding, and
7. Attention management.

We have described four study systems that combine several basic learning strategies in organized approaches to study. The systems we described are:

1. The Survey Q3R system,
2. Dansereau's MURDER system,
3. Jones et al.'s mastery learning system, and
4. Perkins' "knowledge as design" system.

Finally, we described three applications of the learning strategies to hard cases:

1. Learning zoological categories,
2. Learning formulas in physics, and
3. Learning cultural history.

Table 4. A History Matrix

	Music (M)	Religion (R) Philosophy	Science (S)	Literature (L)	Art (A)	Politics (P) Wars
1400	John Dunstable 1369-1453	Nicolas of Cusa 1401-1464	Gutenberg 1398-1468	Death of Chaucer 1400	Fra Angelico 1400-1455	Joan of Arc 1412-1431
1450	Josquin Des Prez 1440-1521	Torquemada 1420-1498	Columbus 1451-1506		Leonardo da Vinci 1452-1519	Lorenzo de' Medici 1449-1492
1500	Thomas Tallis 1505-1585	Martin Luther 1483-1546	Copernicus 1473-1543	Thomas More 1478-1535	Michelangelo 1475-1564	Henry VIII 1491-1547
1550	Palestrina 1525-1594	Giordano Bruno 1547-1600	Gilbert 1540-1603	Shakespeare 1564-1616	El Greco 1548-1614	Elizabeth I 1533-1603
1600	Monteverde 1567-1643	Rene Descartes 1596-1650	Galileo 1564-1642	John Milton 1608-1674	Rembrandt 1606-1669	Oliver Cromwell 1599-1658
1650	Henry Purcell 1659-1695	Benedict Spinoza 1632-1704	Newton 1642-1727	Restoration Comedy	Vermeer 1632-1675	Louis XIV 1638-1715
1700	J. S. Bach 1685-1750	George Berkeley 1685-1753	Benjamin Franklin 1706-1790	Voltaire 1694-1754	Hogarth 1697-1764	Peter the Great 1672-1725
1750	W. A. Mozart 1756-1791	Emanuel Kant 1724-1804	Lavoisier 1743-1794	Goethe 1749-1832	Jacques David 1748-1825	American and French Revolutions
1800	L. Beethoven 1770-1827	J. S. Mill 1806-1873	Faraday 1791-1867	Balzac 1799-1850	Joseph Turner 1775-1851	Napoleon 1769-1821
1850	Tchaikovsky 1840-1893	Karl Marx 1818-1883	Charles Darwin 1809-1882	Tolstoy 1828-1910	Vincent Van Gogh 1853-1890	Queen Victoria 1819-1901
1900						

REFERENCES

Ausubel, D. P. "The Use of Advance Organizers in the Learning and Retention of Meaningful Verbal Material." *Journal of Educational Psychology*, *51*, 267–272, 1960

Barlett, B. J. *Top-level Structure as an Organizational Strategy for Recall of Classroom Text*. Doctoral Dissertation, Arizona State University, 1978.

Dansereau, D. F., McDonald, B. A., Collins, K. W., Garland, J., Holley, C. E., Diekhoff, G. M., and Evans, S. H. "Evaluation of a Learning Strategy System." In *Cognitive and Affective Learning Strategies*, edited by H. F. O'Neil, Jr., and C. D. Spielberger. New York: Academic Press, Inc., 1979.

Flower, L. S., Hayes, J. R., and Swarts, H. *Revising Functional Documents: The Scenario Principle*. Technical Report No. 10, Carnegie-Mellon Document Design Project, Pittsburgh, March, 1980.

Goldman, R., and Hudson, D. A. "A Multivariate Analysis of Academic Abilities and Strategies for Successful and Unsuccessful College Students in Different Major Fields." *Journal of Educational Psychology*, *65*, 364–370, 1973.

Jones, B. F., Monsaas, J. A., and Katims, M. "Improving Reading Comprehension: Embedding Diverse Learning Strategies Within a Mastery Learning Instructional Format." Paper presented at the Annual Meeting of the American Educational Research Association, San Francisco, April, 1979.

Lunch, K. *The Image of the City*. Cambridge: Technology Press, 1960.

Meyer, B. J. F., and Freedle, R. *The Effects of Different Discourse Types on Recall*. Princeton: Educational Testing Service, 1978.

Perkins, D. N. (1986). *Knowledge as Design*. Hillsdale, NJ: Lawrence Erlbaum Associates.

Robinson, F. P. *Effective Study*. New York: Harper & Brothers, 1946.

Table 5. Biographical Notes

1400-1450

M   **John Dunstable**

Nationality: British
Occupation: Composer
Connection: Fought with the British armies in France against *Joan of Arc*.

R   **Cardinal Nicolas of Cusa**

Nationality: German
Occupation: Roman Catholic prelate, mathematician, and philosopher.
Connection: Suggested that the earth might move around the sun. Suggested measuring the speed of falling bodies with a water clock centuries before *Galileo* did.

S   **Johann Gutenberg**

Nationality: German
Occupation: Developed printing press with movable type. He opened the way for widespread literacy.

L   **Death of Chaucer**

Appearance of modern English.

A   **Fra Angelico**

Nationality: Italian
Occupation: Painter of church frescoes.
Connection: Frescoed the Florentine San Marco Monastery, which was reconstructed by the order of Cosimo de' Medici, father of *Lorenzo de' Medici (+1)*.

P   **Joan of Arc**

Nationality: French
Occupation: Led French army to victory against the British. Declared a witch and burned at the stake.

1450-1500

M   **Josquin Des Prez**

Nationality: French-Belgian
Occupation: Composer of the Renaissance.
Connection: *Martin Luther's* favorite composer (+1).

R   **Tomas De Torquemada**

Nationality: Spanish
Occupation: First Grand Inquisitor of Spain. Caused Jews to be exiled from Spain. Authorized torture to obtain confessions.
Connection: Confessor to Ferdinand and Isabella, who financed the voyages of *Columbus*.

Table 5. Biographical Notes—Continued

S   **Cristoforo Columbo**

Nationality: Italian-Portuguese
Occupation: Explored area now known as the West Indies.
Connection: Believed to have introduced syphilis into Europe. *Henry VIII (+1)* contracted syphilis, causing many of his children to be stillborn.

A   **Leonardo da Vinci**

Nationality: Italian
Occupation: Artist, scientist, engineer, inventor. Wrote treatises on perspective, color, anatomy, and many sciences.
Connection: Received patronage from *Lorenzo de' Medici.*

P   **Lorenzo de' Medici**

Nationality: Italian
Occupation: Leader of republican government in Florence. Had popular support, and reformed councils and improved government.

1500-1550

M   **Thomas Tallis**

Nationality: English
Occupation: One of the first composers to write church music in English. Court composer under *Henry VIII*, who named him "gentleman" of Chapel Royal.
Connections: Unsettled times due to the Reformation caused him to switch the language of his compositions, depending on the religion of the current monarch. Was granted a monopoly on printing of music and music paper by *Elizabeth I (+1)*.

R   **Martin Luther**

Nationality: German
Occupation: Ordained priest, composer. Broke away from Catholic Church, established Protestantism.
Connection: Opposed publication of the works of *Copernicus.*

S   **Nicolaus Copernicus**

Nationality: Polish
Occupation: Astronomer. Wrote *On the Revolutions of the Celestial Spheres.* Was the first to strongly propose that the earth revolves around the sun.
Connection: He was 19 when *Columbus* discovered America.

L   **Thomas More**

Nationality: British
Occupation: Author, lawyer. Wrote *Utopia.* He condemned the right of man to interpret the Scriptures freely, and thus sided with the Catholic position in the Reformation.
Connection: Friend of *Henry VIII*, under whom he served as Lord Chancellor. Refused to confirm the oath of the "Act of

201

Table 5. Biographical Notes—Continued

Succession" because it contained a repudiation of papal law.

A	Michelangelo
Nationality:	Italian
Occupation:	Painter, sculptor. Painted Sistine Chapel ceiling.
Connections:	Sculpted the tomb of *Lorenzo de' Medici* (−1). As a young man, he competed with *da Vinci* (−1) to paint a battle scene at the Palazzo Vecchio.

P	Henry VIII
Nationality:	British
Occupation:	King of England, responsible for bringing Protestantism to England.
Connections:	Defended the papacy against *Luther's* attacks. Pressured Pope Clement VII, nephew of *Lorenzo de' Medici* (−1) to accept his divorce from Catherine.

1550-1600

M	Palestrina
Nationality:	Italian .
Occupation:	Composer, master of music at the Villa d'Este.
Connection:	The music of Palestrina was in the serious, anti-secular spirit of the Counter-Reformation. His music was approved by the Council of Trent, which was formulating church discipline for the Counter-Reformation in reaction to *Luther* (−1).

R	Giordano Bruno
Nationality:	Italian
Occupation:	Renegade monk who attacked various church doctrines, including prayer.
Connection:	Was arrested by the Inquisition and burned at the stake. He was a philosopher who borrowed cosmology from Copernicus. Hardened the Church's attitude toward *Copernican* (−1) theories by connecting it with heretical doctrines.

S	William Gilbert
Nationality:	British
Occupation:	Physician and physicist who discovered basic laws of magnetism and static electricity.
Connections:	Personal physician to *Elizabeth I.* One of the first scientists openly to support the work of *Copernicus* (−1) and *Giordano Bruno.*

L	William Shakespeare
Nationality:	British
Occupation:	Famous playwright and poet who wrote both comedy and tragedy.
Connections:	Playwright of the *Elizabethan* era. Wrote a biographical play on the life of *Henry VIII* (−1).

Table 5. Biographical Notes—Continued

A   **El Greco**

Nationality: Greek

Occupation: Artist. Became a court painter in Spain.

Connection: Was a Mannerist painter, that is, one who paints in the manner of *Michelangelo (−1)*.

P   **Elizabeth I**

Nationality: British

Occupation: Queen of England.

Connection: Daughter of *Henry VIII (−1)*, who, during her reign, strengthened the British navy, enabling British to defeat the Spanish Armada.

1600-1650

M   **Claudio Monteverde**

Nationality: Italian

Occupation: Composer, music director at San Marco Cathedral, Venice.

R   **René Descartes**

Nationality: French

Occupation: Philospher, author, scientist.

Connection: He had been planning the publication of a book supporting the views of *Galileo*, but when he learned of Galileo's persecution for his views, Descartes decided against it.

S   **Galileo Galilei**

Nationality: Italian

Occupation: Scientist. Formulated laws of falling bodies and did astronomical observations supporting the work of *Copernicus*.

Connections: Admired the work *De Magnete* of *William Gilbert (−1)*. Discovered a principle of inertia, but credit is usually given to *Descartes*, since Galileo did not fully develop it.

L   **John Milton**

Nationality: British

Occupation: Author. Wrote *Paradise Lost*.

Connections: Met *Galileo* in Italy. There are mentions of Galileo's telescope in *Paradise Lost*. Served as secretary to the Council of State until *Cromwell* came into power.

A   **Rembrandt van Rijn**

Nationality: Dutch

Occupation: Painter. Mastered the techniques of realism which had been developing up to that point, and used them to give expression to profound human emotion.

Connection: His painting, "The Anatomy Lesson of Dr. Tulp," was exhibited the year *Vermeer (+1)* was born.

P   **Oliver Cromwell**

Nationality: British

Occupation: Served as Commander in Chief of British troops and as

203

Table 5. Biographical Notes—Continued

| | Lord Protector to the Commonwealth of England, Scotland, and Ireland. |
| *Connection:* | His uncle, Thomas Cromwell, was Chief Minister to *Henry VIII* (−1). |

1650-1700

M	**Henry Purcell**
Nationality:	British
Occupation:	Court composer, organist and composer for London Theater.

R	**Benedict de Spinoza**
Nationality:	Portuguese-Dutch
Occupation:	Philosopher and lens-maker.
Connections:	Was offered a pension by French officers occupying Holland on the condition that he dedicate a work to *Louis XIV*. Refused the offer. Termed by *Voltaire* (+1) as "less read than famous."

S	**Sir Isaac Newton**
Nationality:	British
Occupation:	Scientist. Revolutionized physics and astronomy.
Connection:	*Voltaire's* (+1) mistress was a mathematician who translated Newton's work from Latin into French. Voltaire invented the apple story about Newton.

| **L** | **Restoration Comedy** |

A	**Jan Vermeer**
Nationality:	Dutch
Occupation:	Painter who perceived reality as a "mosaic of colored surfaces."

P	**Louis XIV**
Nationality:	French
Occupation:	King of France. Revoked freedom of worship of the French Protestants and tried to convert them by force.
Connection:	*Voltaire* (+1) wrote a biography of Louis XIV, and admired him greatly as a youth.

1700-1750

M	**Johann Sebastian Bach**
Nationality:	German
Occupation:	Composer to the court of Prince Leopold of Saxony; organist.

R	**George Berkeley**
Nationality:	Irish
Occupation:	Anglican Bishop. Wrote about the religious and economic problems of Ireland. Asserted that the scientific world

Table 5. Biographical Notes—Continued

	view encouraged atheism, which encouraged vice.
Connection:	Wrote a criticism of *Newton's* (-1) differential calculus.

S   **Benjamin Franklin**

Nationality:	American
Occupation:	Inventor, statesman, writer.
Connection:	Was an avid reader of *Voltaire.*

L   **Voltaire**

Nationality:	French
Occupation:	Author of sociological and political satire.
Connections:	Wrote a biography of *Peter the Great.* Met *George Berkeley* in England. Authored the myth of the apple falling on *Newton's* (-1) head.

A   **William Hogarth**

Nationality:	British
Occupation:	Painter of social satires.

P   **Peter the Great**

Nationality:	Russian
Occupation:	Czar of Russia.
Connection:	Opened Russia to the West.

1750-1800

M   **Wolfgang Mozart**

Nationality:	German
Occupation:	Composer of the Classical Era.
Connections:	*J. S. Bach's* (-1) youngest son became a friend of the Mozart family and influenced the music of Mozart. Mozart's patron later became *Beethoven's* ($+1$) patron.

R   **Immanuel Kant**

Nationality:	German
Occupation:	Philosopher.
Connection:	Criticized the empiricism of the British philosophers such as *Berkeley* (-1).

S   **Antoine Laurent Lavoisier**

Nationality:	French
Occupation:	Chemist. Credited with the discovery of oxygen.
Connection:	Was guillotined during the *French Revolution* on suspicion by the authorities of the revolutionary tribunal.

L   **Johann von Goethe**

Nationality:	German
Occupation:	Philosopher, astrologer. Studied anatomy and optics.
Connection:	Met *Napoleon* ($+1$) in Erfurt. Napoleon was to him a symbol of political order.

Table 5. Biographical Notes—Continued

A	Jacques Louis David
Nationality:	French
Occupation:	Painter of many famous portraits.
Connection:	Painted portrait of *Lavoisier.*

P	American and French Revolutions

1800-1850

M	Ludwig van Beethoven
Nationality:	German
Occupation:	Composer. Marked the end of the Classical Era in music and the beginning of the Romantic Era.
Connection:	Beethoven and *Goethe (−1)* met in 1812, and immediately disliked each other. Beethoven thought Goethe pompous and snobbish; Goethe thought Beethoven wild and unruly.

A	John Stuart Mill
Nationality:	British
Occupation:	Philosopher. One of the founders of the Union of Women's Suffrage Societies.

S	Michael Faraday
Nationality:	British
Occupation:	Invented the dynamo; investigated electromagnetism.
Connection:	Retired to a home given to him by *Queen Victoria (+1).*

S	Honore de Balzac
Nationality:	French
Occupation:	Author. Believed that external circumstances are unimportant in determining how a person's life develops.
Connection:	Wrote about *Napoleon;* said, "What Napoleon achieved by the sword I shall achieve by the pen."

A	Joseph Turner
Nationality:	British
Occupation:	Artist.
Connection:	Went to the Louvre in Paris to study Italian paintings which *Napoleon* captured and brought to Paris.

P	Napoleon I
Nationality:	French
Occupation:	Emperor of European empire which he conquered.
Connections:	*David (−1)* painted portraits of him as a young emperor.

1850-1900

M	Peter Ilich Tchaikovsky
Nationality:	Russian
Occupation:	Composer. Wrote highly emotional and dramatic music. Had several nervous breakdowns.

Table 5. Biographical Notes—Continued

R   **Karl Marx**

Nationality: German

Occupation: Author and philosopher. Wrote *Communist Manifesto.* Was the European correspondent to Horace Greeley's *New York Tribune.*

Connection: Was a great reader of *Balzac (−1).*

S   **Charles Darwin**

Nationality: British

Occupation: Scientist, archaeologist, botanist. Wrote *Origin of Species.*

Connection: *Karl Marx* sent Darwin an inscribed copy of *Das Kapital.*

L   **Leo Tolstoy**

Nationality: Russian

Occupation: Author. Wrote *War and Peace* and *Anna Karenina.*

Connections: Wrote about the invasion of Russia by *Napoleon (−1).* Felt that a classless society would come about through love and moral perfection rather than the philosophy of *Marx.*

A   **Vincent van Gogh**

Nationality: Dutch

Occupation: Post-impressionist painter.

P   **Queen Victoria**

Nationality: British

Occupation: Queen of England. Spent much of her reign in seclusion, lessening the influence of the monarchy on British affairs.

Connection: Napoleon III was a frequent visitor to Victoria.

Table 6. Music Matrix

	England	France	Germany	Italy
1550-1600	William Byrd 1543-1623			G. Palestrina 1525-1594
1600-1650	John Bull 1585-1640		H. Schütz 1585-1672	Claudio Monteverde 1567-1643
1650-1700	Henry Purcell 1659-1695	M. A. Charpentier 1634-1704	J. Pachelbel 1653-1706	A. Corelli 1653-1713
1700-1750	John Gay 1685-1732	J. P. Rameau 1683-1764	J. S. Bach 1685-1750	D. Scarlatti 1685-1757
1750-1800	William Boyce 1710-1779	C. W. Gluck 1714-1787	W. A. Mozart 1756-1792	L. Boccherini 1743-1805
1800-1850		H. Berlioz 1803-1869	L. Beethoven 1770-1827	G. Rossini 1792-1868
1850-1900	Arthur Sullivan 1842-1900	C. Frank 1822-1890	J. Brahms 1833-1897	G. Verdi 1813-1901

III

DECISION MAKING

8

Getting The Facts Straight:
Making Decisions In A Complex World

What should we have for breakfast this morning? What should we wear? Do we have time for another cup of coffee? We can't get through the day without making many small decisions about such practical questions. These decisions are minor ones, but some decisions—choosing a job, college, a business partner—are extremely important. Decision making is a frequent and important human activity. Since most people would agree that this is true, it is puzzling that few of us reflect very often or very deeply about the nature of our decision-making processes, or how they might be improved. Some reflect so little that they are surprised by the idea that they use decision-making processes at all. It never occurs to them that there are alternative decision processes and that they can choose among them.

Decisions are not all of one kind. Procedures for making one decision—for example, buying a home—may be entirely inappropriate for making another decision—for example, what poker bet to make.

In this chapter and the next one we will describe four general types of decisions which require different decision procedures:

1. Decisions under certainty
2. Decisions under risk
3. Decisions under uncertainty
4. Decisions under conflict

This chapter will concentrate on decisions under certainty. In Chapter 9, we will discuss decisions under risk, uncertainty, and conflict.

DECISIONS UNDER CERTAINTY

Imagine that you are searching for an apartment. You have found four, all of which have the same rent—a rent that you can afford. Your task is to rank the apartments in the order of your preference from 1 for best through 4 for the worst. The properties that you should consider important for this decision are shown in Table 1.

Do the problem before proceeding:

rank:	*apartment number:*
1 (best)	
2	
3	
4 (worst)	

Table 1. Student Apartments

	A1		A2
brightness:	always needs artificial lighting	size of rooms:	cramped
		noise level:	usually quiet
cleanliness:	needs vacuuming	general repairs:	needs no repairs
kitchen:	new stove, sink, and refrigerator	brightness:	very bright throughout the day
noise level:	frequently noisy	cleanliness:	needs vacuuming
size of rooms:	average	landlord attitude:	cordial
general repair:	needs no repairs		
distance from place of employment:	15 minutes	distance from place of employment:	60 minutes
landlord attitude:	indifferent	kitchen:	stove, sink, and refrigerator in good condition

	A3		A4
distance from place of employment:	20 minutes	general repair:	needs no repairs
brightness:	fairly bright	brightness:	very bright
landlord attitude:	very friendly	noise level:	often quiet
cleanliness:	ready to move in	size of rooms:	small
kitchen:	stove, sink, and refrigerator old but useable	distance from place of employment:	45 minutes
noise level:	sometimes noisy	kitchen:	stove and refrigerator in good condition
general repair:	needs one week repair work	landlord attitude:	cordial
size of rooms:	comfortable	cleanliness:	ready to move in

Now fill out this chart from the information given in Table 2.

rank: 1 (best)	apartment number:
2	
3	
4 (worst)	

Table 2. Student Apartments

	B1		B2
distance from place of employment:	20 minutes	size of rooms:	small
brightness:	fairly bright	cleanliness:	ready to move in
cleanliness:	ready to move in	brightness:	very bright
landlord attitude:	very friendly	kitchen:	stove and refrigerator in good condition
noise level:	sometimes noisy	general repair:	needs no repairs
kitchen:	stove, sink, and refrigerator old but useable	landlord attitude:	cordial
size of rooms:	comfortable	noise level:	often quiet
general repair:	needs one week	distance from place of employment:	45 minutes

	B3		B4
general repair:	needs no repairs	distance from place of employment:	15 minutes
kitchen:	stove, sink, and refrigerator in good condition	landlord attitude:	indifferent
size of rooms:	cramped	general repair:	needs no repairs
cleanliness:	needs vacuuming	room size:	average
landlord attitude:	cordial	noise level:	frequently noisy
noise level:	usually quiet	kitchen:	new stove, sink, and refrigerator
distance from place of employment:	60 minutes	cleanliness:	needs vacuuming
brightness:	very bright throughout the day	brightness:	always needs artificial lighting

Many people fail to notice that these two problems are really the same. That is, apartment A1 has exactly the same properties as apartment B4 in Table 2; A2 matches B3; A3 matches B1; and A4 matches B2. Now check to see if you have ranked the matching apartments in the same way. If half of your rankings were the same in the two problems, you did as well as the average of a group of 20 faculty members at Carnegie-Mellon University. The purpose of working through examples such as these is to illustrate the sad fact that our decision-making performance is typically imperfect, even in decision-making tasks of a rather familiar sort. Below we will discuss further evidence of the shortcomings of people as decision makers. There is ample room for improvement in human decision making.

In presenting problems in this chapter, we will specify the alternatives from which the decision makers choose, as well as the properties of the alternatives that should be considered in making the decision, such as the size of the rooms and cleanliness, in the above problem. However, in real life, decisions usually don't present themselves in such neat form. More often, the decision maker must actively search out alternatives and evaluate their properties to find those important enough to be considered in making the decision.

We will begin our exploration of decision processes by examining five different methods which are useful for making decisions under certainty. The first four methods are *optimization* methods—that is, they attempt to identify the very best alternative available. The fifth method, *satisficing*, simply looks for the first satisfactory alternative.

OPTIMIZING METHODS

Dominance

Dominance is the simplest of the decision procedures we will discuss. To use it in making decisions, we must first find the dominance relations among the alternatives. One alternative dominates another if both of the following conditions are satisfied:

1. It is *at least as good* as the other on all properties, and
2. It is better on *at least one* property.

Any alternative that is dominated by another is dropped from consideration. Any alternative that dominates all the others is chosen as best.

Now let's apply the dominance procedure to the apartment problem. Table 3 summarizes the information about the four apartments in Table 1. Do any of the alternatives dominate any of the others?

Only one alternative dominates another in this problem: Alternative 4 dominates

Alternative 2. Alternative 4 is as good as Alternative 2 in "kitchen," "general repair," "noise level," "brightness," and "landlord," and it is better in "distance," "size," and "cleanliness." Alternative 1 does not dominate Alternative 2 because, while it is better in some properties, such as "distance," it is worse in others.

Strengths and Weaknesses of the Dominance Method

Dominance is not a very powerful decision-making method because, as the example above illustrates, it usually doesn't eliminate very many of the alternatives. The advantage of the method is that people can agree about which alternatives are dominant. They can do this, even though they may differ about what properties are most important for making the decision. Thus, Jones may feel that the kitchen is the most important property of an apartment while his wife believes that distance from work is most important. Despite these differences, they will agree that Alternative 4 dominates Alternative 2. We can rely on results obtained by the dominance method because, even if we change our minds about how important the various properties are, the dominance relations will be unchanged.

The dominance method is easy to apply, and its results are reliable. Therefore, it can be of value when used to screen some alternatives from consideration before other decision methods are applied to the problem. Any alternative that is dominated by any other may safely be dropped from further consideration since it will never be judged the best alternative by any reasonable decision procedure.

A caution. The most common error people make in using this procedure is failure to apply the definition of dominance strictly. Suppose that Mary scores 100 in math, science, English, history, French, and gym to Fred's zero in all of those subjects, but that Fred gets 96 in stenography, while Mary scores only 95. Clearly Mary is a far better student than Fred, but her grades do not dominate Fred's. The single exception in stenography is enough to spoil the dominance relation.

Exercises

1. If Alternative *A* dominates Alternative *B* and Alternative *B* dominates Alternative *C*, must Alternative *A* dominate Alternative *C*?
2. Use the dominance method to compare the academic performance of the people listed on page 217.
3. Use the dominance method with the data above to compare difficulty of the courses.

The Lexicographic Method

The lexicographic method is so-named because of its resemblance to the proce-

Table 3. Alternatives

Properties	1	2	3	4
Distance in Minutes	15 Min	60 Min	20 Min	45 Min
Size of Rooms	Average	Cramped	Comfortable	Small
Kitchen	New stove, etc.	Stove, etc. in good condition	Stove, etc. old but useable	Stove, etc. in good condition
General Repair	Needs no Repair	Needs no Repair	Needs one Week work	Needs no Repair
Cleanliness	Needs Vacuuming	Needs Vacuuming	Ready to Move in	Ready to Move in
Noise Level	Frequently Noisy	Often Quiet	Sometimes Noisy	Often Quiet
Brightness	Always needs artificial light	Very Bright	Fairly Bright	Very Bright
Landlord	Indifferent	Cordial	Very Friendly	Cordial

Grades

	Al	Betty	Charles	Dorothy	Ellie	Frank
Chemistry	86	90	91	91	84	91
Physics	43	95	90	90	91	90
Calculus	71	99	92	98	97	95
Art	88	88	83	86	87	83
English	61	84	86	88	78	86

dure for ordering words in the dictionary. To decide which of two words comes first, one looks at the first letter. If the two words have the same first letter, then one decides on the basis of the second letter, and so on. In the lexicographic method, one looks first at the most important property. If two alternatives have the same value on this property, then one decides on the basis of the second most important property, and so on.

With the lexicographic method, we must specify the order of importance of the properties of the alternatives. For example, we might order the properties of the apartments as they are shown in Table 3 with distance as the most important property, room size next, and so on. We should be aware that other decision makers might choose to order the properties differently and as a result arrive at different decisions.

To make a decision by this method, consider the most important property first. If one alternative is better than the other alternatives on the most important property, then that alternative is the one chosen. For example, in Table 3, Alternative 1 is chosen because it is better than all of the other apartments in the most important property—distance.

If two or more alternatives are tied on the most important property, then drop the other alternatives from consideration and consider the next most important property in order to break ties. If any ties remain unbroken, then consider the third property, and so on. In Table 3, if the distance for Alternative 1 were 20 minutes rather than 15, Alternatives 1 and 3 would have been tied and we would have dropped Alternatives 2 and 4 from further consideration. We would then have compared Alternatives 1 and 3 on the second most important property—room size—and chosen Alternative 3, since it has larger rooms than Alternative 1.

Notice what would happen if the order of importance of the properties were reversed, that is, if landlord were the most important property, brightness next, and so on. Alternatives 2 and 4 would be tied for the best landlord. These two alternatives are also tied on brightness and noise level. The tie is finally broken in favor of Alternative 4 by the difference in cleanliness. Changing the order of importance of the properties does not always change the alternative chosen as best, but in this case it clearly has.

Exercises

Use the lexicographic method to identify the best student in the previous exercise. Assume that the order of importance of the courses from most to least is:

1. Chemistry, Physics, Calculus, Art, English
2. Art, English, Calculus, Physics, Chemistry

Strengths and Weaknesses of the Lexicographic Method

The lexicographic method is most appropriate when one of the properties out-weighs all of the others in importance. Its major strength under these circumstances is that it is quick and easy to apply. The method is least appropriate when the properties are roughly equal in importance. Under these circumstances the method may lead us to choose an alternative which has a slight advantage in the most important property, even though that advantage is outweighed by big disadvantages in other properties. This happens because the lexicographic method typically ignores all but the most important property.

Additive Weighting

The additive-weighting method takes all of the properties into account but does not give them equal weight. The more important properties receive heavy weights and the less important ones lighter weights.

To use the additive-weighting method, one must have numbers both for weights of the properties and for the values of the properties. For example, in Table 4 we have provided numerical weights for the properties in the right-hand column: 7 for distance, 4 for size of rooms, etc. We have also provided numbers from 1 to 5 for the various values of each of the properties. These are shown in Table 4 in parentheses to the right of each property value. The numerical value 4 is assigned for the 15-minute distance indicating a relatively high or "good" value. The numerical value 1 is assigned to the 60-minute distance, indicating a low or "poor" value. The numbers for the weights and values of the properties are intended to reflect the importance of the properties and property values to the decision maker. Typically, decision makers will differ somewhat in the importance they place on the various properties and value. For example, a tenant who is handy with tools may put a relatively low value on *general repair*, whereas one who is all thumbs may find it much more important. In the same way, a person may not care about the landlord's attitude as long as he isn't actively hostile. Thus, he might want to assign the same numerical value to *indifferent* and *cordial*.

To make a decision by the additive-weighting method, multiply numerical values of the properties by the weights of the properties for each alternative. Then choose the alternative with the largest sum as "best." In Table 4, the products of value and weight are shown in the lower part of each cell. The product for distance for Alternative 1 is the weight 7 multiplied by the value 4, or 28. Alternative 1 has the largest sum of products, 75, and is therefore chosen as the best alternative by the additive-weighting method.

Table 4. Alternative Apartments

Properties	1	2	3	4	Weight
Distance in Minutes	15 Min (4)	60 Min (1)	20 Min (3)	45 Min (2)	7
	28	7	21	14	
Size of Rooms	Average (3)	Cramped (1)	Comfortable (4)	Small (2)	4
	12	4	16	8	
Kitchen	New stove, etc. (5)	Stove, etc. in good condition (4)	Stove, etc. old but useable (3)	Stove, etc. in good condition (4)	3
	15	12	9	12	
General Repair	Needs no Repair (5)	Needs no Repair (5)	Needs one Week work (2)	Needs no Repair (5)	2
	10	10	4	10	

(Continued)

219

Table 4. Alternative Apartments—Continued

Cleanliness	Needs Vacuuming (4) 4	Needs Vacuuming (4) 4	Ready to Move in (5) 5	Ready to Move in (5) 1 5
Noise Level	Frequently Noisy (2) 2	Often quiet (4) 4	Sometimes Noisy (3) 3	Often quiet (4) 1 4
Brightness	Always needs artificial light (1) 1	Very Bright (5) 5	Fairly Bright (3) 3	Very Bright (5) 1 5
Landlord	Indifferent (3) 3	Cordial (5) 5	Very Friendly (4) 4	Cordial (5) 1 5
Sum of Value X Weight	75	51	65	63

Exercises

Apply the additive-weighting procedure to the following problems:

1. Which would be the best apartment in Table 3 if all of the weights were equal?
2. If the weights for the subjects in Exercise 1 were Chemistry 4, Physics 4, Calculus 5, Art 2, and English 3, who would be the best student?
3. If the weights for the subjects were Chemistry 2, Physics 2, Calculus 4, Art 5, and English 4, who would be the best student?
4. You are at the Humane society choosing among three dogs; Spot, Fido and Reginald. The table shows your values for each dog for each of four attributes together with the weight for each attribute.

	Spot	Fido	Reginald	Weight
Appearance	5	3	2	2
Friendliness	4	3	4	5
Health	3	5	3	3
Size	3	4	4	4

Assume that 5 is best and 1 is worst. Choose the best dog by:

a. Lexicography
b. Additive weighting

Does any of the dogs dominate any of the others?

Strengths and Weaknesses of the Additive Weighting Method

The additive-weighting method takes all of the properties into account in making the decision, but it doesn't take the interactions of the properties into account. When we say that two properties interact, we mean that the importance we assign to a value of one property depends on the value whch other properties happen to have. For example, the importance we place on the friendliness of the landlord may depend on the condition of the apartment. If the apartment needs a great deal of repair, it may be very important that the landlord is friendly.

The additive-weighting method can lead to inappropriate decisions by ignoring these interactions, just as the lexicographic method can lead to inappropriate decisions by ignoring the less important properties. However, ignoring these interactions is not really a very serious problem in most cases. This fact is illustrated in the following example, suggested by Yntema and Torgerson's (1961) analysis of decisions.

Suppose that you are a scoutmaster and that you have the task of awarding merit badges to your numerous charges at the end of the year. The realities of life have forced you to concentrate on just three of the 10 boy scout virtues this year: helpfulness, cleanliness, and honesty. During the year, you have given each scout a grade from 1 (low) to 7 (high) for his performance on each of these three virtues. The problem, now, is who gets the badges.

You and the assistant scoutmaster agree that the three virtues are equally important. The assistant suggests that it would be easy to make the decision by additive weighting. "After all," he points out, "if the weights are all equal, we can let them all be 1." Then Merit, M, will just be equal to

1 · helpfulness score + 1 · cleanliness score + 1 · honesty score

or

M = helpfulness + cleanliness + honesty,

or

M = he + cl + ho

He is delighted, but you are worried. You know your troop, and you know that the virtues interact with each other. For example, there was that dirty little kid, Snyder, who was really helpful in the library, but he got the books so dirty that they had to be burned. Helpfulness and honesty interact too. Remember Gionelli, who helped lots of old men across the street and then picked their pockets? In your wisdom you know that the merit contributed by each virtue depends on the values of the other virtues. You know that true merit is measured by this formula:

$$\text{True Merit} = (\text{He} \cdot \text{Cl}) + (\text{Cl} \cdot \text{Ho}) + (\text{Ho} \cdot \text{He})$$

Now that's a lot different from

$$M = \text{He} + \text{Cl} + \text{Ho!}$$

Nevertheless, your assistant seems quite untroubled when you tell him these hard facts of life. "It's true," he says, "those virtues really interact very strongly, but that doesn't mean that the additive-weighting scheme is going to cause us to make lots of mistakes. What we are trying to do is to order the scouts according to their true merit. We make a mistake only when a higher merit scout gets a lower additive-weighting score than a lower merit scout." That is,

if $M_1 > M_2$ (the additive-weighting scores)

but (True Merit)$_2$ > (True Merit)$_1$

Torgerson and Yntema argue that in ordinary circumstances this doesn't happen very much. Suppose we were to select two scouts at random and suppose further that the scouts spread themselves out evenly on the virtue scale. That is, a scout is just as likely to score a 1 on cleanliness or honesty as 2 or 4 or 7. If the true merit of one scout is 6 units greater than the other (which happens 86 percent of the time), Torgerson and Yntema calculate that the additive weighting score, M, will also be greater for the more virtuous scout in 99.5 percent of cases.

What about the remaining 14 percent of cases in which the difference in true merit is less than 6? The additive-weighting procedure can't do worse than chance, so it should get as a minimum an additional seven percent of the decisions right. Thus, even though it ignores interactions, the additive-weighting procedure makes the right choice in at least 93 percent (86% + 7%) of cases in a problem with strong interaction. Further, it tends not to make bad errors. That is, in cases where there is a big difference in true value between the alternatives, the additive-weighting method almost always makes the right decision. We can conclude that the additive-weighting method, even though it ignores interactions, is a reasonably good decision method in general. In particular, it should do a good job for us in assigning merit badges.

The major drawback of the additive-weighting method is that it is time consuming. Obtaining the numbers for the weights and values of the properties is probably the most difficult part of the method. In some cases, these numbers can be derived from objective considerations, such as the posted prices of cars or the caloric content of various foods. In other cases, they must be obtained through subjective estimation. In using the additive-weighting method for Apartments 1, 2, 3, and 4 (Table 4), we had to make eight estimates of property weights and 40 estimates of propert values.

Once the necessary numbers have been obtained, a few minutes worth of multiplying and adding still must be done to find the best choice. All things considered, the additive-weighting method may require between half an hour and an hour to complete. This is likely more time than you would want to spend choosing your dessert in the lunch line. However, it may well be worth spending that amount of time if the decision is an important or expensive one, such as the choice of a graduate school or a new car.

Effectiveness Indices

In some cases, it is important to take into account the interactions which the additive-weighting model ignores. This may happen either because the interactions are especially strong or because errors in decisions are very costly, or both. Both are true in certain medical situations in which the patient must receive two kinds of medication simultaneously. Some pairs of drugs have effects in combination which neither of them has alone. That is, the drugs interact with each other. In some cases, these interactions are life-threatening and must be taken into account in choosing appropriate dosage levels. For cases of this sort, we need a decision method more complex than additive weighting, which will take the interactions into account. We will use the term *effectiveness index* to designate all such "more complex" methods. Often such methods will involve a physical, chemical, or engineering model based on extensive analysis of the situation about which we are making decisions. Designing and implementing such a method may be very expensive indeed.

We will not ask the reader to construct any effectiveness indices. Our purpose in discussing effectiveness indices is simply to point out that when it is very important to get the best decisions, it is possible, though often expensive, to do better than the models we discussed above.

SATISFICING: A NON-OPTIMIZING APPROACH

Decision-making situations that we meet in daily experience are often a good deal messier than the idealized situations we have described above. Perhaps the most important complication we encounter is that, rather than being presented with a predefined list to choose from, we may be forced to search for alternatives. For example, when a teacher assigns a "free" theme, the student's task of deciding what to write about will require that he generate a list of possible topics. Similarly, when a college wants to find a new dean, a search committee is appointed to identify a list of candidates to be considered.

Generating alternatives, examining their properties, and choosing among the alternatives are all activities that may add considerable cost to the decision-making process. In the problem of searching for a dean, these costs include the salaries of the search-committee members and the travel costs of candidates invited from other cities. If the list of candidates that the search committee generates is very large, the costs may also be large. If the search committee takes five years and generates 100,000 names, clearly decision making is going to be very expensive. The decision-making technique described below can be helpful in practical situations where such costs must be considered.

The decision methods we have discussed so far are all optimizing methods, that is, methods designed to find the best available alternative. In this section, we will discuss quite a different approach to decision making called *satisficing*, first described by Simon (1955). This method is *not* designed to identify the best alternative. Rather it is designed to find the *first satisfactory* alternative.

The satisficing method requires the decision maker to identify the worst value he is willing to accept for each of the attributes. He then considers all of the alternatives in order, rejecting any alternatives which fall below the minimal values of the attributes, and accepting the *first* alternative which meets all of the minimal values.

Considering Table 3, suppose that the decision maker's minimal values are:

distance:	45 minutes
room size:	small
kitchen:	useable
repair:	two weeks' repair
cleanliness:	needs some cleaning
noise:	sometimes noisy

brightness: fairly bright

landlord: indifferent

Alternative 1 fails to meet the minimum values for noise level and brightness, and Alternative 2 fails to meet the minimum value for distance and room size. Alternative 3, however, meets all of the minimal requirements and is therefore chosen. Notice that Alternative 4 also meets the minimal requirements but was not chosen or even considered because search was terminated when the first satisfactory alternative was found.

Exercises

1. In the example above, what would be the result if the decision maker insisted in addition to the other minimum requirements that the apartment need no repair? That the stove be new?
2. Use the satisficing method with the data on page 150 to
   a. Find a good all-around student—one who can score 85 in all subjects.
   b. Find a good science student—one who can score 90 or better in math and science.

Strengths and Weaknesses of the Satisficing Method

The satisficing method is particularly useful when we have to choose among a very large number of alternatives and it is not essential to find the best. For example, when we are choosing a dozen apples from a supermarket bin, we don't try to find the 12 best apples. We can't be bothered with examining and comparing all of the apples in the bin. We simply pick the first 12 acceptable apples and go on to use the satisficing method for selecting pepperoni, kiwi fruit, or whatever else we may need. Similarly, in the dean-search task, it is economical to stop the search as soon as a satisfactory candidate is found.

Table 5. Decision Making Methods

Method	Type	Use this method:	Cost of computation required	Number of alternatives examined
Dominance	optimizing	for preliminary screening of alternatives	low	all
Lexicography	optimizing	when attributes are very different in weight	very low	all

(Continued)

Table 5
(Continued)

Method	Type	Use this	Cost of computation required	Number of alternatives examined
Additive Weighting	optimizing	when it is important to find the best alternative	high	all
Effectiveness Index	optimizing	when it is *very* important to get best alternative	very high	all
Satisficing	non-optimizing	when the cost of examining the whole set of alternatives is very high	very low	some

The primary advantage of the satisficing method is that it can yield a satisfactory decision without requiring us to examine all of the alternatives. Thus, compared to optimization methods, it can greatly reduce the cost of search in decision making.

The satisficing method may not yield a decision at all if we set our standards too high. For example, in writing we may find ourselves blocked because we are searching for the perfect word to express our meaning when none may exist. Diogenes seems to have encountered this sort of difficulty in his search for an honest man. As a practical matter what usually happens when we run into difficulty in finding a satisfactory apartment or car or employee is that we change our minds about what is minimally acceptable and set a new but, alas, lower standard.

Table 5 summarizes the properties of the decision-making pocedures described above.

EXPERIMENTAL STUDIES OF DECISION MAKING UNDER CERTAINTY

Do formal decision methods help? The correct choice in any decision situation depends on the decision makers' individual values. If two people make different choices in the same situation, it doesn't mean that one of them is wrong: it may just be that they have different values. This means that we can't tell how good people's decision-making processes are by the choice they make. How then can we measure improvement in decision-making skills?

No matter what people's values are, if they use good decision methods, they should tend to agree with themselves when they make the same decision twice. To test for improvement in decision making, then, we measured self-agreement of students making apartment decisions (see Tables 1 and 2) both before and after they had studied the methods described in this chapter. Of the 71 students tested, 49 were more consistent on posttest than pretest, 14 were less consistent, and eight were unchanged. These results indicate a very reliable improvement in consistency for the group as a result of training in formal decision methods.

INFORMATION-PROCESSING LIMITS IN DECISION MAKING

Often when we are making an important decision, such as what college to attend or where to spend our vacation, we make an effort to get as much information as possible about each of the alternatives. Implicit in this effort is our assumption that more relevant information about the alternatives will enable us to make better decisions. A study by Hayes (1962) indicates that this assumption isn't necessarily true if the decision maker is *not* using a formal decision procedure.

Hayes studied military personnel making decisions about a simulated air-defense situation. The alternatives were characterized by eight equally important relevant properties. For some decisions, information was available about only two of the properties. For other decisions, it was available for four, six, or all eight of the properties. In all cases, the correctness of a decision was scored on the basis of the "real-world situation" measured by all eight properties, whether the decision maker had seen all of them or not.

The surprising result was that the decision makers made just as good decisions when they were given two relevant facts as when they were given four, six, or eight. The subjects must have been deriving useful information from the extra facts, though, because when irrelevant facts rather than relevant ones were added, the decisions became distinctly worse. These results suggest that extra relevant facts both help and hurt. They add extra information, but they also confuse the decision maker. Comparing several alternatives simultaneously on four or more properties appears to be a very difficult task for most people to do in their heads. Decision methods such as lexicography and additive weighting are useful because they allow people to substitute reliable objective procedures for unreliable subjective ones.

REFERENCES

Hayes, J. R. *Human Data Processing Limits in Decision Making.* Technical Documentary Report No. ESD-TDR-62-48. Bedford, MA: Operational Applications Laboratory, July, 1962.

Simon, H. A. "A Behavioral Model of Rational Choice." *Quarterly Journal of Economics, 69*, 99–118, 1955.
Yntema, D. B., and Torgerson, W. S. *Man-Computer Cooperation in Decisions Requiring Common Sense.* IRE Transactions, TGHFE, HFE-2, 20–26, 1961.

PROBLEM SOLUTIONS

Page 215

1. Yes.
2. Betty dominates Al and Ellie
   Dorothy and Frank Dominate Charles
   Dorothy dominates Frank
3. Chemistry dominates (is less difficult than) English
   Calculus dominates physics and English

Page 218

1. Dorothy
2. Betty

Page 221

1. Alternative 4
2. Betty
3. Betty
4a. by lexicography: Reginald
4b. by additive weighting: Fido

None of the dogs dominates any other.

Page 225

1. no repair—alternative 4
   new stove—No satisfactory alternative.
2. a. Dorothy
   b. Betty

9

The Luck of the Draw:
Dealing with Chance in Decision Making

In making decisions under certainty, our task is to figure out which of the alternatives we like best. When we make a choice, we assume that we will get the alternative we want. If we tell the car sales dealer, ''I'll take the yellow Mazda,'' we expect to get it. If they deliver a blue paisley Fiat instead, we would likely be very upset.

BUT, I ORDERED A YELLOW MAZDA !

In this chapter, we will discuss decisions of quite a different sort: What you want *may* be what you get, but then again it may *not*. That is, we will study decisions in which some event not under your control intervenes between your choice and its outcome.

Consider my decision to run for President, for example. It is true that the campaign would cost many millions of dollars, but the job is really a nice one. It provides free housing and, unlike many other jobs, allows one to make State of the Union addresses and be Commander-in-Chief of the armed forces.

Now, even though I'd like the job, I've decided not to invest my millions because I know that this is not a decision under certainty. Even if I were to invest my millions, I would not be *certain* of getting the job. Between my investment and the job lies an election which might not necessarily go my way. In fact, some former friends suggested that my chances are so poor that I would in effect be giving my money away.

My decision then depends not just on finding the alternative I want most, but also on the events intervening between choice and outcome.

Intervening events may be of three different sorts: chance events to which we can assign a probability, such as the flipping of a coin; chance events to which we can't assign a probability, such as the eruption of Mt. St. Helen; and events under the control of an opponent who is trying to beat us, such as the moves of our opponent in a chess game. These three sorts of intervening events correspond to the three types of decisions we will discuss in this chapter: decisions under risk, decisions under uncertainty, and decisions under conflict. Here are examples of each of these three types of decisions:

Risk

Gambling decisions are typical of decisions under risk. In roulette, for example, the gambler chooses a number on which to bet, say, 17. Then a chance event, the position at which a metal ball comes to rest on the roulette wheel, determines the outcome of the gambler's choice. If the ball stops on 17, he wins; otherwise, he loses.

An essential feature of decisions under risk is that we can calculate a probability for the effect of the chance event. In roulette, for example, we know that there are 38 places at which the ball is equally likely to stop. The probability of getting 17, then, is just $\frac{1}{38}$.*

Uncertainty

Like decisions under risk, decisions under uncertainty involve a chance factor. The unique feature of decisions under uncertainty is that we can't calculate a probability for the effect of the chance event. Buying a Christmas present for Aunt Emma, for example, is a decision under uncertainty, if her tastes (the chance factor) are unknown to us.

---

*Appendix II provides an elementary introduction to probability. If you are not familiar with the concept of probability, read Appendix II before proceeding.

For most of us, deciding whether to go on a picnic when the weather looks threatening is making a decision under uncertainty. We know that it may rain, but we don't know enough about weather forecasting to calculate the probability that it will rain. We can change the decision from one under uncertainty to one under risk if we ask the weather bureau to tell us the probability of rain.

Conflict

Decisions under conflict are common in competitive games, like chess and tennis, and in business and war. When you choose a move in chess, or a strategy in tennis, you know that your opponent will do his best to counter your move or foil your strategy.

Each decision type requires a different approach. In decisions under certainty, the main difficulty is deciding which alternative is best. In decisions under risk and uncertainty, the big problem is dealing with the effects of chance; and in decisions under conflict, it is taking account of the hostile action of our opponent. The relations between choice and outcome for all four decision types are diagrammed in Figure 1.

DECISIONS UNDER RISK

Suppose that you have several hundred spare dollars in your pocket and that you are given the choice of playing the following two games as many times as you like. Both games involve tossing a fair coin.

Game 1: You win $2.00 whether the coin comes up heads or tails.

Game 2: You win $10.00 if the coin comes up heads and lose $5.00 if it comes up tails.

Which game should you prefer to play?

One widely recommended technique for making risky decisions like this one is to choose the action which has the greatest *expected value*. The expected value of an action is the average payoff value we can expect if we repeat the action many times.

The average payoff in Game 1 is easy to compute. Since you win $2.00 whether the coin comes up heads or tails, the average payoff has to be $2.00. In Game 2, where the payoffs aren't equal, we can compute the average payoff, or expected value, using the following formula:

1. Expected Value = average payoff = probability of a head ×
payoff for heads +
probability of a tail ×
payoff for tails

or symbolically

$$EV = P(H) \cdot V(H) + P(T) \cdot V(T)$$

where V(H) and V(T) are the values of the payoff for heads and tails.

Since the games involve a fair coin, P(H) and P(T) both equal one-half. The expected value for Game 2, then, is

$$
\begin{aligned}
EV &= \frac{1}{2} (\$10.00) + \frac{1}{2} (-\$5.00) \\
&= \$5.00 - \$2.50 \\
&= \$2.50
\end{aligned}
$$

Notice that this same formula works for Game 1, where

$$
\begin{aligned}
EV \text{ (Game 1)} &= \frac{1}{2} (\$2.00) + \frac{1}{2} (\$2.00) \\
&= \$1.00 + \$1.00 \\
&= \$2.00
\end{aligned}
$$

Since the expected value of Game 2 is greater than the expected value of Game 1, we should choose Game 2 in order to maximize our expected value.

Another Example

Suppose that you are the producer for the local theater company. Long experience has taught you that musicals bring in a lot of money, $10,000, if they succeed, but 80% of the time they fail and, due to high production costs, lose an average of $2,000. Comedies, on the other hand, bring in much less when they succeed, $3,000, but they succeed more frequently, 50% of the time, and lose less—$1,000—when they flop. You are planning a developmental program for your theater, and must decide either on a series of musicals or a series of comedies. Which choice will maximize expected value for your theater?

$$
\begin{aligned}
EV \text{ (musical)} &= 0.2 \times \$10,000 + 0.8 \times -\$2,000 \\
&= \$2,000 - \$1,600 \\
&= + \$400 \\
EV \text{ (comedy)} &= 0.5 \times \$3,000 + 0.5 \times -\$1,000 \\
&= \$1,500 - \$500 \\
&= + \$1,000
\end{aligned}
$$

To maximize expected value, you should choose the series of comedies.

In many situations, we have to deal with more than two possible outcomes. For example, with a single die, we can roll any number from one through six, and with two dice, any number from two through twelve. To compute expected

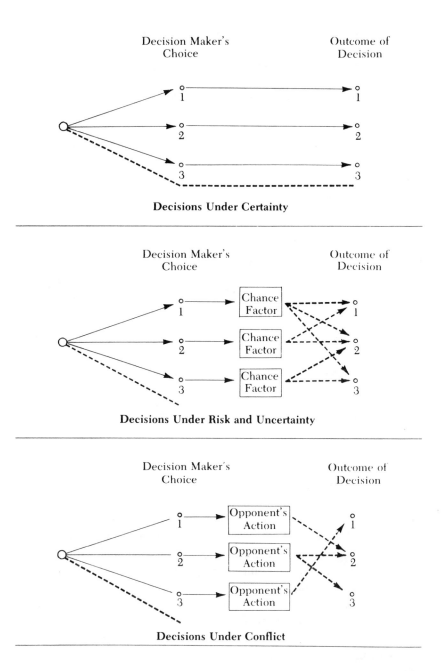

Figure 1. Relations Between Choice and Outcome for the Four Decision Types

values in such cases, we have to expand Equation 1 as follows:

2. $EV = P(1) \cdot V(1) + P(2) \cdot V(2) + P(3) \cdot V(3) + \ldots + P(N) \cdot V(N)$

That is, in a situation with N possible outcomes, the expected value (EV) is simply the probability of each outcome times the value of that outcome added up over all of the possible outcomes.

We can use Equation 2 to compute the expected value for Game 3.

Game 3. Rolling a single die, you win $6.00 if you get a one, $5.00 if you get a two, etc.

For this game, the probability of each outcome is one-sixth, since each of the six numbers has equal probability and the expected value is

$$EV \text{ (Game 3)} = \tfrac{1}{6}(\$6.00) + \tfrac{1}{6}(\$5.00) + \tfrac{1}{6}(\$4.00) + \tfrac{1}{6}(\$3.00) + \tfrac{1}{6}(\$2.00) + \tfrac{1}{6}(\$1.00)$$

$$= \frac{(\$6.00 + \$5.00 + \$4.00 + \$3.00 + \$2.00 + \$1.00)}{6}$$

$$= \frac{\$21.00}{6}$$

$$= \$3.50$$

Since the expected value of Game 3 is greater than the expected values of either Game 1 or Game 2, your should prefer to play Game 3 to the other games in order to maximize expected value.

Exercises

Find the expected value for the following games:

1. If a fair coin comes up heads, you win $1.00; otherwise you lose $1.00.
2. If you roll one die and get a six you win $5.00; otherwise you lose $1.00.
3. On a roulette wheel there are 36 numbered positions and two house positions. If the ball stops on your number, you get your dollar back plus $35.00. Otherwise you lose your dollar.
4. You get $6.00 if you roll a seven on a pair of dice and you lose $1.00 if you roll any other number.*
5. You get $35.00 if you roll a 12 on a pair of dice and you lose $1.00 if you roll any other number.

---

*When rolling two dice, the outcomes from 2 through 12 are not equally likely. If you don't know how to find out what the probabilities are, consult the Appendix on Probabilities.

**Best choice.

DECISIONS UNDER UNCERTAINTY

Sailing, swimming, or tennis?

Suppose that you have to make plans one summer evening whether to play tennis or to go sailing or swimming the next day. The weather forecast is "sunny" but says nothing about winds. You have no idea whether it will be windy or not. Preparations have to be made now, so you can't wait till tommorrow to see what the winds will be like. You know that if the winds are good, sailing will be excellent, but not tennis. If it's not windy, though, sailing will be hot and dull. On the other hand, swimming will be chilly and uncomfortable if it is windy, but perfect if it isn't. To help with the decision you prepare a table like that shown in Table 1. The alternative actions that we are trying to decide among are shown in the rows of the table and the uncertain states of nature which affect the outcomes of these actions are shown as columns. The values of the various outcomes are indicated by the numbers in the cells.

Table 1. Values of Activities in Two Kinds of Weather

	Windy	Calm	Row Minima
Sailing	10	−5	−5
Swimming	−2	8	−2**
Tennis	−3	4	−3

Filtering out Alternatives

Whatever strategy we decide to use in approaching decision problems, it is wise to make a habit of determining if any of the alternatives is dominated by any other alternative and could therefore be eliminated. From Table 1 we can see that swimming dominates tennis because for every state of nature the outcome for swimming is better than the outcome for tennis. The next section will describe four strategies that we can use to determine whether sailing or swimming is the best choice.

FOUR STRATEGIES

We will describe four strategies for making decisions under uncertainty: the mini-max strategy, the maxi-max strategy, the Hurwicz strategy, and the mini-max regret strategy. We will use each of these strategies to arrive at a decision in the sailing-swimming dilemma.

The Mini-max Strategy

This strategy, first described by von Neumann (see Von Neumann and Morgenstern, 1944), is a very conservative, pessimistic strategy which assumes that whatever action we choose, nature is against us and will cause the worst possible outcome. Thus, if we decide to go sailing, the strategy makes the gloomy assumption that the winds will be calm. On the other hand, if we decide to go swimming, then the strategy assumes that the weather will be windy. The values of these worst outcomes, the row minima, are shown in the right-hand column of Table 1.

The mini-max strategy calls for choosing the action that gives us the best (largest) of these minima. That is, it chooses the action whose worst possible outcome is not as bad as the worst possible outcomes of the other actions. Thus, since the worst possible outcome for sailing is -5 and the worst possible outcome for swimming is -2, the mini-max strategy chooses swimming. (Remember, tennis was eliminated because it was dominated by swimming.)

The mini-max strategy has the nice property that it guarantees an outcome which is no worse than the minimum value for the action. The outcome may be better than that minimum, but it will certainly be no worse. However, this strategy, which focuses on preventing disaster, has the unfortunate property that it may eliminate the best outcomes from consideration.

The Maxi-max Strategy

A more adventurous approach to making decisions is to use the maxi-max strategy. This is an optimistic strategy which assumes that nature will cooperate with us to provide the best possible outcome for the action we choose. The values of these best possible outcomes, the row maxima, are shown in the right-hand column of Table 2. The maxi-max strategy chooses the action which yields the best of the best possible outcomes. In this case, it chooses sailing. This strategy has the nice property of guaranteeing you a chance of obtaining the best possible outcome. However, it does not defend you against the possibility that you may obtain the worst possible outcome, as does the mini-max strategy.

Table 2. Values of Two Activities in Two Kinds of Weather

	Windy	Calm	Row Maxima
Sailing	10	-5	10*
Swimming	-2	8	8

The Hurwicz Strategy

This strategy (Hurwicz, 1953) allows a compromise—depending on how optimistic you feel—between the very pessimistic mini-max strategy and the very optimistic maxi-max strategy. To use the Hurwicz strategy, select a value between 0 and 1 for the coefficient of optimism, A. Low values of A, such as 0.1 or 0.2, are pessimistic and reflect a belief that bad things are more likely to happen. High values, such as 0.8 or 0.9, are optimistic. Let's assume that we are being slightly pessimistic and choose A = 0.4. Find *both* the row minima and the row maxima as shown in Table 3.

Table 3. Computations for the Hurwicz Strategy

	Windy	Calm	Row Max.	Row Min.	Weighted Min. & Max.
Sailing	10	−5	10	−5	1
Swimming	−2	8	8	−2	2*

For each row we compute

$$A(Max.) + (1 - A)Min.$$

Thus for sailing we get

$$.4(10) + .6(-5)$$
$$= 4 - 3$$
$$= 1.0$$

For swimming we get

$$.4(8) + .6(-2)$$
$$= 3.2 - 1.2$$
$$= 2.0$$

Now choose the activity which yields the maximum of these computed quantities. In this case, the choice is swimming. Notice that when A is zero, the Hurwicz strategy is the same as the mini-max strategy; when A is 1, the Hurwicz strategy is the same as the maxi-max strategy.

Another Example

Three brothers—Manny, Moe, and Jack—own a bakery. Since the bakery has been making a profit, the brothers decide to invest their surplus. Four investment possibilities occur to them:

1. Expanding facilities to increase bread production
2. Adding a line of pastries
3. Investing in the stock market
4. Starting a bread delivery service.

The brothers recognize that the expected return on their investment will depend on the state of the economy. Table 4 summarizes their estimates of the percent return to be expected for each alternative under various states of the economy.

The brothers can agree to eliminate the delivery service alternative since it is dominated by two of the other alternatives. However, they can't agree on which

---

*Best choice.

Table 4. Percent Return on Four Investments in Three States of the Economy

	Better	Same	Worse	Max.	Min.	Hurwicz
More bread	20	10	2	20	2	11*
Pastries	30	12	-10	30*	-10	10
Stocks	8	6	4	8	4*	6
Delivery	10	4	-20			

of the remaining three alternatives is best because Manny is very conservative, Jack is wildly optimistic, and Moe is a little of each. Since Manny is conservative, he applies the mini-max strategy and decides that the safe and sane thing to do is to invest in stocks. Jack, with visions of a giant industry dancing in his head, applies the maxi-max strategy and decides that making pastries is the route to wealth and power. Moe, whose optimism coefficient is 0.5, applies the Hurwicz strategy and decides that their best option is to increase bread production.

Difficulties with Expected Values

While maximizing expected values seems to be a very reasonable way to make decisions in many cases, there are some situations in which it yields answers that violate our intuitions, answers that just seem wrong. For example, suppose that you had the opportunity to choose between the following offers: either you will receive one million dollars for certain or, depending on the flip of a fair coin, you will receive four million dollars or nothing. In this situation, I would much prefer to take the offer of one million dollars for certain even though the expected value of the other offer is twice as great (the reader should check the difference in expected value, if it isn't clear.) Many others have indicatd that they would make the same choice I have made in this hypothetical situation.

Let's consider a more practical sort of decision—whether or not to buy insurance. Now, we all know that insurance companies make money. The expected value of an insurance policy, then, is positive for the insurance company, but negative for the insured person. Yet many people, perhaps most, choose to buy insurance, and that decision can't be regarded as an error. People are willing to accept a small but certain loss—the payment of the insurance premium—to avoid the risk of a very large loss due to accident or death, even though the expected value of the insurance policy is negative.

Finally, let's consider the problem of lotteries: Here again, we know that people who run them do so to earn money. Though the expected value of buying a lottery ticket is negative, many people buy them week after week.

Why does the expected value technique fail in these cases? Expected values are *averages* of values. They are very appropriate when we are trying to balance values that are close together, e.g., the chance of losing five dollars versus the chance of winning ten. Averages are much less appropriate, though, when we balance values that are very different, such as the cost of a modest insurance pay-

---
*Best choice.

ment versus the risk of being impoverished by a serious car accident, or the dollar price of a lottery ticket versus a prize which would allow us to quit our dull old job and move to Tahiti.

In the four-million-dollar gamble, you were asked to balance the chance of nothing versus the certainty of a $1 million fortune. Most choose the fortune. But suppose you were guaranteed that the gamble would be offered to you 20 times in a row. In this case, most people switch back to maximizing expected values and go for the four million dollars each time. Why? Because with 20 chances, the risk of being left with nothing practically goes away—absorbed by the law of large numbers. Now the choice is between *two* life-changing alternatives and the difference between them is subjectively much smaller than the difference between one million and zero. After all, if it is hard for us to imagine what it would be like to have a million, it is even harder to imagine the difference between one million and four million.

The decision strategy described in the next section may be better designed than maximizing expected value to handle decisions of this sort.

Minimizing Maximum Regret

A decision procedure which works very well for those cases in which expected value fails is the strategy of minimizing maximum regret (MMR). Here regret means pretty much what you would expect. Imagine that you have decided to go sailing and that the wind is calm. There you are at sea—hot, sweaty, and regretting that you didn't go swimming. We can take the difference between the value of the outcome you actually obtained and the maximum value you could have obtained if you had chosen a different alternative as a measure of regret. We can form a regret matrix for the sailing-swimming decision by computing regret for each possible outcome, as shown in Table 5. For example, if it turns out to be windy and we chose sailing, our regret is 0. However, if it is windy and we chose swimming, our regret is 12, the difference between what we could have gotten, 10, and what we actually got, -2. The maximum regret for each action is shown in the right-hand column. If we are to minimize regret in this case, we must choose swimming. Table 6 shows the regret matrix for the bakery problem. Increasing bread production is the action which minimizes maximum regret.

The MMR strategy can be applied to two problems which presented some difficulties for the expected value strategy. These are the Insurance and the Lottery problems. Table 7 shows the payoff and regret matrices for an Auto Insurance Problem, and Table 8 for the Lottery Problem. Using the MMR strategy we would decide both to buy insurance and to be on the lottery.

Exercises

Use the Hurwicz strategy with A values of 0.0, 0.2, 0.4, 0.6, 0.8, and 1.0, and mini-max regret to find the best alternatives for each of the following payoff matrices:

1.   *State of Nature*

	1	2	3	4
A	20	12	8	4
B	26	10	4	−4
C	10	8	7	5

Alternatives

2.   *State of Nature*

	1	2	3
A	1	2	5
B	6	0	3
C	3	2	2
D	4	−1	3

Alternatives

JUDGMENTAL PROBABILITIES

We have made a sharp distinction between decisions under risk, in which we can compute probabilities, and decisions under uncertainty, in which we cannot. Actually, there is a broad range of cases between these two extremes in which, while we can't calculate probabilities precisely, we can estimate them with varying degrees of accuracy. We will call these probability estimates "judgmental probabilities."

The Accuracy of Judgmental Probabilities

People can be quite good at making probability estimates in certain simple situations. For example, in an experiment by Robinson (1964) where people were exposed to a sequence of lights which flashed on the left and the right, they were very accurate in estimating the probability that a flash would be on the left or the right. About two-thirds of the subjects' judgments fell within ±.10 of the true proportions. Further, given long experience, people can make good probability estimates even in complex situations. Peterson et al (1979) and Murphy and Winkler (1974) showed that experienced meteorologists were very good at estimating the probability that the temperature would fall within a specified range. While people in the situations described above were very accurate in estimating probabilities, we should emphasize that people's probability estimates are not universally good. Their success depends on having appropriate information—obtained either through immediate perception or long experience. When people are asked to make judgments about topics in which they are not expert, they may do very poorly. For example, Alpert and Raiffa (1969) asked subjects questions of the following kind: "How many foreign cars were imported into the United States in 1968?

Table 5. Payoff and Regret Matrices for the Sailing-Swimming Problem

| | Payoff Matrix | | Regret Matrix | | |
	Windy	Calm	Windy	Calm	Maximum Regret
Sailing	10	−5	0	13	13
Swimming	−2	8	12	0	12*

Table 6. Payoff and Regret Matrices for the Bakery Problem

| | Payoff Matrix | | | Regret Matrix | | | |
| | Economy | | | Economy | | | |
	Better	Same	Worse	Better	Same	Worse	Maximum Regret
Bread	20	10	2	10	2	2	10*
Pastries	30	12	−10	0	0	14	14
Stocks	8	6	4	22	6	0	22

Table 7. Payoff and Regret Matrices for an Auto Insurance Problem

| | Payoff Matrix | | Regret Matrix | | |
	No Accident	Accident	No Accident	Accident	Maximum Regret
Insure	−5	−5	5	0	5*
Don't Insure	0	−100	0	95	95

Table 8. Payoff and Regret Matrices for the Lottery Problem

| | Payoff Matrix | | Regret Matrix | | |
| | State of World | | State of World | | |
	Lose	Win	Lose	Win	Maximum Regret
Bet	−10	100	10	0	10*
Don't Bet	0	0	0	100	100

*Best choice.

a. Make a high estimate such that you feel there is only a one percent probability the true answer would exceed your estimate.

b. Make a low estimate such that you feel there is only a one percent probability that the true answer would be below this estimate."

They found that in 40 to 50 percent of cases, the true answer fell outside of the
range of values specified by the subject. In short, people were terrible at making
these judgments.

Gambler's Fallacy

Even in simple situations, though, people are subject to systematic errors in
estimating probabilities. Recently a local sports commentator argued that the Oak-
land Raiders were especially likely to win the upcoming Superbowl game because of "the law of averages." He emphasized repeatedly and with considerable
assurance that since they had lost a string of Superbowl games in the recent past,
it was, by the law of averages, their turn to win. Many believe that this law of
averages is a statistical truth. In fact, this so-called law is a very common illusion—
so common that statisticians have named it the "Gambler's Fallacy."

Let's take a very clear case. Suppose we have a fair coin—that is, a coin with
a 0.5 probability of coming up heads and a 0.5 probability of coming up tails.
In a reasonable mood, which is most of the time, we would all agree that the
coin has no memory at all. It is just a metal disk. If we could imagine some way
to ask it, "On your last flip, did you come up heads or tails?" we would have
to believe its answer would be, "What flip? I don't remember any flip!!" Yet
strange things happen to us when we actually begin to flip the coin. Imagine that
the first two flips are heads, and then the third flip is a head, too. We begin to
suspect that the fourth flip will be a tail, but no—another head! What's happening?! Surely the next flip will be a tail, or at least we feel that the probability
is very high. After all, according to the law of averages it's time for a tail to
turn up. We have forgotten, of course, that the coin has no memory. It knows
nothing of the past and is behaving on the fifth flip just as it did on the first.
In both cases, the probability of a tail is 0.5. To avoid the gambler's fallacy,
we should forget the past, just as the coin does, and treat each flip as an event
independent of all previous flips.

Lindsay and Norman (1972) point out that you can use the gambler's fallacy
to earn money:

> In horse racing, this psychological tendency [the gambler's fallacy] suggests that
> you ought to bet on the favorite whenever favorites have been consistently winning
> in the previous few races. The assumption is that the other betters will operate ac-
> cording to the gambler's fallacy. They will assume it less and less likely that yet
> another favorite will win. This tendency would make the odds deviate from the ob-
> jective probabilities and thus provides the opportunity for a good bet. (p. 548)

THE DIFFICULTY OF REVISING AN OPINION

Another difficulty in using probabilities arises because people are often not very effective in using new information to modify old opinions. This ineffectiveness is illustrated clearly in a study by Phillips and Edwards (1966).

Phillips and Edwards showed their subjects a sequence of red and white poker chips drawn from a bag. The subjects knew that the bag contained either 70 red and 30 white chips, or 30 red and 70 white chips. Further, they were told that the probability that the bag was predominantly red was equal to the probability that it was predominantly white. The subjects' task was to make an estimate of the probability that the bag was predominantly red or predominantly white, after seeing each successive chip. Let's assume that the chips are being drawn from a bag of mostly red chips. Before seeing any chips, the subject estimates that the probability is about 0.50 that the bag contains mostly red chips. Typically, as he sees more and more chips, he increases his estimate of the probability that the bag is mostly red. However, he doesn't increase it nearly as fast as he ought to on the basis of the evidence. Edwards estimates that subjects get between one-half and one-fifth of the available information from each chip. What does this mean in terms of accuracy of probability estimates? In this situation, if subjects drew eight red chips and four white ones, they *should* estimate the probability of a mostly red bag at 0.964. In fact, Raiffa (1968) found that his statistics students clustered their estimates around 0.70—nearly 30 percent *too* low.

People aren't always ineffective in using new information (see, for example, Edwards, 1968). However, there are enough situations in which they *are* ineffective to suggest that some aids for revising judgments could be very helpful to decision makers. The aid which we will suggest is Bayes' Theorem.

Bayes' Theorem*

Bayes' Theorem is a procedure for revising opinions on the basis of new evidence. Suppose that we hold some opinions (hypotheses) about the state of the world. For example, if we were medical researchers we might believe that there is a 75 percent chance that a certain disease is caused by organism A (Hypothesis 1) and a 25 percent chance that it is not (Hypothesis 2). Next, we find some new evidence about our hypotheses. For example, we might receive a report that a case of the disease has been observed which does not appear to involve organism A. We now want to revise our opinions on the basis of the new evidence. In particular, we want to reduce the probability of Hypothesis 1 and increase the probability of Hypothesis 2.

To use Bayes' Theorem to do this, we need one more set of probabilities. For each hypothesis, we need to know the probability that the new evidence would have been obtained if that hypothesis were true. In the medical research example, we will need to know two probabilities: we will need to know the probabili-

---

*Many students find the sections on Bayes' Theorem difficult. They may be skipped without spoiling the continuity of the discussion.

ty of observing a case of the disease without observing organism A—first, assuming that Hypothesis 1 is true, and second, assuming that Hypothesis 2 is true. We will call these probabilities $P(E|H1)$ and $P(E|H2)$, which should be read, "the probability of the evidence given that H1 is true," and, "the probability of the evidence given that H2 is true." (The vertical bar is read as "given" or "given that.")

According to Bayes' Theorem, the new probability we ought to assign to H1 given the new evidence is

$$P(H1|E) = \frac{P(E|H1) \times P(H1)}{P(E|H1) \times P(H1) + P(E|H2) \times P(H2)}$$

where $P(H1)$ and $P(H2)$ are our original estimates of the probabilities of H1 and H2.

Now, in the medical research example, assume that there is a small probability, say, .05, that the disease could be observed without finding traces of organism A even if Hypothesis 1 is true. That, is $P(E|H1) = .05$. Assume further that there is a large probability, say, 0.90, that the disease could be observed without finding organism A if Hypothesis 2 is true, that is, $P(E|H2) = .90$. By Bayes' Theorem, our new value for the probability of H1 is

$$P(H1|E) = \frac{(.05)\,(.75)}{(.05)\,(.75) + (.90)\,(.25)}$$

$$= \frac{.0375}{.0375 + .225}$$

$$= 0.143$$

In other words, when we take the new evidence into account, our 75 percent confidence in Hypothesis 1 should be reduced drastically to 14 percent according to Bayes' Theorem.

Why use such a complex procedure to make a simple decision? The reason is that as the Phillips and Edwards study showed, people don't make very good use of new information to modify their previous opinions—they are very conservative about changing their minds. Clearly, people need some help if they are to make adequate use of new information. The computations involved in using Bayes' Theorem, while they would be a nuisance in making a trivial decision, are really well worth the effort if the decision is an important one.

The Fido Caper

Suppose that you left your dog Fido at home to guard your house so that burglars would not break in and steal the 10-pound roast that is defrosting on the counter. When you get back the locks are all in good order, so you know that no burglar has entered. However, the roast is gone. Needless to say, Fido is a prime suspect.

On the basis of past experience, two sessions with the dog psychiatrist, and a certain shifty look in his eye, you judge the probability is 0.95 that Fido did it. However, before forcing Fido to role play as the missing roast, you decide to collect one further piece of evidence. You prepare his ordinary dinner and offer it to him. To your surprise, he gobbles it up to the last crumb. Hardly what you would expect of the thief who just made a 10-pound roast disappear. You estimate that the probability that Fido would do this if he had in fact eaten the roast in only 0.02. Normally, though, he has a good appetite and eats his dinner with a probability of 0.99. How are you to revise your earlier suspicions given the evidence of the readily eaten dinner? Clearly, Bayes' Theorem can come to the rescue as follows: The probability that Fido is guilty given that he just ate his dinner is

$$P(\text{Guilty}|E) = \frac{P(E|\text{Guilty}) \times P(\text{Guilty})}{P(E|\text{Guilty}) \times P(\text{Guilty}) + P(E|\text{Innocent}) \times P(\text{Innocent})}$$

From the story, we know that

$$P(\text{Guilty}) = 0.95$$

$$P(\text{Innocent}) = 0.05$$

$$P(E|\text{Guilty}) \;=\; 0.02$$

$$P(E|\text{Innocent}) \;=\; 0.99$$

Therefore,

$$P(\text{Guilty}|E) \;=\; \frac{(0.02)\,(0.95)}{(0.02)\,(0.95) + (0.99)\,(0.05)}$$

$$=\; \frac{0.0190}{0.0190 + 0.0495}$$

$$=\; \frac{0.0190}{0.0685}$$

$$=\; .28$$

Things looked very bad for Fido before the dinner experiment. However, with the aid of Bayes' Theorem, we were able to take the results of the dinner experiment into account and conclude that Fido was probably innocent. Anyone who loves dogs can see the value of Bayes' Theorem.

The Antique Problem

One day walking past an antique store, you spot what you are certain, well, 80 percent certain, is an antique chair worth about $100. On the other hand, you recognize that there is a 20 percent chance that it is worthless. You know that the owner of the shop is reasonably competent in distinguishing antiques from junk. If it is an antique, there is only one chance in 10 that he will fail to recognize it. On the other hand, if it is junk, there is a very high probability, 0.98, that he will recognize it as junk.

You enter the store and say, "How much for that chair?" The owner says, "Five dollars." Clearly, he thinks it is junk. Using this information, determine

A. a new (Bayesian) estimate of the probability that the chair is an antique, and

B. whether you should buy it or not.

Answer to A. Hypothesis H1 is that the chair is an antique. Hypothesis H2 is that the chair is junk. The new evidence, E, is that the antique dealer thinks it's junk.

Your initial opinions are

$$P(H1) \;=\; 0.8 \text{ and } P(H2) \;=\; 0.2$$

The revised probability is

$$P(H1|E) = \frac{0.10 \times 0.80}{(0.10)\,(0.80) + (0.98)\,(0.20)}$$

$$= \frac{0.08}{0.08 + 0.196}$$

$$= \frac{0.08}{0.276}$$

$$= 0.29$$

The new evidence, then, should reduce your confidence that the chair is an antique.

Answer to B: To buy or not to buy? Now even though you are less confident that the chair is an antique, it could still be a good buy. That is, the risk may be worth the cost. Let's compute the expected value of the purchase. If it is an antique (P=0.29), then you gain $95 ($100 chair minus the $5 purchase price). If it's junk (P=0.71), you lose $5. The expected value of the purchase, then, is

$$EV = (95)\,(.29) - (5)\,(.71)$$

$$= \$27.55 - \$3.55$$

$$= \$24.00$$

If you can scrape together the five dollars, then you ought to take the risk.

How to Understand Bayes' Theorem

Just before the dinner experiment in the Fido Caper, there were four possible outcomes we would imagine, as shown in Table 9. Because these are the only possibilities, the probabilities of these four alternatives sum to 1.

Table 9. Four Possible Outcomes of the Dinner Experiment

Fido guilty and eats dinner P = .0095	Fido innocent and eats dinner P = .0495	Σ = .0590
Fido guilty and doesn't eat dinner P = .9405	Fido innocent and doesn't eat dinner P = .0005	Σ = .9410
		Σ = 1

Since Fido did eat his dinner, the dinner experiment eliminated two of these four alternatives. The eliminated alternatives are the lower two in Table 9. Since one or the other of the remaining two alternatives *must* occur, the probabilities of *these* two alternatives must now sum to 1. That is, the two alternatives whose probabilities summed to .0590 before the dinner experiment must sum to 1 after the dinner experiment. The probabilities of these alternatives must be increased as a result of the new evidence. Bayes' Theorem is just a way of increasing the probabilities so that the new value of each probability is proportional to its original value.

Exercises

1. Suppose Fido had refused his dinner. First, guess the probability that Fido was the roast thief. Next compute the probability using Bayes' theorem.
2. Suppose that a bag has a 0.5 chance of containing 70 green chips and 30 white chips, and a 0.5 chance of containing 70 white chips and 30 green chips. A green chip is drawn from the bag at random and then replaced. What is the probability now that the bag is predominantly green?
3. A second green chip is drawn at random. What is the new probability that the bag is predominantly green?

DECISIONS UNDER CONFLICT

When we play a game against nature, as in the sailing-swimming decision, we can view the mini-max strategy as a conservative one, because we don't really believe that nature is trying to arrange the worst outcomes for us. When we play a game against a human opponent, however, the mini-max strategy isn't at all conservative. We *know* our opponent is actively trying to do us in. The mini-max strategy is the only one we will use for analyzing decisions under conflict.

A Two-Person Zero-Sum Game

Giovanni and Hans, the owners of a town's only two restaurants, are naturally in competition with each other. Each can afford to try any one of a set of strategies to attract customers away from the other (see Table 10). For Giovanni there is G1, a free glass of red wine; G2, waiters who sing Verdi; and G3, half-price pizza. For Hans, there is H1, cheap beer; H2, waiters who yodel; H3, free sauerkraut; and H4, Pumpkin Streudel Night. Table 10, the payoff matrix for Giovanni, shows the percent of the total market that Giovanni can win from Hans when each chooses one of the available strategies. Positive values are good for Giovanni, and negative values are good for Hans. We assume that what Giovanni gains, Hans loses, and vice versa. That is, the sum of Giovanni's gains (or losses) and Hans' losses (or gains) is zero. Such a game, in which the sum of gains and losses added up over all players is zero, is called a *zero-sum game*.

Notice in Table 10 that Hans' strategy H4, Pumpkin Streudel Night (which holds its own only against singing waiters) is dominated by H1 and H3, which have lower scores (better for Hans) for each of Giovanni's strategies. H4 is therefore dropped. The strategies which remain after we have screened for dominance are shown in Table 11.

In Table 11, the row minima are the values of the worst outcomes (from Giovanni's point of view) for each of his strategies. The column maxima are the values of the worst outcomes (from Hans' point of view) for each of *his* strategies. The mini-max decision for Giovanni is G3, half-price pizza, and for Hans, H1, cheap beer. If Giovanni adopts strategy G3, he will pick up at least one percent of the market and he may get more if Hans deviates from his mini-max strategy. If Hans adopts strategy H1, he will lose no more than one percent of the market and he

Table 10. Payoff Matrix in the Giovanni-Hans Conflict

		Hans' Strategies			
		H1	H2	H3	H4
Giovanni's strategies	G1	0	−2	4	4
	G2	−3	3	−4	0
	G3	1	2	3	3

Table 11. Reduced Payoff Matrix

	H1	H2	H3	Row Min.
G1	0	−2	4	−2
G2	−3	3	−4	−4
G3	1	2	3	1*
Column Max.	1*	3	4	

may lose less if Giovanni deviates from his mini-max strategy. In this case, it is best for each participant to adopt a single pure stategy. Giovanni should always use G3, and Hans should always use H1. There are many cases, though, in which the participants should adopt *mixed strategies*. That is, part of the time they should take one action and part of the time another.

Mixed or Pure Strategies?

There is a simple test to determine whether a pure or a mixed strategy is best. If the maximum of the row minima (the maxi-min) equals the minimum of the column maxima (the mini-max), then a pure strategy is best. In this situation, each player does best playing the mini-max strategy. If we play our mini-max strategy, our opponents will always lose by deviating from their mini-max strategy. In the same way, if our opponents play their mini-max strategies, we will always lose by deviating from our mini-max strategy. In the payoff matrix for Giovanni and Hans (see Table 11), the maxi-min and the mini-max both equal 1. Thus, pure strategies are appropriate for this case and they guarantee that Giovanni will win at least 1 (the maxi-min) and that Hans will lose no more than 1 (the mini-max).

For the payoff matrix in Table 12, the mini-max is 1 but the maxi-min is 0. In this game, Alex should gain no less than 0 (the maxi-min), and Bert should lose no more than 1 (the mini-max). Just where the gains and losses will fall between these values will depend on how Alex and Bert play. The mini-max decision procedure we used above would select pure strategies for each participant—Alternative A2 for Alex and Alternative B1 for Bert. But notice that these strategies don't have the nice properties that the strategies chosen for Giovanni and Hans had. If Alex always chooses A2, then Bert is soon going to switch from B1 to B2 so as to lose less with each trial. To keep Bert from doing this,

Table 12. Payoff Matrix in the Alex-Bert Conflict

		Bert's Strategies		Row Min.	Payoff Difference
		B1	B2		
Alex's Strategies	A1	−1	3	−1	3−(−1)=4
	A2	1	0	0*	1−0 =1
Column Max.		1*	3		Σ=5
Payoff Difference		2	3		

*Best choice.

Alex should sometimes use A1 and sock Bert with a loss of 3 points. That is, Alex should use a mixed strategy.

In using a mixed strategy, though, just how often should Alex play A1 and how often should he play A2? There is a fairly simple procedure he can use to find the best proportions for the various strategies. First, he should find the magnitude of the difference in payoff within each row of the payoff matrix. These differences are 4 for the first row, 1 for the second, and their sum is 5. Using these numbers, Alex can now do the following calculations:

$$\text{Strategy A1: } 1 - \frac{4}{5} = \frac{1}{5}$$

$$\text{Strategy A2: } 1 - \frac{1}{5} = \frac{4}{5}$$

and conclude that he should use Strategy A1 one-fifth of the time and Strategy A2 four-fifths of the time. In the same way, Bert can use the differences in payoff in the columns to find the proportions in which he should mix his strategies. Bert calculates as follows:

$$\text{Strategy B1: } 1 - \frac{2}{5} = \frac{3}{5}$$

$$\text{Strategy B2: } 1 - \frac{3}{5} = \frac{2}{5}$$

and concludes that he should use B1 three-fifths of the time and B2 two-fifths of the time.

Each player should conceal his intended action on each trial so that he doesn't forewarn his opponent of his intended move. One way to do this is to let some random process like the throw of the die determine what one will do next.

If each player plays the optimal strategy defined by the method we just outlined, then the value of the game (the amount that Alex can expect to win or the average per game) is easy to determine.

The probability that the payoff is -1 is just the probability that Alex plays A1 and Bert plays B1, that is, $1/5 \times 3/5 = 3/25$. Making these calculations for all the cells of the payoff matrix we can find the expected value of the game as follows:

$$EV = (-1)\left(\frac{1}{5}\right)\left(\frac{3}{5}\right) + 3\left(\frac{1}{5}\right)\left(\frac{2}{5}\right) + 1\left(\frac{4}{5}\right)\left(\frac{3}{5}\right) + 0\left(\frac{4}{5}\right)\left(\frac{2}{5}\right)$$

$$= -\frac{3}{25} + \frac{6}{25} + \frac{12}{25} = \frac{15}{25} = 0.60$$

In this case, the value is 0.6—a value, as we would expect, between 0, the row max, and 1, the column min.

An interesting feature of these strategies is that the value of the game will remain the same as long as either of the players holds to his optimal strategy.

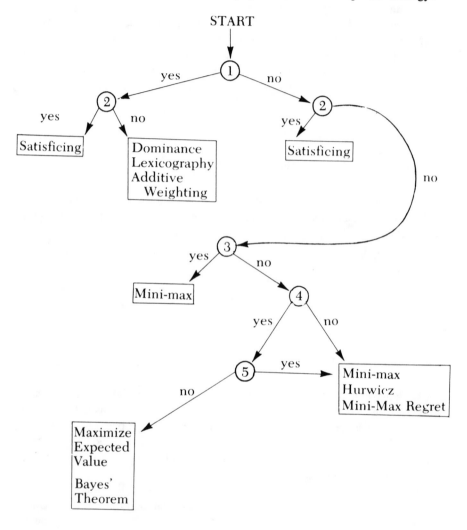

Figure 2. A Decision Tree for Choosing a Decision Procedure

A GUIDE FOR THE BEWILDERED DECISION MAKER

In this and the previous chapter, we have described a number of decision procedures applicable in a variety of situations. Figure 2, a decision tree, can help you find the decision procedure that is appropriate to a specific situation. By answering the following questions, you can work through the decision tree:

1. Is this a decision under certainty?
2. Does it involve costly search?
3. Is this a decision under conflict?
4. Can you estimate the relevant probabilities with reasonable accuracy?
5. Does the decision involve catastrophic outcomes?

Exercises

1. Find the expected value of the following game: You roll two dice. If you get a double, e.g., 1 and 2, and 2, etc. you win ten dollars. Otherwise, you lose a dollar.

2. Use the strategy of minimizing maximum regret to choose the best of the alternative actions below.

	State of the world		
	Economy growing	Economy stable	Economy receding
Invest in stocks	+10	+2	−5
Invest in bonds	+ 4	+3	0
Buy gold	+ 1	+2	+3

3. Electrical troubles have forced you to land your one person spacecraft in alien territory. You have no idea whether the inhabitants are friendly, hostile, or indifferent. You can expend your ship's remaining power in one of three ways: signalling the inhabitants for help, sending an emergency message home, or trying to repair the ship. This table summarizes the values you place on the various outcomes.

	Friendly	Indifferent	Hostile
Contact inhabitants	+12	0	−10
Send message home	+ 2	+6	+10
Repair craft	+ 4	+5	+ 6

Find the best solution by the minimax and the maximax methods and the method of minimizing maximum regret.

4. Your seven year old nephew still believes in the tooth fairy. Actually, his faith is beginning to crack because he has lost all but one of this teeth and the tooth fairy has never paid off. At this critical point in his life, he would estimate that the tooth fairy exists with a probability of 0.8. Last night, after a dinner of Mars bars, his last tooth fell out and he placed it under his pillow. Falling asleep, he decides that if there really is a tooth fairy, the probability is 1.00 that his last tooth will be replaced by a quarter in the morning. He further reasons that if there isn't a tooth fairy, and that this whole business is only a sham of his absent-minded parents, then there is a 0.1 probability that a quarter will appear in the morning where his tooth had been. Alas, when he awoke in the morning, he found his tooth and no quarter. How should he reassess his belief in the tooth fairy?

5. Identify optimal strategies for each player in the following two-person games.

A.

	B1	B2	B3
A1	0	-3	5
A2	2	6	-1
A3	3	5	4

D.

	B1	B2
A1	4	1
A2	2	3

B.

	B1	B2
A1	2	0
A2	0	2

E.

	B1	B2	B3
A1	10	2	0
A2	4	-1	-5
A3	6	8	-4

C.

	B1	B2
A1	4	1
A2	3	2

REFERENCES

Alpert, M., and Raiffa, H. *A Progress Report on the Training of Probability Assessors*. Unpublished manuscript, Harvard University, 1969.

Edwards, W. *"Conservatism in Human Information Processing."* In *Formal Representation of Human Judgment*, edited by B. Kleinmuntz. New York: John Wiley & Sons, Inc., 17–52, 1968.

Hurwicz, L. "What Has Happened to the Theory of Games?" *American Economic Review Supplement*, *43*, 398–405, 1953.

Lindsay, P. H., and Norman, D. L. *Human Information Processing*. New York: Academic Press, Inc., 1972.

Murphy, A. H., and Winkler, R. L. "Credible Interval Temperature Forecasting: Some Experimental Results." *Monthly Weather Review*, *102*, 784–794, 1974.

Peterson, C. R., Snapper, K. J., and Murphy, A. H. "Credible Interval Temperature Forecasts." *Bulletin of the American Meteorological Society*, *53*, 966–970, 1972.

Phillips, L. D., and Edwards, W. "Conservatism in a Simple Probability Inference Task." *Journal of Experimental Psychology*, *72*, 346–357, 1966.

Raiffa, H. *Decision Analysis: Introductory Lectures on Choices Under Uncertainty*. Reading, MA: Addison-Wesley Publishing Co., Inc. 1968.

Robinson, G. H. "Continuous Estimation of a Time-varying Probability." *Ergonomics*, *7*, 7–21, 1964.

von Neumann, J., and Morgenstern, O. *Theory of Games and Economic Behavior*. Princeton, N.J: Princeton University Press, 1944.

PROBLEM SOLUTIONS

Page 234

1. EV = 0
2. EV = 0
3. EV = −2/38
4. EV = +1/6
5. EV = 0

Pages 239–240

Value of A	0.0	0.2	0.4	0.6	0.8	1.0
Best alternative	C	A	A	B	B	B

Value of A	0.0	0.2	0.4	0.6	0.8	1.0
Best alternative	C	C	A	B	B	B

Page 248

1. p = .9946
2. p = .7
3. p = .845

Page 253

1. EV = +5/6
2. invest in stock
3. minimax solution: repair craft

maximax solution: contact inhabitants
Minimizing maximum regret solution: repair craft
4. p = 0.0
5A. A should play A3, B should play B1.
5B. Both players should play each alternative with p = .5.
5C. A should play A2, B should play B2.
5D. A should play A1 with p =.25; and A2 with p = .75
    B should play B1 and B2 with probability p = .5.
5E. A should play A1, B should play B3.

10

Cost-Benefit Analysis

Should saccharin be banned? Should pollution standards be stricter? Are nuclear power plants safe? Should everyone be vaccinated against measles? Are auto seat belts worth the cost? Government agencies and businesses are continually faced with questions such as these. In this chapter, we will describe a decision tool widely used to help answer such questions: Cost-Benefit Analysis. Understanding cost-benefit analysis will:

1. help you to evaluate governmental decisions which affect you, and
2. provide you with a decision-making tool which you can use to make business and personal decisions.

Cost-benefit analysis is based on a very simple idea—the idea that we should take an action only after we have considered all of its costs and benefits. "Certainly *everyone* knows that," you may mutter. While the idea is very simple, it is surprising how often people fail to apply it. When we buy a new puppy, we may fail to consider the wear and tear on the rug or the cat. When a grocer cuts the price of strawberries, he may not consider the possibility that blueberry sales will be reduced as a result.

Suppose that you were trying to decide among several alternative actions, e.g., to add a porch to your house, to insulate it, to take a vacation in Aruba, or to do nothing. To conduct a cost-benefit analysis, you should perform the following steps:

A. For each of the alternative actions,
   1. identify all the important sources of costs and benefits;

257

    2. estimate the values of the costs and benefits;

    3. estimate the probabilities of obtaining the costs and benefits; and

    4. compare the expected values of the costs and benefits.

  B. Choose the action for which *the expected value of the benefits* minus *the expected value of the costs* is greatest.

Each of these steps has its own unique pitfalls into which the unwary cost-benefit analyzer may fall. We will discuss the pitfalls below, but first we will present a highly simplified example to illustrate the mechanics of cost-benefit analysis.

Suppose that you have finally found a potential customer for your $200 car after months and months of trying. You are driving it to your customer's house for inspection when it begins to make a dreadful noise—"Pocketa-queep! Pocketa-queep!" At this point you are approaching the only repair shop in town—"Dishonest Frank's Garage and Mortuary." You know that Frank is a good mechanic who can fix the trouble. Should you stop for repairs or go on? To make the decision you analyze the costs and benefits as follows:

Action 1: Stop at Frank's

  Costs. You estimate that Frank is most likely to charge you $50 (probability = .80), but that the bill may be $100 (probability = .20). The expected value of the costs, then, is

$$EV \text{ (costs)} = (.80) (\$50) + (.20) (\$100)$$
$$= \$40 + \$20$$
$$= \$60$$

  Benefits. You judge that there are three possible outcomes of your sales efforts:

1. The person will be so horrified by the appearance of your car that he will decide not to buy it without even listening to the engine. In this case, the benefit is zero. You estimate that the probability of this outcome is 0.50.
2. The person will be so entranced by the appearance of the car that he will buy it no matter what the engine sounds like. In this case, the benefit is $200. You estimate that the probability of this outcome is 0.10.
3. The person finds the car acceptable only if the engine sounds good. In this case, thanks to Frank, the benefit is $200. You estimate that the probability of this outcome is 0.40.

The expected value of the benefits is

$$EV \text{ (benefits)} = (.50) (0) + (.10) (\$200) + (.40) (\$200)$$

$$= \$100$$

EV (benefits) $-$ EV (costs) $= \$40$.

Action 2: Don't Stop at Frank's

Costs. Zero.

Benefits. The benefits of this action are the same as the benefits for Action 1, with one exception. If the buyer decides to listen to the engine, you will lose the sale. In this case, the benefits will be zero rather than $200.
The expected value of the benefits is

$$EV \text{ (benefits)} = (.50) (0) + (.10) (\$200) + (.40) (0)$$

$$= \$20$$

EV (benefits) $-$ EV (costs) $= \$20$.

Since the expected value of the benefits minus the costs is greater for Action 1 than Action 2, you decide to stop for repairs.

PROBLEMS IN FINDING ALL OF THE IMPORTANT COSTS AND BENEFITS

Some actions have enormously widespread effects which are quite difficult to track down. For example, building a dam may have effects such as improving flood control and transportation, increasing recreational facilities, and providing electric power and irrigation. These effects should result in reduced cost of power and food and increased tourism and industry for the region. These benefits will likely be accompanied by an increase in traffic, in law enforcement problems, in pollution, and in the cost of summer homes. Identifying all the costs and benefits in a complex case such as this may prove very difficult. Before proceeding, try to think of all of the other possible costs and benefits in this case.

Did you think of the potential increase in value of land in areas formerly subject to flooding? Did you think of the possibility that telephone service in the area may be overloaded? Did you think of fire and health services?

A Case Study

Saccharin: To Ban or Not to Ban?

In March of 1977, the Commissioner of the Food and Drug Administration created a minor public uproar when he proposed banning the sale of saccharin. The Commissioner took this action because he judged that saccharin posed a small but definite health hazard for humans. He estimated that the lifetime use of one saccharin-sweetened soft drink per day might cause as many as 1,200 cases of bladder cancer per year in the United States.

The law under which the Commissioner was acting is very specific. The Federal Food, Drug, and Cosmetic Act which regulates food additives contains the so-called Delaney anti-cancer clause (21 USC § 348). This clause states that ". . . no additive shall be deemed to be safe it it is found to induce cancer when ingested by man or animal . . ."

A recently completed Canadian study (1974) provided the Commissioner with reasonably convincing evidence that saccharin does induce cancer in rats. The Commissioner's duty was clear. He *had* to ban saccharin. However, this was not the whole story. As the Commissioner said (*Federal Register*, April 15, 1977),

> Press reports of the announcement of the FDA's intention to withdraw approval of saccharin as an ingredient in foods and beverages have given the impression that the Commissioner is acting reluctantly, based exclusively on the Delaney anti-cancer clause of the Federal Food, Drug, and Cosmetic Act . . . and, further, that the agency's action was triggered solely by the findings of the Canadian study. Neither impression is accurate.

He cited a number of other studies, in addition to the Canadian one, which had independently suggested that saccharin caused cancer. In addition, he stated a rationale for banning even mild cancer-causing agents such as saccharin:

> Although the risk from consumption of saccharin is small compared to that of other health hazards, e.g., cigarette smoking, saccharin is only one of a potentially large number of hazards present in our environment. The Commissioner believes that reduction of prolonged, general exposure to a number of weakly carcinogenic substances in our environment as they are discovered may be essential to reduce the total incidence of cancer. (*Federal Register*, April 15, 1977)

The proposed ban received a considerable amount of unfavorable comment. Marvin Eisenstadt, executive president of Cumberland Packing Corporation, the nation's largest producer of low calorie sweeteners, charged that the "outrageous and harmful action" was based on "flimsy scientific evidence." Public opinion polls showed that a majority of consumers believed that the animal tests were either irrelevant or not conclusive. (As we will see, the public was wrong on both counts, but not necessarily wrong in their opposition to the ban.)

Criticism of the scientific evidence varied in sophistication. On the simpleminded end was the popular joke, "What the studies show is that rats shouldn't drink diet cola." The ugly fact is that agents that cause cancer in rats are very likely to cause it in humans, too. A more sophisticated criticism concerned the saccharin dosages involved in the study. The amount of saccharin the rats were given was, taking their body weight into account, about 1,000 times greater than the amount a human would typically use. This criticism seems impressive on first hearing. However, it loses much of its force when one considers the rationale of animal studies. First, the life span of a rat (two years) is much shorter than that of a human (75 years). If we are interested in lifespan effects, then it is reasonable to use higher dosages in the rat who is exposed over a much shorter time than the human.

Further, in a human population, an incidence of one case of cancer in 1,000 or in 10,000 would be considered important. Animal researchers typically conduct their experiments with only 50 or 100 animals. If animal researchers used a dosage of saccharin which produced only one case in 1,000 or one case in 10,000, there is a very good chance that none of their one hundred rats would show any signs of the disease. To have a reasonable chance of observing an important cancer-producing effect, the researchers must either use a very large number of animals or increase the effect by using a high dosage. The researchers' decision to use high dosages is entirely justified.

Most of the criticism of the FDA ruling was directed at the validity of the evidence that saccharin caused cancer. This criticism appears to have been overly severe. Recent studies have confirmed the conclusion that saccharin does cause bladder cancer. Does it follow then that we should ban saccharin? What do you think?

We know that using saccharin has a cost—namely an increased incidence of as much as 1,200 cases of bladder cancer a year. But what about the benefits of saccharin? There are two major uses of saccharin: 1. to help diabetics keep to their sugar-free diets, and 2. to help dieters keep their weight down. We will discuss only the second benefit.

Excess weight may seem a trivial health problem compared to cancer, but in this case, it may not be trivial at all. Excess weight has important implications for health and life. People who are overweight die younger than other people. Bernard Cohen (1978) has compared the benefits of saccharin in controlling weight with its costs in causing cancer. Using the FDA data, Cohen calculated that due to cancer risk, each soft drink reduced one's life expectancy by about nine seconds. To put this in perspective, each cigarette reduces life expectancy by about 12 minutes, or about 80 times as much. Drinking a diet drink every day over a whole lifetime would reduce life expectancy by about two days.

Now, life insurance statistics show that every pound of excess weight a person carries decreases life expectancy by 29 days. Substituting one saccharin-sweetened drink for a sugar-sweetened drink every day would reduce weight enough to cause a 200-day increase in life expectancy—100 times as large as the two-day decrease due to cancer risk. Thus, even without considering the benefits of sugar-free drinks for diabetics, it appears that the benefits of saccharin are much greater than its costs.*

---

*We may want to question Cohen's analysis of the healthful effects of diet drinks. For example, we might want proof that overweight people actually do reduce their intake of calories as a result of using diet soft drinks. There are enough reports of people who diet by eating large quantities of diet foods in addition to their regular meals to make us question this assumption. Whether Cohen's analysis is accurate or not, it serves to alert us that health costs due to excess weight may be considerable, and should be accurately evaluated and taken into account in making the saccharin decision.

What can we learn from a case such as this? *At least* two things.

1. A law, like the Delaney anti-cancer clause, which focuses narrowly on avoiding one particular kind of cost, may be more harmful than helpful. By failing to look at *all* the costs and benefits, it may kill more people than it saves. This point becomes dramatically evident in the case of Vitamin A, a substance *necessary* to life. Vitamin A has been shown to have mild cancer-causing effects. If we tried to stamp out Vitamin A because of this particular cost, we would do vast harm.

The point applies not just to laws, like the Delaney clause, but to decision procedures generally. Whenever we focus narrowly on avoiding a particular cost and don't take all the important costs and benefits into account, we may make very bad decisions.

2. A second lesson to be derived from the saccharin case is that people often fail to look for all the costs and benefits. The proposed ban focused entirely on the cancer issue, as did objections to the ban. This writer was appalled to see his favorite news commentators looking very serious about the controversy, scrunching up their eyebrows, saying, "Well, just how good *is* the evidence that saccharin causes cancer?" and completely missing the point that there might be costs as well as benefits in banning saccharin.

   Delaney didn't consider all the costs and benefits of saccharin when he was writing his law, the FDA Commissioner didn't consider them when he proposed his ban, and the public didn't consider them when they criticized the ban. Cost-benefit analysis may seem a very elementary and obvious idea, but people surely have failed to use it in cases where it was appropriate.

In the saccharin case, applying the technique of cost-benefit analysis would have broadened people's perspective on the problem by leading them to search actively for costs and benefits. It would by no means have guaranteed that they would find them all, however.

PROBLEMS IN ESTIMATING PROBABILITIES

We have already discussed some of the problems caused when people make subjective judgments of probability, as with the gambler's fallacy (Chapter 9). Measuring objective probabilities can cause problems as well. This is particularly true when we are dealing with new technology. If we wanted to measure the probability of failure of a 1970's automatic transmission, for example, we could count the number of units that failed after one year, after two years, and after three years, and compute the appropriate probabilities. For a new transmission just developed this year, though, we don't have the data to make these probability measurements. Customers might like to have them now, but we simply can't deliver them.

When nuclear reactors were first developed, engineers wanted to know the probabilities that various materials such as steel and concrete would be weakened by intense radiation. Many years of experience with the new technology were required before the answers could be provided.

Other cases in which it is difficult to get adequate probability estimates are situations involving large risks which have a very small probability of occurring, such as airplane crashes and oil spills. Suppose that you are considering buying a house just below a new dam. It is important for you to know whether the probability that the dam will break in the next 10 years is one in one hundred, one in ten thousand, one in a million or less. You ask an engineer who says, "Well, that's a new kind of dam, and only 20 of them are 10 years old. Since none has broken yet, I suppose that means that the probability of failure is between zero and one in 20, or five percent." Unfortunately, this is nowhere near the accuracy you need to make your decision. A great deal of experience is needed in making decisions of this kind, and sometimes that experience just isn't available.

In evaluating nuclear power, a major cost to be considered is the possibility of a disastrous nuclear explosion. To evaluate this cost, analysts must try to identify all of the ways in which an accident could occur. To do this, they may start with the standard operating procedure of the plant and ask what can go wrong in the procedure. For example, they may ask, "What would happen if the reactor heat-control pump should fail?" or, "What would happen if the reactor heat-control pump *and* the reactor temperature-warning system should both fail?" By working through the potential failures and combinations of failures in the standard operation of the plant, the analysts can arrive at an estimate of the likelihood of an accident. This is a difficult task even if we assume that the operators are following standard procedures. If they are not, the difficulties are enormously increased. For example, violation of standard procedure was an important factor in the fire at the Brown's Ferry Nuclear Power Plant. This fire narrowly missed causing "many casualties and radiation contamination of a large part of Alabama and Tennessee" (Comey, 1975). Technicians in the plant had been searching for air leaks. One ingenious technician was using a candle to aid the search, grossly violating standard operating procedure, but improving the efficiency of the search. The candle caused the fire, and fire, together with a few other malfunctions, almost caused a major nuclear disaster.

Clearly violations of standard procedure can lead to accidents. Unfortunately, it's very hard for an analyst to predict all of the ingenious ways in which people will violate standard procedure.

Taking the saccharin and the Brown's Ferry cases together, we can see that cost-benefit analysis can help in complex decisions, but we should recognize clearly that it is subject to error. Just because someone has done a cost-benefit analysis doesn't guarantee that they have done it right.

THE PROBLEM OF COMPARING
DIFFERENT SORTS OF VALUES

One of the drawbacks of cost-benefit analysis is that it is sometimes difficult to compare values of different sorts. For many things, money provides a convenient scale for comparison. Since it is our medium of exchange, many things are assigned money values or prices. These prices give us a way of deciding how many "X's" are worth a "Y". Money values allow us to "compare apples and oranges" in everyday commerce.

There is still a "comparing apples and oranges" problem, however, because there are many important things for which we do not ordinarily set a price. For example, a new dam may provide facilities for water sports as one of its benefits. How do we compare the pleasure people get from water sports with the dollar cost of the dam? A new subway system may provide a quieter, less crowded ride than the old. How do we compare the increased comfort of the riders with the dollar cost of the new system? An intensive care unit may save some lives which otherwise might have been lost. How do we compare the value of these lives with the cost of the intensive care unit?

In this last case, some people will state flatly that you can't put a value on a life—certainly not a money value. There are two things such a statement might mean. First, it might mean that there really is *no* way to compare the value of a life to the value of, say, ten dollars. By this interpretation, if we ask the question, "Is Smith worth ten dollars?" the answer must be, "I don't know and there is no way to decide." I think this answer is unacceptable. Most of us would agree readily that a life is worth much more than ten dollars, even though we all know a few exceptions.

The other interpretation is that a life is worth more than any amount of money we can imagine. While this interpretation has a certain attractiveness, it is surely false. Consider the following difficult problem. Suppose that the life of a child depended on a very expensive kidney machine—so expensive, in fact, that it required all of the nation's resources to keep it running. Given a vote, would you vote to devote all of the nation's resources to saving this child's life? If you did, you would be voting for impoverishment, suffering, and death for a great many other people. Money runs hospitals, money grows crops, money pays for immunizations and prenatal care. Money represents resources and the ugly fact is that resources are limited. If we spend a million dollars to save Smith, we may not have the million dollars that would be required to save Cincinnati.

What can we conclude from the kidney-machine example? We are forced to the difficult conclusion that we can't *sensibly* spend unlimited amounts to save a particular person's life. To do so would cost many more lives than it would save. Well, then, how much should we spend to save a life? We know we should spend more than ten dollars and we know that we shouldn't spend so much that we cause the deaths of lots of other people, but how much *should* we spend?

There is no clear answer to this question. Nonetheless, to reveal the nature of the problem a little more clearly, let's examine the kidney-machine problem in a smaller context—the context of a single family. Imagine a family with five children. One of the five will die if he doesn't have the kidney machine. Should the parents provide the money for the machine if it means that

1. The other four will die?   Yes ( )   No ( )

or

2. The other four will live in abject poverty with greatly decreased life expectancies?   Yes ( )   No ( )

or

3. The other four will live in abject poverty with a strong probability that they will become criminals, perhaps murderers?   Yes ( )   No ( )

or

4. The other four, who are blind, will have to give up remedial surgery?   Yes ( )   No ( )

or

5. The other four will have to drop out of high school before graduation to take menial jobs?   Yes ( )   No ( )

or

6. The other four, though promising students, will have no chance to go to college?   Yes ( )   No ( )

or

7. The family won't be able to buy a piano or a car?   Yes ( )   No ( )

These are horrible questions to ask. We ask them only because they reveal something of the nature of a very important problem. Most people will answer "no" to the first question and "yes" to the last, but may differ on their answers to the questions in between.

In order to answer these questions we have to compare human values of very different sorts. We have to compare certain death with a probability of death, or with life-long suffering, or with lost opportunities. People differ from one another in these decisions, perhaps because their values differ, or perhaps they aren't quite sure at any given moment what their values are in these difficult comparisons. Low-income people may place more importance on curing blindness and less on graduating from high school than do high-income people. People seem to place a higher value on lives if the individuals are identified than if they are anonymous. As Zechhauser (1975) points out, we are very unlikely to send astronauts on one-way trips into space even though it would greatly cut costs. We are much more likely to reduce expenses for highway safety where the victims, while more numerous, die in comforting anonymity.

What can we conclude about comparing values such as life, happiness, and money? Such comparisons are very difficult. People will not agree with each other and they will not agree with themselves at different times and in different situations. However, we cannot avoid such comparisons. We make them frequently whether we do so in full consciousness or not. Governments do so when they establish pure food and drug laws, or set airline safety standards. Individuals make these comparisons when they decide whether or not to ride a motorcycle or to enter a high-risk profession such as police work. Cost-benefit analysis won't make the difficulty of these value comparisons go away. However, the framework of cost-benefit analysis can help us as individuals and as a society to be clearer and more systematic about what we are doing when we make these comparisons.

Dealing with Value Comparisons in Practice

There are some situations in which we can get around difficult value comparisons by using a dominance rule. For example, consider a diabetes detection program. The costs of such a program include financial costs—such as wages for physicians and technicians, testing materials, carfare and wages lost by the persons tested—and human comfort costs—such as the annoyance of waiting in the office. Similarly, the benefits of the program include the financial benefits of avoiding the expenses of hospitalization and lost wages, and the human comfort benefits of avoiding blindness and pain. We can apply the dominance rule in this decision as follows: If the benefits are greater than the costs in one of the two areas and no worse than the costs in the other, then the program should be undertaken. Thus, if the financial costs and benefits were the same, but the human comfort benefits were greater than the costs, then the total benefits would be greater than the costs.

Suppose it costs as much in dollars to immunize people against a disease as it does to treat them for the disease. Since it is better in human terms for people to avoid the disease than to have it, the total benefits of immunization would exceed its costs.

The Direct Approach to Value Comparison

Another way to deal with value comparison is the direct approach. We can ask people to tell us how much they would be willing to pay for the pleasure of going fishing, or for relief from hayfever, or for a less risky job. Consider the following decision. Suppose you are offered two summer jobs as bank guard at different branches of the same bank. One job in the suburban branch where there is zero risk to your life pays $5,000 for the summer. The other job is in a busy urban area and involves a one percent risk to your life over the summer. How much would the job in the urban branch have to pay to be as attractive as the surburban job? Would an extra $100 be enough? How about an extra million? While measurements such as these are not very precise, they do give us some idea of how the individual compares very different values, and allow us to proceed with a cost-benefit analysis. (For a more detailed discussion of these methods, see Zechhauser, 1975.)

PROBLEMS IN COMPARING COSTS AND BENEFITS RECEIVED AT DIFFERENT TIMES

In doing cost-benefit analysis, we frequently have to compare costs and benefits received at different times. For example, suppose that on January 1 of year zero the Jones Company invests $3,200 in a machine which earns $1,000 a year, payable on January 1 of years 1, 2, 3, and 4, and then it wears out. At first glance it appears that the benefits outweigh the costs by $800 (Table 1), *but this isn't right!* The benefits received in years 2, 3, and 4 are not directly comparable to the costs in year 1. To understand why they are not directly comparable and how they *can* be compared, we will have to discuss interest and its relation to the present and future value of money.

Computing Interest

Interest—Simple and Compound

Suppose that you put $100 in the bank at 6% interest and then every year you receive a check for $6.00. This is called "simple" interest. If you invest P dollars at i% interest for n years, the total amount of money you will have after n years, F, is

*F*uture value = *P*rincipal + (*P*rincipal × *i*nterest × *n*umber years)

or

1. $F = P + Pin$

Table 1

	Jan. 1, yr. 0	Jan. 1, yr. 1	Jan. 1, yr. 2	Jan. 1, yr. 3	Jan. 1, yr. 4
costs (spent)	3200				
benefits (received)		1000	1000	1000	1000

This may also be written as

$$F = P(1 + in)$$

If we invest $100 at 6% simple interest, in 10 years we will have

$$F = P + Pin$$
$$= \$100 + \$100 \times (.06) \times 10$$
$$= \$100 + \$60$$
$$= \$160$$

Suppose on the other hand you invest $100 in the bank at 6% interest, but rather than receiving an interest check each year, you have the interest added to the amount already in the bank. Thus, the interest will also collect interest. This is called "compound" interest. If you invest P dollars at i% interest for

n years, the total amount of money you will have after n years, F, at compound interest is

2. $F = P(1 + i)^n$

If we invest \$100 at 6% compound interest, in 10 years we will have

$$F = P(1 + i)^n$$
$$= 100(1 + .06)^{10}$$
$$= \$179.08$$

Table 2 compares the value of F for simple and compound interest over 20 years. Clearly compound interest has an increasing advantage over simple interest as time passes. We will be concerned primarily with compound interest in this discussion.

Table 2

	\multicolumn{8}{c}{Number of Years}							
	1	2	3	4	5	10	15	20
6% simple interest on \$100	106	112	118	124	130	160	190	220
6% compound interest on \$100	106	112.36	119.10	126.25	133.82	179.08	239.66	320.71

Table 3 shows the value of F at compound interest at several interest rates and for various numbers of years.

If we take P as the present value of a sum of money and F as its future value, Equation 2 shows us how to get future value from present value. Often we want to work backwards, that is, we are given the future value and we want to compute the present value from it. Equation 3 shows how to do this. It is derived directly from Equation 2.

Table 3

Compound Interest on \$100	\multicolumn{8}{c}{Number of Years}							
	1	2	3	4	5	10	15	20
at 4%	104	108.16	112.49	116.99	121.67	148.02	180.09	219.11
at 6%	106	112.36	119.10	126.25	133.82	179.08	239.66	320.71
at 8%	108	116.64	125.97	136.05	146.93	215.89	317.22	466.09
at 10%	110	121.00	133.10	146.41	161.05	259.37	417.72	672.75

3. $P = \dfrac{F}{(1 + i)^n}$

Now back to the Jones Company. Using Equation 3 and assuming an interest rate of 10%, we can compute the present value (that is, the value on Jan. 1, year 0) of $1000 received on Jan. 1, in years 1, 2, 3, and 4. A thousand dollars received on Jan. 1, year 1, is the future value of the unknown present value, P_1, and after one year's interest. Thus

$$P_1 = \frac{1000}{(1 + .10)} = \$909$$

Similarly,

$$P_2 = \frac{1000}{(1 + .10)^2} = \$826.45$$

$$P_3 = \frac{1000}{(1 + .10)^3} = \$751.31$$

and

$$P_4 = \frac{1000}{(1 + .10)^4} = \$681.01$$

The sum of these values is $3,169.77, which is less that $3,200! Thus, the *present value* of the earnings to be received over four years is actually less than the present value of the investment in the machine. The Jones Company would do better to invest their money at 10 percent and forget about buying the machine.

Summary

Cost-benefit analysis is a decision procedure in which we compare the expected costs and benefits of alternative actions. It involves the following steps:

A. For each of the alternative actions:
   1. identify all the important sources of costs and benefits;
   2. estimate the values of the costs and benefits;
   3. estimate the probabilities of obtaining the costs and benefits; and
   4. compare the expected values of the costs and benefits.
B. Choose the action for which *the expected value of the benefits* minus *the expected value of the costs* is greatest.

When we do cost-benefit analysis, we may encounter a number of practical problems. These include:

1. difficulties in identifying *all* of the important costs and benefits;
2. difficulties in estimating probabilities (especially when dealing with new technology); and
3. difficulties in comparing values of different sorts, e.g., the value of a job opportunity versus the value of a life.

SAMPLE PROBLEMS

Problem #1

In an article in the *Journal of the American Medical Association*, Kirkland (1977), questioned the usefulness of screening patients over 65 for syphilis. He said:

> The economics of hospital care have now made the scrutiny of all expenses, no matter how small, necessary.
>
> At Emory University Hospital, screening for syphilis has had the sanctity of tradition and official requirements. At the time of this study, an 'admissions package' given to each new patient by the admissions office included a requisition for an automated reagin test (ART) [a test for syphilis].

Kirkland reviewed the folders of 300 patients 65 or older, and found that only one case of syphilis had been detected and treated. The patient was a 71-year-old woman admitted to the hospital with serious heart trouble. He continued:

> Therefore, at $3.50 per ART, a minimum of $1,050 was spent to detect and treat that one patient. It is highly questionable whether or not that treatment will have any effect on her longevity or well-being; she probably just got upset at being told what it was for.
>
> It therefore seemed wasteful to continue routine screening in this age group, and such screening was discontinued at this hospital as of January, 1975. It seems improbable that this move will constitute a major public health hazard or will substantially affect the health of the individual patients.

What costs and benefits were considered in this case?

Problem #2

Suppose that you put $500 in the bank at 6% *simple* interest. How much will you have in 10 years? How much will you have if the interest is compound?

Problem #3

What would the answers be in problem #2 if the interest rate were 9%?

Problem #4

How much money would you have to have put in the bank 10 years ago to have $1,000 now? Assume 8% compound interest.

Problem #5

Assuming a 10% interest rate, what is the future value 5 years from now of $1,000 invested today? What is the future value 5 years from now of a $1,000 investment if we invest $500 of it today *and* $500 a year from today?

Problem #6

Your company has an opportunity to buy a duplicating machine that will last through 5 years of use. It costs $20,000 and will bring in $5,000 in business payable at the end of each year. Taking the costs and benefits into account, what is the present value of this purchase? Assume a 10% interest rate.

Problem #7—Hayes' Disease

You are a public health officer in your last year at your present post. As your final act, you must decide whether or not to launch a one-shot (i.e., one time) immunization campaign against a newly discovered respiratory affliction called "Hayes' Disease." Hayes' Disease in uncomfortable but generally not serious. Its most usual symptoms are fever and coughing and temporary hearing loss, although sometimes more serious complications occur. However, it is extremely contagious. In an epidemic year, essentially every susceptible person will contract it. Epidemics are believed to occur every 5 years. Since the disease has only recently been recognized, you don't know when the last epidemic in your region occured.

To make your decision, you assemble the following facts concerning costs and benefits of the program.

Costs
vaccine $3/patient (assume that it is 100% effective)
office costs $4/patient
advertising for campaign $1/patient

Benefits
The benefits of the program are calculated from the costs which patients would

have incurred if they had contracted the disease. These costs are as follows:

65% of patients—no expense

25%—one $15 office visit

5% contract pneumonia; of these, 1/20 require $500 hospitalization, 19/20 require 2 office visits @ $15 and $5 medication

5% contract otitis (ear trouble) requiring 2 office visits @ $15 and $5 medication

Since you don't know when the next epidemic will occur, these benefits may be realized this year or in any of the four following years. For purposes of computation, you assume that 20% of the benefits will be realized this year and 20% in each of the four following years. You assume an interest rate of 10% to find the present value of the future benefits.

Do a cost-benefit analysis on the basis of these figures to decide whether or not you should launch this campaign.

REFERENCES

Cohen, B. L. "Relative Risks of Saccharin and Calorie Ingestion." *Science*, *199*(3), 983, 1978.

Comey, D. D. "How We Almost Lost Alabama." *Chicago Tribune*, August 31, 1975. *Federal Register*, 42(73), 19996-20006, 1977.

Kirkland, J. *Journal of the American Medical Association*, *238*(5), 399, 1977.

Toxicity and Carcinogenicity Study of Orthotoluenesulfonamide and Saccharin, Project E405/405D, Department of Health and Public Welfare of the Canadian Government, February, 1974.

Zechhauser, R. "Procedures for Valuing Lives." *Public Policy*, *23*, 419-464, 1975.

PROBLEM SOLUTIONS

Pages 271-273

2. $800
3. $950
4. $463.20
5. $1,610.51
6. $1,056.52
7. Average cost per patient = $8.41
   Average benefit per patient = $6.37
   Answer: Don't launch the campaign.

IV

CREATIVITY AND INVENTION

11

Cognitive Processes in Creative Acts

In the next two chapters, we will approach creativity from two very different points of view. In this chapter, we will define creativity and discuss four of the cognitive processes underlying creative acts: problem finding, idea generation, planning, and preparation. In addition, we will describe some procedures which can increase your problem finding and idea generation skills. In the next chapter, we will discuss the social conditions of creativity—that is, we will describe how society treats people differently according to their sex, religion, and race, and how this difference in treatment encourages or discourages creative activity.

The main point that we want to make in both of these chapters is that you can exercise some control over the cognitive processes and the social conditions which influence your creative abilities. To this extent, you can increase your chances of becoming a creative person.

WHAT IS A CREATIVE ACT?

Creative acts come in a great variety of forms. A creative act may be quite ordinary and inconsequential—for example, it might be something as simple as making up a bedtime story to tell our children—or it may be world shaking—as was Galileo's invention of the science of physics. A creative act may involve years of concentrated work—consider the decades Darwin devoted to developing the evidence for the theory of evolution—or it may be brief—condensed into a sudden flash of insight—the sort of insight that drove Archimedes naked from his bath shouting, ''Eureka!''

What is there about these very different acts that leads us to call them all ''creative''? Typically, we apply fairly stringent criteria in judging creativity. In most cases, we require an act to pass three tests before we call it creative. First, we must believe that the act is *original*. Second, we must believe that it is *valuable*. And third, it must suggest to us that the person who performed the act has special mental *abilities*. For example, when we see what the person has done, we ask overselves, "How did she ever think of that?" or, "How did he have the patience to work all that out?"

Let's examine these conditions in order.

Originality

We certainly wouldn't judge a painter creative who simply copied the pictures of other painters. To be judged creative, painters must use their own resources to shape the painting. They must paint their *own* pictures.

We don't mean though that everything in a creative work must be original. Painters, writers, and inventors routinely use ideas borrowed from others. However, the creative person combines or interprets these borrowed ideas in ways that are original. Renaissance artists very frequently painted the Madonna and Child, but each great artist presented the theme in an individual way.

Sometimes a person will do something original which is not new. For example, a scientist may make a discovery, quite independent of other people, only to find later that the discovery has been made several times before. In our society newness *is* important. We are very careful to give special credit to the person who is *first* to invent something. Still, we attribute creativity to the scientist above on the grounds of originality, even though the discovery is not new.

Value

Even if an act is original, we won't consider it creative unless we also judge it to be valuable. Suppose, for example, you were to turn all the furniture in your house upside down. That would be original, but it would hardly be valuable. Your friends would not ask admiringly, "How did you think of that?" Rather, they would ask, "Why did you think of that?" and worry a bit about your mental health.

Judging whether something is valuable or not is tricky. Perfectly reasonable people may disagree with each other about the value, say, of contemporary music. Further, opinions change over time. In the 1860's, both the critics and the public much preferred the painters of the French Academy to the Impressionists. Now both critical and popular judgment is reversed. Today the work of Impressionists such as Renoir, Degas, and Monet is much better known than that of French Academy painters such as Greuze or Gérôme.

If judgments of value can change with time, then judgments of creativity can change, too. An act which is judged creative by one generation may not seem so to the next.

Abilities

Our final condition for judging an act creative is that it must suggest that the person who performed the act has special mental abilities. Imagine the following scene: A housepainter is retouching the ceiling in a museum gallery. Just as he is about to finish, his foot slips. He knocks over the ladder, splattering paint everywhere and does a double flip into a potted palm. He regains consciousness several hours later, just in time to hear members of the museum selection committee saying, "Brilliant!" "A work of genius!" "What freedom of movement!" Peering through the palm fronds, he sees that they are referring to the aftermath of his accident on the wall.

Now, while the housepainter produced something original and valuable, we can't call his act creative. Falling off the ladder doesn't in any way cause us to admire the housepainter's mental abilities. It only suggests that he may have a tendency toward clumsiness.

You might be inclined to say that the housepainter's act wasn't creative because it was unintentional. You should notice, though, that some very creative acts are unintentional. For example, Becquerel's discovery of radioactivity was unintentional. He had no idea that uranium ore would fog a photographic film. We admire Becquerel for making the discovery because, while it was unintentional, he had the wit to recognize its significance.

CREATIVITY AND IQ

If creative acts require special mental abilities, we might expect that creative people have especially high IQ's. While creative people do have higher than average IQ's, the relation between creativity and IQ is complex. The simplest way to summarize it is to say that people with below average IQ's tend not to be creative. However, if we look just at people above a certain IQ level, such as 120, then there is very little relation between creativity and IQ. It is as if there is a certain minimum IQ required for creativity, after which IQ doesn't matter.

An alternative view (see Hayes, 1978) is that IQ has nothing to do with creative ability, and that the reason people with low IQ's are not creatively productive is that they aren't given the opportunity. IQ does predict how well a person will do in school. People who do poorly in school may have difficulty getting into good schools and getting good jobs in which there is a chance to be creative. Thus, our society may actually *prevent* people with low IQ's from being creative.

The important point about creativity and IQ that you should understand is this: You shouldn't give up on yourself as a creative person just because your IQ is not outstanding. For example, the IQ's of such famous people as Copernicus, Rembrandt, and Faraday have been estimated at 110 or less!

CREATIVITY AND ILL-DEFINED PROBLEMS

In discussing the nature of a creative act, we will follow the lead of Newell, Shaw, and Simon (1964). These authors proposed that a creative act is a special kind of problem solving, that it is the act of solving an ill-defined problem.

In Chapter 1, we defined ill-defined problems as ones which require problem solvers to contribute to the definition of the problem from their *own* resources. To solve an ill-defined problem, you may be required either to make decisions based on your own knowledge and values (gap-filling decisions) or to discover new information through your own active exploration of the problem (jumping in), or both.

Your solutions to ill-defined problems are very much *your* solutions. They depend on your knowledge and your values. Other people would almost certainly have arrived at different solutions because their knowledge and values differ from yours. It is just because we put our own knowledge and values into the solution of ill-defined problems that it is possible to solve them creatively. It is by drawing on private resources—different in each person and largely hidden from the outside viewer—that we are able to produce solutions which dazzle and astound.

COGNITIVE PROCESSES UNDERLYING CREATIVE ACTS

Creative acts depend on a great many of our cognitive processes working together in harmony—processes of representation, search, memory, and decision making. We will focus on just four of these processes which are especially important for creativity: problem finding, idea generation, planning, and preparation.

Problem Finding

Many problems come to us with neat labels which say in effect, "Solve me. I'm a problem!" Problems in exams, IQ tests, and puzzle books are like that. When we open an exam booklet, we are likely to find labels such as "Question #1" or "Problem 3." Whether we can solve the problems or not, we have no trouble finding them.

Some problems aren't as neatly labeled, though. There is a special class of ill-defined problems in which what we have to contribute to the definition of the problem is the discovery that there *is* a problem.

Here is an uncomplicated example in which I discovered a problem: Over the years, I have searched through the theater pages of the newspaper hundreds of times to find what was playing at my local theater. On the average, the search involved examining about half of the ads before finding the one I wanted. While this was a minor annoyance, until recently I hadn't seen it as a problem—that is, as a difficulty for which one could find a sensible solution. When I did see it as a problem—when I finally said to myself, "Something could be done about that"—it was easy enough to think of solutions, e.g., standardize the positions of the ads or alphabetize them. Finding this problem was a great deal more difficult than finding methods for its solution.

PROBLEM FINDING AND CREATIVITY

The process of problem finding plays a very important role both in artistic and in scientific creativity. For example, in the early 1900's, a group of American artists called the "ashcan school" discovered esthetic values in the everyday appearance of the city—people shopping or crossing at an intersection. They took it as their problem to capture these values in their paintings. No one told them to do this. In fact, a horrified artistic establishment told them not to. They had to discover their artistic problem for themselves.

Problem finding is important in scientific discovery as well. Einstein and Infeld (1938) comment:

> Galileo formulated the problem of determining the velocity of light, but did not solve it. The formulation of a problem is often more essential than its solution, which may be merely a matter of mathematical or experimental skill. To raise new questions, new possibilities, to regard old problems from a new angle, requires creative imagination and marks real advance in science.   (p. 95)

Here are three cases in point.

Case 1

In the heyday of the telegraph, hundreds of operators listened to the dots and dashes of the Morse ticker and transcribed them into words on paper. When the connection was bad, the messages were hard to hear. Most simply shrugged their shoulders and did the best they could in a difficult situation. Edison distinguished himself from the others by seeing the difficulty as a problem to be solved. He solved it by constructing a device which would record the dots and dashes as visible marks on a rotating disk. When the device was complete, however, others didn't necessarily see it as the solution to a problem. Edison's employers, for example, thought that reading from a disk rather than listening to the ticker was a complete waste of time.

The pattern of events that led to Edison's invention has been repeated in a number of scientific discoveries. What many had observed and dismissed as a trivial annoyance, one person recognized as an important problem to be solved.

Case 2

As many bacteriologists do, Alexander Fleming was growing colonies of bacteria on sterile agar plates. An accident, such as must have happened thousands of times in other laboratories, contaminated some of the plates with dust. The bacteria Fleming was trying to grow died in the neighborhood of the dust specks. Rather than throwing the plates out as "spoiled," Fleming saw that they posed an interesting problem—"Why did the bacteria die?" The answer was that the dust contained the mold which produces Penicillin—a substance whose existence was unknown at that time. Thus a major medical discovery depended on someone seeing a problem in some spoiled agar plates.

Case 3

As a part of a study of digestion, the physiologist, Ivan Pavlov, investigated the salivary reflex in dogs. Dogs salivate automatically when food is put into their mouths. The experiments went well at first, but then to Pavlov's surprise, the dogs began to salivate before they had any food in their mouths at all. He found that they would salivate at the sight or sound of the food dishes or to any other signal that had frequently been associated with feeding. These developments seriously complicated Pavlov's experiments. But, rather than seeing them simply as an annoyance, as most would have done, he saw that they revealed an important problem—"What was the nature of these anticipatory responses?" Pavlov received stern warning from his colleagues that he would be risking his very promising career in physiology if he pursued these "unscientific" psychological interests. Fortunately, Pavlov had the courage to ignore these warnings and to continue to work on the problem he had discovered. This work on conditioned reflexes earned him the Nobel prize.

IMPROVING YOUR PROBLEM-FINDING SKILLS

The three procedures we are about to describe are not likely to earn you a Nobel prize, but they can help to make you a better problem finder. The first is intended as an aid to aspiring inventors. The second and third are *critical thinking* techniques, that is, techniques for finding flaws in arguments. Critical thinking skills are important for creativity because detecting a flaw in an accepted theory can be a very powerful source of inspiration for creating a new theory. Critical thinking skills are also very useful in such mundane activities as defending ourselves against politicians and encyclopedia salesmen.

Bug Listing

Bug listing is a technique that Adams (1974) recommends to help inventors find promising problems to work on. The basic idea is that things which bother you, such as ice cream cones that drip or typewriters that won't spell, probably bother other people as well. An invention created to solve one of your bugs could have a wide market.

A bug list is simply a list of things that bother you. To make a bug list, you should carry a notebook with you so that you can record the bugs when you notice them. (Bugs are often so commonplace that they are hard to remember.) Here is a representative bug list:

1. remembering to mail letters
2. taking out the trash
3. fastening seatbelts
4. putting tops back on toothpaste, ketchup, etc.
5. changing the cat box
6. washing dishes
7. making my bed
8. keeping clean and dirty laundry separate
9. turning off lights
10. sliding doors that stick
11. cupboard doors that don't close
12. crumbs on the table, counter, and floor
13. cat fur
14. people with dirty ears
15. hanging up my coat
16. restaurants with dim lights that make your eyes go buggy
17. places that are crowded
18. stupid teachers
19. people in pants that are too tight
20. shorts that are too short
21. men who wear their shirts open to the navel
22. music in supermarkets
23. fight songs
24. stupid radio and television personalities
25. sour milk
26. sunburn
27. tangled hair
28. razor stubble
29. dirty glasses
30. dirt under contact lenses

31. food that drips on your clothes (like tacos)
32. getting teeth cleaned at the dentist
33. dark nail polish
34. dirty fingernails
35. registering for classes
36. drying my hair
37. humid days
38. crying babies
39. dripping faucets
40. passport photos

Each of these bugs can be viewed as a problem to be solved, and as the potential source of a useful invention.

SEARCHING FOR COUNTEREXAMPLES

The Employment Argument

This argument is not very popular today, but it was widely accepted in the '50's. "When a company is filling a job, it should hire men in preference to women, because men have to support families."

A common way for people to test an argument is to search for positive instances (Wason, 1968)—that is, to think of a case in which the argument seems right. For example, a person might say, "Well, if a man is supporting a wife and three kids, it *is* more important for him to have a job than for a single woman to have one." Having found a positive instance, many stop their search and accept the argument.

While searching for positive instances is a very common technique, it is, unfortunately, a very uncritical one. It ignores cases in which the argument is false. A much more critical approach to testing arguments is one widely used by philosophers and mathematicians—searching for counterexamples. A counterexample is a case in which the argument we are testing is false. A person searching for a counterexample to the employment argument might say, "Well, a woman who is supporting her crippled husband certainly deserves to have a job as much as a bachelor does." Clearly, we are much less likely to accept a faulty argument if we test it by searching for counterexamples. Here is another case.

The Pre-cognition Argument

Some claim that certain people can have accurate knowledge of events before they happen.

Positive Instance: "Yeah! Last week my aunt dreamt that something good was going to happen to me and today I won the lottery!"

Counterexample: "Sure, but two weeks ago, she dreamt that your turtle was going to have puppies."

Searching for counterexamples is only one of many techniques which philosophers have developed for detecting problems in arguments. An interesting and highly readable introduction to some of these techniques is provided by Thomas Schwartz in his book, *The Art of Logical Reasoning* (1980).

SEARCHING FOR ALTERNATIVE INTERPRETATIONS

Our second technique for finding problems in arguments borrows from the critical spirit of scientific research. It is the technique of searching for alternative interpretations.

Case 1: Singing the Baby to Flab

Suppose that someone tried to convince us that singing to children makes them grow. They tell us that they have systematically observed 20 kindergarten children whose mothers sing to them every day, and that over a period of eight months, these children gained an average of four pounds.

Fortunately, the main problem in this argument is easy to find. We know that kindergarten children are growing rapidly, so we can readily formulate an alternate interpretation of the data. Those children might have gained four pounds even if they hadn't been sung to.

The problem with the argument is that the observations do not include *control* measurements, for example, weight gains of 20 kindergarten children whose mothers do *not* sing to them. We would be much more inclined to accept the argument if the children who were sung to gained *more* than the children who were not.

Case 2: Hypnotizing Chickens

Once, in my wasted youth, I ran across an enterprising salesman who was selling a device for hypnotizing chickens. Indeed, the device was impressive. The salesman held a chicken down on a table and placed the device, which emitted a soft buzzing, next to the chicken's head. When he released the chicken, it just lay there and stared as if all active chicken thoughts had been chased from its head. It was completely gorked out. Then, after 30 seconds of complete immobility, it suddenly scrambled up and ran off.

One can easily understand that many people, perhaps even the salesman himself, would be convinced of the efficacy of the device—some to the extent of buying one.

I wasn't convinced, however, because I had an alternative interpretation of the demonstration. For no good reason, at that time, I was the local expert on "animal hypnosis." I knew that various animals—guinea pigs, snakes, alligators, and yes, chickens, could be "hypnotized" simply by putting them into certain postures. In particular, a chicken can be hypnotized by holding its head down on a table for a few seconds. My alternative interpretation was that what we were seeing was just another case of animal hypnosis and that a control observation in which the chicken's head was held on the table *without* the buzzer would have produced the same result, i.e., a gorked-out chicken.

Case I Revisited: Singing to Children

Suppose that the person studying singing and weight gain had made the control observation we suggested above. Suppose that they had found that children of mothers who sing to them gain two pounds more on the average than children of mothers who do not. Would we then be forced to accept the argument that singing to children makes them grow? The answer is "No." The argument still has problems as we can see by considering some alternative interpretations. Perhaps there were other differences between the two groups of mothers. Perhaps if we interviewed the mothers, the non-singers would say, "Sing to my kid? Hell, I don't even feed 'm!'', while the singers insist that a healthy child needs at least nine meals a day.

Clearly, searching for alternate interpretations can help us to find problems in persuasive arguments.

Summary

In some cases finding a problem is the most difficult part of solving it. Many discoveries depend on finding a problem that others have ignored. We frequently hear persuasive arguments that have problems hidden in them. If we fail to find the problems, we are likely to be persuaded of something that is false. By asking the following three questions, we can increase our chances of finding such problems:

1. Can I think of a counterexample?
2. Have appropriate control measurements been made?
3. Are there alternate interpretations of the result?

Exercises

1. Design a study of singing and weight gain that would avoid the problems we found above.

2. What problems can you find in the following arguments?
   a. Nine out of 10 doctors interviewed said that they prescribe our brand in preference to all others. Buy our brand.
   b. In clinical tests, eight out of 10 felt relief within 10 minutes after using our brand. Buy it.
   c. Four leading pain relievers contain 650 mg of aspirin per tablet, but our brand contains 800 mg. Buy our brand.

GENERATING IDEAS

Many of the difficulties in creative problem solving arise not in finding the problem but in generating ideas for a solution. When faced with a problem like The Loser (Remember the man who always lost at gambling because the fortune teller cast a spell on him?), some people are terrific at thinking up ideas and some are terrible. This section is designed for people who have trouble generating dieas.

Many methods have been proposed to help make ideas flow. We will discuss just two:

1. brainstorming, and
2. finding analogies.

Brainstorming

Brainstorming is a technique developed by Alex Osborn, an executive of a major New York advertising firm, and first described in his book, *Your Creative Power* (1948). It is designed to increase the flow of ideas in small group meetings. The most important principle underlying brainstorming is that the process of generating ideas is completely separated from the process of evaluating them. Brainstorming sessions take place in two phases—an *idea generation* phase and an *idea evaluation* phase. During the idea generation phase, all judging and criticism of the produced ideas is eliminated—or rather deferred—until the evaluation phase.

In most conferences, such as town meetings and informal planning sessions, the standard format is debate, that is, proposal and criticism. This format is not notably successful in producing new ideas. Typically in such sessions, each new idea is met with a welter of criticism. Brainstorming is quite different from most meeting situations.

During the idea generation phase:

1. All criticism of ideas is withheld until the evaluation phase.
2. Wild or even silly ideas are welcomed.

3. Quantity of ideas is encouraged.
4. Participants are encouraged to combine or improve on ideas already suggested.
5. The group acts as a whole, not breaking up into several small groups.
7. One person acts as a secretary to record the list of ideas.

A brainstorming group needs a leader who will enforce the rules. The first and most important task of the leader is to be sure that criticism is withheld. There seems to be a strong tendency in many people to respond to an idea by saying, "Oh, that won't work because. . . ." An idea which is proposed as a joke may not be useful in itself as a solution of the problem, and yet it may aid the solution by suggesting a new dimension of the problem or by opening a new line of inquiry.

In a typical brainstorming session, the members of the group are allowed to propose ideas whenever they please. The possibility exists in this situation that one or a few of the group members will dominate the session, with the result that others may be prevented from contributing all that they could. To eliminate this possibility, Bouchard (1972) has modified the typical brainstorming procedure by adding a sequencing rule in which the members of the group take turns in offering ideas. He reported that groups using the sequencing rule produced more ideas than groups that did not use it.

If the group begins to run out of ideas during the idea-generating phase, it sometimes helps to review the list of ideas already suggested. When the group's ideas have been exhausted, it is time to move to the evaluation phase.

In the evaluation phase, each idea is reviewed critically to determine if it is in fact a practical solution. A list of the ideas that the group considers most practical is then submitted as the group's problem-solving recommendations.

Osborn feels that brainstorming is helpful in producing new ideas for two reasons. First, the reduction in criticism during the generation phase allows ideas to be born and developed that otherwise might never have been suggested, or might have been rejected before they had received sufficient positive consideration. Second, Osborn feels that brainstorming sessions promote a kind of social contagion in which one person's idea inspires a better idea in another—an idea that the second person wouldn't have thought of otherwise.

Studies reviewed by Stein (1975) indicate that groups using the brainstorming technique do produce more ideas than groups that generate and evaluate ideas simultaneously. Further, most of these studies also show that the brainstorming groups produce more high-quality ideas.

We should note that Osborn recommends brainstorming only for certain types of "simple and talkable" problems—problems like, "How can we prevent stealing from the library?" and, "How can we get more foreign visitors to come to the United States?" Indeed, research on group problem solving suggests that groups do better than individuals on some kinds of problems but not on others. Individuals are as good or better than groups in solving arithmetic problems (Hudgins, 1960), and in solving problems where each individual has all the necessary information. Groups are superior to individuals in tasks where the pooling of skills and information is important. For example, groups are superior to individuals for remembering a complex story (Perlmutter, 1953), and for solving prejudice-provoking syllogisms (Barnlund, 1959). Barnlund suggests that the group is more objective than the individual because prejudices are not completely shared among the members of the group.

Exercise

Form a group and conduct a brainstorming session. Suggested topics are:

- ways to save time
- ways to keep the city clean
- uses for discarded styrofoam cups

Individual Brainstorming

While the brainstorming technique was designed to be used with groups, it can also be used by a single person in private idea-generating sessions. The principles to be applied are the same. Separate idea generation from evaluation. Start with the idea generation phase, writing down ideas as they occur, without criticism. You should welcome wild or silly ideas, and you should try to combine or improve ideas that were generated earlier. The hard part in this phase is to control your internal editor—the internal voice of criticism which may lead you to ignore an idea that seems too dumb or trivial.

Just as with group brainstorming, when you begin to run out of ideas, you can review the list as a source to stimulate further production. When the ideas really have stopped coming, it is time to move on to the evaluation phase. Here you review each idea to select those that seem best for solving the problem.

Exercise

Conduct a brainstorming session by yourself. Suggested topics:

- how to increase your own efficiency
- how to make your favorite annoyance less annoying
- how to persuade someone to give you a job

Individual brainstorming sessions can be very helpful when you are writing (see Flower, 1980). Suppose that you are planning a magazine article on architecture for a teenage audience. To brainstorm, first generate all of the ideas you can think of that a teenager might find interesting or important about architecture. As you do this, scratch down rapid notes in the form of scattered words and phrases that will remind you of the ideas. When idea generation is complete, evaluate the ideas—that is, decide which ideas you want to include in your article—and then organize them into an outline. At this point, you are well started in producing your article.

DISCOVERING ANALOGIES

Analogies are an important source of ideas when we are searching for problem solutions. Several systems have been proposed for stimulating the discovery of useful analogies. In essence, all of these systems employ some checklist of analogy types. The user of the system works through the checklist and tries to find analogies of each type.

In Gordon's synectics system (Gordon, 1961), the checklist consists of four analogy types: personal, direct, symbolic, and fantasy. Suppose that we were members of a synectics group looking for ideas to improve automobile brakes. First, we would try to form personal analogies in which we put ourselves directly into the problem situation. For example, we could imagine ourselves as the brakes of a car. Next, we would search for a direct analogy if the same function is accomplished in some other setting, such as a cat trying to stop on a slippery floor. Third, we would try to form symbolic analogies. I would tell you about this kind of analogy if I could, but unfortunately, I have been unable to find an intelligible description of it.

Finally, we think of fantasy analogies in which anything including magic and science fiction are allowed, for instance, claws reaching out of the road to grab our wheels.

In Koberg and Bagnall's (1974) attribute analogy system, the checklist is a list of attributes of an object—its name, form, function, color, and material. If we are trying to improve some object, say, a fireplace, we first list its attributes and then attach analogies to each one. Table 1 illustrates the process.

As yet there appears to be no solid experimental evidence that either synectics or attribute analogies actually work. However, the synectics system has received a good deal of favorable comment from users in industry (see Stein, 1975).

PLANNING AND CREATIVITY

A plan is a set of directions we use to guide us in solving a problem. The more effort we put into planning, the more likely we are to construct a good map which will guide us efficiently to the best solution. Since creative acts are problem solving acts, it shouldn't surprise us that planning is also important for creativity. Flower and Hayes (1980) have shown that good expository writers plan much more effectively than do poor writers.

Table 1. The Attribute Analogy System (from Koberg and Bagnall, 1974)

Assuming the problem is to improve a fireplace, its attributes are: *Name:* Fireplace *Form:* Geometric, angular, conical, etc. *Function:* Heat room, psychologically soothing, etc. *Color:* Black, brick red, etc. *Material:* Steel, masonry, etc. *Analogy Chains* (similarities) *Name:* Combustion chamber, tea pot, auto engine, cigarette lighter, etc. *Form:* Architectural constructions, crystals, prisms, etc. *Function:* Cat on lap, robe, intimate friend, etc. *Ideas Produced* (for improving fireplace) Change name to energy transformer. Try forms which are derived from crystal structures. Use robe insulation principle to conserve radiant heat, etc.

A path-breaking study by Getzels and Csikszentmihalyi (1976) indicates that planning is critically important in art. They showed that the amount of planning* that an art student did in preparing to draw a picture predicted not only the quality of the resulting picture, but also whether or not the student would become a productive artist years later.

The investigators tested 31 male second- and third-year students at a prestigious art school. Each student was brought into an experimental room supplied with drawing materials, an empty table, and a variety of objects. The students were asked to select any of the objects they wanted, arrange them on the table as they chose, and then to draw a picture. They were told, "The important thing is that the drawing should be pleasing to you."

The experimenter then noted three things about the students' behavior before they started drawing and three things about their behavior while they were drawing. These six behaviors (listed in Table 2) were chosen to reflect the amount of planning the students did in executing the drawing. For example, students were scored high on planning if they examined many objects or if they made many drafts and took considerable time in arriving at the final structure of their drawings.

BEFORE DRAWING:

B1. How many objects were manipulated?

B2. Were unusual objects chosen—that is, did a student choose objects which few other students chose?

B3. How carefully did the student examine the objects?

WHILE DRAWING:

W1. How much time elapsed from the beginning of drawing to the time at

---

*These authors claim to measure problem finding rather than planning. However, as these terms are used in this text, and, I believe, in cognitive science generally, it is more appropriate to say that they have measured planning.

which the final structure appeared? (judged later by looking at a sequence of timed photographs)

W2. Did the subject start the drawing over or change the arrangement of the objects?

W3. Was the drawing simply a copy of the arrangement of objects, or were the objects in the drawing modified in size, position, or number?

The drawings that the students produced were then evaluated independently by five art critics for originality, craftsmanship, and overall value. Table 3 shows the correlations between the average of the five critics' judgments and the planning behaviors. Five of the six planning behaviors show strong correlations with the critics' judgments. (In this study, a correlation of 0.3 or larger should be considered significant.) Planning, then, appears to be very helpful in creating a good drawing.

In a follow-up study seven years later, Getzels and Csikszentmihaly tried to determine how successful the 31 students were in pursuing artistic careers. By contacting art critics, directors of art galleries, and the students themselves, they found that about half of the students had dropped out of art completely. The rest were pursuing careers in the fine arts with varying degrees of success. Seven were using their skills in related professions, such as teaching art, but had not yet exhibited their work publicly. The remaining nine had all exhibited. Some were represented by major galleries and one had achieved a very notable degree of success. His work is hung in the best galleries, and articles about his work appear in the most respected art journals.

The last column of Table 1 shows the correlation between success as an artist and the planning behaviors measured seven years earlier. Four of the six behaviors

Table 3. Correlations Among Planning Behaviors,
The Quality of the Drawing, and Later Success
Art Critics' Judgments

Planning Behaviors	Originality	Craftsmanship	Overall Worth	Success (7 years later)
B1—number of objects	.52**	.17	.48**	.45**
B2—unusualness of objects	.42**	.21	.35*	.21
B3—careful examination of objects	.58***	.34*	.44**	.43**
W1—delay in final structure	.08	−.18	.09	.48**
W2—restarts and changes in arrangement	.37*	.01	.22	.31*
W3—difference between drawing and arrangement	.61***	.37*	.44**	.20

*There is only one chance in 20 that a correlation this large would be obtained by chance.
**There is only one chance in 100 that a correlation this large would be obtained by chance.
***There is only one chance in 1,000 that a correlation this large would be obtained by chance.

show strong correlations with success. The simplest way to interpret this remarkable result is to assume that the successful artists habitually make planning part of their approach to artistic problems. Planning leads to high quality in all their artistic work just as it led to high quality in the experimental drawings.

CREATIVITY AND PREPARATION

In Chapter 2, we reviewed research indicating that skillful chess players employ an enormous amount of chess-pattern knowledge. To acquire this knowledge, the chess player must spend thousands of hours of preparation—playing chess, reading chess magazines, and studying chess positions. Simon and Chase (1973) note that it is very rare for a person to reach the grandmaster level of skill with less than 10 years of intensive study.

If chess masters require a long and intensive period of preparation to acquire their skill, what about painters and composers? Certainly painting and composition require large amounts of pattern knowledge. The painter must know how a face will look from a multitude of angles and how colors clash or harmonize. The composer must know the timbres of the various instruments and the sound, look, and feel of chords and key structures. Do creative artists then also require intense preparation before they can produce works of real merit? Does creative productivity depend on preparation, or can geniuses produce masterworks right from the beginning of their careers? To answer this question, I decided to examine the lives of famous composers.

I started my investigation with the incredibly precocious Mozart, because he is the composer who seems least likely to have required a long period of preparation. He began to study music at four and wrote his first symphony at the age of eight.

I have graphed the number of works that Mozart produced in each year of his career in Figure 1. The figure shows that Mozart's productivity increased steadily for the first 10 or 12 years of his career. It also shows that Mozart did produce works in the very early part of his career when he had had only a year or two of preparation. If these are works of very high quality, then we could conclude, for Mozart at least, that he didn't require long preparation to be outstandingly creative. However, these early works may not be of oustanding quality. Perhaps they have been preserved for their historical rather than their musical value.

To obtain some measure of the quality of Mozart's work, I turned to Schwann's *Record and Tape Guide*. I reasoned that an excellent work is likely to be recorded more often than a poor one. The decision to record a work presumably reflects both musical judgment and popular taste—that is, it reflects the musical judgment by a conductor that the work is worthwhile and the belief of the record companies that the record will sell.

Figure 2 shows the number of recordings listed in Schwann's guide (August,

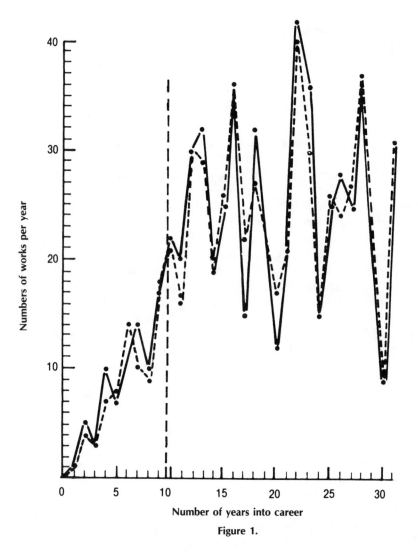

Figure 1.

1979) of works written in each year of Mozart's career. While about 12 percent of Mozart's works were written in the first 10 years of his career, only 4.8 percent of the recordings came from this early period. Further, many of the recordings of early works are included in collections with labels such as, ''The Complete Symphonies of Mozart.'' Perhaps the early works were included for reasons of completeness rather than excellence. When recordings included in complete collections are omitted from the calculations, the percentage of recordings in this early period drops to 2.4. These observations suggest that Mozart's early works are not of the same high quality as his later ones. The music critic, Harold Schonberg, is of the same opinion. He says (1970)

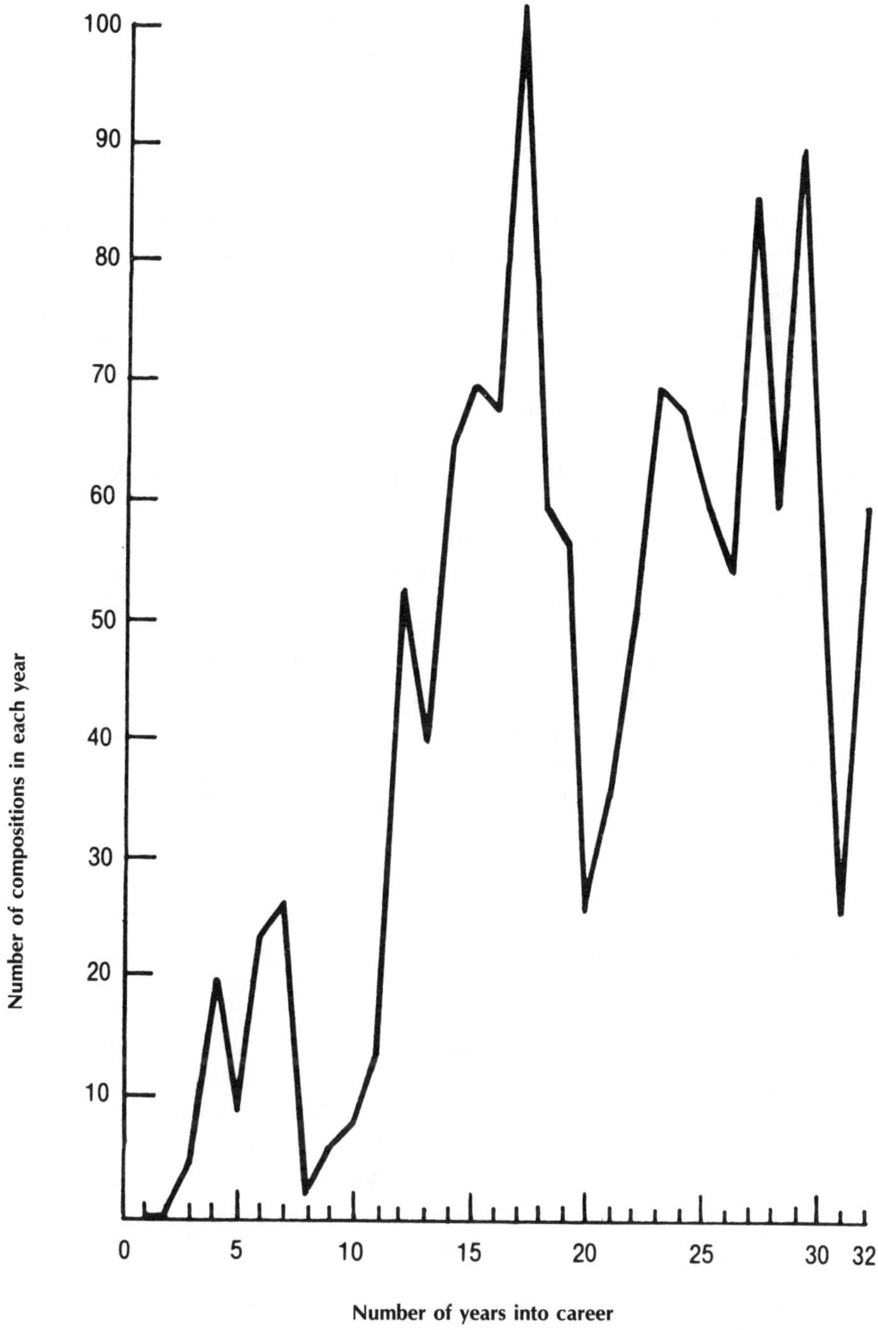

Figure 2.

295

It is strange to say of a composer who started writing at six, and lived only 36 years, that he developed late, but that is the truth. Few of Mozart's early works, elegant as they are, have the personality, concentration, and richness that entered his music after 1781. . . ."

In 1781, Mozart was in the 21st year of his career.

Some works are recorded two or three times in different complete collections. Therefore, to weed out works which may be recorded for reasons other than musical quality, I defined a masterwork (for the purposes of this study) as one for which five different recordings are currently listed in Schwann's guide. By this definition, Mozart's first masterwork was written in the 12th year of his career.

To explore the question about creativity and preparation more generally, I searched for biographical material about all of the composers discussed in Schonberg's *The Lives of the Great Composers* (1970). For 76 of these composers, I was able to determine when they started intensive study of music. Incidentally, all of these composers had at least one work listed in Schwann's guide, and 64 had one or more works which were available on five different records.

In Figure 3 all of the careers of the composers are shown on the same scale. That is, the 10th year of Handel's career is graphed in the same place as the 10th year of Brahms' career. The figure shows that very few composers produced masterworks with less than 10 years of preparation. There are just three exceptions: Satie's "Trois Gymnopédies," written in year 8; Shostakovich's Symphony #1, and Paganini's Caprices, both written in year 9. Between year 10 and year 25, there is an enormous increase in productivity.

Figure 4 shows that composers maintain their productivity through the 40th year of their careers. Figure 5 indicates that a decline in productivity begins at about the 50th year of their careers. Productivity can continue far beyond the 50th year, however. For example, Albeniz's first masterwork was written in the 72nd year of his career!

It is reasonable to ask whether the important factor in the composers' productivity is really preparation or if perhaps the important factor is simply age. It is conceivable, for example, that composers have to be, say, 16 or 22, before they can write good music. Perhaps it is experience in life rather than experience in music that is critical. To test this possibility, I divided the composers into three groups. The first consisted of 14 composers who had begun their careers between the ages of 3 and 5. The second group consisted of 30 composers who began their careers between 6 and 9 years of age. The third group consisted of 20 composers who began their careers at 10 or later.

I reasoned that if age were the critical factor, then those who started their careers early would have to wait longer to produce good work than those composers who started late. In fact, this was not the case. The median number of years to first notable composition was 16.5 for the first group, 22 for the second group, and 21.5 for the third group.

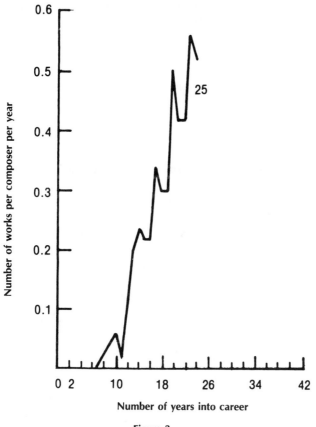

Figure 3.

It appears, then, that what composers need to write good music is not maturing but rather musical preparation. The results make it dramatically clear that no one composes outstanding music without first having about 10 years of intensive musical preparation.

These results *do not* mean that there is no such thing as genius. They *do not* mean that just anyone with 10 to 25 years of experience can write great music. They *do* mean that even a person endowed with the genius of Mozart or Beethoven will need 10 years or more of intense preparation to be creative.

These results have the following practical implications:

1. If you have been working hard in your chosen area for several years and haven't yet received a Nobel or even a Pulitzer prize, don't despair. Think in terms of decades rather than years.
2. If you have decided to go into creative work because you are "basically lazy," you have made a ghastly mistake. Creative scientists typically work

70-80 hours a week. You would do better to be a plumber or mechanic. These are honorable professions and they pay much better per hour than science or art.

Summary

A creative act is one which:

1. is original,
2. valuable, and,
3. suggests that the person performing the act has unusual mental abilities.

A creative act is a problem solving act, and, in particular it is the solution of an ill-defined problem. Four cognitive processes especially important for creativity are: problem finding, idea generation, planning, and preparation.

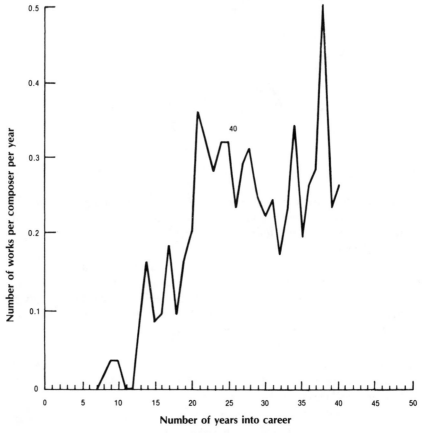

Figure 4.

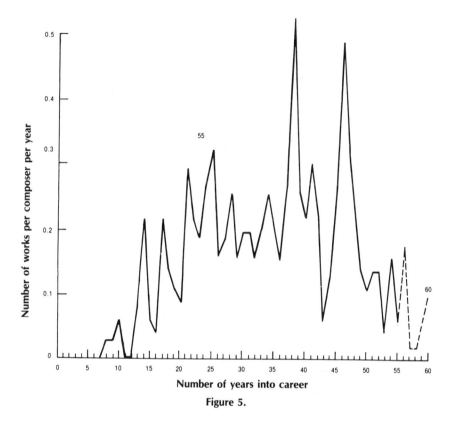

Figure 5.

Problem finding—the discovery of a new problem not suggested by anyone else—is important in initiating new directions in science and art. Three procedures than can help us to find problems are: bug listing, searching for counterexamples, and searching for alternative interpretations.

Sometimes, when we are trying to solve an ill-defined problem, we are blocked by difficulty in *generating ideas* for solution. Brainstorming and discovering analogies may help us out of this difficulty.

Planning is important in creative activities as it is in any form of problem solving. Good writing and good art depend on good planning.

Extensive *preparation* is essential for acts of outstanding creativity. Composers require about 10 years of preparation before they can produce works of outstanding quality.

REFERENCES

Adams, J. L. *Conceptual Blockbusting*. San Francisco: W. H. Freeman & Co., 1974.
Barnlund, D. C. "A Comparative Study of Individual, Majority, and Group Judgment." *Journal of Abnormal and Social Psychology, 58*, 55-60, 1959.

Bouchard, T. J., Jr. "A Comparison of Two Group Brainstorming Procedures." *Journal of Applied Psychology*, *56*, 418–421, 1972.

Einstein, A., and Infeld, L. *The Evolution of Physics*. New York: Simon and Schuster, Inc., 1938.

Flower, L. *Problem Solving Strategies for Writing*. New York: Harcourt, Brace, Jovanovich, Inc., 1980.

Flower, L., and Hayes, J. R. "The Cognition of Discovery: Defining a Rhetorical Problem." *College Composition and Communication*, 2(31), 21–32, 1980.

Getzels, J. W., and Csikszentmihalyi, M. *The Creative Vision: A Longitudinal Study of Problem Finding in Art*. New York: John Wiley & Sons, Inc., 1976.

Gordon, W. J. J. *Synectics*. New York: Collier, 1961.

Grove's Dictionary of Music and Musicians, Fifth Edition. New York: St. Martin's Press, Inc., 1955.

Hayes, J. R., *Cognitive Psychology: Thinking and Creating*. Homewood, IL: The Dorsey Press, 1978.

Hudgins, B. B. "Effects of Group Experience on Individual Problem Solving." *Journal of Educational Psychology*, *51*, 37–42, 1960.

Koberg, D., and Bagnall, J. *The Universal Traveler*, Third Edition. Los Altos, CA: William Kaufmann, Inc., 1974.

Koechel ABC, Fifth Edition. Wiesbaden: Breitkopf and Hartel, 1965.

Newell, A., Shaw, J. C., and Simon, H. A. "The Processes of Creative Thinking." In *Contemporary Approaches to Creative Thinking*, Third Edition, edited by H. E. Gruber, G. Terrell, and M. Wertheimer. New York: Atherton Press, 1964.

Osborn, A. *Your Creative Power*. New York: Charles Scribner's Sons, 1948.

Perlmutter, H. V. "Group Memory of Meaningful Material." *Journal of Psychology*, *35*, 361–370, 1953.

Schonberg, H. C. *The Lives of the Great Composers*. New York: W. W. Norton & Co., Inc., 1970.

Schwann-1 Record and Tape Guide. Boston: ABC Schwann, August, 1979.

Schwartz, T. *The Art of Logical Thinking*. New York: Random House, Inc., 1980.

Simon, H. A., and Chase, W. G. "Skill in Chess." *American Scientist*, *61*, 394–403, 1973.

Stein, M. I. *Stimulating Creativity*, Volume 2. New York: Academic Press, Inc., 1975.

Wason, P. C. "Reasoning About a Rule." *Quarterly Journal of Experimental Psychology*, *20*, 273–281, 1968.

12

How Social Conditions
Affect Creativity *

Creativity can occur on a variety of levels, as pointed out in Chapter 11. When we speak of creativity in this chapter, we mean the very highest level of creativity—the level at which a symphony is produced, a scientific discovery made, or a Pulitzer-prize-winning play is written.

We are in no way suggesting that people who aspire to and achieve this high level of creativity are better, happier, or more personally fulfilled than the rest of us. And we certainly have no magic formula to insure that people can become a Rembrandt or an Einstein or a Mozart.

Still, we do know some factors that are important for achieving high-level creativity. In the last chapter we discussed the importance of knowledge, planning, and hard work; in this chapter we will discuss how social conditions affect creativity.

INTRODUCTION

When we compare groups of people in the United States, we find enormous differences among them in creative productivity. Men achieve more than women; Jews, more than Christians; Orientals, more than whites; and whites, more than blacks and native Americans.

Some claim that these differences are innate. For example, Jensen (1971) has argued that racial differences in intellectual performance, particularly on IQ tests, are due in part to heredity. However, Brody and Brody (1976) have carefully reviewed the research on racial differences in intelligence. They found no evidence to suggest that the differences are hereditary.

---

*This chapter was written with Sandra J. Bond, of Carnegie-Mellon University.

We believe that differences in high-level creativity between groups are due largely to differences in environment. Some environments foster creativity and some do not. As we see it, society has been conducting some very large-scale "natural" experiments on creativity. Men and women in our society are raised differently, even though they may be raised in the same household. Jews and Christians are taught different attitudes toward learning. Blacks and whites are given different economic opportunities. All of these differences can influence creative productivity. By examining the experiences of people in these groups, we can gain some insight into how this happens.

MEN AND WOMEN

Historically, men have been more creative than women, as Table 1 shows. This is true not only for the sciences and politics, but for the arts as well. Although there are about equal numbers of men and women in our population (49 percent, male; 51 percent, female), men have clearly overshadowed women in creative accomplishment. Are women less creative than men by nature? We feel that there is really no reason to believe so. Our culture treats men and women very differently. Women are given far less opportunity and encouragement to be creative than are men. In the following sections, we will argue that these differences in treatment can make an enormous difference in creative output.

Some Prerequisites for Creativity: Interest, Self-Confidence, and Time

In Chapter 11, we found that even Mozart and Beethoven required more than 10 years of intensive preparation before they could begin to produce their masterworks. In any field, people who want to be creative must expect to invest enormous amounts of time and effort in their profession and even then it may not be enough. The effort involved goes far beyond the hours a normal job requires. For example, University of California professors spend an *average* of 60 hours weekly on teaching and research (Harris, 1972). Some spend much more time. Herbert Simon, 1978 Nobel Laureate in Economics, spent about 100 hours a week for years doing the work for which he eventually won the Nobel prize (personal communication). Since there are only 168 hours in a week, it is obvious that intensive creative work of this type necessarily takes precedence over everything else—including sleep!

People who can invest this sort of intense effort in a field must have:

1. Sufficient interest in the field that they *want* to invest the time;
2. sufficient self-confidence to believe that they are not simply wasting their time; and

Table 1. Achievements by Men and Women

	MEN	WOMEN
Nobel Prizes (1901-1987)		
physics	128	2
chemistry	106	3
physiology or medicine	138	4
economics	23	0
National Academy of Science Awards		
Carty Medal in Science(1932-1986)	18	0
Draper Medal in Physics (1886-1986)	42	1
Elliot Medal in Zoology or Paleontology (1917-1986)	46	2
Kovalenko Medal in Medical Science (1952-1986)	13	0
Thompson Medal in Geology or Paleontology (1921-1986)	29	0
National Medal of Science (1962-1979)	153	2
AMA Distinguished Service Award (1938-1986)	49	0
Total	745 (98%)	14 (2%)
Nobel Prizes (1901-1987)		
literature	83	5
Pulitzer Prizes		
fiction	57	18
drama	71	7
poetry	60	15
music	40	3
biography	71	7
Priz de Rome (music)	131	8
Total	513 (89%)	63 (11%)
Nobel Prizes (1901-1987)		
peace	72	7
U.S. Senators (1986)	98	2
Members of the House of Representatives (1986)	412	23
Governors (1986)	47	3
Total	629 (95%)	35 (5%)
Listings in *Who's Who in America* (1982-1985)	94%	6%

Left margin labels: *Science*, *The Arts*, *Politics*

Percent of population in the United States: men, 48.7%; women, 51.3%.
Population figures for 1984: males, 115.2 million; females, 121.4 million.

3. sufficient freedom from other responsibilities so that necessary time is available to them.

Our culture makes it far more likely that men will meet these criteria than women.

A Taste of History

To understand current attitudes, it is often helpful to remind ourselves of attitudes held in the not too distant past. The following is a chapter on "the equality

of the sexes" taken in its entirety from T.S. Arthur's "*Advice to Young Ladies*"
published in Boston in 1851.

Equality of the Sexes

Singularly enough, we have in this day a class of intellectual ladies, who boldly
contend for the absolute equality of the sexes, and who write books for the purpose
of proving this doctrine, and spreading it throughout society. As far as we are able
to understand what they do believe, we infer that they hold the only radical difference that exists between a man and a woman to be the difference of physical
conformation—the social difference that is seen every where, arising from man's
superior physical power, by which he is able to keep woman in subjection. They
claim for woman equal civil and political privileges with man, and see nothing but
tyranny in the law, or usage that has the force of law, which keeps a woman out
of her country's legislative halls. Every where would these reformers place women
in contest with men for the honors and emoluments which society bestows upon
the successful;—in the camp, on the bench, at the bar, in the pulpit, in the dissecting-
room, or hospital, with the operator's knife in her hand,—in fact, wherever strong
nerve, powerful intellect, decision, and firmness are required.

Some of the books written by advocates of these doctrines contain views of a
most pernicious character, striking still more deeply at the very foundations of social well-being. As might be supposed, few of their writers understand or teach
what is true in regard to marriage. And this is no matter of wonder; for how can
any one, who is not able to see the true difference between the sexes, teach what
is true in regard to their union?

In order to guard our young friends against the false reasonings, and equally
false conclusions, of these advocates of the equality of the sexes, we will, in as
plain and comprehensive a way as possible, set forth what is the true relation of
one sex to the other; and in doing this we must explain the radical difference. As
to equality in itself, this, no doubt, exists; but it is in the equal right of both to
be useful and happy in the particular spheres for which God created them. The main
point of equality which is contended for, and upon which all the rest is made to
depend, is *intellectual* equality; and here the great error is committed, and it is committed by "intellectual" or "masculine" women, who hold the same false relation
to their sex, that "effeminate" men hold to theirs. It is a little curious that the first
use made, by these intellectual women, of their great mental powers, is to lead their
followers into a most dangerous error!

That there does exist as great a difference between the mental as between the
physical structure of the sexes, is clear, from common perception, to almost every
one. That it must be so, will be seen from this: Every physical form that we see
in nature is the outbirth of some spiritual and invisible cause; and the peculiarity
of its form and quality depends solely upon the peculiarity of its cause. The cause
that produces a rose is different from that which produces a lily, and ever remains
different. The cause that produces a lion is different from that which produces a
lamb. It is not circumstances, the peculiarity of education, nor any other external
thing, that makes this difference, for it is radical. And as this is true in the broader,
so is it true in all the minuter, shades of difference that exist in the world of nature.

If there be any difference in form, there is a corresponding difference, be it ever so minute, in the producing cause. Keeping this in view, it may readily be seen, that what makes man a man, and woman a woman, is not the body, but the mind; and, as the body is formed from, by, or through the mind as a cause, the mind of a man must be different from the mind of a woman, because he has a different external conformation. This difference is not a slight one; it is a difference that pervades every part of the body.

The question now comes—"In what does this difference specifically consist?" Before attempting to answer this fully, let it be remarked, that this difference is a *uniting* difference, not a separating one; and that inherent in the two sexes is an instinct that tends to a union of one with the other. This union, let it be further stated, is necessary to the formation of a perfect being: until it does take place, both the man and the woman must be, in a certain sense, imperfect—he only a thinking man, and she only a loving man. But when it is effected, then both unite to form one truly perfect man, with thought and affection in their fullest power.

As clearly as it is possible for us to do it, will we now endeavor to show in what the difference of the sexes consists. The mind is composed of two faculties, Will and Understanding; the one the seat of affection, and the other of thought. The brain is that organ by which the mind acts, and is marked by two grand divisions, the cerebrum and the cerebellum. The cerebrum occupies the highest and anterior part of the skull, while the cerebellum, or little brain, as it is sometimes called, occupies the lower and posterior part of the skull. It is by means of the cerebellum that the will acts, and by means of the cerebrum that the understanding acts. By the will, affections are excited; and by the understanding, thoughts. The will feels, or loves; the understanding thinks. The understanding is the agent of the will, and bodies forth or gives forms to its peculiar affections. The will is man's life or love, and the understanding is only the means by which the life or love of a man comes into activity, and thence into power.

By keeping this division in the mind, the difference between the sexes, when stated, will be clearly apparent. A man has will and understanding, and a cerebellum and cerebrum by which they act; and so has a woman. In this they are alike. But in man the understanding predominates, and in woman the will; and here they are different. If this be so, we may, of course, expect to find a larger development of the cerebrum, or upper brain, in man, and a larger development of the cerebellum, or lower brain, in woman; and this is so. A man's head is higher, and fuller in front, than a woman's; while a woman's head is broader and larger behind than a man's.

From this it will be seen that man has a will and an understanding; and so has a woman;—that both are thinking and loving beings, but that in one the understanding or intellect preponderates, and in the other the will or affections; and therefore to claim mental equality is absurd. A man is not equal to a woman, nor a woman equal to a man. As to the question of superiority, we leave that for others to decide; merely stating, however, that the will has reference to good, and the understanding to truth; the affections regarding quality or good, and the understanding being merely the discriminating power by which truth is perceived. Some think good higher than truth; and this is our own opinion. Good is, in fact, the essence, and truth the form, of a thing.

The true difference between the sexes is that which we have just stated. Now, let any sensible woman reflect upon the nature of this difference, and she will at once see that the claim of equality which is set up is altogether an erroneous one, and that the attempt to make woman equal in the way some contend that she should be, would be to do the greatest possible wrong, both to herself and society. That she has not the strong intellectual power that man possesses, no woman, but one blinded by her own pride and self-love, will for a moment attempt to maintain. There are men of weak intellect, and women of strong intellect; but take the whole mass of women and the whole mass of men, and every one can see that there is an immense preponderance of intellect in the one over the other. By *intellect* do not understand us to say *mind*: we are only speaking of a *faculty* of the mind by which man is peculiarly distinguished. *Love*, the sweeter, purer, stronger quality of mind, is woman's.

In the beginning, God made man male and female. There is a deep significance in this peculiar language. It is said in the Bible, speaking of a man and his wife, that *They twain shall be one flesh*. And the common perception of mankind, brought down into common language, is, that "a man and his wife are one." This is not a mere figure of speech, a beautiful idealism. It is the truth. A man and his wife, *truly* so, are one. Now, how can two things, precisely alike, become one? A man and a man are alike, and so are a woman and a woman; but they cannot become one. There needs to be a uniting difference; and this we have in the preponderance of intellect in man, and affection in woman; and their union, mystical and holy, is needed to make one truly perfect, effective man.

Of the nature of this mystical union we had thought of speaking here at some length; but the subject is rather difficult of comprehension, and hardly in place in a work like this.

It follows, from what has been said, that marriage is essential to human perfection. This we firmly believe; and we also believe that where marriage is opposed from principle, (it never is from any other than a selfish principle,) the mind becomes perverted from its true order, and the intellect weakened.

It may seem to some, that to say *equality* of the sexes is not the true mode of speaking, as a denial of this equality, leaves on the mind an idea of inferiority of one to the other. To some, the terms used will doubtless convey this meaning. The difficulty of choosing terms that express with perfect exactness what we desire to convey, is often very great, especially as to the same set of terms different persons attach peculiar, and sometimes very important, shades of difference. By *equal*, as used in this chapter, is meant being alike as to mental conformation and mental power—which is denied. As to which is highest or lowest, superior or inferior, that is another matter. Here we believe woman to be the equal of man; not born to obedience, but to be his intelligent and loving companion.

Let no young woman be deceived by the class of reformers, to which we made allusion in the commencement of this chapter. Some of them, stepping out of the sphere for which God and their own peculiar mental qualities designed them, are assuming the place of men as itinerant and public lecturers; and most of them speak almost with a species of scoffing of the holy state of wedlock. No good, in any case, has ever arisen, but much evil, from the promulgation of their pernicious doctrines. Man they are too much in the habit of representing as a selfish tyrant, and woman as his plaything or slave; and they are full of intemperate appeals to their sex to throw off the yoke that man has placed upon their necks. That there are men who are selfish tyrants, and makes slaves of their wives, is not to be denied; but just as many women tyrannize over their husbands. These form the exceptions, not the rule; and to judge of all, by these exceptions, shows either a weak head or a bad heart.

As far as we have observed these social reformers, we find that the great evil complained of, the head and front of all the wrong they suffer, lies in the necessity there is for the female sex to attend to domestic duties, while man steps abroad into the world, and makes himself a name and a place therein. They complain that every avenue to wealth, place, and preferment, is blocked up by men, and that a woman is not permitted, by the absurd customs of society, to contend for honors and wealth, but must meekly withdraw into her little circle at home, and be content with her husband's honor, or the portion of his wealth he may choose to dole out to her.

With this idea set steadily before their minds, at the same time that they are profoundly ignorant of what really makes the difference between man and woman, they see nothing but wrong and oppression in the usages of society, and charge upon man the authorship of what is only the legitimate result of a law impressed by the hand of God upon the human mind.

In thus speaking, it is not meant to deny that many evils exist in society, and that women do not suffer sorely from these evils. This, alas! we know too well. But that which is pointed out by the persons we allude to, as the cause, is not the true one.

There is something really so absurd and revolting in the idea of taking woman out of her present sphere, and her present high and holy uses in society, and placing her side by side with man in the world's rough arena, and in contest with him for honor, and fame, and wealth, that we cannot seriously argue against it. We have deemed it sufficient to show that, in the very nature of things, such can never be the case.

The extreme views expressed in Arthur's chapter seem out of date now. However, as we see in the following sections, they are not as out of date as we might like to think.

Education of Females: The Early Years

By tradition, males and females have very different roles in our culture—roles they are expected to play from very early childhood on. When we hear of a child being born, we are almost always told its sex. Sexual identity is taken very seriously, and the child is rarely allowed to forget it. As infants, boys are dressed in blue and have boys' names, while girls are dressed in pink and have girls' names. As four-year-olds, boys are expected to be interested in trucks; and girls, in dolls. In the primary grades, boys are expected to show more interest in science than girls do. These expectations mold children's interests. Torrance (1960) found that girls are reluctant to work with science toys and often say that these toys aren't suitable for them, and that boys suggest twice as many ideas as girls in experiments with science materials. By changing the teaching conditions, though, Torrance was able to reduce this difference significantly. He concluded that social forces were at work even at early ages to turn girls away from certain fields.

Not only does society guide girls' interests away from science—it also directs them very powerfully toward other occupations in which it is difficult to pursue high-level creative activities. Chief among these "women's jobs" is "wife-and-mother." According to the cultural ideal, the wife-and-mother is a homemaker—she cleans, sews, cooks, and washes at home, is "fulfilled" by raising babies, and admires and supports her husband. It is easy to guess that there is little about this occupation that fosters the creative effort necessary to produce a masterwork. If a wife-and-mother does work outside the home, society encourages her to enter women's occupations such as domestic helper, nurse, secretary, and teacher. These occupations have relatively low status and low pay, and offer little opportunity for creative achievement.

Self-Confidence

Experiences during the early years not only shape children's interests, they also help to determine whether children will develop sufficient confidence in themselves to compete in creative fields.

It is traditional in our culture to believe that as a group women suffer from certain intellectual deficits. It is said that women can't handle abstract ideas and that they can't think logically. A corollary of these beliefs is that women can't do well in math- or science-related fields such as engineering, medicine, or finance. If a young girl's parents believe these things, it may be difficult for her to develop confidence that she could succeed in any of these fields.

In a study of successful and unsuccessful women, Bond and Hayes (1978) found that parents of successful women don't share this cultural stereotype. One of the successful women, a psychiatrist, says:

> My father shared the view that women should do whatever work they were equipped to do and gave me faith in myself, determination, and moral support.
> (Rossi and Calderwood, 1973)

Another, a successful chemist, states:

> It was always assumed that I would pursue a scientific career, since I showed some talent in that direction. I cannot say that I was encouraged to have professional aspirations, as much as that it was assumed that I would fulfill them. (Kundsin, 1974)

A pediatrician recalls:

> To my father and mother, it was important that people are what they are—and that being who and what I was was good. As a woman, I was told, I would be able to do whatever I wanted.   (Kundsin, 1974)

A noted physician says:

> During adolescence and college, it was taken for granted by everyone, including myself, that I would go into medical school. No one seemed to have any doubts at all that I would go, and retrospectively, the most extraordinary factor I can now recognize is that never once while I was growing up do I remember anyone at any time ever suggesting that there was something I could not do simply because I was female. Everyone I knew or every came in contact with simply took it for granted that whatever I wanted to do, I could do. (Kundsin, 1974)

Role Models

It is helpful for people planning to enter a difficult field to have role models—that is, people they admire and want to imitate, who can show them what it is to lead the sort of life to which they aspire. If you want to be a physician, you will have a real advantage if a parent, close relative, or friend is a physician. You will be able to learn firsthand what sorts of problems doctors face and how they deal with them.

There is no question that the people we select as role models have a powerful effect on the direction our life can take. Two of the successful women in our study—the first, a physician; the second, an electrical engineer—talk about their role models:

> At the age of 11, I was taken in by [a doctor's family] to live with them in New York. This is where my academic intellectual life and my interest in medicine began, for [the doctor] loved to talk over his cases with me. I often went on his rounds with him. (Kundsin, 1974)

> My professional career can be said to have started with freshman physics. My performance in that class impressed my teacher enough so that she, on her own, started to offer me professional counseling. She suggested I pursue a career in science. This professor maintained an interest in me throughout my undergraduate days at Hunter College and broadened my horizons by many orders of magnitude. (Kundsin, 1974)

Women may be better role models for other women because they can show them how to deal effectively with the special difficulties that women encounter—sexism, role conflicts, etc. Unfortunately, because there are relatively few women in creative fields now, there are relatively few women who can serve as role models for young females who want to enter these fields.

For a woman, her most signifcant role model may be her mother. It should come as no surprise that "mothers who stay home to raise a family usually have daughters who want to do just that" (Angrist and Almquist, 1975). Of college women who aspire to careers, only 20 percent have mothers who had never worked outside the home. For college women who do not aspire to a career, the comparable figure is 50 percent (Angrist and Almquist, 1975). Mothers who work outside the home not only convey to their daughters that working is valued, but they also serve as examples of how to successfully combine career and mother-hood. Here is how two successful women (the first, a psychiatrist; the second, a college administrator) put it:

> All of the women in my family worked. It was expected that I would. Both of my parents were professionals and this influenced my choice to take up a profes-sional occupation.   (Rossi and Calderwood, 1973)

> I don't believe it has ever occurred to anyone on either side of the family that a woman could be or ought to be 'a mere housewife,' and hardly a man in the fami-ly would be likely to choose a wife who saw herself in that single role. It is a family in which every woman is supposed to be *somebody*. (Rossi and Calderwood, 1973)

In contrast, here are two statements from non-career-oriented college women with mothers who had never worked outside the home:

> I would like to get married and have a family and I don't want to be a career woman. That is a very potent statement. I think my mother is a good example of what I would like to be and I have several girlfriends whose mothers are the same. They are not career women yet they are very active in the community. I think you can keep up with what is going on in the world and you don't have to work all your life.   (Almquist and Angrist, 1971)

and:

> Our family life has been kind of strange. My father even has a little bell he rings and my mother comes running and brings him coffee and he will call her from another room to change the television station. And it has been so successful. He is so happy and she is happy doing it. Why not treat him like a king because the male ego is kind of a sensitive thing to go tampering with. My life is probably not going to make that much difference on society, but maybe what my husband and children do will. I don't feel that I am that important, but if I had the time left over, I would like to do volunteer work or spend time on my own hobbies. *If* I have the time left over.   (Angrist and Almquist, 1975)

It is hardly surprising that women from such families might find it especially difficult to think of themselves in a career outside the home. However, as we will see, there are people who have overcome even more serious difficulties.

Getting Credentials

Suppose that a woman survives or escapes early discouragement and decides to obtain professional training. (Some do—about one Ph.D. in 10 is earned by a female.) Now she faces another hurdle. In professional school she is likely to feel isolated and unwanted. Here are some experiences reported by successful women.

[They] were interviewing graduate students in the political science department. The professor there said to me: "Well I guess we are going to have to take you. We don't like older women, we don't think you are worth our investment, but this is a state school, you have the grades and you have the letters of recommendation, so we are going to have to take you."

That was discouraging, so I walked across the street to the sociology department and asked if they had a graduate advisor.

They said: "No, but Dr. Dalton will talk to you."

When I went in and presented my credentials, he said: "You know you have to take statistics."

I said: "Yes, I understand that."

Then he asked: "You know what getting a Ph.D. is like?"

I said: "Yes, I do."

He said, "Well, you are willing to go through this?" I said, "Yes."

He said, "Well, we are delighted to have you."

And I said, "Well, I am old."

And he said, "Oh, no, no. (He happened to be twenty years older than I) You are not old." I was afraid to mention that I was a woman.

So the reason I am a sociologist today is because there was sex discrimination in the political science department at UCLA, but not in the sociology department.

(Cantor, 1974)

A physicist reports:

During my first year of graduate school, what seemed to me like an infinite number of professors, teaching assistants, and colleagues, none of whom were women, told me that women can't think analytically and I must, therefore, be husband hunting. The resultant discouragement was great as or greater than any I've known since; hence the solid determination with which I emerged with my Ph.D . . . It needed to be solid, because it seems that a woman in physics must be at least twice as determined as a man with the same competence, in order to achieve as much as he does.   (Kundsin, 1974)

A mathematician recounts:

As a woman mathematician—a mathematical logician—my existence apparently refutes a commonly held conviction. It is generally believed that a woman is not logical, but acts on the basis of intuition alone...

This point of view, so prevalent during the fifties and early sixties, was reinforced when I went from an all-female environment to an all-male environment when I enrolled in Harvard University Graduate School. I recall very vividly my first day in class: three seats in front of me, three seats in back of me, and two seats on either side were left vacant. I was a complete pariah in that social setting. The reason was quite simple. The men were positively unable to interact with me. They were accustomed to dating girls and talking to them about sweet things and even speaking to them about more intellectual subjects such as politics, history, and sociology. But to converse about a purely masculine subject such as physics or mathematics as one equal to another was something they had not previously experienced . . .

My first colloquium at Harvard University was a memorable event. The tea, which preceded the actual lecture, was held in the library and was a rather formal affair. As I entered, all eyes sank lower into the teacups in a great effort not to seem to notice me. Needless to say, no one talked to me at all. At the end of the tea the chairman flipped the light switch up and down as a signal for the colloquium to begin. As he did so he turned to me and said, with a twinkle in his eye, "Your presence is noted here."   (Kundsin, 1974)

Currently, conditions are far from ideal for the creative woman. However, we don't want to give the impression that there has been no progress. Things have been worse. Mary Somerville became a scientist in England in the 1800's, but she had to put up with a lot to do it.

One day Mary saw a magazine in which she found an algebra problem. She yearned to know what the X's and Y's meant—she had never heard of algebra—and no one could tell her anything more. Her rescue came by accident: she overheard a painter telling people to study Euclid for perspective and mathematics. She knew, then, she needed "Euclid"—but social mores forbade a young lady of 16

"Your presence is noted here."

to go to a bookseller. She found a man who could do for her what she could not do herself: buy Euclid for her and help her with problems. But she ran into opposition at home. She sat up late reading Euclid and the servants complained about how many candles she was using. Her candles were taken away, so she was forced to memorize Euclid. She worked problems in her mind every night before going to sleep. Her father warned that they would have to stop Mary's studies 'or we shall have Mary in a strait jacket one of these days.' For women in the 1800's in England, too much learning was considered a very dangerous thing. (Toth and Toth, 1978)

This is hardly the sort of warm, enthusiastic support which a talented but uncertain person may need to continue on a difficult path.

Marriage and Creativity

Since 93 percent of men and 95 percent of women marry, most creative people combine career and marriage. A study by B.W. Hayes (1980) suggests that it is much easier for men to combine career and marriage than it is for women to do so. She compared 174 men with 174 women listed in *Who's Who*. Table 2 shows the percentage of these men and women who had ever married.

Table 2. Percent Married in *Who's Who* Sample

[Data compiled by B. W. Hayes (1980).]

	men	women
single	9.7%	37.9%
ever married	90.3%	62.1%

Successful men marry about as often as men in the general population, but successful women are more than seven times as likely to remain single as other women.

Table 3 shows that successful married men have about the same number of children as married men in the general population.

Table 3. Percent of Marriages in *Who's Who* Sample with Various Numbers of Children

[Data compiled by B. W. Hayes (1980).]

No. Children	Men	Women
0	9%	34%
1	12%	21%
2	29%	19%
3	18%	16%
4	15%	7%
5 or more	7%	2%
Average no. children per family	2.48	1.46

Successful married women, however, have fewer children than other married women. Of all the women in the *Who's Who* sample, 50 percent are childless. A similar pattern is found in women who have Ph.D.'s. Only 45 percent of women with doctorates are married; 38 percent have never been (Astin, 1969). Of the female Ph.D.'s who are married, 80 percent are married to professional men, and 30 percent have no children (Simon, Clark, and Galway, 1967). This is twice the childless rate for the general population.

Women, then, seem to have more difficulty than men in combining marriage with a successful career. Why should this be so?

Imagine that you have just begun your career as a microbiologist at a prestigious university. You work full-time, are married, and have a young child. Your boss has agreed to pay your expenses for a week-long conference that will allow you to keep abreast of recent developments in your field. What do you do?

If you are a man, you would probably say to yourself, "What's the problem? I'm going!" But if you're a woman, the decision would not be so simple. Most likely it would involve juggling a lot of factors both in reality and in your mind. Who would do the cooking and washing? Would you be able to find adequate child-care arrangements for an entire week? Would you be able to leave your child for a whole week without worrying about the child or about the possibility that you aren't a good mother for doing so? Many married women who face just this type of situation find that a supportive husband is a tremendous asset. In this situation, a supportive husband may be one who will tell you, "Of course you should go. I'll take care of the baby," or, "Great idea. I'll go with you. Let's call your folks (or mine) and see if they can come and stay with the baby for that week." A non-supportive husband might say something like, "Well, your working is one thing, but being gone for a whole week and leaving the baby here with me is another," or "I don't think it's a good idea for you to go."

Married female Ph.D.'s, even those with no children typically spend about 50 hours a week doing housework. Married male Ph.D.'s, even those with children, spend less than 10 hours a week on household chores (data compiled by Gribben and presented by Sells and Patterson in Rossi and Calderwood [1973], pp. 79-91). People who work 100 hours a week on research and 50 more on housework won't survive very long, let alone win a Nobel prize!

About eight percent of women Ph.D.'s allow a time lapse of over 27 years between the B.A. and the Ph.D. Only seven percent finish in the normal four-year period, while the majority of men do. On the average, women Ph.D.'s obtain their degrees five years later than men (Astin, 1969). This means that, on the average, women Ph.D.'s have five years less than men to devote to research. Only 81 percent of female Ph.D.'s work full-time, as compared with 98 percent of male Ph.D.'s, and 21 percent of women Ph.D.'s interrupt their life's work for an average of 14 months (Astin, 1969).

These differences between male and female Ph.D.'s are not bizarre or unexplainable. They are accounted for by the fact that women take time off to have

and care for babies. Of course, men share in having children, but it rarely interrupts their career.

Until now, we have been discussing factors within marriage which can im-
pede the careers of creative women. Sometimes, though, marriage can stop a
career dead! Here are some experiences reported by unsuccessful women in the
study by Bond and Hayes (1978):

> My husband was in favor of my returning to work, but now he is ambivalent.
> He feels it is too tiring for me and that if we need more money, he should get a
> second job.   (Ginzberg and Yohalem, 1966)

> I could not complete my doctorate because when my husband completed his
> Ph.D., he found a job in another city and I was obliged to take over the care of
> his four-year-old child by a previous marriage. (Ginzberg and Yohalem, 1966)

> All of my credits for the Ph.D. were completed and qualifying exams passed
> by 1952. All that had to be done was the thesis. However, my husband had ob-
> tained his Ph.D. and was leaving Columbia for post-graduate work at California
> Institute of Technology. Of course, I went with him.(Ginzberg and Yohalem, 1966)

In her book, *Silences*, Olsen (1978) makes a very powerful case that many
creative women writers have been silenced by the demands placed on them by
their roles as wives and mothers. Here she describes her own circumstances as
a writer and mother:

> Circumstances for sustained creation are almost impossible. Not because the ca-
> pacities to create no longer exist, or the need (though for a while as in any fullness
> of life the need may be obscured), but . . . the need cannot be first. It can have
> at best only part self, part time . . . Motherhood means being instantly interrupti-
> ble, responsive, responsible. Children need one *now* (and remember, in our socie-
> ty, the family must often try to be the center for love and health the outside world
> is not). The very fact that these are needs of love, not duty, that one feels them
> as one's self; *that there is no one else to be responsible for these needs*, gives them
> primacy. It is distraction, not meditation, that becomes habitual; interruption, not
> continuity; spasmodic, not constant, toil. Work interrupted, deferred, postponed
> makes blockage—at best, lesser accomplishment. Unused capacities atrophy, cease
> to be.

For the professional woman who does marry, marrying someone with similar
goals, interests, and occupational status is extremely important. Doing so increases
the likelihood that her partner will understand, accept, and encourage what she
is trying to do. Men who are also engaged in creative professional work are in
a good position to realize its inherent value and that it requires lots of time and
hard work.

Even with a supportive husband who shares chores and childcare, it still isn't
easy for women in our society to combine a career, marriage, and a family. (Men,

we might note, have been doing so for years.) Childcare can be very expensive. Some employers still have nepotism rules which prevent a husband and wife from working at the same institution. Well-meaning people may still tell career women that they are ruining their children's lives. It isn't easy—but it can be done. Of the 17 professional women in our study, 16 stated that they were glad they chose to combine a career with marriage and a family, and that they were happy with their lives. Of the 14 nonprofessional women in our study, nine reported dissatisfaction with their lives.

Summary

Historically, women have been much less creative than men. This does not mean that women are less creative than men by nature. Our culture provides far more opportunity and encouragement to men to be creative than to women.

1. Our culture discourages women from taking an interest in science-related fields and encourages them to be interested in homemaking.
2. Our culture tends to undermine the confidence of women in their ability to compete in certain creative fields.
3. There are relatively few female role models in creative fields.
4. Males may resent and discriminate against females in professional education and at work.
5. In our culture it is much more difficult for women to mix marriage and career than it is for men. This is due to the assumptions that domestic duties such as cooking and child care are more the responsibility of women than men, and that the husband's career is more important than the wife's and, therefore, any conflict of interest must be resolved in favor of the husband's career.

These factors, taken together, may well account for the observed differences in creativity between men and women.

THE CREATIVE ACCOMPLISHMENT OF JEWS

In the western world, Jews constitute a very small proportion of the general population (less than one percent in Europe and less than three percent in the United States). They constitute a much larger proportion of the creative population. Table 4 shows this clearly.

Why are Jews so creative? We believe that the place to look for the answer is in the Jewish family.

Jews have a lower divorce rate, higher income, and fewer children than other people (Goldstein and Goldscheider, 1968). Most Jews live in urban areas. All of these factors—stable homes with both parents present, high income, small family size, and living in an urban environment are associated with high IQ (Lipset and Ladd, 1974; Patai and Wing, 1975). However, there are two factors which we believe are more important than all of these. The first is Jewish respect for scholarship, and the second is the importance of the child in the Jewish family.

Respect for Scholarship

Historically, the Jewish respect for scholarship has centered on the sacred writings of the Talmud. The Talmud and Talmudic scholars have always been highly esteemed by Jews, even by those who are not themselves educated. Patai and Wing (1975) say, "Throughout the Middle Ages and down to the nineteenth cen-

Table 4. Accomplishments of Jews

[Based on data from Arieti, 1976; Ladd and Lipset, 1975; Lipset and Ladd, 1971, 1974; Patai and Wing, 1975; and Sherman, 1965.]

In the U.S., where less than 3% of the population are Jews:
1. Jews have won 27% of Nobel Prizes awarded to Americans.
2. Jewish violin virtuosos occur at 12 to 25 times expectancy.
3. 16% of Jews are professionals, compared to 10% of the entire population.
4. 10% of all college faculty members are Jews; 19% of faculty members at elite colleges are Jews.
5. 70% of Jewish faculty members are at research-oriented universities.
6. 32% of Jews are at the highest quality universities, compared to 9% of non-Jewish faculty.
7. 33% of Jewish faculty members have over 10 publications, compared to 11% of Catholic and 15% of Protestant faculty members.
8. 28% of Jewish faculty members are full professors and at a younger age (38 versus 40) than non-Jewish faculty.
9. 25% of law professors are Jewish.
10. 22% of medical faculty are Jewish.
11. 21% of biochemistry faculty are Jewish.

In Europe, where less than 1% of the population are Jews:
1. Sarton's list of scholars in Europe to 1400 A.D. listed 10.6% Jews—three times their proportion in Europe at the time.
2. Jews have won 16% of all Nobel Prizes (1901-1972) and have won 60% of the Prizes in Economics, 24% in Physiology and Medicine, and 20% in Physics. The ratio of Jewish Laureates is 28 times greater than the rest of the world population.
3. In pre-Nazi Germany, 25% of mathematicians, medical researchers, and physicists were Jewish—30 times their population proportion.
4. In Italy in the 1930's, 50% of mathematicians were Jewish.
5. In 1937, 9% of Soviet scholars were Jewish.
6. In 1947, 16% of Stalin science awards and 14% of Stalin art and literature awards went to Jews.
7. 3.5% of British faculty are Jewish, although Jews constitute less than 1% of the British population (1965).
8. 7% of members of Britain's scientific honor society, the Royal Academy of Science, are Jewish (1971).

tury . . . Jews considered Talmudic scholarship the greatest of achievements.''

On the Sabbath, Jews may not work but they may study. Study is not restricted to religious matters: It may include secular things such as homework. Thus
the respect for religious scholarship extends to scholarship generally.

The Importance of Children

During the early part of this century, when infant mortality rates were still
high, Jews had the lowest infant mortality rate of any group, although they were
mostly poor immigrants (Lipset and Ladd, 1974). Special care was taken not only
with the children's physical well being, but with their mental growth as well.
Patai and Wing (1975) say

> . . . The average Jewish parents did, and still do, everything they can to stimu-
> late and advance the intellectual development of their child. They surround him
> from birth with an enriched environment, including nowadays the latest fads in educa-
> tional toys and games, talk to him a lot, fondle him, and implant in his mind at
> a very early age the ideas that he must excel in his studies, and ultimately become
> a rabbi, a doctor, a lawyer, a scientist, or some other type of intellectual giant.
> Needless to say, they will also do everything possible to send him to the best schools
> and to create in the home the best of circumstances conducive to doing all home-
> work in the most satisfactory manner. In addition to all this, Jewish parents simply
> assume that their child will do well in school, which communicates itself to the
> child and thus becomes a self-fulfilling expectation.

and again,

> The appreciation of scholarship was inculcated into the children to such an ex-
> tent that, generally speaking, all the boys who had the mental capacity endeavored
> to achieve . . . scholarly status.

There is another side to this strong support for intellectual activities. Aspiring
to non-intellectual pursuits can carry severe repercussions. Here is one man's
account of what is (*and* what is not) rewarded in the traditional Jewish home:

> There was Leo's brother, Oscar, who was special. If I had available to me then
> the words I have now I would have described Oscar to my friends as smart-smart.
> That's the way the family regarded him. But Oscar posed a real problem because
> he played football, and extremely well. He was as good in football as he was in
> the classroom. That Oscar was on the small side was only one reason for family
> opposition to playing football. It was important because he might get "good and
> hurt," not be able to go to school, and maybe not even go to college. The more
> important point was that nice Jewish boys, particularly if they were smart-smart,
> didn't play football. That was for the gentiles (goys), who were by nature not
> smart . . .

> One Saturday morning I walked into [Oscar's] apartment . . . and I heard my aunt yelling and screaming . . . she was telling him and the world what she thought of a Jewish boy who was going to play football for his high school *on Saturday.* What had she done to deserve such punishment? What would *they* think? "They" referred to all her Jewish friends and neighbors who, she was sure, would both blame and sympathize with her on one of the worst fates a Jewish mother could experience. How could a mother stand by and watch her child, with such a "good head," go straight to hell? (Sarason, 1973)

The channelling of the child's energies toward scholarly pursuits and away from distracting activities seems to work. The following figures, based on data from Ladd and Lipset (1975) and Sherman (1965), show that a larger percentage of Jews in the U.S. go to college than non-Jews, and when they get there they perform better than non-Jews.

1. 62 out of every 100 college-age Jews are in college, compared to 27 out of every 100 non-Jews.
2. Jewish college students are proportionately in better schools than non-Jewish students.
3. Jews have better grade-point averages than non-Jews.
4. Jews are in Phi Beta Kappa at twice their undergraduate proportion.

In our society, scholarship is an important route to success. Advanced education often leads to a professional career, a good income, and an opportunity to do creative work. Traditionally, scholarship has been highly respected by Jews, and the Jewish family has been very effective in teaching this value to the Jewish child. We believe that it is by transmitting respect for scholarship to the young that Jewish culture has succeeded in producing such a large number of creative people.

THE ASIANS

Asians are another highly creative minority within American culture. While they constitute less than one percent of our population, they are one percent of the undergraduate population and two percent of the graduate population (Kitano, 1976). Four Asian Americans have won Nobel prizes (all in Physics). A remarkable number of Asian Americans have become outstanding musicians. Many Asian Americans are professionals—21 percent of Japanese males and 30 percent of Chinese males, as compared to 15 percent of non-Asian American males (Almquist, 1979).

There are many similarities between Asian and Jewish subcultures in our society. Both have an ancient heritage which esteems scholarship and a stable family environment which encourages children to pursue scholarly careers.

For the Jews, scholarship has strong religious overtones. For the Asians, it has strong moral connections.

> For many centuries [the Chinese] revered written characters, which they be-
> lieve to have been created by past sages. There were many 'societies for saving
> papers with written character.' These societies employed collectors who roamed
> around town, with forks in hand and baskets on their backs, gathering such scat-
> tered pieces. The bits were then burned at the local Confucian temple. It was be-
> lieved that a person who used inscribed papers for toilet purposes would be struck
> dead by lightning. And one who accidentally stepped on a book must pick it up
> and place it on his head momentarily for propitiation.   (Hsu, 1970)

The ultimate achievement was wisdom, and the Confucian way to wisdom was by studying. Asian students were exposed to stories of scholars who let nothing interfere with their desire to learn: "the man who put a rope around his neck and tied it to the ceiling to keep from falling asleep or the man who used a cage-ful of fireflies to study at night or the man who poured ice water on his body in winter to stay awake to study" (Dore, 1965; Horinouchi, 1967). While Western-ers may find these stories excessive or gruesome, they illustrate the degree to which scholarship was esteemed by Asians.

The Family

Asians have the lowest divorce rate (1.6 percent) of any group in the United States. They have a high marriage rate, high home ownership, high income, and high occupational status. Unemployment is rare and family size is small. This pattern resembles that found among Jews.

Respect for learning is interwoven with respect for the family and for the Confucian values of diligence and hard work. Consider the first admonition in a Japanese school:

> To be born human and not be able to write is to be less than human. Illiteracy
> is a form of blindness. It brings shame on your teacher, shame on your parents
> and shame on yourself. The heart of a child of three stays with him till he is a hundred
> as the proverb says. Determine to succeed, study with all your might, never forget-
> ting the shame of failure.   (Dore, 1965)

The precept was also taught at home: "By learning well, you will honor your family name" (Horinouchi, 1967). One young man recalled:

> When I was sent to school I was expected to try my best and to get good grades—
> there was no question about this in my or my parents' mind. I guess it's just like
> my mother and father—if Mom ironed a shirt, she had to do best; if my Dad dug
> a ditch he had to do it just right. So did all of the other Nisei kids. I guess that's

why so many of us were on the Honor Roll.   (Kitano, 1976)

Like the Jews, Asians encourage some activities and discourage others. The Asian community reinforces the family in enforcing its values. One man recalls how the community dealt with an instance of delinquency:

> I knew these two brothers who were pretty wild. They would get drunk . . . were always fighting, always in trouble and were uncontrollable. Finally, their father came to talk to my father and other Japanese families in the neighborhood . . . all agreed that these boys would hurt the reputation of the other Japanese and provide poor models for the younger boys . . . so even though the brothers were already young adults and out of high school, they were sent back to Japan in 1937. As far as I know, they never came back to the United States.   (Kitano, 1976)

The Asians have the lowest crime rate in the United States. It is probably no accident that they have the lowest school drop-out rate of any group in the country. Dropping out of high school "is considered a disgrace in an Asian community" (Horinouchi, 1967).

Conclusion

Asians, like Jews, form a remarkably creative subculture in America. Like the Jews, Asians have an ancient heritage which places a high value on scholarship and, like the Jews, they provide a stable family environment in which children are encouraged to work hard and to pursue scholarly careers. Further, in both groups deviations from this ideal pattern, e.g., dropping out of school, are actively discouraged.

BLACKS

There are several factors which can seriously thwart creative effort:

1. lack of education
2. lack of opportunity
3. lack of support

Unfortunately, blacks have been the victim of all three. Physically removed against their will from their native land, they were made to serve a society which would neither teach them how to become its members, nor allow them to retain their heritage. As a consequence, blacks have been doubly denied a culture and cultural values.

Inadequate Education

When the slaves were freed, they were barred by law from many jobs and from most schools. Eager to learn, they set up their own schools, but these were generally staffed by blacks with little more education than their pupils.

Segregated schools were the norm until the Supreme Court ruled in 1954 that separate is not equal. In the 1960s, most blacks still attended segregated schools. In Alabama, Louisiana, and Mississippi, less than one percent of black students attended school with whites (Pinkney, 1969). In the North in 1966, 65 percent of black first graders attended schools which were 90 to 100 percent black (U.S. Department of Health, Education, and Welfare, 1966). About 60 percent of black college students attended black colleges, of which there are 123. However, only 63 percent of them are accredited (U.S. Department of Commerce, 1966). In five southern states in 1954, there were 1.8 books per pupil in black school libraries, but 4.8 per pupil in white school libraries (Ashmore, 1954). In black high schools, in 1966, 20 percent were without physics equipment compared to six percent of white schools (U.S. Department of Health, Education, and Welfare, 1966).

Although only about 25 percent of blacks lived in rural areas, in 1900, 90 percent did (U.S. Bureau of the Census, 1966). Many adult blacks attended a school like the one described below in an excerpt from *Growing Up in the Black Belt*. And it is not as though urban blacks have it any better. Fully two-thirds are members of the lower class and attend predominately black schools (Pinkney, 1969).

> It is in a dilapidated building, once whitewashed, standing in a rocky field unfit for cultivation. Dust-covered weeds spread a carpet all around, except for an uneven, bare area on one side which looks like a ball field. Behind the school is a small building with a broken, sagging door. As we approach, a nervous middle-aged woman comes to the door of the school. She greets us in a discouraged voice marred by a speech impediment. Escorted inside, we observe that the broken benches are crowded to three times their normal capacity. Only a few battered books are in sight, and we look in vain for maps or charts. We learn that four grades are assembled here.   (Johnson, 1941)

In the face of all this, it is a tribute to the perseverance of black people that they have reduced their illiteracy 70 percent in about 70 years. Unfortunately, to be creative in a technologically advanced society like ours, that is not good enough. To compete for the creative occupations, blacks need education and training equal to whites. So far, society has not provided that.

Lack of Opportunity

Malcolm X recounted in his autobiography an all too typical example:

> I know that he [the teacher] probably meant well in what he happened to advise me that day. I doubt that he meant any harm. It was just in his nature as an Ameri-

can white man. I was one of his top students, one of the school's top students—but all he could see for me was the kind of future 'in your place' that all white people see for black people.

He told me, "Malcolm, you ought to be thinking about a career. Have you been giving it thought?"

The truth is, I hadn't. I never have figured out why I told him, "Well, yes, sir, I've been thinking I'd like to be a lawyer." Lansing certainly had no Negro lawyers—or doctors either —in those days, to hold up an image I might have aspired to. All I really knew for certain was that a lawyer didn't wash dishes, as I was doing.

Mr. Ostrowski looked surprised, I remember, and leaned back in his chair and clasped his hands behind his head. He kind of half-smiled and said, "Malcolm, one of life's first needs is for us to be realistic. Don't misunderstand me, now. We all here like you, you know that. But you've got to be realistic about being a nigger. A lawyer—that's no realistic goal for a nigger. You need to think about something you *can* be. You're good with your hands—making things. Everybody admires your carpentry shop work. Why don't you plan on carpentry? People like you as a person—you'd get all kinds of work."

The more I thought afterwards about what he said, the more uneasy it made me. It just kept treading around in my mind.

What made it really begin to disturb me was Mr. Ostrowski's advice to others in my class—all of them white. Most of them had told him they were planning to become farmers, like their parents—to one day take over their family farms. But those who wanted to strike out on their own, to try something new, he had encouraged. Some, mostly girls, wanted to be teachers. A few wanted other professions, such as one boy who wanted to become a county agent; another, a veterinarian; and one girl wanted to be a nurse. They all reported that Mr. Ostrowski had encouraged whatever they had wanted. Yet nearly none of them had earned marks equal to mine.

It was a surprising thing that I had never thought of it that way before, but I realized that whatever I wasn't, I *was* smarter than nearly all of those white kids. But apparently I was still not intelligent enough, in their eyes, to become whatever I wanted to be.

It was then that I began to change—inside.   (Malcolm X, 1964)

No matter how bright or hardworking an individual is, if opportunity to be creative is denied, there can be no creativity.

Lack of Support

Blacks have higher unemployment, lower income, less education, and more children than white people. Only one-third own their own homes. The divorce rate among blacks is 23 percent, the illegitimacy rate is 25 percent, and 25 percent of black households are headed by females with no male present (Pinkney, 1969; U.S. Department of Labor, 1965). How do these grim statistics affect the black child?

First, such a pattern allows little chance for escape. Children who grow up in an impoverished environment have little exposure to the range of options society can offer. Role models are likely to be the toughest kids on the block, rather than scholars. Children in an impoverished environment are probably not surrounded by books or stimulating toys. They may neither be encouraged to study nor rewarded for doing so. Chances are that the people they interact with on a daily basis—their friends and neighbors—are in the same predicament they are. They probably attend an ill-equipped school which offers little stimulation. As a result of being raised in a broken home, they may not learn the values and behaviors necessary to achieve success in our society (Comer, 1967). Further, the absence of a strong male role model may make it difficult for male children to develop good work habits (Ginzberg, 1956).

Children from such an environment may still aspire to achieve—indeed, many do (Pinkney, 1969), and many have. But to do so requires overcoming tremendous odds. Without money, a good education, a stable home, a strong value for scholarship, and without encouraging friends and family, the task seems enormous.

There is hope of breaking this pattern, but most of the changes must come from sources external to blacks.

More and better jobs, especially jobs which pay and promote nondiscriminately, would help. In 1966, a black with some college education was still earning less than a white with an eighth-grade education (Fein, 1966). Better housing and more accessible home ownership could add a sense of stability and security. An improved environment can increase a child's IQ; a depressed environment can make it go down (Patai and Wing, 1975). Better equipped and staffed schools could help equalize the educational situation. Studies show that as schools improve, performance improves (Patai and Wing, 1975). These changes, though, must come from the larger society.

From within the black community, help can come from blacks who have succeeded and who are willing to work with those who have not, and thereby serve as role models.

Help can also come from the church, as it has in the past, in the drive for civil rights. The church has been the outstanding social institution in the black community, the place where blacks have found refuge and emotional relief. Its role in the future must be even more demanding if blacks are to break the pattern we have discussed.

Bleak as the picture may be, it has some positive notes. Blacks are progressing and indeed have made tremendous contributions in literature, music, sports, entertainment, and dance. Four blacks (two Americans) have won the Nobel prize. About 10 percent of blacks are professionally employed (Almquist, 1979).

Further, fully 80 percent of mothers of black college students work outside the home (Willie and McCord, 1972). While many probably do so by necessity, nonetheless, as we have seen in our discussion of women, a working mother is the best assurance that her children, especially her female children, will also work.

In those black families which are stable and middle class, education is emphasized and encouraged. More blacks are attending college, setting higher goals, and getting better jobs than ever before (Willie and McCord, 1972).

The major difference between black and white families appears to be one of class, not color. "As soon as blacks enter the middle class, family patterns associated with the lower class tend to disappear. The differences between black and white family patterns, then, are largely the result of status in the society" (Pinkney, 1969). Because the black lower class is so large, problems loom large. Perhaps as status improves, the creative potential of blacks will likewise improve.

COMPARING ASIANS AND BLACKS

Asians are sometimes held up to blacks as "model minorities" (Almquist, 1979), the implication being that if Asians could become successful, blacks can, too. However, as Almquist points out, there are a number of ways in which this implication is unfair.

First, many Asians came to this country as highly skilled workers. Over 60 percent of Asian immigrants in the 1950's were classified as white collar workers (Almquist, 1979). Second, Asians are less than one percent of our population, or 1.3 million people. Blacks, numbering 20 million, are not as easily absorbed by the work force.

Third, while Asians have been subjected to discrimination (for example, the internment of Japanese Americans during World War II), it can in no way be compared to 200 years of slavery which deprived an entire people of their dignity, heritage, civil rights, and property. Fourth, Asians chose to come here and viewed the United States as a place of opportunity. Fifth, the strong Asian communities can accommodate newcomers and provide them with housing and jobs.

Asian creative achievement is certainly to be emulated, but it is unfair to suggest that if Asians have "made it," blacks should have "made it," too. The problems that blacks have faced are extremely severe ones and they are by no means solved. Despite these difficulties, blacks have made very respectable progress.

AMERICAN INDIANS

Statistics on American Indians are not encouraging. The average educational level among Indians is 9.8. Only one-third finish high school. Many are functionally illiterate (Wax, 1971). One-third live in poverty, making them the ranking poverty group in this country (Almquist, 1979). Unemployment is chronic, and has at times reached 80 percent among those living on reservations, as over 60 percent do (Wax, 1971). Indians have the highest birth rate and lowest life expectancy of any group in our country.

When Europeans occupied the North American continent, the Indian population was greatly reduced—from over one million in 1492 to 220,000 in 1910 (Alm-quist, 1979)—and their usual means of livelihood was removed.

> When the buffaloes were destroyed . . . the Sioux were deprived not only of food, but also of culturally significant activities. The tribal societies concerned with war and hunting lost their functions and atrophied. The arts and techniques sur-rounding the buffalo hunt . . . which had once been sources of social status and of pride in workmanship, were now rendered useless.   (Barber, 1941)

Indian cultures are quite diverse. There are hundreds of distinct tribes which may differ greatly from one another in language and customs. Unlike Jewish cul-ture, though, Indian cultures typically do not mesh well with the dominant Ameri-can culture. Consider this letter sent to the Virginia Commission in 1744 regarding an invitation for six Indian children to attend William and Mary College:

> Several of our young people were formerly brought up at Colleges of the North-ern Provinces; they were instructed in all your sciences; but when they came back to us, they were bad runners, ignorant of every means of living in the woods, un-able to bear either cold or hunger, knew neither how to build a cabin, take a deer, or kill an enemy, spoke our language imperfectly, were therefore neither fit for hunters, warriors, or counsellors, they were totally good for nothing. We are, however, not the less obliged by your kind offer, though we decline accepting it; and to show our grateful Sense of it, if the Gentlemen of Virginia will send us a Dozen of their Sons we will take care of their education, instruct them in all we know, and make Men of them.   (Noel, 1968)

Although this letter was written over 200 years ago, it voices the attitudes of many Indians today. The "White Man's" education is still not viewed as worth-while. For Indians, the school dropout rate is very high. In many cases, drop-ping out can be attributed directly to conflicts between the local Indian culture and the dominant culture. For example, many southwest Indians do not believe in making decisions for other people or in advising them.

> Indians do not believe that one person should tell another what to do or that endless hours should be wasted in persuading another. From infancy, Indians are taught to respect the rights of others and to avoid interfering with other people. Even if another person is placing himself or herself in great physical danger, the Indian will not tell the person what to do. Passengers in an automobile will remain silent rather than warn the driver of a rock slide or a steer in the road. To warn the driver would constitute interference.   (Almquist, 1979)

This aspect of their culture leads Indian children to drop out of school and, further, to make the decision to drop out of school on their own, without discus-sion or parental guidance.

Being barely literate and not esteeming the values of the larger society has made finding employment difficult for Indians. Wax (1971) says

He may be a shrewd judge of human character, be strong, loyal, reliable, and willing to work, but he will be lucky if he gains even the most menial and poorly paying employment.

Their own culture makes it difficult for native Americans to obtain education and employment in the United States. Further, it makes it unlikely that they would be able or inclined to be creative within the framework of our culture.

CONCLUSION

If your society

1. values intellectual activities,

and

2. encourages you to be interested in intellectual activities,

and

3. encourages you to believe that you can succeed in intellectual activities,

and

4. helps you to obtain necessary education,

and

5. does not impose other occupations on you which preempt your time, then your chances of becoming a creative person will be much better than average. However, if any of these conditions is violated because you are a black, a woman, a Native American, or for whatever reason, then your chances of becoming a creative person will be greatly reduced.

These observations about the social conditions of creativity have implications both for the individual and for society as a whole.

First, individuals should be aware of social pressures which may tend to block their creative development. Ask yourself these questions about your upbringing:

- In high school, was it more important to be a good student or a good athlete?
- Did your friends consider it unfeminine to be intellectual?
- Were you worried that you might lose your religion if you thought too deeply about science or philosophy?
- Have you modeled your own career on someone you knew well?
- Was there pressure on you at home to get good grades?
- Did your parents expect you to become a professional?
- Were your parents interested in intellectual things?

In answering these questions, most people can identify many social pressures which have pushed them either toward or away from intellectual pursuits. Being aware of the pressures which have influenced you and which may influence you in the future can help you to take a more active role in determining your own creativity.

If society suggests that you can't be creative because of your race or sex, you needn't be deterred if you understand that the fault is in society and not in you. You can set goals for yourself—as Malcolm X and Mary Somerville did—far beyone the goals others might try to set for you. You can consciously seek a role model for yourself among the people you know who are outstanding in your field or by reading biographies. You can seek out people in your field and ask them how they "made it." You can resist pressures from your friends to be "regular" and choose instead to be special.

The observations in this chapter should lead us to ask some very serious questions about our culture. Clearly, our culture depends on the work of creative people for its well-being. It depends on them to solve problems of pollution, of population, of food and energy production, and of disease. It depends on them to produce new music, art, dance, and literature. While our society depends on creative people, it does not appear to be very interested in fostering their development. For example, why do basketball superstars earn more than Nobel prize winners? Is it because basketball players do more to reduce disease or increase food production? Why do advertising executives earn more than college professors? Do they contribute more to art and knowledge? Why does our society insist that women, regardless of their potential creativity, raise their children personally, rather than be provided with adequate child-care facilities? Why are there athletic scholarships? Wouldn't the money be better spent on people who are good at intellectual rather than athletic skills? Why does our school system put such emphasis on its athletic programs? Why is it that when we look at our high schools, we are very likely to see a sign saying, "Home of the Fighting Wombats," but nothing about the school's academic achievements?

There are many such questions to ask. Asking them and providing sensible answers could be crucial for the survival of our society.

REFERENCES

Almquist, E. M. *Minorities, Gender, and Work*. Lexington, MA: Lexington Books, 1979.

Almquist, E. M., and Angrist, S. S. "Role Model Influences on College Women's Career Aspirations." In *The Professional Game*, edited by A. Theodore. Cambridge, MA: Schenkman Publishing Co., Inc., 1971.

Angrist, S. S., and Almquist, E. M. *Careers and Contingencies*. New York: Dunellen, 1975.

Arieti, S. *Creativity: The Magic Synthesis*. New York: Basic Books, Inc., Publishers, 1976.

Arthur, T. S. *Advice to Young Ladies*. Boston: G. W. Cotrell & Co., 1851.

Ashmore, H. S. *The Negro and the Schools*. Chapel Hill, NC: The University of North Carolina Press, 1954.

Astin, H. S. *The Woman Doctorate in America*. New York: Russell Sage Foundation, 1969.

Barber, B. "Acculturation and Messianic Movements." *American Sociological Review*, 6(10), 653–673, 1941.

Bond, S. J., and Hayes, J. R. *A Comparison of Successful and Unsuccessful Professional Women.* Unpublished manuscript, 1978.

Brody, E. B., and Brody, N. *Intelligence: Nature, Determinants, and Consequences.* New York: Academic Press, Inc., 1976.

Cantor, M. "Why I am a Sociologist." In *Graduate and Professional Education of Women.* Proceedings of AAUW Conference, Washington, D.C., May 1974.

Comer, J. P. "The Social Power of the Negro." *Scientific American, 216*(4), 21-27, 1967.

Dore, R. P. *Education in Tokugawa Japan.* Berkeley: University of California Press, 1965

Fein, R. "An Economic and Social Profile of the Negro American." in *The Negro American,* edited by T. Parsons and K. Clark. Boston: Houghton Mifflin Company, 1966.

Ginzberg, E. *The Negro Potential.* New York: Columbia University Press, 1956.

Ginzberg, E., and Yohalem, A. M. *Educated American Women: Self-Portraits.* New York: Columbia University Press, 1966.

Goldstein, S., and Goldscheider, C. *Jewish Americans.* Englewood Cliffs, NJ: Prentice-Hall, Inc., 1968.

Harris, S. E. *A Statistical Portrait of Higher Education.* New York: McGraw-Hill, Inc., 1972.

Hayes, B. W. *Family Patterns in Successful Men and Women.* Unpublished manuscript, 1980.

Horinouchi, I. "Educational Values and Preadaptation in the Acculturation of Japanese Americans." Paper 7, Sacramento Anthropology Society, Fall, 1967.

Hsu, F. L. K. *Americans and Chinese: Reflections of Two Cultures and Their People.* Garden City, NY: Doubleday & Co., Inc., 1970.

Jensen, A. R. "The Race X Sex X Ability Interaction." In *Contributions to Intelligence,* edited by R. Cancro. New York: Stratton Intercontinental Medical Book Corporation, 1971.

Johnson, C. S. *Growing up in the Black Belt.* Washington, D.C.: American Council on Education, 1941.

Kitano, H. H. *Japanese Americans,* Second Edition, Englewood Cliffs, NJ: Prentice-Hall, Inc., 1976.

Kundsin, R. B. (Ed). *Women and Success: The Anatomy of Achievement.* New York: William Morrow & Co., Inc., 1974.

Ladd, E. C., Jr., and Lipset, S. M. *The Divided Academy.* New York: McGraw-Hill, Inc., 1975.

Lipset, S. M., and Ladd, E. C., Jr. "Jewish Academics in the United States: Their Achievements, Culture and Politics." In *American Jewish Yearbook 1971,* Vol. 72, edited by M. Fine and M. Himmelfarb. New York: The American Jewish Committee, 1971.

Lipset, S. M., and Ladd, E. C., Jr. "Jewish Academics in the United States." In *The Jew in American Society,* edited by M. Sklare. New York: Behrman House, Inc., 1974.

Malcolm X. *The Autobiography of Malcolm X.* New York: Grove Press, Inc., 1964.

The Negro Family. U.S. Department of Labor, Washington, D.C.: U.S. Government Printing Office, March, 1965.

Noel, D. L. "A Theory of the Origins of Ethnic Stratification." *Social Problems, 16,* 157-172, 1968.

Olsen, T. *Silences.* New York: Delta/Seymour Lawrence, 1978.

Patai, R., and Wing, J. P. *The Myth of the Jewish Race.* New York: Charles Scribner's Sons, 1975.

Pinkney, A. S., and Calderwood, A. (Eds.). *Academic Women on the Move.* New York: Russell Sage Foundation, 1973.

Rossi, A. S., and Calderwood, A. (Eds.). *Academic Women on the Move.* New York: Russell Sage Foundation, 1973.

Sarason, S. B. "Jewishness, Blackishness, and the Nature-Nurture Controversy." *American Psychologist, 11,* 962-971, 1973.

Sherman, C. B. *The Jew Within American Society.* Detroit: Wayne State University Press, 1965.

Simon, H. A. Personal Communication, 1978.

Simon, R. J., Clark, S. M., and Galway, K. "The Woman Ph.D.: A Recent Profile." *Social Problems, 15,* 221-236, 1967.

Torrance, E. P. *Creativity: Second Minnesota Conference on Gifted Children.* Center for Continuation Study, University of Minnesota, Minneapolis, 1960.

Toth, B., and Toth, E. "Mary Who?" *Johns Hopkins Magazine, XXIX*(1), 25-29, 1978.

U.S. Bureau of the Census. *Current Population Reports,* Series P-20, No. 155, "Negro Population: March, 1965." Washington, D.C.: Government Printing Office, 1966.

U.S. Department of Commerce, Business and Defense Services Administration. *A Guide to Negro Marketing Information.* Washington, D.C.: Government Printing Office, 45–50, 1966.

U.S. Department of Health, Education, and Welfare, Office of Education. *Equality of Educational Opportunity.* Washington, D.C.: Government Printing Office, 1966.

U.S. Department of Labor, Bureau of Labor Statistics. *The Negroes in the United States: Their Economic and Social Situation*, Bulletin No. 1511. Washington, D.C.: Government Printing Office, 1966.

Wax, M. L. *Indian Americans.* Englewood Cliffs, NJ: Prentice-Hall, Inc., 1971.

Who's Who in America, Forty-First Edition. Chicago: Marquis Who's Who, 1980–1981.

Willie, C. V., and McCord, A. S. *Black Students at White Colleges.* New York: Praeger Publishers, Inc., 1972.

The World Almanac and Books of Facts 1980. New York: Newspaper Enterprise, 1979.

APPENDIX I
Time Management

Time management is important because it can influence your problem-solving efficiency in a number of ways:

1. The simplest and most obvious way is that through poor scheduling, you allow insufficient time to work a problem through to solution or, perhaps, you never get to it at all. No matter how bright you are, it you don't work on a problem, you won't solve it.

2. Even if you do schedule enough time to solve the problem, you may not schedule the best time to solve it. For example, you may schedule work on a problem at the very last minute before the problem is due. The pressure that results from such scheduling can cause inefficient problem solving by limiting the amount of planning that you feel you can do at the beginning of the solution process or by discouraging you from examining alternative solution paths in sufficient depth. Certainly, such scheduling would eliminate the very valuable practice of reviewing and criticizing the solution process immediately after the solution is achieved. A far better time to schedule problem solution is right after class. At this time, facts and ideas which may be forgotten in a few hours can be used and consolidated.

3. If your time management is generally poor, your ability to solve problems may suffer because you have failed to acquire an essential piece of knowledge or because you have not attained sufficient mastery of a basic skill. Students sometimes try to save time by attempting to solve problems after only a quick glance at the relevant chapter or without working through the practice problems. While this corner-cutting technique sometimes al-

lows you to get by, in the long run it is likely to reduce your problem-solving efficiency.

While there is very little glamour in time management, the techniques are simple and they work. For some, they can produce considerable gains in problem solving efficiency. According to Crawley (1936), time management is the most useful skill that students acquire in courses on study-skills.

TECHNIQUES OF TIME MANAGEMENT

Time management employs two major techniques:

Time planning: alloting specific blocks of time during the day or week to specific tasks according to their importance and the time they require.
Efficiency: getting a great deal accomplished in the available time.

Let's start our discussion with time planning. The first serious step in time planning is to find out how you spend your time now. Perhaps the simplest way to do this is to keep a time chart such as this:
You should record your activities in the chart for at least one complete week, since for most people time usage varies a good deal from day to day. Weekends, for example, are usually scheduled quite differently from weekdays. Since the record is entirely for your benefit, it is worth making it as complete and accurate as you can. Take the data sheet with you wherever you go so that you can make the entries as soon after the activity as possible. Be unsparingly honest about such questions as, "Was I studying or really just reading magazines?"
One would expect most college students to spend 12 to 15 hours in class each week and 25-30 hours in study.
Once you have an idea of how you use your time, you may be delighted and impressed, or you may decide that you want to design a better schedule. You may find, for example, that you spend more time in casual recreation than you thought and want to convert some of those hours to study use. You may find that you are putting undue emphasis on one topic at the expense of others or that some topics are suffering because they are being left for the last minute. If any of these things is true, you will likely profit by making a time plan and sticking to it.
To make a time plan, you should establish a fixed weekly schedule in which specific topics are assigned to specific time slots. The amount of time you assign to each topic should depend on its importance to you and on the difficulty you have with it. Deciding on the relative importance of the topics is very important and therefore worth considerable thought. Making these decisions sensibly may be the most valuable aspect of time planning.

TIME SCHEDULE FOR WEEK

Date: _____

Hour	Monday	Tuesday	Wednesday	Thursday	Friday	Saturday	Sunday

Try to place the time slot for studying a topic as close as possible after the lecture on the topic. Try to schedule topics that require a great deal of problem solving or concentration at times when you are most alert. Leave routine activities and recreation for times when you are likely to need relaxation.

Your schedule should include a weekly review and planning session to see where you have gotten during the past week and where you are going during the next.

Your scheduling of recreation should be realistic rather than idealistic. You may feel that it is noble to spend no time at all on foolish things like TV watching, but if missing your favorite programs turns you into a self-pitying blob, the sacrifice probably isn't worth it academically or otherwise. On the other hand, if you find that you reward yourself with an hour of TV for every hour you study, you are clearly being wildly self-indulgent. Be reasonable! Give yourself enough recreation to stay efficient but not too much more.

Once you have established your time plan, you should try to follow it closely. Of course, it may need adjustments. You may find that you have too much of something or too little of something else. If an emergency comes up, say in the form of an exam, you have to borrow time from one topic to work on another. The borrowed time should always be paid back, however.

You may find it helpful to continue your time diary so that you can see the extent to which your actual time usage approximates your plan. Keeping the diary for at least one week once your plan is in operation certainly should be informative.

Given a satisfactory schedule of work and recreation, the next problem is to insure that you get the maximum benefit out of the hours you work. Efficiency requires both organization and concentration.

ORGANIZING YOUR WORK

Most of us have had the experience of settling down to work only to discover that necessary papers are missing or that we have lost the assignment. Or we may be working along at high speed on a paper and have to stop for 10 minutes to search for a dictionary under heaps of papers and record jackets. The purpose of organizing your work is to reduce the amount of time you spend doing things like searching through various heaps for things you need right now. Some of the following rules may help:

1. Keep a shelf (or fixed place) for frequently used reference books and make a habit of returning them to their places after use.
2. Keep a separate, clearly marked notebook or folder for each topic.
3. Date your papers, and number the pages.
4. Keep your personal library in some reasonable order, e.g., arranged by topic or alphabetically by author.

5. If you can't complete a job in one session, divide it into subparts which can be completed in one session.

6. When you finish a work session on a given topic, you should plan what to do next when you return to that topic and leave yourself a note as a reminder. It may save you some time in reorienting yourself to the topic.

CONCENTRATION

The other aspect of efficiency that we will consider is concentration. Trying to make yourself concentrate is a much more difficult task to get hold of than attempting to organize your work. Some authors simply throw up their hands and say, "The only way to concentrate is to concentrate." There are some kinds of advice in the "How to Study" literature, however, which you may find useful.

1. Once you establish your work schedule, stick to it. One author draws an analogy with eating. If you regularly eat a certain times of the day, you will be hungry at those times. If you regularly work at certain times of the day, you will be ready for work at those times.

2. While it is not absolutely essential, a quiet work place does help. Keep TV and friends out of your study area. Use a radio only if the music drowns out sounds that are more distracting.

3. Use your work space only for work. If you have a moment for relaxation, do it somewhere else.

4. Schedule short rests and make good use of them: stretch, walk around, do something different from what you have been doing.

5. Don't work more than two hours at a time on the same topic if you can help it.

6. Schedule your work hours for those times of the day when you are most efficient. It may be worth trying different times to discover if, even though you pass yourself off as a night owl, you are really a latent morning person, and vice versa.

7. When you have worked through a problem, take time to review what it was that gave you difficulty and how you overcame it. Reflection just after you have solved a problem is a very valuable aid in remembering newly discovered solution techniques, so that you don't have to discover them anew each time the same sort of problem comes up.

8. Avoid daydreaming. If daydreaming becomes a problem in reading—if you notice that your eyes have moved over the page but you haven't understood a thing—try summarizing each paragraph to yourself as you come to the end of it. If daydreaming is a problem at other times, e.g., while working physics problems, try using a kitchen timer which you keep reset-

ting before it rings—when it does ring, it will bring you back from your daydream.

9. If daydreaming becomes a severe problem during a study session, work on a more interesting topic, or stop studying altogether for a while.

REFERENCES

Crawley, S. L., *Studying Efficiently*. Englewood Cliffs, NJ: Prentice-Hall, Inc., 1936.

APPENDIX II

Probabilities

This appendix is designed for readers who feel that their knowledge of elementary probability theory is shaky or absent. After studying this appendix, readers should be able to do the following four things:

1. define probability,
2. state three elementary properties of probabilities,
3. estimate probabilities for some simple events, and
4. compute probabilities for some complex events.

PROBABILITY DEFINED

Many, perhaps most, of the events in our everyday experience have outcomes which we can't predict with certainty. For example, we can't be certain that our favorite football team will win today's game or that a recently purchased plant will survive our care. We can think of plant raising as an activity which can have either of two outcomes: the plant will live or it will die. If we have had poor success in the past, we may have little confidence that the new plant will live. If we have been generally successful in the past, we may be moderately or even strongly confident of success. In any case, we will realize that we can't predict *with certainty* whether or not the new plant will live.

In some cases, it is possible to describe the uncertainty of an event by specifying probabilities for the various possible outcomes of the event. *The probability of an outcome is defined as the proportion of times the outcome will occur given that we observe an indefinitely large number of events.* Thus, if the probability that our team will win is actually 0.80, then if we observe many games, our team will win about 80 percent of them.

When we know the probability, we still don't know with certainty whether or not our team will win its next game. The useful thing that we do know is that if we bet on our team many items, we will win eight bets out of ten. In general, knowing the probability of an outcome is useful for predicting the number of times that outcome will occur when the event is repeated many times.

Probabilities are related to odds, but the two shouldn't be confused. The odds of an outcome is the ratio of the number of times the outcome occurs, N, to the number of times it doesn't occur $\overline{N}$. ($\overline{N}$ may be read as N-BAR or as *not* N.) That is,

$$\text{Odds (outcome)} = \frac{N}{\overline{N}}$$

The probability of an outcome is the ratio of the number of times the outcome occurs, N, to the total number of events, T. Since the total number of events is the sum of N and $\overline{N}$, then

$$\text{Prob (outcome)} = \frac{N}{T} = \frac{N}{N + \overline{N}}$$

Usually probabilities are stated as decimal fractions whereas odds are stated as the ratio of whole numbers. Thus, the probability that our team will win is 0.80, but the odds that it will win are eight to two, or, reduced to lowest terms, four to one.

THREE PROPERTIES OF PROBABILITIES

1. A probability is a number between zero and one. An outcome which can never occur has a probability of zero and an outcome which always occurs has a probability of one. Most outcomes have probabilities which fall between these two. A probability can never be a negative number.

2. The probabilities of all of the outcomes of an event add up to one. Suppose that an event has a number of possible outcomes—say five. For example, if we put five cards numbered from one to five into a hat, then drawing one card from the hat could have any one of five outcomes. Suppose that we have observed the event an indefinite number of times, T, so that we can calculate the probabilities of the outcomes. If outcome 1 occurred N_1 times, outcome 2, N_2 times, and so on, then

$$P_1 = \frac{N_1}{T}, \; P_2 = \frac{N_2}{T}, \text{ etc.}$$

Since every event must have one of the five outcomes, $N_1 + N_2 + N_3 + N_4 + N_5 = T$. Now, the sum of the probabilities of the outcomes is given by

$$P_1 + P_2 + P_3 + P_4 + P_5 = \frac{N_1}{T} + \frac{N_2}{T} + \frac{N_3}{T} + \frac{N_4}{T} + \frac{N_5}{T}$$

$$= \frac{N_1 + N_2 + N_3 + N_4 + N_5}{T}$$

$$= \frac{T}{T} = 1$$

3. Suppose that we observe some event, X, which has several possible outcomes, one of which we will call A. Suppose we observe the event T times, and that event has the outcome A N out of T times. As T increases, the proportion of time A occurs, N/T, approaches a fixed probability, called the probability of A, more and more closely.

Table 1 shows the results of tossing a coin repeatedly. As the number of tosses increases, the proportion of heads obtained approaches 0.5. Thus, in a million tosses of a fair coin, we should obtain a proportion of heads very close to 0.5. If the coin had been biased, the proportion of heads would have settled down to some other value.

Table 2 shows the result of tossing a biased coin. From these results, we can estimate that for this coin, the probability of a head is about 0.53. The value 0.53, is only an estimate of the probability, since we can never toss the coin the infinite number of times required to find the "true" probability. However, the estimate will approach the true probability more and more closely as we increase the number of tosses. The fact that the estimate will approach the true probability in this case is an instance of an important law about probabilities called *the law of large numbers: the proportion of times an event has a particular outcome approaches the true probability for that outcome as the number of events increases.*

ESTIMATING PROBABILITIES
FOR SIMPLE OUTCOMES

Probability estimates come from two sources: experience and rational models. The previous discussion of the biased coin illustrates the use of experience to make probability estimates. An event is observed a number of times; the proportion of times a particular outcome occurs is calculated and that proportion is used as the estimate of the probability of the outcome. The more important it is that we have an accurate estimate, the larger the number of events we will want to observe. If we want to be sure that a drug has a low probability of causing harm-ful side effects, we give it extensive testing (observe lots of events) before releasing it to the public.

Rational models are the other source of probability estimates. In a rational model, we try to identify sets of equally probable outcomes for an event. Suppose that we come from a distant country where coin-flipping is unheard of. When we are approached for the first time to bet on the flip of a coin, we will be at a distinct disadvantage if we can't estimate the probability of obtaining a head or a tail. What can we do with zero experience in coin-flipping? By examining the coin, we can see that the two sides are quite symmetrical. There is no reason to believe it will land heads more often than it lands tails. We reason, therefore, that heads and tails are equally likely alternatives, or more formally,

$$P \text{ (heads)} = P \text{ (tails)}.$$

Since heads and tails are the only alternatives,

$$P \text{ (heads)} + P \text{ (tails)} = 1$$

and

$$P \text{ (heads)} = P \text{ (tails)} = 0.5$$

In the same way, if we were unfamiliar with dice, we could quickly estimate the probability of rolling a three or a five by noticing that a die is a cube with six equal faces. We estimate that each side is equally likely to turn up on a roll and conclude that the probability for each side is one-sixth. If the die had been irregular, with faces of various sizes and shapes, we could not have made this prediction.

In general, rational models for estimating probabilities such as these make extensive use of arguments about symmetry or equivalence of alternatives.

COMPUTING PROBABILITIES FOR COMPLEX OUTCOMES

Sometimes outcomes are complex in the sense that they are combinations of other simpler outcomes. For example, rolling a die to get a number greater than four is a complex outcome which consists of two simpler outcomes: rolling a five *or* rolling a six. Outcomes combined in this way are said to be "ORed" (pronounced to rhyme with "roared") together. In the same way, rolling a twelve on a pair of dice is a complex outcome which consists of two simpler events: rolling a six on the first die *and* rolling a six on the second die. Outcomes combined in this way are said to be "ANDed" (pronounced to rhyme with "band-ed") together.

Many complex outcomes involve both methods of combining simpler outcomes. Rolling a ten on a pair of dice consists of rolling a four on the first die *and* a six on the second, *or* a five on the first die *and* a five on the second, *or* a six on the first die *and* a four on the second. Here simple outcomes are ANDed together to form complex outcomes which are, in turn, ORed together to form more complex outcomes. In this section, we will show to compute the probabilities of complex events from the probabilities of the component simpler events. First, we will discuss outcomes which are ORed together. Then, we will discuss outcomes which are ANDed together. For clear exposition, we will need to consider a fairly complex example such as the following.

Suppose that you have a box containing 100 identical balls labeled from 1 to 100. Imagine that you shake the box thoroughly and then draw out one ball without looking. It is easy to construct a rational model for this event which indicates that the 100 alternative outcomes are equally probable and that each has a probability of 1/100.

Suppose that balls 1 through 30 are red, balls 31 through 60 are white, and balls 61 through 100 are blue. Further, suppose that balls 1 through 50 are made of wood and that balls 51 through 100 are made of plastic (see Figure 1).

To Compute Probabilites for Outcomes Which are ORed Together

1. Identify clearly the set of outcomes and their relations for which you want to compute a probability. For example, if asked to find the probability of rolling a 3 or a 5 you can write "Find Prob (3 or 5)."
2. Determine whether or not the outcomes are *mutually exclusive*. Two outcomes are mutually exclusive if they can't occur together. It is impossible to get both a head and a tail with a single toss of a coin. Therefore, "head" and "tail" are mutually exclusive outcomes of this event. In the same way, getting a three and a five on the roll of a single die are mutually exclusive outcomes. In probability terms, if A and B are mutually exclusive outcomes, then Prob (A *and* B) = 0, that is, the probability that the two occur together is zero.

Events that are Mutually Exclusive

If the outcomes are mutually exclusive, then the probability of the ORed outcomes is the sum of the probabilities of the separate outcomes. That is,

Prob (A or B or . . . or K) = Prob (A) + Prob (B) + . . . + Prob (K).

Example:

What is the probability of rolling a three *or* a five on a single roll of a die?

	Wooden	Plastic
red	①②···㉚	
white	㉛···㊿ ㊿①㊿⓪	
blue		⑥①⑥②··· ⑩⓪

Solution

Step 1. Find Prob (3 *or* 5)

Step 2. These outcomes are mutually exclusive as we noted above

Step 3. Prob (3 *or* 5) = Prob (3) + Prob (5)
$$= 1/6 + 1/6$$
$$= 1/3$$

Example:

What is the probability of drawing a white ball in the situation described above?

Solution

Step 1. Find Prob (white). This is a complex outcome which consists of drawing ball number 31 or ball number 32 or . . . ball number 60. Thus, Prob (white) = Prob (31 or 32 or . . . 60)

Step 2. These outcomes are mutually exclusive since we have assumed that only one ball is to be drawn at a time.

Step 3. Prob (31 or 32 or . . . or 60)
$$= \text{Prob (31)} + \text{Prob (32)} \ldots + \text{Prob (60)}$$
$$= 1/100 + 1/100 \ldots + 1/100$$
$$= 30/100$$
$$= 0.30$$

Exercises:

Compute the probabilities of the following complex outcomes:

1. Drawing a blue ball.   (answer: 0.40)

2. Drawing a wooden ball.   (answer: 0.50)
3. Obtaining a head or a tail on a coin flip.   (answer: 1.0)[1]
4. Getting a number less than 3 on a single roll of a die.   (answer: 0.33)

Example:

What is the probability of drawing a red ball or a blue ball?

Solution

Step 1. Find Prob (red *or* blue)

Step 2. These are mutually exclusive outcomes since a ball can't have
two colors

Step 3. Prob (red or blue) = Prob (red) + Prob (blue)
$$= 0.30 + 0.40$$
$$= 0.70$$

Events Which are not Mutually Exclusive

If two outcomes are *not* mutually exclusive, then the probability of the ORed
outcomes is the sum of the probabilities of the separate outcomes *minus* the probability that the two occur together. That is,

$$\text{Prob (A } or \text{ B)} = \text{Prob (A)} + \text{Prob (B)} - \text{Prob (A } and \text{ B)}$$

Example:

Find the probability of drawing a white ball or a wooden ball.

Solution

Step 1.   Find Prob (white *or* wooden)

Step 2.   These outcomes are *not* mutually exclusive since we can draw
a ball which is both white and wooden.

Step 3.   Prob (white or wooden)
= Prob (white) + Prob (wooden) −
Prob (white *and* wooden)
= 0.30 + 0.50 − Prob (31 or 32 or . . . or 50)
= 0.80 − 0.20
= 0.60

The reason that we must subtract Prob (A *and* B) for outcomes that are not mutually exclusive is that otherwise some outcomes would be counted twice. In the example above, to find the probability that a ball is wooden, we add up probabilities for outcomes 1 through 50. To find the probability that a ball is white, we add up the probabilities of outcomes 31 through 60. Now, to find the probability of drawing a ball which is white *or* wooden, what we really want to do is to add the probabilities of outcomes 1 through 60. By adding the probability of drawing a white ball and drawing a wooden ball, we are in effect counting outcomes 31 through 50 twice. These are just the outcomes which are both white *and* wooden. This error is corrected by subtracting Prob (white *and* wooden) = Prob (31) + Prob (32) + . . . + Prob (50).

For some, the diagrams in Figure 2 help to clarify the difference between outcomes which are mutually exclusive and those which are not.

To Compute Probabilities for Outcomes Which are ANDed Together

1. Identify clearly the set of outcomes and their relations for wich you want to compute a probability, e.g., Prob (A *and* B *and* C).
2. Determine whether or not the outcomes are *independent* of each other. An outcome is independent of another outcome if the probability of the second outcome is not influenced by the occurrence or non-occurrence of the first. For example, the probability that there will be an eclipse of the moon tomorrow does not depend on whether or not I am kind to my cat. The two outcomes are unrelated and independent. However, the probability that I wear a raincoat tomorrow is *dependent* on the weather. If the weather is rainy or overcast, the probability that I will wear a raincoat is much higher than if it is sunny.

Independent Outcomes

If the outcomes are independent, then the probability of the ANDed outcomes is the product of the probabilities of the separate outcomes. That is,

Prob (A *and* B *and* . . . *and* K) = Prob (A) × Prob (B) x . . . x Prob (K)

Example:

Find the probability of tossing a head on each of three successive flips of a fair coin.

Solution

Step 1. Find Prob (head *and* head *and* head)

Step 2. Successive coin flips are independent of each other. Coins have no memory for previous events.

Step 3. Prob (head *and* head *and* head)
= Prob (head) × Prob (head) × Prob (head)
= 1/2 × 1/2 × 1/2
= 1/8

Exercises:

Compute the probability of rolling a three on one die and a four on a second die. (answer: = 1/36)

Compute the probability of getting a head, then a tail, then a head, and finally a tail in four successive coin flips. (answer: = 1/16)

Dependent Outcomes

If the outcomes are *not* independent then we have to take the dependencies into account. We can express the dependence of outcome B on outcome A as follows:

$$\text{Prob } (B|A) \quad \text{Prob } (B|\bar{A})$$

This should be read as the probability of B given that A has occurred is not equal to the probability of B given that A has not occurred ($\bar{A}$ may be read *as not* A). Prob (B|A) is called the *conditional* probability of B given A.

First, we will show how to calculate conditional probabilities. Then, we will use the conditional probabilities to calculate the probabilities of ANDed outcomes when the simple outcomes are *not* independent.

Calculating Conditional Probabilities

Suppose we know that a wooden ball has been chosen but we don't know what color it is. The probability that it is white is the conditional probability of white given wooden; that is, Prob (white|wooden). When we learn that a wooden ball has been chosen we know that one of the outcomes 1 through 50 has occurred but we don't know which one. Of these 50 outcomes, 20 are white. We can conclude then that Prob (white|wooden) = 20/50 = 0.40.

Exercises:

What is the probability of obtaining

1. a red ball given that a wooden ball had been chosen?
   (answer: 0.60)
2. a white ball given that a plastic ball had been chosen?
   (answer: 0.20)
3. a wooden ball given that a white ball had been chosen?
   (answer: 2/3 = 0.66)

Calculating Probabilities for Dependent Outcomes

If two outcomes A and B are not independent, the probability of the ANDed outcome is the probability of A times the conditional probability of B given A, that is, Prob (A *and* B) = Prob (A) × Prob (B|A)

Example:

What is the probability of drawing a ball that is both wooden and white?

Solution

Step 1.   Find Prob (wooden *and* white)
Step 2.   These outcomes are not independent since
           Prob (wooden/white) ≠ Prob (wooden/not white)
Step 3.   Prob (wooden *and* white)
        = Prob (wooden) × Prob (white|wooden)
        = 0.50 × 0.40 = 0.20

Notice that the order in which we consider the outcomes doesn't matter. Thus,

           Prob (white *and* wooden)
        = Prob (white) × Prob (wooden|white)
        = 0.30 × 2/3
        = 0.20

just as we find for Prob (wooden and white).

Exercises:

Calculate the probability of drawing a ball that is

1. red and wooden   (answer: 0.60)
2. white and plastic   (answer: 0.20)

3. plastic and white   (answer: 0.20)

Many problems involve both ANDing and ORing of outcomes. Such problems can be solved by successive applications of the rules we have been using.

Example:

What is the probability of getting a 10 when rolling a pair of dice?

Solution

Step 1. Find Prob (10) = Prob [(4 *and* 6) *or* (5 *and* 5) *or* (6 and 4)]

Step 2. The ANDed outcomes are independent and the ORed outcomes are mutually exclusive.

Step 3.   Prob (10)
       = Prob [(4 *and* 6) *or* (5 *and* 5) or (6 *and* 4)]
       = Prob (4 *and* 6) + Prob (5 *and* 5) + Prob (6 *and* 4)
       = Prob (4) × Prob (6) + Prob (5) × Prob (5) + Prob (6) × Prob (4)
       = 1/6 × 1/6 + 1/6 × 1/6 + 1/6 ×1/6
       = 1/36 + 1/36 + 1/36
       = 3/36
       = 1/12

GENERAL REVIEW EXEPCISES
2

1. Define probability, odds.
2. What is the law of large numbers?
3. Compute the probability of
    a. an alternating sequence of heads and tails four long, e.g., HTHT or THTH   (answer: 1/8)
    b. getting a seven by rolling a pair of dice.   (answer: 1/6)
4. In an ordinary well-shuffled deck of 52 cards, what is the probability of drawing
    a. a two of diamonds? (answer: 1/52)
    b. a two of any suit?   (answer: 4/52 = 1/13)
    c. a diamond?   (answer: 13/52 = 1/4)
    d. a two or a diamond?   (answer: 16/52 = 4/13) (If you got 17/52 what was your error?)

TABLE 1

Number of tosses	10	100	300	500	1,000	10,000
Number of heads	4	54	138	235	484	4,983
Proportion of heads	0.40	0.54	0.46	0.47	0.48	0.498

TABLE 2

Number of tosses	10	100	300	500	1,000	10,000
Number of heads	5	57	147	256	519	5,309
Proportion	0.50	0.57	0.49	0.51	0.52	0.531

Author Index

Numbers in *italics* refer to bibliographic references.

A

Adams, J. L., 282, *300*
Almquist, E. M., 309, 310, 319, 324, 325, 326, *328*
Alpert, M., 241, *253*
Angrist, S. S., 309, 310, *328*
Arieti, S., 317, *328*
Arthur, T. S., 304, 307, *328*
Ashmore, H. S., 322, *328*
Astin, H. S., 314, *328*
Atkinson, R. C., 161, *171*
Ausubel, D. P., 179, *199*

B

Baddeley, A. D., 116, 170, *172*
Bagnall, J., 290, 291, *300*
Banks, W. P., 114, *146*
Barber, B., 326, *328*
Barber, G., 114, *146*
Barenfeld, M., 73, *88*
Barnes, J. M., 135, *146*
Barnlett, T., 114, 115, *147*
Barnlund, D. C., 289, *300*
Bartlett, B., 175, 177, 178, *199*

Bates, A., 114, 115, *147*
Bereiter, C., 97, 99, *106*
Binks, M. G., 14, *32*
Blaustein, A., 102, *106*
Bond, S. J., 102, 103, *107*, 301, 308, 315, *329*
Bouchard, T. J., Jr., 288, *300*
Bousfield, W. A., 131, *146*
Bower, G. H., 125, 140, 142, 143, *146, 147*
Bracewell, R., 99, *106*
Bridwell, L. S., 99, *106*
Brody, E. B., 301, *329*
Brody, N., 301, *329*
Brooks, L. R., *147*
Brown, R., 129, *147*
Burtt, H. E., 132, *147*

C

Calderwood, A., 308, 310, 314, *329*
Cannizzo, S. R., 127, *147*
Cantor, M., 311, *329*
Carey, L., 99, 100, *106*
Carpenter, P. A., 73, *88*
Carroll, J. S., *171*
Chase, W. G., 56, *67*, 124, *147*, 293, *300*
Cherry, E. C., 117, *147*

349

Subject Index